LSAT Workout

LSAT Workout

Bob Spruill

First Edition

Random House, Inc.
New York

www.PrincetonReview.com

The Princeton Review, Inc.
2315 Broadway
New York, NY 10024
E-mail: booksupport@review.com

ISBN: 0-375-76459-3

Editor: Suzanne Markert
Production Editor: Patricia Dublin
Production Coordinator: Effie Hadjiioannou

Manufactured in the United States of America.

10   9   8

First Edition

ACKNOWLEDGMENTS

Thanks for their help in producing this book belongs, first, to the fine folks in our publishing department, especially to Suzanne Markert for her tireless editing efforts and to the hardest-working production department in test prep, including Patricia Dublin and Effie Hadjiioannou. Thanks also to the reviewer, Mindy Myers.

Most of all, I would like to thank the excellent staff and students of The Princeton Review for providing me with the opportunity over many years to learn so much about the LSAT and teaching smart approaches to it. The list of those who deserve thanks in this regard is too long to include here, but I would like to single out Shannon Lamm, Ian Stewart, Fritz Stewart, and Tricia McCloskey for particular thanks. They have all, in different ways, contributed significantly to developing and sharpening the understanding of the LSAT that informed this book.

And special thanks to Adam Robinson, who conceived of and perfected the Joe Bloggs approach to standardized tests and many of the other successful techniques used by The Princeton Review.

CONTENTS

PART I

The LSAT

How to Prepare for the LSAT

THE TEST

The Law School Admission Test (LSAT) is a nearly four-hour exam required for admission to virtually all law schools in North America. It consists of five multiple-choice sections, 35 minutes each—four scored, one unscored—and an unscored 30-minute essay that will be sent to schools along with your LSAT scores. The LSAT is a paper-and-pencil exam, administered four times a year: June, September/October, December, and February.

Each multiple-choice section contains questions of one of three types: Logical Reasoning, Analytical Reasoning, or Reading Comprehension. Of the four scored sections, two will be Logical Reasoning sections (we call them "args"), one will be Analytical Reasoning (we call it "games"), and one will be Reading Comprehension (we call it "RC"). The unscored "experimental" test section will be one of these three types, but your performance on this section will not affect your score. Since you won't know which of the sections is experimental, you'll always need to do your best on every section.

Section Type	Minutes	Counts Toward Score?
Logical Reasoning	35	Yes
Logical Reasoning	35	Yes
Analytical Reasoning	35	Yes
Reading Comprehension	35	Yes
Experimental	35	Yes
Essay	30	No

To arrive at your score, LSAC (the Law School Admission Council, the organization that writes the LSAT) will first compute a raw score by adding up the number of multiple-choice questions you answer correctly on each scored section. You are not penalized for incorrect answers, so you should always answer every question on every section, even if you have to guess. Choose the same answer choice every time you guess. Using this strategy, you're less likely to deviate significantly from the average of 20 percent of your guesses.

LSAC analyzes the raw scores of everyone who took the test during your administration to create your "scaled" score for that test, which can range from 120–180 (the average is 150, with a standard deviation of around 10 points). You can compare scaled scores across any three-year period, since different exams may have slightly different scales. You'll only receive the one scaled score; there is no breakdown by question type or section. About two-thirds of test takers score between 140–160, while only two percent score 170 or above. The tight nature of the scoring scale and the extreme competitiveness of law school admissions make your LSAT performance an important determining factor in how your application is handled.

HOW TO PREPARE

Doing well on the LSAT isn't a matter of knowing facts; it's a matter of strategy, technique, and extensive practice. Since LSAC will report all of your LSAT scores along with an average of all those scores, it is very important not to take the LSAT "just to see how you do." Although of course you might find it necessary to take the exam more than once, the best approach is to prepare as if you only had one shot.

If you elect to take advantage of one of the coaching programs available, such as The Princeton Review's Hyperlearning course, your teacher or tutor will provide you with various resources and a plan for how to use them. If you're preparing on your own, you'll need to make some decisions for yourself.

Keep these golden rules of LSAT prep in mind as you study:

1. Don't leave your preparation for the last minute. Short-term crash preparation is ineffective, and may actually cause your score to go down. Give yourself plenty of lead time. Develop a study plan and stick to it.

2. Set reasonable goals. The simple fact is that not everyone is capable of achieving a 170. You would never start training for the hundred-yard dash by deciding you had to get within a quarter-second of the world record; instead, you'd develop a training plan calculated to improve your performance and reach your best possible result. Focus on the goal of personal improvement, not on some absolute end score.

3. Take advantage of the fact that LSAC releases three of its tests every year. Recent tests can be rather expensive on a per-question basis, but regardless of how you're otherwise preparing for the LSAT, past tests should be part of your preparation. Use them as practice tests, and take them under conditions that are as realistic as possible. While past LSATs don't provide a great deal of guidance about strategy and approaches, they are an invaluable barometer of your progress.

4. Remember that practice by itself may not be adequate to provide significant improvement. You must also carefully analyze your performance and look for opportunities to improve your approach. Discerning the patterns and basic ideas underlying many questions—and evaluating your instinctive response to them—is important to making sure that you correct flaws in your approach to the exam. Preparation books that focus on techniques, such as The Princeton Review's *Cracking the LSAT*, can give you valuable ideas about how you might improve in this aspect. In combination with practice, these adjustments are your best chance of significantly changing your LSAT score.

5. Be persistent and tough. It may sound trite, but preparing for the LSAT can be a frustrating and discouraging process. This is a difficult exam, and improvement can be equally difficult to come by. Often it comes suddenly, unexpectedly, and only after a great deal of effort. Success on the LSAT requires a positive attitude.

How to Use This Book

This book is not intended as a substitute for past LSATs or for preparation books like *Cracking the LSAT*. Although past LSATs are a great source of practice problems, you would have to buy many tests to get a complete overview of the methods used by test writers. Similarly, although books such as *Cracking the LSAT* are valuable for presenting and describing techniques, they too tend not to focus on the basic patterns of construction of test questions, especially the most difficult ones. This book is meant to fit into the gap between practice exams and technique-oriented preparation materials.

Each section of this book is devoted to one of the three kinds of multiple-choice questions on the exam. (Since the writing sample is unscored, it is not particularly important for your preparation, and no discussion of it is contained in this book.) Each section leads off with a compact description of The Princeton Review's fundamental techniques and strategies. These chapters are as close as is reasonably possible to being exhaustive, and as such are packed with information that you may find difficult to process fully on a first reading. It is recommended that you return often to these technique descriptions, especially if an explanation for a problem relies on terminology or ideas that don't make sense to you. Since this book is not intended to provide a step-by-step introduction to techniques, you may find it useful to pick up a copy of *Cracking the LSAT* for further explanations and details.

If you're already familiar with The Princeton Review's techniques or if you're simply looking for some challenging practice for the exam and more advanced discussions of test ideas, this is the book you need. The nearly 400 example questions contained in this book are, as a group, far more difficult than the ordinary mix of questions on the LSAT; although the questions taken individually are consistent with the more difficult LSAT questions in terms of their construction and contents, you should not expect that complete LSAT sections are as uniformly difficult as the questions in this volume. Basically, if you can handle these, then you should be able to handle anything the writers of the LSAT throw at you.

Every problem is accompanied by a full explanation. Within the chapters, examples are grouped to highlight broad ideas found in LSAT questions. At the end of each section are timed, LSAT-style exercises. We have not included scoring scales for these exercises, since they are more difficult than the mix of questions you'll experience on the actual test.

If you can grasp and become comfortable with the ideas presented here and use them without consuming too much time, you should have no problem achieving a top score on the LSAT.

PART ◆ II

Logical Reasoning

2

Arguments Strategy

LOGICAL REASONING

Each of the scored Logical Reasoning ("Args") sections of the LSAT will have 24 to 26 questions, leaving you a bit less than a minute and a half to answer each. This isn't enough time for many people. One smart way to maximize your time is to leave the most time-consuming questions for last. You must keep moving on this section and make decisions without second-guessing yourself. On the other hand, when you're down to two or three answer choices on an args question, you'll need to slow down and carefully consider the choices before you make your decision. On many of these questions, the real work doesn't start until you've eliminated a few choices.

Every args question consists of three basic parts: the argument or passage you'll be working with, the question stem, and the possible answer choices. Each time you work an args question, you should follow the same four-step process:

1. Evaluate the Question Task

2. Analyze the Argument

3. Apply the Strategy

4. Use Process of Elimination

1. EVALUATE THE QUESTION TASK

There are ten major types of questions that can appear on an LSAT Arguments section, along with a host of other minor or variant types. First things first: Read the question. The question indicates what the relationship between the argument and the credited answer choice needs to be, and different questions may require you to do different kinds of work on the argument to prepare for the choices. Basically, the question tasks come in five fundamental varieties.

Some questions require you to identify or draw **conclusions** based on the passage material. An Args section tests your ability to apply deductive reasoning, and the staple of deductive reasoning is combining several facts or premises to arrive at a new, true statement. When you're drawing your own conclusions, stay away from leaps of logic, and don't go beyond the material presented in the passage.

The majority of args questions require you to work with a **flaw** or **gap** in the original argument's reasoning—a place where the test itself makes leaps of logic. Some of these questions may ask you to evaluate (identify) the fact that is required to correct the flaw, while others will ask you to pick a new item of information that would either help or hurt the argument's conclusion. One key concept in all of these question types is relevance: Your answer must have a direct impact on the argument's stated conclusion in order for it to have a chance.

Many args questions will ask you to **describe** features of the argument. Some may simply ask you to pick a correct description of how the argument arrives at its conclusion, but most of these questions ask you to identify what the argument does wrong.

Virtually all of the args questions you encounter will ask you to do one of the three things mentioned above. However, there are two other tasks that you will see on a few args questions.

One task, which appears at the rate of 1–4 questions per test, asks you to **explain** a situation presented in the passage. On these, the passage will describe a set of facts that don't seem to be compatible with one another; your answer must explain how they can be.

The last task, which appears at the rate of 2–3 questions per test, asks you to **parallel** the reasoning in the original argument. These questions are often more difficult—and virtually always more time-consuming—than others on the section. If time is a problem for you on LSAT Args, you should definitely leave questions that involve this task for last on the section.

2. ANALYZE THE ARGUMENT

No matter what question task you're facing, once you know what you have to do, it's time to attack the passage with that task in mind. Different question tasks require different approaches at this step, which is a big reason why you want to read the question stem first. There are two basic ways you may need to analyze an argument.

The first and by far most prevalent type of analysis required on args is identifying the **parts** of an argument. As mentioned above, the LSAT is a test of deductive reasoning, in which one or more premises are used to arrive at a conclusion. The conclusion is the point of an argument—the thing that an argument is constructed to convince you of—and is the most important thing to find. Very often, a sentence in the argument will explicitly state the conclusion. In this case, the exact wording of the conclusion sentence will be important to working the question. Whenever a conclusion is explicitly stated, mark it.

When you've correctly identified the conclusion, it should be supported by other statements in the argument, which provide reasons to accept the truth of the conclusion. These are the argument's premises, the facts that you'll have to work with. Not everything that's included in an argument is a conclusion or a premise. While it may be important for you to understand definitions of terms, historical background, and parenthetical comments, these play no role in an argument's logical structure. On the LSAT, this supporting material must be separated out from the premises of the argument; very often, it's strategically placed to make the argument's gap or flaw more difficult for you to find.

In many cases, the correct answer will relate to the gap: the possibility the argument leaves out, the unwarranted assumption it makes, the misinterpretation or misuse of a key premise. As you'll see in the chapters ahead, the writers of the LSAT have many different ways (some of them fiendishly clever) for constructing arguments with flawed reasoning. Whenever you encounter it, you'll always have a better chance on the question if you can identify, as specifically as possible, what's wrong with an argument before you move to the answer choices. You won't be able to identify an argument's flaw all the time, even in cases when the question indicates that the argument is flawed, but you should always make the attempt before moving on.

There are cases on LSAT Args, however, when the passage on which a question depends isn't a complete argument. For some of the question tasks, the passage may simply be a collection of facts, or a series of premises that appear to lead up to an unstated conclusion. In these cases, the passage won't have parts you can identify, but you should still at the very least **paraphrase** or **summarize** the passage in your own words. The exact wording of the passage is always important on LSAT Args, but you'll have a better chance of narrowing down the answer choices if you have a better understanding of the passage's contents.

3. APPLY THE STRATEGY

The strategy will depend, once again, on the exact question task you're facing, but the general idea in every case is to **predict**, as well as you can, what the right answer will be like. In certain cases—where the question asks you to identify the main point of the argument—your predictions may be quite specific, and will closely resemble the answer. In others—such as a weaken question, when the task is to pick a new fact that would make the conclusion less likely to be true—you will only be able to predict general features of the right answer. In still others—on many inference questions, for example—you may not be able to predict very much at all about the right answer. On the other hand, there are some inference questions—those that involve a series of related conditional statements—for which you'll need to do quite a lot at this stage to prepare to evaluate the choices.

Whichever situation you face, however, you must do everything you can to develop a sense of what choice you're looking for before you move to the answer choices. The choices are where the hard work begins on an args question, since the writers of the LSAT are extraordinarily adept at devising appealing choices that don't accomplish the task at hand. The more specific a notion you have of what you're looking for, the less likely you are to fall into traps the test writers set for you.

4. USE POE

Process of Elimination (POE) is essential on every args question because, in many cases, you'll be better able to identify wrong answers with confidence than you will the right answer. Mark out the letters of answer choices as you eliminate them; this will help you focus your attention on the work you have left to do before you can settle on your answer. Always examine all five answer choices; there will be cases when more than one answer choice fits your prediction, or appears to do what the question task requires. When you're down to two choices, compare the remaining choices if you can, and never hesitate to go back to the argument to examine parts of it more carefully. The exact wording of some statements may be crucial to answering the question, and you'll find that there are times when you realize you've skimmed past things on your initial reading that turn out to be very important.

Although different question tasks may require slightly different approaches to POE, there are some things you will always want to be conscious of when you evaluate the choices.

Be attentive to the **strength of language** in each answer choice. The LSAT does not exaggerate or use language figuratively; when a statement involves the word *all*, it means in every case, without exception. There are some situations in which you'll want to lean toward strong statements like these, and others in which you'll want to steer clear of them. The strength of language you want will be determined by the question task and by the strength of language in the original argument, but you must always register how strong or weak the wording in an answer choice is.

When a question task involves determining the impact of statements on an argument's conclusion, the concept of **relevance** or **scope** is key. No matter what the question task, if it's one where the impact on the conclusion is important, then you'll carefully need to eliminate any choice that doesn't directly relate. This may sound easy, but the exact wording of an argument's conclusion may make its scope significantly narrower than you think it is on a first reading. It's never a waste of time to go back to the conclusion you've marked and make certain of how sweeping or specific it is.

Watch out for **wonderful answers to different questions**. For example, you might see a great answer that strengthens the conclusion on a question that asks you to weaken it. These answers can be tempting because they are clearly relevant to the argument, and because even though they don't do what is required, they are more appealing to you on a first reading.

Finally, never eliminate **answer choices you don't understand**. At its worst, the language on LSAT Args can be bafflingly labyrinthine. Under the timed conditions of the test, there may be no need to spend time unraveling the language in particularly difficult answer choices, but if you skip past a choice because of its difficult language, you can't eliminate it. There will be some cases in which you realize, by POE, that a choice you don't fully understand has to be the right one!

If you've ever cast a play or put together a starting lineup, then you've already had some training for the kinds of negotiations and comparisons required to do POE effectively. You begin the process with a more or less distinct notion of exactly what you need to do the job at hand; then reality sets in, and you're given a choice from among a few alternatives. Sometimes you find exactly what you want, and the other alternatives are clearly inferior. Sometimes, though, none of the alternatives is exactly what you wanted, and you have to go back to the drawing board, reexamine the situation, and look for a choice that will work even if it isn't perfect. In still other cases, several of the choices seem to be what you wanted, and then you have to make comparisons on the basis of things that didn't initially seem crucial.

SUMMARY OF ARGS STRATEGIES

The charts below provide quick summaries of the strategies and methods that are most effective on each type of LSAT args question. Remember, there's no substitute for experience and practice on this section. As you work through the exercises in later chapters, you may want to return to these charts to refresh your memory.

MAIN POINT OR MAIN CONCLUSION

The Question Says	"the main point is" "the main conclusion is" "the argument leads to the conclusion that" "statements commit X to the position that"
The Task Is to	identify the argument's conclusion: what the person making the argument wants you to believe
Analyze and Apply by	finding the conclusion, if it's explicitly stated; if not, the opposite of the conclusion may be stated instead
Avoid Choices That	are worded more strongly than the argument; go beyond the conclusion; are premises of the argument
Look for Choices That	bring the whole argument together; are specific rather than general

CONCLUSION *VARIANTS*: POINT AT ISSUE OR AGREE/DISAGREE

The Question Says	"the main point at issue is" "an issue in dispute is" "are committed to disagreeing about" "expresses a point of agreement"
The Task Is to	find a statement about which the participants in a conversation definitely hold different opinions or, possibly, the same opinion
Analyze and Apply by	finding the conclusion and premises for each participant's argument; summarizing the exact thing they're arguing about
Avoid Choices That	pertain to one side of the conversation but not the other; rely on implication; answer the wrong question (agree rather than disagree)
Look for Choices That	pertain to what's explicitly stated; are clearly something about which the participants would say "yes" or "no"

ID REASONING

The Question Says	"the argument proceeds by" "a method of reasoning employed by the argument" "a technique of reasoning employed by the argument"
The Task Is to	describe how an argument supports its conclusion
Analyze and Apply by	finding the conclusion and the premises, then summarizing the process used in the argument
Avoid Choices That	do not match the argument closely, especially the main point or purpose of the argument
Look for Choices That	match the argument piece by piece; correctly describe the relationship between the premises and the conclusion

ID REASONING *VARIANT*: ID RESPONSE

The Question Says	"X responds by" "responds in which one of the following ways" "uses which one of the following techniques in countering"
The Task Is to	in a conversation, describe how a response relates to the first person's argument in the conversation
Analyze and Apply by	finding the conclusion and the premises of both parts of the conversation, then summarizing the relationship between them as specifically as possible
Avoid Choices That	pertain to the first argument rather than the second; identify flaws in the first argument not exploited in the response; do not match the response closely; get the relationship between the two arguments wrong
Look for Choices That	match the response piece by piece; correctly describe whether the two participants agree or disagree; correctly identify the point of agreement or disagreement

ID Reasoning *Variant*: Role of the Statement

The Question Says	"the role of the statement X in the argument is" "the statement X figures in the argument in which one of the following ways"
The Task Is to	describe the indicated part of an argument in terms of its overall logical structure
Analyze and Apply by	finding the conclusion and the premises, then summarizing which of these two roles the statement plays; if neither, summarizing the relationship between the statement and the premises and conclusion
Avoid Choices That	do not match the argument closely; mistakenly identify the conclusion; mistakenly identify a statement as the main conclusion when it is only a step in the argument's chain of reasoning
Look for Choices That	match the argument piece by piece; correctly describe the relationship between the indicated statement and the conclusion

Inference

The Question Says	"must also be true" "can most properly be concluded" "most strongly support the inference" "which of the following conclusions can be properly drawn"
The Task Is to	find a statement that has to be true on the basis of passage information; note that these passages are often not arguments
Analyze and Apply by	summarizing the passage; if it seems to lead to a specific conclusion, you should find it before moving on; some may involve a series of related conditional statements that can be diagrammed
Avoid Choices That	are too strongly worded; use terms with no clear relationship to passage material; are too specific or demand too much input to be relevant; involve questionable comparisons
Look for Choices That	are wishy-washy and say as little as possible; are specific, but not too specific; include stipulations or qualifications; seem to restate passage material

INFERENCE VARIANTS: COULD BE TRUE/MUST BE FALSE

The Question Says	"which one of the following could be true" "each of the following could be true EXCEPT:" "CANNOT be true"
The Task Is to	usually find a statement that is directly contradicted by passage information; occasionally, find a statement that is not contradicted by passage information
Analyze and Apply by	summarizing the passage; it is unlikely that you will be able to predict the right answer
Avoid Choices That	Could Be True: are broad or strongly worded; are contradicted by a specific example presented in the passage Must Be False: (or Could Be True EXCEPT): could even possibly be true; involve instances not dealt with by the passage; are qualified or wishy-washy
Look for Choices That	Could Be True: could even possibly be true; involve instances not dealt with by the passage; are qualified or wishy-washy Must Be False (or Could Be True EXCEPT): are broad or strongly worded; are contradicted by a specific example presented in the passage

INFERENCE VARIANT: FILL-IN

The Question Says	"most logically completes the argument" "provides a logical completion" (the argument ends with _____)
The Task Is to	usually supply the conclusion logically supported by the passage statements; occasionally, find the assumption required by the argument; occasionally, apply a rule in the argument to a specific case
Analyze and Apply by	summarizing the passage; if it seems to lead to a specific conclusion, you should find it before moving on
Avoid Choices That	are too strongly worded; use terms with no clear relationship to passage material; are too specific or demand too much input to be relevant
Look for Choices That	bring all the passage material together; involve terms mentioned in the argument; are specific rather than general

ASSUMPTION

The Question Says	"an assumption on which the argument depends" "is assumed by the argument" "is required in order for the conclusion to be properly drawn" "relies on the fact that"
The Task Is to	find a statement that has to be true in order for the argument's conclusion to be true
Analyze and Apply by	finding the conclusion, the premises, and any gap or flaw in the reasoning; find the most specific notion of the argument's problem that you can
Avoid Choices That	weaken the argument; explain why or how too specifically; are more strongly worded than the argument's conclusion; are not directly relevant to the conclusion
Look for Choices That	help the conclusion; logically connect pieces of the argument to one another; if false, weaken the conclusion; are weakly worded; eliminate a possible weakness of the argument

WEAKEN

The Question Says	"most seriously weakens the argument" "undermines the conclusion" "calls into question" "casts doubt upon" "conclusion would not follow if" "overlooks the possibility that"
The Task Is to	find a new fact that, if true, would make the conclusion unlikely to be true
Analyze and Apply by	finding the conclusion, the premises, and any gap or flaw in the reasoning; you will not be able to predict the correct answer's exact contents, but you should be able to say what it must tell or show
Avoid Choices That	are not directly relevant to the conclusion; strengthen; are trying to weaken but do not attack the conclusion strongly; require extensive explanations to show relevance; attempt to contradict a premise
Look for Choices That	strongly attack the conclusion; present a specific instance in which the conclusion is incorrect; present a sweeping contradiction of the conclusion; present a possibility the argument overlooks

STRENGTHEN

The Question Says	"most strengthens" "most strongly supports the conclusion" "allows the conclusion to be properly drawn" "follows logically if which one of the following is assumed"
The Task Is to	find a new fact that, if true, would make the conclusion certain, more likely to be correct, or, at the very least, less likely to be incorrect
Analyze and Apply by	finding the conclusion, the premises, and any gap or flaw in the reasoning; you will not be able to predict the correct answer's exact contents, but you should be able to say what it must tell or show
Avoid Choices That	are not directly relevant to the conclusion; weaken; restate premises in different words
Look for Choices That	present a sweeping assurance that the conclusion is correct; state assumptions; logically connect pieces of the argument; present a specific instance in which the conclusion is correct; explain why or how the conclusion is correct; support the conclusion using a method not employed in the argument; eliminate a possible weakness of the argument

WEAKEN/STRENGTHEN *VARIANT*: EVALUATE

The Question Says	"would be most useful to know in evaluating the argument" "the answer to which one of the following questions would contribute to an evaluation" "in evaluating the argument, it would be most useful to know whether"
The Task Is to	identify a statement that, if true, either weakens or strengthens the conclusion and, if false, does the other; if in the form of questions, a "yes" answer to the choice will do one, a "no" answer will do the other
Analyze and Apply by	finding the conclusion, the premises, and any gap or flaw in the reasoning; you will not be able to predict the correct answer's exact contents, but you should be able to say what it must tell or show
Avoid Choices That	can only weaken or can only strengthen; do not pertain directly to the conclusion; can at best contradict or restate premises
Look for Choices That	stick closely to the argument's reasoning; have direct impact on the argument's conclusion; pertain closely to a clear weakness of the argument

PRINCIPLE

The Question Says	Justify: "principle, if established, would most help to justify"
	"principle provides the strongest support for the conclusion"
	Conform: "conforms to which one of the following generalizations"
	"reasoning most closely conforms to which one of the following principles"
The Task Is to	always, find a general statement that supports the argument's conclusion/judgment; for conform, also match the method of reasoning as closely as possible
Analyze and Apply by	identifying the conclusion/judgment in the argument and the premises/situation on which it is based; you will most likely not be able to predict the exact contents of the correct answer
Avoid Choices That	are incapable under any circumstances of matching the judgment made in the conclusion; make reference to items of information not known about the situation presented in the premises; for conform, support the conclusion using a method the argument does not
Look for Choices That	for justify, support as strongly as possible, even if it goes beyond the argument; for conform, match the method of reasoning used in the argument as closely as possible without going beyond it

Principle *Variant*: Use the Principle

The Question Says	Justify: "the principle above most strongly supports which one of the following arguments" "the principle above would justify which one of the following judgments" Conform: "which statement most closely conforms to the principle stated above" "is an application of the principle above"
The Task Is to	identify which argument in the answer choices correctly uses the rule stated in the passage; whereas most principle questions provide one argument and five possible principles, these provide one principle and five possible arguments; they can be very time-consuming
Analyze and Apply by	summarizing the principle at hand; the answer choices are where you'll do your work on these
Avoid Choices That	have main points that don't match the kind of conclusion the principle can allow you to draw; do not match the provided principle closely; do not include information essential to making the judgment allowed by the principle
Look for Choices That	match the principle's requirements as closely as possible; correctly use necessary and sufficient conditions in the principle

Flaw

The Question Says	"argument is flawed because" "commits which one of the following errors of reasoning" "reasoning is questionable because" "is most vulnerable to criticism on the ground that"
The Task Is to	describe the way in which the argument's reasoning is incorrect
Analyze and Apply by	finding the conclusion, the premises, and any gap or flaw in the reasoning; the more specific a notion you have of the argument's problem, the better
Avoid Choices That	do not match what the argument does; demand further information or support in cases where it is not needed; refer to things the argument does that are not wrong; rely on a mistaken understanding of the argument's conclusion
Look for Choices That	match the gap you've identified as closely as possible; cannot be eliminated for a definite reason

RESOLVE/EXPLAIN

The Question Says	"most helps to resolve the apparent paradox" "most helps to explain the apparent discrepancy" "provides a resolution to the apparent inconsistency"
The Task Is to	find a new fact that, if true, would explain why an apparently impossible state of affairs exists
Analyze and Apply by	summarizing the contents of the passage; articulating as precisely as possible what paradox or discrepancy needs to be explained
Avoid Choices That	make the paradox worse; only explain one side of the paradox; aren't relevant to the situation; require you to make too many assumptions
Look for Choices That	explain as explicitly as possible; describe how or why; include new considerations not addressed in the original passage

PARALLEL

The Question Says	"most closely paralleled by" "most similar in its logical structure to" "pattern of reasoning is most similar to"
The Task Is to	find an argument whose logical structure most exactly matches the structure of the original; these are most often time-consuming and difficult
Analyze and Apply by	finding the conclusion and premises of the original argument; summarizing the method used in the argument; finding the skeletal structure of the argument
Avoid Choices That	do not have similar main points to the original; have skeletal structures that involve a different number of key terms from the original; contain flawed logic
Look for Choices That	parallel the method while possibly rearranging the order of the statements; employ the most similar theme or principle to the original

PARALLEL VARIANT: PARALLEL-FLAW

The Question Says	"exhibits a flawed pattern of reasoning most like" "contains questionable reasoning that is most similar to" "questionable reasoning is most closely paralleled by"
The Task Is to	find an argument whose logical flaw most exactly matches that in the original argument; most often time-consuming and difficult
Analyze and Apply by	finding the conclusion, premises, and flaw in the original; finding the skeletal structure, especially when conditionals are involved; stating the flaw as precisely as possible
Avoid Choices That	are not flawed arguments; do not have similar main points to the original; have skeletal structures involving a different number of key terms from the original
Look for Choices That	parallel the problem while possibly rearranging the order of the statements

3

Drawing Conclusions

HOW TO DRAW CONCLUSIONS

A number of LSAT args questions test your ability to identify conclusions, draw conclusions from presented evidence, or see how a conclusion is supported. Although each of these three tasks requires some slightly different skills, there are a few things you should always keep in mind.

CONCLUSIONS ARE NOT TOO BROAD

When presented with evidence, most people have the impulse to draw the most interesting or provocative conclusion they can. The LSAT takes advantage of this impulse by providing you with statements that, although more interesting, are not truly supported. On the LSAT, conclusions are specific statements, not general ones. Stick to what's there, and try not to inject anything of your own.

CONCLUSIONS BRING TOGETHER ALL THE PRESENTED EVIDENCE

If an argument's text prominently includes advertising, bicycles, and springtime, then the conclusion probably will as well. LSAT args questions are most often arranged so that there are no "loose ends." If you find yourself picking an answer that makes you wonder why they were talking about advertising at all in the argument, then it's likely you're falling into a too-specific trap answer.

CONCLUSIONS ARE OFTEN COUCHED IN QUALIFIED LANGUAGE

There are exceptions to this, of course. Generally, though, if you're given a choice between a strong, definite, absolute statement of an argument's conclusion and one that seems wishy-washy, bland, or tentative, go bland. It's much easier to defend a soft statement than it is to defend a sweeping one.

Let's look more specifically at each of the three tasks.

1. Find the Conclusion

This batch of questions consists of those whose primary task is to figure out what the conclusion of the argument is. On other types of LSAT args questions, you will often find the conclusions marked with words such as *therefore, thus,* or *so.* In this batch, you will need to be a bit warier of such markers; sometimes they're meant to lure you into picking a statement that doesn't include the entire argument.

Keep in mind that LSAT conclusions are often particular kinds of statements: Recommendations, predictions, and moral or practical judgments should all, when you encounter them, attract particularly close attention. They're often the conclusions of arguments in which they appear.

Finally, be alert for one of the LSAT's favorite tricks in presenting conclusions on these types of questions. Although elsewhere on the test you can usually expect to see the conclusion of an argument explicitly stated, here the test writers often deviate from that pattern. Instead of stating the conclusion directly, these types of arguments may often state its opposite, in the form of an alternative viewpoint the argument is intended to refute. Keep an eye out for marks of disagreement: *but, although, yet,* and so forth.

Try the problems on the next page. Answers can be found in Chapter 20.

DRILL #1

1. Recent studies have shown increased health risks to children in households that own two pets or more. One recent study examined groups of children in households with no pets, with one pet, and with two or more pets. Although the study found that the incidence of streptococcus infections was twice as high for children in the third group as it was for children in either of the other two groups, these results cannot be considered convincing, since the number of children involved in the study was less than fifty.

Which one of the following most accurately expresses the main conclusion of the passage above?

(A) It is unlikely that the number of pets in a household has any effect on the incidence of streptococcus infection among children in that household.

(B) The results of at least one recent study of the effect of pet ownership on childhood illness cannot be considered convincing, since it concerned only streptococcus infections and excluded other health risks.

(C) More studies need to be done on the effects of pet ownership on health risks to children.

(D) A recent study fails to demonstrate that there is a causal link between the number of pets in a household and the illnesses of children in those households.

(E) If a recent study had included more children in each of its study groups, the study would have conclusively shown that owning two or more pets presents an unacceptable health risk to children.

2. X: It is ridiculous to suggest that anyone other than the historical person named William Shakespeare wrote the plays attributed to him. Although various other playwrights of the time have been proposed as possible authors, all of them were famous in their own right. Why would any famous author wish to conceal his or her authorship of plays as wonderful as Shakespeare's?

Y: Why do you think that a single person must have written all of Shakespeare's plays? It is possible that Shakespeare's name became attached to plays written by several different authors, or perhaps by committees of authors working together.

The main point at issue between X and Y is whether

(A) any other playwright of the time could have been responsible for writing the plays attributed to William Shakespeare

(B) the plays attributed to William Shakespeare could have been written by committees of authors working together

(C) the assertion that the historical person named William Shakespeare did not write all of the plays attributed to him could be correct

(D) any other author who was involved in writing the plays attributed to William Shakespeare could have wished to conceal that fact

(E) X's assumption that a single person wrote all of the plays attributed to William Shakespeare could be correct

3. Most economists agree that government subsidies
    to food producers are justified, since they serve
    to maintain both low prices and a reliable food
    supply. In the absence of such subsidies, the normal
    business cycle coupled with the unpredictability of
    weather would result in shortages and, therefore,
    deprivation for the poorest members of society. Yet
    these economists overlook the fact that government's
    main obligation is to use its resources in the most
    efficient manner possible. There can be no doubt
    that supplying food to those in need in times of crisis
    would require far fewer government resources than
    paying farmers to produce unprofitable crops year
    after year.

    The argument above is structured to lead to which
    one of the following conclusions?

    (A) Most economists are misguided in at least one
        of their beliefs.
    (B) The government's main concern in the
        expenditure of its revenues should be
        efficiency.
    (C) The removal of government subsidies to food
        producers would result in deprivation for the
        poorest members of society.
    (D) A policy that provides food to the poorest
        members of society at times of crisis would
        represent an efficient use of government
        resources.
    (E) The normal business cycle tends to lead to
        a more efficient use of resources than that
        produced by any system of government
        subsidies.

4. Not all accidental consequences of an action are
    ones for which the person performing the action can
    be held blameless. Responsibility for an aggressive
    or violent act, for example, extends also to its
    unforeseen and unintended results. Thus, although
    an accidental consequence is typically defined by
    the fact that it is not intentional, intent is not entirely
    irrelevant to the question of whether or not an
    individual can be held responsible for an accidental
    consequence of his or her action.

    Which one of the following most accurately
    expresses the main conclusion of the argument?

    (A) Someone who performs an action which has
        unintended consequences may nevertheless be
        responsible for those consequences.
    (B) Aggressive and violent actions differ in at least
        one respect from all other actions.
    (C) Any consequence of an action that cannot
        be considered accidental is an intended
        consequence of that action.
    (D) If someone performing an action can be held
        blameless for the unintended consequences of
        that action, then that action must be neither
        aggressive nor violent.
    (E) The responsibility for an accidental
        consequence of an action may depend in
        at least some cases upon what the intended
        consequences of that action were.

5. Inez: There is no reason to refurbish our home to meet the new, more stringent fire codes. Even if these codes had been in place last winter, and we had refurbished our home to comply with them, they would not have prevented the furnace fire and the resulting property damage. Moreover, the amount it would cost us to refurbish our home is much greater than any amount the city could fine us for not complying with the new codes.

Jacques: The purpose of the new fire codes is not to protect property, but to save lives. If either of us had been in the house at the time of the fire last winter, we might not have been able to escape in time. If our home had met the new codes, however, we would not have been in serious danger.

The main point at issue between Inez and Jacques is

(A) the purpose of the city's new fire codes
(B) what reason, if any, there is to refurbish their home to comply with the new fire codes
(C) whether the expense of refurbishing their home to meet the new fire codes is justified
(D) what danger, if any, the furnace fire in their home last winter posed
(E) whether the new fire codes provide adequate protection against injury and property loss

6. Most students who study physics think of time as a quantity that is invariant and objective, in which events appear to occur in the same order to all those who witness them. Without a more precise understanding, however, this perception of time is bound to lead to contradictions. While it is true that time cannot become so disjointed that the rules of cause and effect are violated, it is relatively easy to show that two events perceived by one observer to be simultaneous may not appear simultaneous to an observer moving relative to the first. Strange though the fact may seem, this violation of the usual assumptions about time is necessary to ensure that both observers witness sequences of events that are completely consistent with one another.

Which one of the following most accurately restates the main point of the passage?

(A) Contrary to a belief held by many who study physics, time is not governed by predictable laws, since an observer may identify as a cause an event that is perceived by a different observer to be an effect.
(B) It is not precisely correct to think of time as invariant and objective, since a chronology of events perceived by one observer may not be in all ways identical to a chronology of events perceived by an observer moving relative to the first.
(C) Recent discoveries in physics have changed commonly held notions of time and space.
(D) If an event is perceived by one observer to be simultaneous with another event, then it is impossible for any other observer to witness the same two events simultaneously.
(E) If two observers witness at the same time an event that is a cause of some other event, then these two observers cannot witness that effect at the same time.

7. Economist: I refuse to accept this report's conclusion that the unemployment problem in our country is growing worse. The report itself states that job losses are smaller now than they have been at any time in the past two years. Moreover, surveys have indicated that our citizens are paying off debt and saving at greater rates than at any time in the past decade. It is clear that the report's findings were politically motivated.

The economist concludes that the report

(A) is in large part false
(B) makes unacceptable assumptions
(C) raises doubts about the actual unemployment rate
(D) is called into question by economic data
(E) is merely propaganda

8. Geneticist: We are on the verge of being able to treat some hitherto intractable mental illnesses. Studies of excessive anxiety in pointers, for example, have revealed the defective gene responsible for the disorder in these dogs. It is clearer than ever that the causes of anxiety have nothing to do with a person's experience or environment, but are instead the result of heredity and biochemistry.

Psychoanalyst: This particular type of anxiety in pointers has only a few symptoms in common with the most prevalent type of anxiety that afflicts humans. Moreover, researchers believe that the function of the gene that is defective in these pointers is carried out by multiple genes in humans.

Which one of the following most accurately states the main point of the psychoanalyst's response?

(A) The causes of excessive anxiety in humans are not the result of heredity and biochemistry.
(B) The defective gene responsible for excessive anxiety in pointers is responsible only for those types of anxiety in humans that have similar symptoms.
(C) It is unlikely that a gene defect similar to that found in some dogs is responsible for cases of excessive anxiety in humans.
(D) Only defects in several human genes could give rise to the same symptoms of excessive anxiety found in some pointers.
(E) Anxiety in humans is a complex disorder that most likely results from a combination of factors, including heredity, biochemistry, environment, and experience.

2. Drawing Unstated Conclusions

Instead of asking you to identify the stated or intended conclusion of a given argument, many LSAT questions will present you with a set of facts and then ask you to draw your own conclusion from it. Generally speaking, the kinds of statements you'll be looking for in the answer choices are similar: qualified and not too broad.

But there are important differences in how you approach these questions. When a question asks you merely to identify an argument's intended conclusion, you don't need to worry about how well supported that conclusion is. An argument that includes huge assumptions, lack of logic, or weak support may nevertheless intend to reach a conclusion that its reasoning does not properly justify. When it's your turn to draw a conclusion, though, leaps of logic are definitely not allowed. In fact, some of the answer choices will try to tempt you to take steps beyond the presented material and lure you into concluding too much.

When you're working these questions, be especially vigilant about words that indicate quantity or frequency. When an argument or answer choice uses the words *none, all, never, only,* and so on, interpret those words quite literally. Although in our daily lives we routinely engage in exaggeration, you shouldn't do that on the LSAT. Consider soft statements—those including *some, many, seldom*—carefully. Often the right answer on these questions will seem an understatement of the conclusion supported by the facts.

Try out the problems on the next page. Answers and explanations can be found in Chapter 20.

DRILL #2

1. Naturalist: Some have suggested that the tendency of some species to prey on their own young is the result of evolutionary pressure to prevent overpopulation when resources are scarce. Yet it is well established that a behavior becomes widespread in a population of animals only when that behavior increases the reproductive success of the individuals that exhibit it. The only kind of evolutionary pressure that could result in a species preying on its own young would be one that allows individual animals of the species who exhibit that behavior to produce, in the long run, more offspring that survive and reproduce than individuals who do not.

The naturalist's statements, if true, provide the greatest support for which one of the following conclusions?

(A)   The evolutionary pressure to prevent overpopulation when resources are scarce could encourage a behavior in some species that appears to decrease the reproductive success of individuals of those species.

(B)   The tendency of some species to prey on their own young when resources are scarce is not the result of an evolutionary pressure for individuals of that species to maximize the number of their offspring that survive and reproduce.

(C)   An individual animal that preys on its own young when resources are scarce diminishes competition for those resources, thus ensuring that the animal will survive to produce offspring at a later time when resources are abundant.

(D)   Evolutionary pressure to prevent overpopulation when resources are scarce cannot have resulted in the behavior of those species that prey on their own young.

(E)   Animals that prey on their own young when resources are scarce do not engage in this behavior when resources are abundant.

2. Executive: The original rationale for discontinuing our old product line and introducing the new one was that the demand for products like those in our old line was predicted to decline within the next two years. Now, two years later, it has become apparent that demand for products like those in our old line has not declined, whereas overall company sales are less now than they were when we changed our product line. Therefore, _____.

Which one of the following most logically completes the executive's argument?

(A)   the decision to change product lines has been a complete failure

(B)   the original rationale for discontinuing our old product line was insufficient to prompt such a radical response

(C)   if the goal of our company is to maximize sales, then it is unlikely that the decision to change product lines has served that goal

(D)   the executive who made the decision to change our product lines should be demoted or fired

(E)   products like those in our old line are more attractive to consumers than are those in our new product line

3. Four years ago, only five percent of those who cast votes in the mayoral election voted for anyone other than the candidates nominated by the two major parties. Over the intervening four years, both major parties have experienced widely publicized scandals, and as a result three thousand fewer votes were cast in this year's mayoral election than were cast four years ago. This time, candidates other than those nominated by the same two major parties received ten percent of the votes cast.

Which one of the following can most properly be concluded from the statements above?

(A) The widely publicized scandals that afflicted the two major parties are at least partly responsible for the fact that they received a smaller share of the vote in this mayoral election than they did in the election four years ago.

(B) Third-party nominees received more votes in this year's mayoral election than third-party nominees received in the election four years ago.

(C) Neither major party was substantially damaged by the widely publicized scandals that it experienced within the past four years.

(D) This year, a greater percentage of the city's population supported candidates who were not nominated by one of the two major parties than did so four years ago.

(E) Fewer people cast votes in favor of the major-party nominees in this year's mayoral election than cast votes in favor of the major-party nominees in the mayoral election four years ago.

4. Engineer: The most important concern in planning the surface probe's mission is to maximize its likelihood of success. Although the chaotic region north of the equator is an area of substantial scientific interest, any effort to explore it would be extremely risky. Therefore, some other region should be chosen for the surface probe's landing.

Scientist: It is true that exploring the chaotic region poses a significant risk of mission failure, but the success of the mission is irrelevant if it offers only marginal scientific benefits. There are many other regions we might choose where a landing would be less hazardous, but none of them is entirely free of risk, and the scientific benefits of exploring any of these regions would be negligible compared to those we could expect from exploring the chaotic region.

By their statements above, the scientist and the engineer are committed to disagreeing about the truth of which one of the following statements?

(A) Some factor other than the likelihood of success must contribute to a determination of whether or not the chaotic region is selected as the surface probe's landing site.

(B) Some region might be chosen for the surface probe's landing that poses no risk to the success of its mission.

(C) Although the scientific benefits of landing the surface probe outside the chaotic region may be less than those associated with a landing within the chaotic region, the scientific benefits of a successful mission are greater than those associated with any failed mission.

(D) The likely scientific benefits should be the most important factor in planning the surface probe's mission.

(E) In planning the surface probe's mission, it is impossible both to minimize the risk of failure and to maximize the possible scientific benefit of its results.

5. It is widely believed that the newly approved medication developed by PharmCorp for other purposes can also cure certain kinds of cancer. Previous estimates that the medication would be effective for this purpose at the dosage recommended by PharmCorp have been shown in recent trials to be incorrect, and the medication is extremely toxic at the dosages needed to be effective against cancer. Safety studies conducted on this medication show that the incidence of side-effects would be too high to receive approval at any dosage higher than that recommended by PharmCorp.

The statements above, if true, most strongly support which one of the following conclusions?

(A) Previous safety studies conducted on PharmCorp's new medication reached erroneous conclusions.

(B) The incidence of toxic side-effects for PharmCorp's new medication is higher than the incidence of toxic side-effects of other medications developed for the same purposes.

(C) The danger of harm to patients due to toxic side-effects is greater for PharmCorp's new medication than is the danger to patients posed by the types of cancer this medication might be used to cure.

(D) Either PharmCorp's new medication will never be used as an effective treatment for cancer, or it will be administered in a way that could be considered dangerous by some standard.

(E) The safety requirements a drug must satisfy in order to be used to treat cancer are more stringent than the requirements a drug must satisfy in order to be used for other purposes.

6. In selecting a home to buy, Loretta has definite requirements for several of the home's important features, including location, price, size, and age. She plans to select a home according to the following principle: I may select a home which does not ideally suit my requirements with respect to one or more of the important features as long as the other homes I am considering all fail to suit my requirements with respect to a greater number of these features; otherwise, I may not select any home that fails to suit every one of my requirements. Loretta has seen three homes so far. One of the homes is large enough but not in an ideal location, another one is in an ideal location but is too small, while the last is ideal in terms of both location and size but is the only one of the three that was constructed too long ago to meet her age requirement.

If the statements in the passage are true, and if exactly two of the three homes described are too expensive but the other one meets her price requirement, then which one of the following, if true, would definitely allow Loretta to select one of the three homes mentioned in the passage?

(A) Location, price, size, and age are not the only four features of a home for which Loretta has definite requirements.

(B) In addition to location, price, size, and age, Loretta's only other requirement concerns the accessibility of her home to public transportation, and none of the three homes meets this requirement.

(C) The fourth home Loretta sees does not meet her requirements for either size or age.

(D) Loretta may be willing to dispense with her requirement concerning her home's age if she does not eventually find a home that suits every one of her requirements.

(E) It is not reasonable to expect that Loretta will find a house that suits every one of her requirements.

7. A recent study conducted on college students to measure their use of illegal drugs and their television viewing habits has yielded interesting results concerning the interactions between these behaviors and the students' living situations. Illegal drug use occurred among both high-viewing and low-viewing students, but drug users were more likely to be high-viewing than they were to be low-viewing. Students who lived in an apartment or house with two or more other students were also more likely to be high-viewing than they were to be low-viewing. The lowest rates of television viewing occurred among students who did not engage in drug use and who shared a dormitory room with exactly one other student.

Which one of the following conclusions is best supported by the findings of the study described above?

(A) Pairing college students together and having them share dormitory rooms would be the most effective way for colleges to reduce their students' use of illegal drugs.
(B) Living conditions are the most important determining factor in both a student's television viewing habits and their use of illegal drugs.
(C) Drugs users who share an apartment or house with two or more other students are more likely to experience academic problems than other students are.
(D) A college student's use of illegal drugs cannot be predicted from his or her television viewing habits alone.
(E) All college students watch at least some television, although not all of them engage in the use of illegal drugs.

8. Rex: I enjoy Earache's songs, but their music cannot be considered truly original popular music. No matter how memorable their tunes may be, their lyrics are simply too repetitive.

Phil: In order to be considered original, popular music need not have inventive lyrics. It must, however, demonstrate a greater range of style and tempo than Earache seems capable of.

Rex's and Phil's statements provide the most support for holding that they would agree about the truth of which one of the following statements?

(A) Earache's popular music should be considered original.
(B) If at some later time Earache's music begins to display a greater range of style and tempo, then it would meet at least one criterion for originality that it does not now meet.
(C) In addition to having a memorable tune, demonstrating a range of style and tempo, and not having repetitive lyrics, there may be other criteria that popular music must meet in order to be considered truly original.
(D) Earache's music cannot be considered truly original because of its repetitive lyrics.
(E) Earache's music does not demonstrate a wide range of style and tempo.

9. Last year, Center City was both socially progressive and fiscally healthy. In order to remain fiscally healthy, Center City must take in at least as much revenue in taxes this year as it expends for supporting social programs. In order to remain socially progressive, however, Center City must expend at least as much money for supporting social programs as it collected in taxes last year.

Which of the following can most properly be inferred from the information in the passage above?

(A) Center City will cease to be either socially progressive, or fiscally healthy, or both.
(B) In order to remain both socially progressive and fiscally healthy, Center City must collect more revenue in taxes this year than it collected in taxes last year.
(C) If Center City is able to find sources of revenue other than taxes, it will be able to remain both socially progressive and fiscally healthy.
(D) If Center City collects less revenue in taxes this year than it collected in taxes last year, then it will be more important for the city to remain fiscally healthy than to remain socially progressive.
(E) By collecting as much in tax revenue this year as it collected in tax revenue last year, Center City may be able to remain both fiscally healthy and socially progressive.

3. Describing Arguments

Some of the more difficult questions concerning an argument's conclusion require you to identify correct descriptions of the reasoning that leads up to it, or identify in what specific way it is not well supported. Descriptions of an argument, or of the role a particular statement plays in the argument, often use general, convoluted language that can be extremely difficult to decipher.

It's important on these questions to spend time breaking down the argument. You'll need, first, to correctly identify the conclusion, and then examine the relationship of the premises to it. When a question asks how an argument is flawed, you'll also need to have an idea of what improper leap of logic is involved. If you don't have a solid understanding of the argument to start with, it'll be very difficult for you to recognize the correct answer when you read it.

Spend plenty of time with the answer choices, too. Even if you understand the argument inside and out, the writers of the LSAT are very skilled at writing credited responses that sound bad or are all but indecipherable. Your POE skills will be crucial here; very often, you'll settle on your answer by finding four others you know it can't be. Be sure to take every answer choice one piece at a time and examine each piece carefully. If you read through quickly and just try to get a sense of what each answer choice is saying, on some of these questions you'll wind up hopelessly baffled.

Try out the questions on the next page. Answers and explanations can be found in Chapter 20.

DRILL #3

1. Aid worker: Rampant crime and a deteriorating infrastructure in many areas of Erronia is causing harm to its economy and extreme hardship for its citizens. Many people argue that, since the declining economy of Erronia is likely only to accelerate the deterioration of conditions in the country, a full-fledged humanitarian disaster is inevitable. In Erronia's provincial city of Nod, however, the impact of this decline has been minimized by the organization of all-volunteer neighborhood safety councils and local citizen groups that make certain food and medical aid is distributed efficiently to those in the greatest need. Thus, officials in Nod have proven that the worsening economic conditions in Erronia need not lead to chaos and privation for its citizens.

The aid worker's argument proceeds by

(A) appealing to an economic expert to refute a widely held belief
(B) questioning the evidence on which an opposing position is based
(C) proposing an alternative explanation for a worrisome state of affairs
(D) showing that a set of conditions that leads to a series of effects in one case need not lead to the same series of effects in all cases
(E) presenting a counterexample to a general claim

2. Senator: The increasingly frequent and explicit portrayals of violence in our popular culture must be addressed by legislation. Although studies have failed to establish a definitive link between portrayals of violence and violent behavior among individual children and young adults, any reasonable person would agree that a child who is exposed to frequent portrayals of violence is more likely to engage in such behavior himself. The vast majority of people are willing to accept limits on free speech in instances where public safety is at risk, and this is unquestionably such an instance.

The senator's argument above conforms most closely to which one of the following principles?

(A) In cases where public safety conflicts with the protection of free speech, legislation should curb free speech only as much as is necessary to protect public safety.
(B) In cases where a reasonable person would agree that a certain activity threatens public safety, definitive proof of that threat is not required in order for legislative action to be permissible.
(C) In cases where an activity widely considered a threat to public safety cannot be definitively proven to pose a threat, legislative action against that threat is nevertheless required, as long as the majority of people are willing to accept limits imposed by the legislation.
(D) In cases where an action negatively affects the public as a whole, that action need not be proven to harm individuals in order for reasonable people to agree that the action poses a threat to public safety.
(E) In cases where a fundamental right would be limited by legislative action, that action is acceptable whenever a majority of citizens agree to that limitation.

3. Four years ago, the population of endangered panthers indigenous to this region was shrinking. Today, it is once again experiencing growth, but it cannot thereby be concluded that the panther population has been stabilized. Efforts to prevent destruction of the panthers' habitat have largely succeeded, and the recent growth of the population can be attributed directly to the success of these efforts, but the population of prey animals on which the panthers depend is shrinking as fast as ever. Unless something is done about this decline, it will soon be the food supply, not habitat, that will impose a limit on the panther population, and thus the panthers will once again find themselves facing the prospect of extinction.

The statement that the panther population has been stabilized plays which one of the following roles in the argument?

(A) It is the conclusion of the argument.
(B) It is a statement whose truth is required in order for the argument's main conclusion to be true.
(C) It provides the context in which the main conclusion of the argument can best be understood.
(D) It is a statement that the argument is advancing in order to refute.
(E) It is a statement whose truth cannot be directly verified.

4. Jackson: Clearly, biologists do not understand genes as well as they pretend to. Although the purported genetic causes of disorders such as hemophilia and cystic fibrosis have been identified, successful treatments remain elusive. So-called gene therapy has been an abject failure, and trials of it have been called to a halt after it was found that the treatment caused leukemia in many of its subjects.

Mikulski: Certainly the early efforts at gene therapy have included tragic side-effects, but you are overlooking the cases in which it has been successful. Some participants in these trials appear to have been cured of illnesses that are otherwise untreatable, and would eventually have cost them their lives. The technology of gene therapy is by no means mature, but it is based on sound science.

Mikulski employs which one of the following argumentative techniques in countering Jackson's argument?

(A) calling into question the accuracy of evidence used to support Jackson's conclusion
(B) characterizing Jackson's generalizations as too broad
(C) presenting additional evidence that contradicts the evidence on which Jackson relies
(D) exposing an assumption of Jackson's argument that is unlikely to be true
(E) introducing a relevant distinction that undermines Jackson's conclusion

5. The tiny countries of Titania and Oberon have the same population and the same per capita income. Titania has a healthy economy and an extremely low rate of poverty. One hundred percent of Titania's citizenry is literate, less than five percent of the working-age population is unemployed, and the quality of life in Titania is among the highest in the world. No doubt Oberon, like Titania, enjoys similar benefits of its citizens' prosperity.

The reasoning in the argument is most vulnerable to criticism on the grounds that the argument

(A) presupposes the truth of the conclusion it sets out to prove
(B) mistakenly identifies as a cause some factor that is more properly understood as an effect of other causes
(C) fails to recognize that having identical per capita income is consistent with great differences in the prosperity of citizens overall
(D) does not acknowledge that education and employment may not be the only factors relevant to the overall health of a country's economy
(E) disregards the possibility that two countries that are identical in some respects may not be identical in every respect

6. Spokesperson: The Tremendous Corporation has received intense scrutiny from the federal government. In a report released this week, the investigating commission found no evidence of illegal trade practices on our part. There can thus be no doubt that the accusations recently made by Scrappy, Inc., concerning The Tremendous Corporation's trade practices are completely false.

Journalist: The only thing that can be called "completely false" is your own statement. In testimony before the investigating committee, several Tremendous Corporation executives admitted to making illegal campaign contributions to candidates for national office. There can be no doubt that the accusations made by Scrappy, Inc., which include charges of official corruption, are in fact true.

The journalist's response

(A) reveals a mistaken belief that the spokesperson's statement characterizes the accusations of Scrappy, Inc., as being entirely without merit
(B) employs excessively emotional language in pointing out a flaw in the spokesperson's statement
(C) fails to demonstrate that the accusations of Scrappy, Inc., are in some part true
(D) resorts to attacking the character of individuals associated with The Tremendous Corporation rather than addressing the content of the spokesperson's statement
(E) succeeds in undermining the spokesperson's assertion by pointing out a relevant consideration that it overlooks

7. If no student had heard more about the schedule changes than any other student, then no student could secure a place that should be open to all students on a first-come, first-served basis. All any student has heard about the schedule changes is what the Registrar has told them. If the Registrar had told every student everything about the schedule changes, then no student would have heard more about the schedule changes than any other student. Unfortunately, the Registrar did not tell any student everything about the schedule changes. Therefore, some student can secure a place that should be open to all students on a first-come, first-served basis.

    The argument's reasoning is flawed because it fails to recognize that which one of the following is possible, given the facts presented in the argument?

    (A) The Registrar did not tell everything about the schedule changes to every student.
    (B) Even if some student knows more about the schedule changes than every other student, that student may not wish to secure a place that should be open to all students on a first-come, first-served basis.
    (C) Some student may have heard information about the schedule changes that the student shared with every other student.
    (D) The Registrar may not have a complete knowledge of the schedule changes.
    (E) Every student has heard everything about the schedule changes that any other student has heard.

8. Philosopher: Every tree in the garden is taller than every flower in the garden. Every piece of statuary in the garden is both shorter than the shortest tree in the garden and taller than the tallest flower in the garden. Therefore, since at least one thing in the garden is both taller than the tallest statue and shorter than the shortest tree, the garden must contain something in addition to flowers, trees, and statuary.

    Which one of the following is a principle of reasoning employed by the philosopher's argument?

    (A) If the members of a collection all possess a particular attribute to a greater or lesser extent, then any member that possesses this attribute to a greater extent than every member of a group within the collection must not belong to any group within the collection.
    (B) If one member of a collection possesses an attribute that is not possessed by any member of all the known groups within that collection, then the collection cannot be composed solely of members of the known groups.
    (C) If two groups within a collection are known to have at least one member in common, then it cannot be said that either group possesses any attribute to a greater or lesser extent than the other group.
    (D) If a collection is composed entirely of known groups, then anything that is not a member of at least one of these known groups must also not be a member of the collection.
    (E) If a collection is composed of known groups, then the number of members in the collection cannot be less than the number of members in the largest known group.

4

Language Shifts

WHAT IS A LANGUAGE SHIFT?

Many conclusions in LSAT args questions are not supported by the given premises. The test writers construct these flawed arguments in lots of different ways, but one of their favorites is to shift the language being used, sometimes quite subtly. Broadly speaking, a language shift happens when an argument pretends that one word, phrase, or idea means exactly the same thing as another one used in the argument. The shift can happen between the premises and the conclusion or within the premises themselves, and sometimes involves a premise being "forgotten" on the way to the conclusion. Here are some things to keep in mind when you approach an argument that contains one of these types of gaps.

Focus on the Conclusion

One small mercy of these arguments is that the conclusion is almost always explicitly stated. It is absolutely essential that, when it is, you locate this statement and closely examine its language. Not only will this make it much easier for you to find many of the language shifts on the LSAT, it will also tell you what the exact scope of the argument is—the precise set of issues that are relevant to the conclusion. The LSAT test writers love to write appealing wrong answers by addressing issues that lie just outside the argument's actual scope.

Take Out the Garbage

Not everything in an argument is essential to its reasoning. Historical background, definitions of terms, and parenthetical commentary may help to clarify an argument's content, but this sort of garbage usually isn't part of the premises or the conclusion, which are the only structurally significant parts of an argument. The test writers often strategically position this garbage to separate the two statements involved in a language shift. Some shifts that would be jarring in two adjacent statements become much more difficult to notice when the statements are distant from one another.

Allow Paraphrases, Synonyms, and Specific Instances

Not every difference in language represents a gap, assumption, or flaw. If a premise of the argument concerns "human institutions" and the conclusion involves "a national government," this difference in language is most likely not a fatal language shift; after all, a national government *is* a type of human institution. The first step in finding a language shift is of course to note differences in language, but the key second step is to ask whether the two terms actually refer to the same thing.

With these ideas in mind, let's look more specifically at three different ways the LSAT can shift the language within an argument.

1. New Stuff in the Conclusion

Some of the more blatant, and most common, language shifts seen in LSAT arguments involve differences between the terms used in the premises and those used in the conclusion. As usual, the most important step in finding these is to look carefully at the conclusion as it's stated. If there's a key word, phrase, or idea in the conclusion that appears there for the very first time, you've found a language shift that's very likely to be the gap around which the question is constructed.

Once you've found the language shift, keep in mind that your job isn't quite done. Depending upon the question being asked, the answer you're looking for may have different relationships to the gap indicated by the shift. On an assumption question, for example, the answer will identify the shift fairly directly; on a strengthen question, the answer may explain why the language shift makes sense, or provide a specific case in which the two terms used really are closely linked. But on a weaken question, the right answer will disconnect the two terms from one another; a flaw question's right answer will describe why the shift really is a problem. Make sure the answer you pick is going in the right direction to answer the question that's being asked. Many of these questions include distracting, wrong answers that do a wonderful job of answering some other question.

Finally, keep an eye out for language that involves judgment or prediction. If a conclusion includes a *should* or a *will*, that sort of language must also appear in the premises in order for the conclusion to be properly drawn. This sort of language is very often the new stuff to be found in the conclusion.

Now try out the drill on the following page. Answers can be found in Chapter 20.

DRILL #1

1. Editorial: Candidates for political office often campaign on matters of economic policy, but nothing could be more inappropriate. Recent surveys indicate that only 25 percent of voters know enough about economic concepts to understand even newspaper articles on the subject, much less the complex theories and arguments concerning the relationship of cause and effect in this difficult area. It is clear that a majority of those who vote do not know enough about economics to evaluate the truth of a candidate's economic claims or to make informed decisions about the economic policies candidates propose.

Which one of the following, if true, most weakens the editorial's argument?

(A) Even those who know enough about economic concepts to understand newspaper articles on the subject are not in all cases able to evaluate the truth of economic claims made by a candidate for political office.

(B) Although a majority of individual voters may not be able to make informed decisions about the economic policies proposed by the candidates for political office, a majority of votes may nevertheless be cast for the candidate with the greatest understanding of the relationship of cause and effect in matters of economic policy.

(C) It is inappropriate for candidates for political office to campaign on any matter of policy about which a majority of voters cannot be expected to make informed decisions.

(D) A voter who does not understand newspaper articles on the subject of economic policy may nevertheless be able to evaluate the truth of economic claims made by a candidate for political office.

(E) Some voters who do not know enough about economic concepts to evaluate the truth of economic claims made by a candidate for political office may nevertheless be able to make informed decisions about the economic policies that candidate proposes.

2. Use of performance-enhancing drugs by professional athletes in all sports is rampant. Not only do such drugs pose health risks for those who use them, but also when some athletes in a particular sport use these drugs and others do not, the quality of competition in that sport suffers, and fan interest declines. Since fan interest in any sport is crucial to the sales of tickets and merchandise, it is therefore imperative for every sport's financial health that stringent systems of testing for performance-enhancing drugs and penalties for those who use them be instituted.

Which one of the following is an assumption on which the argument depends?

(A) The financial health of a sport depends in part upon the sales of tickets and merchandise related to that sport.

(B) Stringent systems of testing for performance-enhancing drugs and penalties for those who use them will be equally effective in decreasing the use of these drugs in every sport.

(C) The use of performance-enhancing drugs by some of a sport's athletes does not result in increased sales of merchandise related to those individual athletes.

(D) If every athlete in every sport made use of performance-enhancing drugs, then performance-enhancing drugs would pose no threat to the financial health of any sport.

(E) Systems of testing for performance-enhancing drugs, no matter how stringent, cannot prevent all athletes in every sport from using these drugs.

3. In order to be called just, a legal system need only be consistent. A legal system is consistent when all those who are found guilty of the same crime receive the same punishment, and when all those who are accused of the same crime are pursued with equal vigor. Most international agencies are therefore incorrect when they claim that the legal system in the country of Vigona is excessively harsh. In Vigona, those found guilty of crimes are exiled without exception, and no country pursues those accused of crimes more zealously than Vigona does.

The reasoning in the argument is flawed because the argument

(A) fails to establish that the legal system in the country of Vigona satisfies at least one known requirement for a legal system to be just
(B) attacks the motives of international agencies in criticizing the legal system of Vigona rather than the substance of those criticisms
(C) presupposes without warrant that any legal system that can be said to be excessively harsh must also be unjust
(D) accepts the vigor with which a country pursues those accused of crimes as incontrovertible proof that that country also metes out equal punishment to all offenders
(E) interprets the fact that Vigona's legal system meets criteria that guarantee its consistency as meaning that every consistent legal system must also meet these criteria

4. All bivalves are mollusks, and all mollusks possess both a muscular foot and a visceral mass. It follows that all bivalves possess both a muscular foot and a visceral mass. It thus also follows that the sea cucumber is not a bivalve.

The final conclusion above follows logically if which one of the following is assumed?

(A) Anything that possesses both a muscular foot and a visceral mass is a mollusk.
(B) There are no mollusks that are not bivalves.
(C) The sea cucumber does not possess a visceral mass.
(D) The sea cucumber possesses a muscular foot.
(E) There are no bivalves that are not mollusks.

5. Inspector: In this apartment building, every floor has the same layout and is partitioned into individual apartments in precisely the same way. Nevertheless, the price of an apartment on the second floor is lower than the price of the equivalent apartment on the fifth floor, and both are substantially less expensive that the equivalent apartment on the fifteenth floor. It must be true that apartments located higher above the street are more desirable to prospective tenants.

Which one of the following, if true, provides the strongest possible support for the inspector's conclusion?

(A) Apartments located higher above the street provide a wider view of the surrounding area, and a wider view is invariably associated with a higher price.
(B) Apartments located higher above the street are less accessible to firefighters, and thus may be more dangerous for their tenants.
(C) The price of an apartment is determined by many factors, some of which depend on the layout of the building in which the apartment is located.
(D) Every apartment in a given building is more desirable than any apartment in a building situated in a less desirable location.
(E) The price of an apartment is a reliable indicator of its relative desirability to prospective tenants.

6. A rule that applies to all city parks requires that pets be kept on leashes. Many parks are in areas with several nearby roads, and unleashed animals are liable to run out into traffic and become involved in accidents that are dangerous both to the animal and to drivers. Some pets may chase or even attack people who walk or jog along the park's paths, and leashes are necessary to prevent these occurrences. Also, some animals behave aggressively toward one another, and leashes are necessary to protect the other pets in the park. This park, however, is different: there is no road nearby, only pet owners use the park, and all the animals that frequent the park are gentle-natured and never behave aggressively. This park should thus be exempt from the rule requiring pets to be kept on leashes.

Which one of the following principles, if established, would most strongly support the position advocated above?

(A) Citizens should be exempt from following rules that provide no clear benefit to them.

(B) Rules governing the use of a public resource should apply in only those specific instances where the reasons for instituting the rule apply.

(C) Even if citizens who currently use a public resource do not use it for a specific purpose, they should not therefore be prevented from using it for that purpose in the future.

(D) If the reasons for instituting a rule cease to exist, the rule should immediately be repealed.

(E) Rules governing the use of a public resource can be instituted when the foreseeable result of not instituting that rule would be injury to some person or animal.

7. W: Poetry has ceased to serve a useful purpose in our society. This cannot be said to be the fault of contemporary poets; today's poetry retains the same ability to inspire reflection, evoke feeling, and engage the imagination that poetry has possessed throughout history. Nevertheless, today the majority of people in our society seek these pleasures in popular music, whereas only a very few read poetry.

Y: Only a very few people in our society comprehend mathematical statistics, can read ancient Greek, or know how to design a microchip. Yet each of these activities, in its own way, makes essential contributions to our society.

Y responds to W by

(A) invoking a generalization relevant to W's conclusion

(B) exposing a bias that underlies W's reasoning

(C) questioning W's use of vague terminology

(D) drawing an analogy that casts doubt on the basis of W's judgment

(E) providing additional evidence that sheds new light on W's claim

8. The law states that a person cannot be held responsible for a harmful action if that person is incapable of distinguishing right from wrong. Although this fact may seem cruel to the family and friends of those harmed by such an action, it would be far crueler to punish someone who is incapable of understanding why that action merits punishment. Smith, however, can be held responsible for his action. In his own statement, he acknowledges that he now knows that what he did was wrong.

Which one of the following is an assumption upon which the argument relies?

(A) If failing to punish a harmful action would be crueler than punishing it would be, then that action merits punishment.

(B) Smith cannot be punished for his action without holding him responsible for that action.

(C) Smith can be held responsible for his action if he was able to distinguish between right and wrong at the time he took that action.

(D) Smith's action was harmful.

(E) Smith does not meet any criteria, including the inability to distinguish right from wrong, that would prevent him from being held responsible for his action.

9. Even after adjusting for inflation, Americans today earn higher incomes than they did fifty years ago. They own far more labor-saving appliances and are able to enjoy many more luxuries than Americans have in the past. Yet, at the same time, surveys indicate that Americans are more dissatisfied with their lives than ever before. The meaning of these trends is clear: Not only does material prosperity provide no guarantee of happiness; it actually stands in the way of real happiness.

Each of the following, if true, weakens the argument above EXCEPT:

(A) Income, ownership of certain types of property, and the enjoyment of luxuries are not the most important measures of material prosperity.

(B) Feelings of dissatisfaction are not inconsistent with real happiness.

(C) The same surveys mentioned in the argument showed that rates of dissatisfaction were highest among those who enjoyed the least material prosperity.

(D) Factors such as public safety, a pleasant living environment, quantity of leisure time, and meaningful family relationships are not related to material prosperity.

(E) Increased access to communications media has led Americans to be satisfied with levels of material prosperity that are attained by many fewer individuals than was the case fifty years ago.

2. Internal Shifts in Language

Often the problematic language shift in an LSAT argument doesn't take place between the premises and the conclusion, but instead within the premises themselves. Although in essence the flaws in these arguments work the same way as those in the previous section, they can be more difficult to spot. You can't rely on the red flag of a new word, phrase, or idea appearing suddenly in the statement of the conclusion to tip you off.

The thing you'll need to do to find this sort of gap is pay close attention to the relationship of the premises to one another. Sometimes they form a chain of reasoning in which a link is missing between two of the crucial terms. Sometimes the premises include a general rule but not the statement that assures you the rule can be applied in the specific case discussed by the argument.

However the test writers choose to make use of this type of flaw, the tip-off will always be a difference in terminology. Sensitivity to the language used in every part of the argument is the most important skill for you to work on in the next drill. Answers can be found in Chapter 20.

DRILL #2

1. Opponents of nuclear energy overlook an inescapable fact: no matter how stringently safety regulations are enforced, no method of power generation is completely safe. Contrary to popular sentiment, the wastes produced by nuclear power are actually less dangerous to the environment than those produced by fossil fuels, which account for almost all of the power generation in our country. Since most people agree that the dangers of generating power with fossil fuels are acceptable, they must also be willing to accept the dangers associated with nuclear power.

Which one of the following, if true, provides the strongest additional support to the argument above?

(A) The dangers associated with waste produced by nuclear power are outweighed by the benefits of lower fuel costs and decreased dependence on foreign sources of fuel.

(B) Although accidents at power plants using fossil fuels take place more frequently than do accidents at nuclear power plants, the effects of accidents involving fossil fuels are usually not widespread and dissipate more quickly.

(C) Technology associated with increasing the safety of nuclear power generation offers additional potential benefits in the areas of medicine, space exploration, and electronics.

(D) Any technology that represents an advance in human understanding must be developed and employed.

(E) No danger associated with power generation is greater than that posed by the waste products of the fuels used.

2. Activist: The prison system in this country has become a major source of political and economic power. Legislators pass laws that mandate ever longer sentences, and as a result prison populations grow ever larger. The rapid growth of this population provides increased profits to corporations that build prisons and provide services to them. As their profits grow, these corporations make ever larger contributions to political candidates, and thus gain increasing influence over the legislative decisions these candidates make while they are in office. Unless something is done to break this cycle, the prison population in this country will continue to grow for the foreseeable future.

Which one of the following is an assumption required by the argument?

(A) The rate at which crimes are committed in this country will not decline in the foreseeable future.

(B) Some corporations will make use of their political influence to encourage legislation that may increase their profits.

(C) Corporations that are able to spend a greater proportion of their profits on political contributions will do so.

(D) Action must be taken to curb the excessive accumulation of political and economic power in any one area of government.

(E) The longer sentences mandated by recent legislation are not justified.

3. Maria's parents plan to institute a system of monetary rewards to encourage her to improve her grades, which are currently below average. For every A she receives, Maria will be given $100; for every B, she will receive $50. Also, for every A or B she receives in a course that state education standards require for graduation, she will be given an additional $25. Maria has often complained that her parents do not give her enough money to purchase the things that she and her friends enjoy, so this solution should satisfy everyone. As long as she works hard to earn A's and B's, her parents will be satisfied with her improvement, and Maria will finally be able to afford the things she wants.

The answer to which one of the following questions would be most relevant in evaluating the likely success of the system devised by Maria's parents?

(A) What grades are currently considered average under state education standards?
(B) Do Maria's friends primarily earn A's and B's?
(C) Would the ability to purchase the things she wants prevent Maria from being dissatisfied with the amount of money her parents give her?
(D) Would the rewards associated with an average number of A's and B's provide Maria enough money to afford the things she wants?
(E) Does the approval or disapproval of Maria's friends provide sufficient encouragement for Maria to work hard?

4. Transportation authorities have recently begun searching passengers' luggage and their persons at all of the nation's airports and train stations. Although some claim that these searches represent an intolerable violation of privacy, there can be no doubt that the law permits such searches, and that they are successful at preventing certain acts of sabotage and terrorism. Since the primary purpose of the transportation authorities is to prevent all such acts, there can be no doubt that the transportation authorities have fulfilled their purpose by instituting these searches.

The reasoning in the argument above exhibits which one of the following errors of reasoning?

(A) It dismisses valid objections to a course of action on the basis of the fact that the objections are inconsistent with the purpose of that course of action.
(B) It draws a definite conclusion on the basis of facts that concern only what is possible or likely to be true.
(C) It treats one representative type among a class of events as if that type were the only one belonging to that class of events.
(D) It improperly infers from the fact that a policy is legally permissible the conclusion that the policy is thereby legally required.
(E) It supports its conclusion using evidence that also may be used to support the opposite conclusion.

5. Mandel: Legal authorities defend the light sentences given to perpetrators of corporate crime such as securities fraud and tax evasion by pointing out that these crimes are nonviolent, since they do not pose a threat to the health or safety of other citizens. Nothing, however, could be further from the truth. Corporate crime results in the loss of billions of dollars in government revenue annually, and these revenues pay for health coverage and police protection for this country's citizens. Although the threat may not be direct, corporate criminals are nevertheless responsible for the illness and violent death of literally thousands of their fellow citizens every year.

Schwartz: Your standard of so-called responsibility applies as well to violent offenders as to the nonviolent criminals you mention. When the police respond to a bank robbery or an assault, they are taken away from their normal duties of protecting health, life, and property. The resources devoted to prosecuting violent criminals could be spent instead on medicine or other forms of public welfare. We must either hold no criminal responsible for the diversion of resources involved in enforcing the law, or hold every criminal responsible for it. Whichever you choose, the major difference between violent and nonviolent crime remains: one constitutes a direct threat to the health and safety of citizens, whereas the other does not.

Which one of the following, if true, presents a relevant distinction that would most support Mandel in responding to Schwartz's objections?

(A) The quantity and type of resources involved in pursuing nonviolent corporate criminals are substantially different from those required to pursue violent criminals.

(B) Although all crimes result in the diversion of resources attendant upon their pursuit and prosecution, only nonviolent corporate crime poses a direct threat to the overall quantity of resources available for protecting the health and safety of citizens.

(C) Crimes that result in loss of property cannot be considered as serious as those that harm the health or safety of other citizens.

(D) Unlike violent crime, nonviolent corporate crime causes a loss of confidence in the integrity of the country's economic systems overall, resulting in economic weakness that harms every citizen, regardless of income or employment.

(E) Unlike violent crime, nonviolent corporate crime may have a net positive effect on the profits of corporations within a country, resulting ultimately in an overall increase in government tax revenues that may be used to protect public health and safety.

6. Commentator: It is widely known that chemical imbalances cause certain physical disorders in humans. Many biologists believe that chemical imbalances are also responsible for some behavioral disorders. While it is true that naturally occurring chemicals are involved in both behavior and in physical processes, in the case of physical disorders the effects of these chemicals are entirely involuntary and must be controlled by chemical means. Humans, however, are conscious beings, and therefore are capable of monitoring and controlling their own behavior. It is thus clear that chemical imbalances do not play the same role in causing behavioral disorders as they do in producing physical disorders.

The commentator's argument requires the assumption that

(A) a disorder that cannot be fully attributed to chemical causes must have no symptoms that can be attributed to a chemical imbalance

(B) a disorder that can be consciously monitored and controlled must not be caused by a chemical imbalance

(C) only humans are capable of monitoring and controlling their own behavior

(D) no unconscious factor can play a role in any disorder that can be consciously monitored and controlled

(E) every conscious human is capable of monitoring and controlling his or her own behavior

7. The purpose of every business decision is to maximize profit. When a corporation makes a charitable contribution, it realizes tax benefits from the contribution and also receives public attention that serves the same essential function as paid advertising. Although corporate contributions to charities do have beneficial effects for society, nevertheless the choice to make those contributions is in all cases a business decision.

Which one of the following, if true, most weakens the argument?

(A) The potential benefit to society is not relevant to every corporation's business decisions.

(B) The increased revenue that the best available advertising opportunity can be expected to generate exceeds that associated with any charitable contribution of equivalent price.

(C) The combined tax savings and increased revenue a corporation expects from a charitable contribution is exceeded by the cost savings that would be realized by devoting an equal amount to capital improvements that increase productivity.

(D) No other equivalent expenditure provides a profit benefit to the corporation that exceeds the profit benefit associated with relatively small charitable contributions.

(E) A corporation's motives in making a charitable contribution are less important to an evaluation of that contribution than are its resulting benefits to the corporation and to society.

8. Judges not only may, but should, disregard sentencing guidelines in cases where mitigating circumstances are relevant to the commission of a crime. Although Lewis was undoubtedly guilty of the crime of which she was convicted, her primary motive in committing the crime was not to enrich herself, but instead to provide her daughter with needed medical care she could not then afford. The judge should therefore disregard the sentencing guidelines associated with Lewis's crime.

Which one of the following, if true, would most support the recommendation above concerning Lewis's sentencing?

(A) Committing the crime was the only foreseeable way in which Lewis could afford her daughter's medical treatment.

(B) In all cases where a judge may disregard sentencing guidelines, the judge should do so.

(C) The motives for committing a crime may be considered in evaluating the mitigating circumstances for that crime.

(D) Sentencing guidelines should be considered invalid in those cases where following the guidelines would result in unduly harsh punishment.

(E) A person committing a crime should not receive the maximum sentence for that crime unless no mitigating circumstances are relevant to its commission.

3. The Disappearing Premise

This last, and most difficult, of language shifts occurs when a requirement, stipulation, or condition included in the premises is glossed over as the argument proceeds to its conclusion. It often occurs when an argument applies a general rule or principle to a specific situation. A gap in this kind of reasoning can be difficult to spot because the rule appears to be applied correctly; what's missing is a guarantee that the rule actually *can* be applied to that specific case.

These sorts of "outside the box" assumptions also occur in some arguments where evidence is explained or interpreted. The argument may disregard a possible explanation that the premises explicitly allow. If one premise leaves open a possibility that none of the other premises really exclude, then you'll need to be alert for answer choices that pertain to that possibility. Again, these can be difficult to spot because the reasoning used doesn't have a blatant internal flaw; it just doesn't consider all of the possibilities.

You won't always spot one of these types of gaps at first sight, or in some cases not even at second or third sight. Process of elimination is crucial in any case where the question guarantees you that something's wrong with the argument, but you can't figure out on your own what that thing is. Keep an open mind, and check the argument's premises carefully as you examine the choices. It may be that something you think is true isn't actually stated in the argument, and as you've undoubtedly learned by now, the only things we know for certain are the facts stated in the premises.

Try out the following drill. Answers can be found in Chapter 20.

DRILL #3

1. Property owner: I regret that a small amount of cash was stolen from your apartment while it was being repainted. However, your lease states that except in the event of negligence or misconduct on the part of me or my employees, I cannot be held responsible for any loss or damage of property contained in the apartment. At the time the apartment was repainted, you had moved all but a few of your possessions out, and under those circumstances the terms of the lease permit me and my employees to enter your apartment to make it ready for future tenants. The painters were employed by me, so under the terms of the lease they were permitted to enter the apartment, and I cannot be held responsible for your loss.

Which one of the following, if true, would most weaken the property owner's contention?

(A) A tenant's having moved all but a few possessions out of an apartment does not constitute evidence of the intent to abandon the apartment.

(B) The term of the lease had expired by the time the owner's employees entered the apartment to repaint it.

(C) One year before, the owner had requested that all tenants allow the owner's employees access to their apartments to repaint them, whether or not those apartments could be expected to have new tenants in the near future.

(D) The owner was negligent in not ensuring that the property contained in the apartment remained secure after the owner's employees finished repainting the apartment.

(E) The theft of money from the apartment represents an instance of misconduct.

2. The head of the accounting department and the independent auditor were the only other people present at the single meeting in which the CEO discussed her plan to mislead the company's investors. Without leaked information from that meeting, the plan could never have been reported in the press. Without the scandal that resulted from the press's revelations, the CEO would never have been forced to resign. It seems clear, then, that the CEO's downfall was the result of a single strategic mistake: she should never have invited the independent auditor to participate in that meeting.

Which one of the following most accurately describes a flaw in the argument's reasoning?

(A) treating as the foreseeable result of some course of action an undesirable outcome that was merely one of several possible results of that course of action

(B) confusing a set of conditions necessary to produce a given outcome as if they were by themselves sufficient to produce that outcome

(C) asserting that since one event preceded other events to which it has been shown to be related, the first event must therefore have been the cause of all the others

(D) interpreting a set of facts as leading to one explanation of a state of affairs when those facts provide equally strong support for a potential alternative explanation

(E) imputing error to an individual in a case where that individual's course of action led to an undesirable outcome without considering the likely undesirable outcomes associated with any alternative course of action

3. Doctor Ellis: A fundamental principle of scientific investigation states that the most commonly believed explanation for a natural phenomenon may be rejected when reproducible experimental observations indicate that this explanation is extremely unlikely to be correct. A theory has been advanced that purports to explain the mechanism by which atoms of an element, when excited to higher-energy states, emit light only at certain wavelengths, a characteristic called the element's emission spectrum. This theory, however, is wildly unsuccessful at predicting the emission spectrum for any element other than hydrogen, and is thus unlikely to be correct. Therefore this theory may be rejected.

Doctor Cho: Even if its predictions are not entirely accurate, an explanation may not be rejected when it is the only one available that is consistent with other well-supported explanations of related phenomena. The theory you mention agrees with tenets of physics and chemistry that have never been discredited, and upon which our entire understanding of the universe has long been predicated. Although its details require some refinement, the basic explanation this theory offers must be accepted as almost certainly correct.

Which one of the following best describes a flaw found in the arguments of both Doctor Ellis and Doctor Cho?

(A) drawing conclusions about the rejection of a given theory without considering relevant aspects of other theories advanced to explain the same phenomena

(B) failing to establish that no theory other than the one described is consistent with the explanations offered by well-supported theories concerning related phenomena

(C) overstating the degree to which the theory in question either is or is not valuable by the competing standards presented in their respective arguments

(D) assuming without warrant that the theory in question is the most commonly believed explanation for the characteristic emission spectra exhibited by excited atoms

(E) accepting that a theory's predictive value is the only aspect relevant to the decision of whether to accept or reject that theory

4. All that is needed to ensure a successful party are fascinating guests, delicious food and drink, and music with wide appeal that creates an upbeat mood. That is why Norm's party is sure to be a success. His choice in party music appeals to nearly everyone, he has spared no expense in acquiring the tastiest food and drink available, and he has invited only the most sociable and interesting people he knows.

Which one of the following arguments contains flawed reasoning most similar to that in the argument above?

(A) Veronica's trip to Paris is certain to be enjoyable. In order to be enjoyable, a trip need only include first-class accommodations, beautiful and historic surroundings, and plenty of time to enjoy them. Veronica has lots of time off from work and a reservation at one of the world's best hotels, and no city is more beautiful or historic than Paris.

(B) Miguel's new film is sure to be a commercial success. Every commercially successful movie has an exciting plot, engaging characters, and is superbly filmed and edited. Miguel's film includes the very best cinematography, and the script and acting talent are both excellent, featuring a gripping plot and wonderful characters.

(C) WorldAuto's new sports car features original styling, excellent handling and road feel, and an exceptionally powerful engine. It is sure, therefore, to become a classic sports car. All any sports car needs to become a classic is plenty of power, good handling and road feel, and a sleek, original appearance.

(D) Lots of snow, great trails with plenty of lifts, and inexpensive, comfortable accommodations guarantee a profitable ski resort. That is why Bobcat Mountain is sure to be a profitable ski resort. Bobcat Mountain meets every one of these requirements.

(E) A successful opening requires a large, well-lit gallery, superb art, and plenty of publicity. Nora's art is striking, and her opening is taking place at one of the largest and best-lit galleries in the city, but unfortunately the opening has not been well publicized, so it probably will not be as successful as it could have been.

5. After purchasing a radar detector at a store in Union County, Tricia was informed by a county sheriff that she would not be allowed to use it, since state law forbids the use of type-3 electronic devices, and a Union County ordinance classifies the model of radar detector she purchased as a type-3 electronic device.

Which one of the following, if true, most strongly undermines the county sheriff's argument?

(A) It is not illegal to sell the model of radar detector Tricia purchased in Union County.

(B) Tricia does not live or work in Union County.

(C) Both state law and county ordinances must be consulted in order to determine whether or not a particular activity is permitted in Union County.

(D) In any case where a county ordinance conflicts with state law, the county ordinance can be considered invalid.

(E) Tricia would be permitted to use some model of radar detector in Union County other than the model she purchased.

6. The executive vice presidents of Giganticorp have decided to reorganize some departments within the management division in order to make the company more responsive to changes in its most important markets. Although the disruptions associated with reorganization have a potential to hurt employee morale, the executive vice president in charge of personnel has ample evidence that three of the largest departments within the management division are very poorly organized, and morale among these employees could not be any lower. Hence, the reorganization of the management division will not hurt employee morale at Giganticorp.

The conclusion drawn above depends upon which one of the following assumptions?

(A) It is possible to improve the poor organization of the departments within the management division that have low employee morale.

(B) The reorganization of Giganticorp's management division will include departments in which evidence indicates that employee morale is lowest.

(C) The reorganization of the worst-performing departments within Giganticorp's management division will have the effect of making the company more responsive to changes in its most important markets.

(D) Any improvement to employee morale at Giganticorp requires that three of the largest departments in its management division be reorganized.

(E) Employee morale has a measurable effect on the products and services offered by any company to its customers.

7. These defective components show significant carbon scoring. Every component receives high-voltage testing both by the manufacturer and by the distributor, from whom we purchased these components. Evidence on the components' packaging indicates that they must have shown this same amount of carbon scoring when the distributor received them from the manufacturer, but the distributor claims that these components passed all high-voltage tests. The manufacturer conducts precisely the same tests that the distributor does, and we can be certain that the manufacturer would never ship a defective component. There can be no doubt, then, that the distributor is lying about the results of the high-voltage tests the distributor conducted on these components. The distributor must have known that the components were defective when they were shipped to us.

    Which one of the following, if it were known about the components and their testing, would most strongly undermine the main conclusion drawn above?

    (A) High-voltage testing of the components could not have resulted in the significant carbon scoring they exhibited.
    (B) The manufacturer incurs additional costs when high-voltage testing reveals that a component is defective, whereas the distributor does not.
    (C) Rough handling of the components can result in damage that both causes carbon scoring and causes the components to fail some high-voltage tests conducted by the distributor and the manufacturer.
    (D) The defective components made up less than a quarter of all the components received in the distributor's last shipment.
    (E) Jostling experienced during delivery can cause components that have previously passed all high-voltage tests to become defective.

8. The idea at the root of Einstein's theory of special relativity can be explained in terms of a simple thought experiment: imagine that you are inside a train car whose interior is completely isolated from the universe outside, moving along a straight and level track at a constant velocity. Under these conditions, there is no known experiment you could conduct that would demonstrate that you are moving relative to the ground outside. From this fact, Einstein concluded that an experimenter's perception, or awareness, of physical laws does not depend upon his or her constant velocity relative to any fixed reference point.

    If Einstein's conclusion and the facts on which he based it are correct as they are presented in the passage above, then which one of the following statements must also be true?

    (A) Every experiment that is capable of demonstrating an experimenter's motion relative to any fixed reference point is known.
    (B) An experimenter's perception of his or her motion does not depend upon the physical laws that govern that motion.
    (C) Unless the interior of a train car can be completely isolated from the universe outside, Einstein's theory of special relativity cannot be demonstrated to be correct.
    (D) No experiment exists that could demonstrate the motion of an experimenter within a train car isolated from the universe outside even if the train car is not moving at a constant velocity.
    (E) If Einstein's theory of special relativity is incorrect, then there exists some fixed reference point in the universe at which normal physical laws do not apply.

5

Interpretations of Evidence

HOW DO YOU INTERPRET EVIDENCE?

As you saw in the previous chapter, many LSAT arguments involve applications of abstract principles or chains of reasoning where structure and language end up being more important than what the premises and conclusions are actually saying. Although you'll want to be on the lookout for little differences in language on the LSAT, content is still relevant to the argument's reasoning. Arguments that identify causes or reasons for an occurrence, that explain how or why something is happening, or that recommend solutions on the basis of such things involve interpretation of the evidence at hand. On the LSAT, these interpretations are never the only possible way to look at the material presented in the premises. Whenever an argument's conclusion offers an explanation of the facts, you'll need to keep a couple of key things in mind.

BE SKEPTICAL

No matter how reasonable, plausible, or likely an interpretation of evidence may seem, you'll do best if you start out with the attitude that the argument is trying to fool you. Most args questions—assumption, flaw, weaken, strengthen, and principle particularly—depend upon there being a gap in the argument. When one of these questions is asked about an argument that interprets evidence, the right answer will relate to a possible error in the interpretation.

LOOK FOR ALTERNATIVES

An error in an interpretation of evidence usually involves some consideration or possibility that the argument doesn't consider. The game on these questions is to pick the answer that relates to an alternative explanation, or an unforeseen consequence. Even though these arguments don't usually involve misuses of language similar to those we've already seen, the language of the premises and the conclusion will still sometimes provide clues as to where you should look for the gap.

DON'T ELIMINATE TOO HASTILY

Because right answers on these often involve a competing explanation of the given facts, they may seem out of scope when you first encounter them. Remember that the final deciding factor in whether or not an answer choice is in scope is whether or not that choice relates to the argument's *conclusion*. Don't reflexively eliminate choices that bring in things not mentioned in the argument; for an interpretation of evidence, this is often what's needed to point out the argument's weakness.

In this section, we'll start with a particular kind of interpretation that pops up in a lot of LSAT arguments: causal arguments. The second batch of examples will deal with interpretations of evidence more generally.

1. Causes and Motives

Many interpretations of evidence on the LSAT boil down to picking out some individual factor or event that caused the others. As a general matter, cause is very difficult to prove. Correct answers on these questions will often relate to a different possible cause, or another possible motivation, that could have been responsible for the facts the argument is attempting to explain. The most general thing to look for, then, is something else that could have caused the evidence to be the way it is.

There are other ways the LSAT plays with these arguments, though. A claim that one event caused another can sometimes be undermined if we find a situation in which the cause occurs without leading to the supposed effect. Similarly, if the effects can be present without the cause, that may also weaken the argument's claim, depending upon how strong that claim is. These types of weaknesses are especially seen in arguments that make predictions on the basis of a perceived cause-effect relation, or that propose a solution to a problem on the basis of one.

Finally, there is a special class of causal arguments that comes with two standard possible weaknesses. Often, the premises in an argument will present a correlation. One example we hear about a lot is the strong association between diabetes and obesity among people in the United States. This correlation is often interpreted to mean that obesity contributes to causing diabetes, but realize that the fact that they often occur together doesn't provide definite support for that interpretation. Without further evidence, we might just as easily conclude that the causation is reverse—namely, that diabetes contributes to causing obesity. Alternatively, it's possible that obesity and diabetes are effects both caused by some X-factor—perhaps some gene that these individuals share, or maybe a staple of the diet they consume. When you see a correlation-cause argument, keep these two specific alternate possibilities in mind.

Now, work on the following drill. Answers can be found in Chapter 20.

DRILL #1

1. Since the ruling Aventa party in Trirene was ousted in a military coup earlier this year, the reported incidence of problems in Trirene's provincial villages has increased substantially. International observers have found that famine, violent crime, and disease are all widespread in these areas. Hence there is reason to believe that the policies of the new central government have diverted the country's resources away from the provinces in order to maintain its tenuous hold on power.

   Each of the following, if true, weakens the argument above EXCEPT:

   (A) The new military government has abandoned long-standing policies by the ruling Aventa party that made it exceptionally difficult for international organizations to monitor conditions in provincial Trirene.
   (B) Members and former allies of the Aventa party remain within all levels of Trirene's provincial governments, leading to widespread corruption that prevents money and other resources from reaching the people in these areas.
   (C) Devastating storms during this year's rainy season have led to flooding that has caused food shortages, epidemics of serious disease, and civil disarray in countries around Trirene.
   (D) Armed rebels remain active in Trirene's cities, requiring increased efforts on the part of the military government to prevent civil war from breaking out there.
   (E) Internal displacement of people as a result of the earlier military coup has caused the complete collapse of Trirene's economy, and actions of the outgoing Aventa party have drained the treasury and left the country so deeply in debt that it is unable to secure international loans.

2. Although this state's wetlands have shrunk steadily over the past decade, the change cannot plausibly be blamed on the development and growth of the state's major cities. Throughout the decade, all such development has proceeded in accordance with a state law that requires every acre of wetlands drained by developers to be compensated for by the construction of new wetland habitats elsewhere in the state. While it is true that the majority of development in our state has taken place in the cities, the greatest losses in wetland acreage have occurred not in the vicinity of the cities, but instead in the rural farming areas of the state.

   Which one of the following is an assumption required by the argument?

   (A) Development in accordance with laws requiring replacement of wetland habitats cannot have failed to lead to an increase in wetland acreage throughout the state.
   (B) Small variations in annual rainfall can result in significant losses of wetland acreage.
   (C) If located adjacent to existing wetlands, new landfills built to accommodate growing city populations can change runoff patterns in such a way that these wetlands are threatened.
   (D) The loss of the state's wetlands cannot plausibly be blamed on any activity taking place in a portion of the state where the greatest losses in wetlands have not occurred.
   (E) The artificial wetlands mandated by state law are not all constructed in such a way that they can reasonably be expected to dry up in less than a decade.

3. Literary critic: Without the revolutionary aesthetic ideas first propounded by Druiard almost a century ago, the novels written by Billups would never have received the critical acclaim and substantial attention they enjoyed when they were first published. In interviews, Billups has indicated that she is familiar with Druiard's ideas. It is clear, then, that Billups was influenced by Druiard in writing her novels.

The literary critic's argument commits which one of the following errors in reasoning?

(A) concluding that, since one event preceded another related event, the earlier event must have been responsible for the later event

(B) assuming that a condition identified as necessary to a particular result made that result inevitable

(C) failing to establish that a present state of affairs also obtained at some past time with regard to which a conclusion is drawn

(D) employing a hypothetical situation in support of a conclusion that is presented as definite

(E) accepting as true statements that, in the light of other evidence, are more likely to be false

4. The Crazy Land theme park is losing money, and if this situation continues, it will have to close. Its admission prices are the lowest of any theme park in the area, but its operating costs are actually higher than those of some of the other parks. The good news is that Crazy Land will be able to avoid closing if it raises its admission prices.

Which one of the following is an assumption on which the argument depends?

(A) If it raises its admission prices, at least some patrons who would have chosen to visit Crazy Land will visit another theme park instead.

(B) The additional revenues generated by Crazy Land's increased admission prices will not be offset by declines in the sale of food, beverages, and souvenirs.

(C) Crazy Land could not become profitable by retaining its current admission prices and closing its most expensive ride to operate.

(D) The fact that Crazy Land's facilities are in poor repair is not responsible for the theme park's declining popularity.

(E) The other theme parks with which Crazy Land competes are not also losing money.

5. A year ago, federal authorities enlisted the aid of one city pharmacy in a sting operation meant to identify doctors who write illegal prescriptions, and the patients who obtain medicine with their help. The operation has been successful, resulting in an estimated fifty percent decrease in the number of illegal prescriptions being written in the city. Nevertheless, the number of illegal prescriptions received by this pharmacy has grown throughout the period of the operation, and now is larger than ever before.

Which one of the following, if true, most helps to explain the results of the operation described above?

(A) The pharmacy in question accepts prescriptions not only from its own area, but also from other areas via phone, fax, and Internet.

(B) The prosecutions have been conducted carefully so that the pharmacy's role in the sting operation is not revealed to offenders.

(C) Increased advertising has led to an increase in the legitimate business conducted by the pharmacy throughout its period of participation in the federal operation.

(D) Recent legislation has made low-cost prescription drugs available to those who have previously been unable to afford them.

(E) Estimates of the sting operation's effect on the local trade in illegal drugs are difficult to obtain, and may not be completely accurate.

6. City Education Commissioner: Mandated increases in the proportion of education funding that is spent on direct instruction of students are having their intended effect. Before we instituted this mandate, our students' test scores in three important areas were much lower than those of comparable students in other cities throughout the country. Now, our students' scores in these three areas are in line with the national average. The quality of instruction our students receive has clearly improved.

Which one of the following, if true, would provide the greatest support for the city education commissioner's conclusion?

(A) Along with the new funding mandates, the city education commission also instituted new guidelines that govern which city students are exempt from testing.

(B) The increased funding for direct instruction did not result in a decrease in the average class size throughout the city.

(C) The test scores of students comparable to those in the commissioner's city do not significantly exceed the national average scores of students on those tests.

(D) Changes in test scores in the three areas referred to do not necessarily reflect changes in the quality of instruction delivered to students who take those tests.

(E) A recently imposed regime of nationwide testing has resulted in a change to the standards by which quality of instruction is measured.

7. Sunspots have long been known to interfere with AM radio signals. Throughout the day, I have been hearing static and odd sounds in the background whenever I tune to my favorite AM station. We must be experiencing a period of high sunspot activity.

Which one of the following arguments exhibits flawed reasoning most similar to that in the argument above?

(A) We know that smoking causes emphysema. Emerson is a heavy smoker, and he has a recurrent cough. Unfortunately for Emerson, it seems certain that his cough is an early symptom of emphysema.

(B) Emerson has recently been diagnosed with emphysema. Emerson must certainly be a smoker, since everyone knows that smoking causes emphysema.

(C) Throughout the past year, Emerson has experienced a troublesome cough. Everyone knows that smoking causes emphysema, and that one early symptom of emphysema is a troublesome cough. Fortunately, Emerson is not a smoker. Therefore his troublesome cough must not be a symptom of emphysema.

(D) Emerson coughs every time he smokes. Since smoking has long been known to cause emphysema, Emerson must be well on his way to developing emphysema.

(E) Although Emerson has a recurrent cough, the doctors have recently reassured him that it is not a symptom of emphysema. Emerson must not be a smoker, then, since everyone knows that smoking leads to emphysema.

8. Murray has argued in favor of the ballot initiative that would extend certain rights to illegal aliens in this country. Murray is also a known member of the Renewal Party, which advocates the violent overthrow of the government. Therefore, although it is not immediately clear how, this ballot initiative will likely lead to a destabilization of the government if it is passed.

Which one of the following principles, if established, would provide the strongest basis for casting doubt on the truth of the argument's conclusion?

(A) No government can legitimately refuse to extend any right to any person unless the extension of that right poses a threat to the stability of the government.
(B) Establishment of the reasons for a belief requires that all plausible reasons for that belief be considered.
(C) Evidence of an individual's support for a general goal is insufficient to predict the likely result of any course of action supported by that individual.
(D) Not all those who are members of an organization that advocates for a course of action necessarily support that course of action.
(E) Any action that tends to undermine the respect of individuals for a ruling authority leads in time to a destabilization of that authority.

9. Art dealer: Since his death, Patrona's paintings have commanded ever higher prices at auction. At the same time, the works of Patrona's friend Avlov have not increased in value. There can be no doubt that Patrona's work displays a lasting quality that Avlov's simply does not.

Which one of the following, if true, would most undermine the art dealer's argument?

(A) The tastes of those affluent individuals and institutions that influence the art market prefer Patrona's intellectual style to Avlov's grace and spontaneity.
(B) Avlov has sold dozens of new paintings since his friend Patrona's death.
(C) The high prices paid for some Patrona paintings auctioned immediately after his death make his work likely to be a good long-term investment.
(D) Recent work in art criticism has led to a greater appreciation of Patrona's paintings in the years since his death.
(E) The materials Avlov used in executing his paintings tend to decompose relatively quickly, leading to unavoidable changes in their appearance.

10. Advances in technology have enabled independent directors to use sophisticated filming and editing techniques that were previously available only to directors of big-budget movies. The result of this change is that more independent films than ever are attracting large audiences and enjoying commercial success. Whereas before, independent productions were likely to seem clumsy and amateurish, now they seem as polished and professional as their big-budget competitors.

Which one of the following, if true, would most strongly support the argument?

(A) Advances in technology have not resulted in the development of new editing techniques that audiences have come to expect from polished, professional productions.
(B) Films do not enjoy commercial success unless they have a professional appearance.
(C) Changes to the business of distributing and marketing films guarantee that big-budget movies will continue to attract larger audiences than independent films.
(D) The amount of money available for making a film is a determining factor in the degree of commercial success it is likely to enjoy.
(E) In the past, some movies that did not use sophisticated filming and editing techniques were nevertheless able to attract large audiences.

2. How and Why

Many interpretations of evidence you'll encounter on the LSAT don't directly involve descriptions of cause or motivation, but instead involve explanations of how or why the evidence appears as it does. You should approach this more general category of interpretations in much the same way you do causal arguments: by looking for other explanations, a different way or reason the evidence looks the way it does.

These arguments don't all fall into neat subcategories, but there are a few kinds of evidence that pop up on these questions pretty often. Surveys and polls, for instance, are sometimes used to draw conclusions about preferences or likely outcomes. A survey only makes for good evidence of these preferences if the group surveyed is representative of the group about which the conclusion is drawn. The classic example of a skewed sample was the telephone polling that gave us the historic headline "Dewey Defeats Truman" in a presidential election Truman won; since the poll was conducted at a time when not all Americans had phones, and those who had them were affluent and more likely to vote for Dewey, the sample wasn't representative of the larger group of people who cast ballots, and the conclusion the pollsters drew was inaccurate. Similarly, watch out for respondents in opinion surveys who have an ulterior motive or incentive to give false answers. A poll concerning prison conditions conducted by the prison guards themselves is likely to result in a rosier picture than one conducted independently.

Generally, watch out on this test when an argument uses evidence that involves percentages and numbers. Percentages can be slippery things, increasing while the raw number on which they are based decreases, or vice versa. Words like *rate*, *frequency*, and *proportion* are all words that indicate percentages are being talked about. Keep in mind that the crime rate can go down while the number of actual crimes committed goes up; the missing piece to the equation is another number: the overall population. If the population grows by a greater percentage than the number of crimes committed does, then the crime rate will go down. As you can imagine, the increase and decrease of percentages are played with in LSAT args as well. When an argument includes percentages, be extremely skeptical.

There are certainly other types of evidence that the LSAT enjoys playing with. Analogies between dissimilar things, chronologies, statements concerning the knowledge of individuals or groups, and anything with numbers in it should be scrutinized very carefully. These are a few of the LSAT writers' favorite things when it comes to fooling you into believing that the argument's explanation of how or why something is happening is correct.

Now see if you can decipher the evidence in the following drill. Answers can be found in Chapter 20.

DRILL #2

1. Pundit: Law enforcement's warnings about identity theft are clearly overblown. Despite the fact that they have spent so much energy and effort explaining what identity theft is and the various ways it is done, the activities they describe have resulted in very few crimes. The number of confirmed cases of identity theft last year in this country was less than 6,000. Several other types of fraud that received less publicity claimed many more victims. It is clear that these efforts against identity theft are more effective at increasing public approval of law enforcement authorities than they are at actually protecting citizens.

The reasoning in the pundit's argument is flawed because this argument

(A) employs inflammatory rhetoric to support its contention rather than verifiable evidence

(B) fails to acknowledge that steps taken by law enforcement to prevent identity theft may be effective against other types of fraud as well

(C) asserts that the ineffectiveness of law enforcement's action is sufficient to conclude that some motive other than preventing crime prompted law enforcement to take that action

(D) assumes that all those whose identities have been stolen are currently aware that they are victims of a crime

(E) overlooks the possibility that law enforcement's efforts against identity theft were effective at preventing such crimes from being committed

2. Reviews of economic data show that tax cuts are effective at stimulating the long-term growth of a nation's economy in every case where these cuts do not result in crippling national debt. So the solution to Jennona's economic problems is clearly to continue cutting taxes.

Which one of the following, if true, most seriously undermines the argument's stated conclusion?

(A) Nations with healthy economies are able to manage debt while cutting taxes because of growth in activity, whereas nations whose economies are experiencing stagnation must increase taxes to avoid crippling debt.

(B) Jennona's aging infrastructure makes it difficult for short-term economic growth to be sustained.

(C) Recent tax cuts in Jennona have not resulted in the increase of its national debt.

(D) Jennona's economic problems are serious enough to merit changes to its tax code, although past efforts to reform its treatment of high-income individuals and profitable companies have been largely unsuccessful.

(E) Jennona's economy has remained relatively stable over the past two years.

3. Recent construction beneath the bank building has revealed signs that a Roman bath once stood on this site. It was known that one of the bank building's cornerstones was extremely old, but now we can be sure that this stone was part of the Roman building that once stood here. Recent analysis of the stone's chemical weathering indicates that it has been in place for at least 2,600 years. It has long been believed that the Romans first came to this area approximately 2,000 years ago, but these new discoveries make it clear that they were here earlier.

Which of the following is an assumption required by the argument?

(A) The analysis of chemical weathering cannot result in an error of more than 600 years in its determination of how long a particular stone has been in place.

(B) Rates of chemical weathering in industrialized areas have not increased significantly over the past 200 years.

(C) The bank's cornerstone is not a remnant of a construction that was in place on the site when the Romans first came to the area.

(D) Comparison of the cornerstone with the remains of the Roman bath beneath the bank building indicates that both were quarried at a place along the known route of a road built by the Romans.

(E) The time of the Romans' arrival can be definitively established by determining the age of buildings they constructed.

4. Some scientists have recently concluded that there was once liquid water on Mars. Since Mars has polar ice caps, it has long been clear that there is currently water on the planet, although it remains in solid form because of the low surface temperature. Exploration of the Martian surface now indicates the presence of the mineral hematite, which forms on Earth almost exclusively in the presence of liquid water. These same explorations have also shown, embedded in Martian rocks, spherical concretions that could have been formed when liquid water percolated through cracks in the rocks, depositing dissolved minerals as it flowed.

Which of the following, if true, would most strengthen the conclusion reached by the scientists mentioned in the passage above?

(A) The formation of polar ice caps requires the presence of water vapor in a planet's atmosphere.

(B) The surface of Mars features several large volcanoes, indicating that the planet once had a molten core, and that in at least some regions its surface temperatures were once substantially higher.

(C) Comets and meteorites from the nearby asteroid belt, many of which contain water, are known to have impacted Mars throughout its history.

(D) Spherical formations resembling the concretions found on Mars are also found in the vicinity of known impact craters on Earth, when molten rock thrown into the air solidifies as it falls to the ground.

(E) Conditions on Mars are similar enough to conditions on Earth that it is reasonable to expect that the mechanisms of hematite formation are the same on both planets.

5. Pollster: This year's nationwide parliamentary elections will heavily favor the Future Party. Surveys of the nation's voting-age population indicate that more than sixty percent of people prefer the Future Party's position on the issue they identify as most important to the position advocated by any other party.

Strategist: Support for the Future Party is highest in the cities, whereas the majority of parliamentary representatives come from districts in the nation's rural areas. The Future Party will certainly win a large number of seats, but they will remain a minority party in the parliament.

Which one of the following, if known, would most support the pollster's contention against the strategist's response?

(A) Recent actions taken by the ruling majority party have enraged many Future Party supporters who have not voted in past parliamentary elections.

(B) The survey to which the pollster appeals was based on a representative sample of the nation's population, including both those who live in cities and those who live in the nation's rural areas.

(C) Voters in a parliamentary election cast their votes primarily on the basis of positions advocated by the parties whose representatives are candidates in the election.

(D) Among all the nation's parties, only the Future Party has a candidate on the ballot in every parliamentary district where votes will be cast.

(E) In more than half of the nation's parliamentary districts, the Future Party candidate is running unopposed.

6. The ancient epic of Gilgamesh includes a story about a massive flood that destroyed virtually all life. Similar stories appear in the traditional texts of many ancient religions. Geological evidence indicates that, at some point after the last Ice Age, a natural dam near what is now called the Bosporus Strait collapsed, causing the Mediterranean to fill a deep basin beyond and form the Black Sea. Underwater explorations have recently found the remains of primitive human settlements on the floor of the Black Sea. There can be little doubt that the ancient flood stories, which have traditionally been thought of as mythological or figurative, instead provide accounts of actual past events in human history.

Which one of the following, if true, would most weaken the argument's conclusion?

(A) Tools retrieved from the submerged settlements are similar to those found at other human settlements known to date to the last Ice Age.

(B) Both the epic of Gilgamesh and the traditional texts that include flood stories were first recorded in places geographically distant from the Black Sea, long after the collapse of the land bridge.

(C) Although by geological standards the flooding of the basin is considered rapid, evidence indicates that it took place over a period of several months.

(D) All known flood accounts include descriptions of the flood waters eventually receding.

(E) The flood accounts in both the epic of Gilgamesh and in the traditional texts of ancient religions were based on earlier folk tales that were prevalent throughout the region surrounding the Black Sea.

7. An independent commission is investigating the events surrounding the collapse of the elected government in Menae, and our country's role in them. Although the foreign affairs minister has already replied to the commission's questions in writing, she has refused to testify in person. There must be at least some truth to the accusations made by some journalists and foreign politicians that our foreign affairs office undermined Menae's elected government.

The argument's reasoning is fallacious because the argument

(A) calls into question the motives for advancing an argument without considering that argument on its merits

(B) takes as positive proof of a contention a fact that is merely not inconsistent with that contention

(C) assumes what it sets out to prove, without attempting to provide factual support for its contention

(D) makes an assumption concerning the purpose of an action without any proof that the purpose would be desirable to achieve

(E) accepts the likely truth of a fact whose accuracy has not yet been independently established

8. Studies have shown that an interviewer's initial impression of a prospective employee is formed within the first minute of a face-to-face job interview. Personal references and resume materials can refine that impression, but it is extremely rare that these sources of information result in the candidate being hired if the interviewer's initial impression of that candidate is negative. Therefore, there is no reason for an interviewer to extend any face-to-face interview beyond the first minute, if after that time the interviewer has a negative impression of the prospective employee.

Which one of the following is an assumption required by the argument?

(A) The content of the interview after its first minute is not the most important factor in an interviewer's decision to hire a prospective employee.

(B) There is no reason for an interviewer to engage in an activity related to hiring if that activity is unlikely to change the interviewer's initial decision not to hire a candidate.

(C) Personal references and resume materials are not the most important factor in determining whether a prospective employee is qualified for the job for which he or she is a candidate.

(D) Any prospective employee an interviewer decides not to hire is not the best candidate for the job.

(E) The candidate an interviewer hires is one who made a positive impression on that interviewer within the first minute of a face-to-face interview.

9. Health experts indicate that increasing physical activity and decreasing sedentary activities such as watching television or playing video games lead to greater general health and longer life. Encouragingly, recent reports show that many people are taking this advice to heart. The number of new memberships issued by commercial gyms and other athletic training facilities has grown at a rate two to three times as fast as the population, and surveys have shown that people are feeling healthier than they ever have before.

Each of the following, if true, would weaken the argument above EXCEPT:

(A) Increased competition among commercial gyms has led people who have always engaged in physical activity to change gym memberships at unprecedented and rapidly growing rates.

(B) Many employers have begun to include among their employee benefits the opportunity to obtain gym memberships at substantial discounts.

(C) Record sales of video game systems and rapidly increasing rates paid for advertising reflect substantial increases in the amount of time the average person spends in front of his or her television set.

(D) The surveys mentioned in the passage also indicate that those who are exercising more at commercial gyms and other training facilities find time for these activities by walking less and participating in fewer free physical activities such as playing sports with their children.

(E) Increased feelings of health are consistent with changes to diet and the purchase of gym memberships, even among those who do not engage in increased physical activity.

10. Over the past five years, repression of civil rights and free expression in the country of Piranhia has grown substantially. At the same time, most international aid agencies agree that the quality of life in Piranhia is greater than at any time in the past century.

Each of the following, if true, could contribute to an explanation of the apparent paradox above EXCEPT:

(A) Increased effectiveness of Piranhia's law enforcement has led to substantial decreases in government corruption and organized crime in the country.

(B) Greater security has allowed the recent exploitation of Piranhia's native oil reserves, the revenues from which have primarily been devoted to improving the housing and medical care of Piranhia's citizens.

(C) Until five years ago, warring factions in Piranhia embroiled the country in a devastating civil war in which suppression of free expression, along with most other types of government control including public safety protection, have been absent.

(D) Increased media reporting on the plight of Piranhia's citizens has led to a marked increase in the attention paid by international aid agencies to the country over the past five years.

(E) Stability directly attributable to the government's activities has allowed Piranhia's economy and its people's average income to grow at record levels over the past five years.

11. Some recent findings of planets beyond our own solar system have relied on what astronomers call occultation—the fact that, when a planet passes between the Earth and a star, it obscures the star from view for a limited period of time. When a planet is part of a distant system, its occultations occur regularly and involve only the star it orbits. New observations, however, have shown a pattern of occultations with several stars, taking place over time. Some astronomers have concluded that these observations indicate the existence of an undiscovered planet within our own solar system, orbiting slowly beyond Pluto and passing between Earth and several different distant stars sequentially.

Which one of the following observations would be LEAST consistent with the conclusion attributed to the astronomers in the passage?

(A) The pattern of occultations mentioned in the passage does not recur within any of the astronomers' lifetimes.

(B) Several of the stars that are part of the pattern mentioned experience occultations that cannot be explained by the existence of an undiscovered planet in our own solar system orbiting beyond Pluto.

(C) Some large comets, which orbit the Sun but are not considered planets, are large enough to obscure the view of distant stars from Earth.

(D) It is exceedingly unlikely that the stars that are part of the pattern mentioned in the passage all have planets of their own that could be responsible for occultations in precisely the sequence they were observed.

(E) Dust clouds beyond the orbit of Pluto sometimes obscure the view of distant stars from Earth at times that cannot be predicted.

12. Sandy: *The Sun* was irresponsible in its reporting on Representative Smith's possible violation of ethical standards in accepting gifts from lobbyists and campaign contributors. The ethical standards in question do not prohibit the acceptance of gifts, and in fact disclosure documents filed by other representatives indicate that virtually all of them have accepted similar gifts in the past. Since the disclosure documents relevant to Representative Smith's case have not yet been released, it has not been shown that the allegations have any merit whatsoever.

Pat: It is the responsibility of newspapers such as *The Sun* to report news stories that are also covered by other media outlets and that have become part of the public debate. Representative Smith has always been a controversial figure, and although the allegations against him have not yet been fully investigated, every other serious media outlet has reported on them in recent days.

The answer to which one of the following questions would be most helpful in evaluating the merit of Sandy's argument in light of Pat's response?

(A) What disclosure do ethical standards require of representatives with regard to gifts accepted from lobbyists and other campaign contributors?

(B) Did *The Sun* represent the allegations that Representative Smith violated ethical standards as true?

(C) To what extent is the propriety of Representative Smith's electoral practices a matter of public debate?

(D) Were *The Sun*'s readers aware of the allegations concerning Representative Smith before it chose to report on them?

(E) Is it necessary for allegations to have been proven true in order for any media outlet's report of those allegations to be anything but irresponsible?

13. State legislators raised the minimum legal drinking age in response to a large increase in the rate of drinking-related accidents and arrests among people between the ages of sixteen and twenty in the state. In the four years immediately after the change, the number of drinking-related accidents in this age group continued to increase. Legislators agree, however, that their response to the problem was both adequate and successful.

Which of the following, if true, would provide the best possible explanation of the legislators' judgment, as it is presented in the passage above?

(A) It is adequate to address a problem by imposing harsher legal penalties on those who contribute to the problem, whether or not those penalties are successful at diminishing the problem.

(B) The increase in the minimum legal drinking age took place at a time when demographic data indicated the population within the state of those between the ages of sixteen and twenty was due to increase substantially over the following four years.

(C) Drinking-related arrests of those between the ages of sixteen and twenty also increased substantially over the four-year period immediately following the raising of the state's minimum legal drinking age.

(D) The success of the state's legislative action led most other states to raise their own minimum legal drinking ages within four years.

(E) Studies indicate that the age of consent—the time at which young people first try alcohol—is typically three to four years lower than the state's minimum legal drinking age, and the legislative action in question was successful at raising the age of consent within the state to sixteen years of age.

14. The poverty line is currently set at twenty percent of the worldwide median income. By this standard, fully fifty percent of our country's citizens live below the poverty line. Studies published ten years ago indicated that approximately thirty percent of our citizens lived below the poverty line then. It is clear that the ruling party's actions over the past ten years have led to a greater disparity in incomes between the country's richest and poorest residents.

Which one of the following, if true, most strengthens the argument?

(A) Over the past ten years, the wealth of the country's richest residents has increased rapidly, while the income of its poorest residents has remained unchanged.

(B) The ruling party's actions over the past decade have included the institution of a flat tax, which imposes the same rate of taxation on all citizens, regardless of their income.

(C) The country's average income is less than twenty percent of the worldwide average income.

(D) The richest of the country's citizens have almost all left the country and given up their citizenship over the past decade due to the government's excessively harsh tax policies.

(E) The country's median income is less than twenty percent of the world's median income, although the income of the richest five percent of the country's citizens is comparable to that of the richest five percent of many other countries' citizens.

15. Until recently, Graves was the owner of many irreplaceable works of art. During a period of mental illness, however, Graves destroyed several of them, and was only stopped from destroying the others by the intervention of law enforcement authorities. Courts subsequently ruled that, since the works of art belonged to Graves, their destruction was not illegal, and law enforcement had no justification for attempting to prevent the destruction of the others. Their intervention was justified, however, because after receiving treatment Graves expressed regret for having destroyed the irreplaceable works, and thanked law enforcement for having prevented him from destroying the others.

The argument above conforms most closely to which one of the following principles?

(A) Law enforcement authorities are justified in intervening to prevent irreversible harm from being done, even when that intervention is subsequently found by courts to be unjustified.

(B) Law enforcement authorities are not justified in intervening to prevent actions that, although harmful, are not illegal.

(C) Law enforcement authorities are justified in preventing any action that prevents the destruction of property that, although privately owned, is properly seen as the collective cultural property of some larger group.

(D) Law enforcement authorities are justified in intervening to prevent an action from taking place as long as their intervention does not itself prevent the action from being performed at some later time with the same eventual result.

(E) Law enforcement authorities are justified in intervening to prevent someone from performing an action that, although it is not illegal, would have been regretted had the person not been prevented from performing it.

6

Formal Logic

STYLE, NOT SUBSTANCE

In two of our earlier Args sections—"Drawing Conclusions" and "Interpretations of Evidence"—we dealt primarily with the *content* of arguments. That is, we read the argument text in much the same way we might read a magazine or an editorial, with the purpose of discerning the meaning of the passage text, imagining what situation or idea the text was meant to convey.

In the section on "Language Shifts," however, we focused instead on the precise terms or phrases that the argument used. Even though some of the shifted language might have seemed to refer to the same thing—or something reasonably similar—we had to recognize that the use of different terms opened up the possibility, at least, of a gap. In other words, for these passages the *structure* of the argument was of primary importance. The structural flaws in these arguments were all in some basic sense the same: They involved the substitution or deletion of key terms as the argument moved from its premises to its conclusion.

This last group of arguments questions depends exclusively on the logical structure of the argument. Of course a sort of rough-and-ready logic has been important on all of the questions we've seen so far, but these questions emphasize logic and use language that is, in the end, arbitrary. Many of these questions and their answers sound like gibberish, because the ideas around which they're based have little or nothing to do with the nouns and verbs used; they depend instead on the use of certain key terms and phrases such as *if, only if, unless,* and a host of others. As you'll see, in the test they mean something pretty different than what they mean in everyday life.

HOW TO LEARN FORMAL LOGIC

Our purpose in this section isn't to try to turn you into a logician. The serious study of formal logic involves specialized terminology, proofs, and all sorts of other things that aren't necessary to deal with the formal logic on this test. What is necessary is sensitivity to the language that indicates that considerations of formal logic are important to the question, and so to highlight this fact, the examples we'll use in introducing each drill will involve nonsense statements that, hopefully, will draw your attention to the language that's important in each. The more sensitive you become to this language, the better you'll get at some of the most challenging and confusing questions on the LSAT.

1. Necessary Conditions, Sufficient Conditions

The basic staple of formal logic is the conditional statement. Here's a good one to start with:

If I scratch my arm, **then** the crickets will sing.

It's important to understand what this statement does—and doesn't—mean. For the sake of ease, let's call the statement *I scratch my arm* the **condition**, and the statement *the crickets will sing* the **result**. Like all premises on the LSAT, we take this if/then statement to be an absolutely true statement. Given that fact, let's start by taking a look at two hypothetical situations.

Suppose I scratch my arm. By this statement, I can be guaranteed that the crickets will sing. I've satisfied the condition, and because of the type of statement we're given to work with, that fact is **sufficient** to assure the result.

Suppose, alternatively, that I don't scratch my arm. Will the crickets sing? They might, but then again they might not. This sufficient condition provides us a way to guarantee the result, but it does not provide us the information that this is the only way to achieve the result.

Now, let's work with hypotheticals involving the result. Suppose we observe the crickets singing. Did I scratch my arm? Certainly, if I had, then the crickets would have started singing. But, using the same reasoning we used just a moment ago, our sufficient condition doesn't assure us that scratching my arm is the only thing that might result in the crickets' singing. Maybe the spirit moved them; who knows? So I might or might not have scratched my arm; other things could conceivably be responsible for the result.

Suppose, alternatively, that the crickets are not, at this moment, singing. In this case we do know something. If I'd scratched my arm, then by the statement we're given, we know the crickets would be singing. But they're not singing, so I must not have scratched my arm.

Here's one way we could sum up all the things we know from our statement of a sufficient condition:

Sufficient Condition	Result
I scratch my arm.	The crickets will sing.

When I Know That...	I Can Conclude That...
I scratch my arm	the crickets will sing
I don't scratch my arm	the crickets may or may not sing
the crickets are singing	I may or may not have scratched my arm
the crickets aren't singing	I didn't scratch my arm

In summary, then, a sufficient condition provides us a way of guaranteeing the result, but the sufficient condition may not be the only way to achieve the result.

So far, this probably seems fairly intuitive to you. The other type of condition is usually the one people have a harder time using. Here's an example of this type:

Only if a star falls will my baby come home.

It's sometimes more difficult to parse this type of conditional statement. Here, the condition is *a star falls*, and the result is *my baby will come home.* We call this statement a **necessary condition** because it describes a minimum requirement that must be met in order for the result to be possible. In conversation, we tend to overinterpret such phrases; we make them mean more than the LSAT means them to be. As before, let's use some hypothetical situations to illustrate how a necessary condition is different from the sufficient condition we saw a moment ago.

Suppose a star falls. Will my baby come home? Possibly; possibly not. Our statement tells us that the only way our baby could ever come home is if a star falls, but it does not provide a guarantee. The condition is just a prerequisite—a minimum requirement.

How about if a star doesn't fall? Then there's no way my baby is coming home, because the minimum requirement hasn't been met. Compare this pair of hypotheticals to the similar one we saw before with a sufficient condition. Do you see the difference? Before, we could draw a conclusion just in the case where we knew the condition was met; here, we can draw one just in the case where it's not met.

Suppose my baby really does come home. We know then that a star must have fallen. Why? Because the condition is something that's necessary in order for the result to be possible. Here we observe the result, so the necessary condition must have been met.

What if my baby doesn't come home? As you've hopefully guessed by now, we can't conclude either way about whether or not a star has fallen. As we've seen before, meeting the necessary condition doesn't guarantee us the result. It's possible that the star fell, and yet sadly my baby didn't come home after all.

Here's a comparable chart to the one we saw before with our sufficient condition:

Necessary Condition	Result
A star falls.	My baby will come home.

When I Know That...	I Can Conclude That...
a star falls	my baby may or may not come home
a star doesn't fall	my baby won't come home
my baby came home	a star fell
my baby didn't come home	a star may or may not have fallen

There are a number of different ways the LSAT can use to state necessary or sufficient conditions. The following list of examples, although by no means exhaustive, should give you a good sense of the language and ideas for which to be alert.

Sufficient

If the sky is red, **then** Augustus dances.

The world will rejoice **if** they install more fire hydrants.

The clock strikes **whenever** I fall asleep.

Pretzels are **enough** to keep me happy.

Every rose has its thorn.

All dogs have fleas.

Catching an aphid **will** make you lose your car keys.

Necessary

You will be fortunate **only if** it's snowing outside.

Only the good die young.

Prices **must** rise to keep the Emperor well fed.

Good posture is **required** for winning at poker.

Nobody will leave **unless** Zorro takes off his mask.

Keep an eye out for these types of language in the following drill, and throughout LSAT args. Even questions that don't center on the necessary/sufficient difference sometimes have an answer choice or two that use these ideas. The better you get at identifying conditional language, the more you'll see that a great number of LSAT args questions use it. Answers can be found in Chapter 20.

DRILL #1

1. In order to qualify for the Olympic team, a distance runner must be able to run a mile in less than five minutes. Only ten percent of the population can run a mile in less than five minutes, but fortunately Roderick is part of that ten percent. Thus Roderick will certainly succeed in his effort to become a distance runner on the Olympic team.

Which one of the following most accurately describes an error of reasoning committed by the argument?

(A) It relies on evidence that concerns only percentages of a population to draw a definite conclusion about a single member of that population.

(B) It fails to specify the distance of the Olympic running event for which Roderick is seeking to qualify.

(C) It draws a conclusion about a future event on the basis of evidence concerning past occurrences of similar events.

(D) It interprets statements as ensuring an outcome, which merely fail to exclude the possibility of that outcome.

(E) It ascribes to an entire group some attribute that can only properly be ascribed to the individual members of that group.

2. The only people who can read ancient Sanskrit are those who have studied at a university, and the only people who have studied at a university are those who are familiar with a broad range of topics. It thus follows that anyone who understands ancient Sanskrit must also be familiar with a broad range of topics.

Which one of the following is most similar in its argumentative structure to the argument above?

(A) Everyone who can play ice hockey must be able to ice skate, and everyone who can ice skate must possess superb balance. It is thus clear that anyone who possesses superb balance could also play ice hockey.

(B) Only people who work on the top floor live in the suburbs, and everyone who lives in the suburbs owns a car. Therefore, everyone who works on the top floor must own a car.

(C) Anything that is impermanent must eventually end, and anything that eventually ends must also have begun at some definite time. So anything that is impermanent must have begun at some definite time.

(D) Only those who know calculus can truly comprehend physics, and only those who truly comprehend physics correctly understand the nature of gravity. Thus, anyone who does not know calculus must not correctly understand the nature of gravity.

(E) Everyone who reads poetry possesses an active imagination. It is clear, then, that everyone who reads novels must also read poetry, since only those who possess an active imagination read novels.

3. Without a molten core, a planet cannot generate a magnetic field. Earth's magnetic field is crucial to life as we know it, since in the absence of a magnetic field a planet's surface is bombarded with ionizing radiation that is harmful to all such life. Recently, astronomers have discovered a planet in a nearby solar system. Observations of this planet's orbit and spin have led astronomers to conclude that it does not possess a molten core.

Which one of the following can most properly be concluded from the information in the passage above?

(A) The spin of a planet with a molten core is more rapid than the spin of a comparable planet that does not possess a molten core.

(B) Any life that exists on the newly discovered planet mentioned in the passage must be located beneath the surface, where it is protected from the bombardment of harmful ionizing radiation.

(C) If there is life on the surface of the newly discovered planet mentioned in the passage, then that life is dissimilar from life on Earth in at least one crucial respect.

(D) Any subsequently discovered planet that possesses a molten core will be capable of supporting life.

(E) The orbit and spin of a planet are the main determining factors in whether or not that planet is capable of supporting life that can be considered Earthlike.

4. Forester: Before the institution of fire-prevention measures, fires caused predominantly by lightning played an essential role in maintaining the health of the nation's forests. Forest fires clear dead trees that inhibit new growth, help recycle nutrients, and foster the spreading of topsoil more evenly across the forest floor. Now, though, human intervention has limited both the frequency and the scope of natural forest fires. A newly instituted program of controlled burning, which produces the beneficial effects of natural forest fires without incurring the attendant risks to property and life, will restore the health of the nation's forests.

Which one of the following, if assumed, would allow the forester's conclusion to be properly drawn?

(A) It is possible to institute a program of controlled burning without threatening the life and property of residents in or near the forests where that program is applied.

(B) The loss of beneficial effects associated with natural forest fires constitutes the only factor that prevents the health of the nation's forests from being restored.

(C) The benefits associated with natural forest fires cannot be restored to the nation's forest by any means other than a program of controlled burning.

(D) Reintroducing the beneficial effects of natural forest fires is necessary to restoring the health of the nation's forests.

(E) Past fire-prevention measures, such as fuel removal and the creation of firebreaks, have been responsible for limiting the frequency and scope of natural forest fires.

5.   Every new marketing initiative introduced by a
      company creates at least some temporary confusion
      in the market. When there is temporary confusion
      in the market, overall sales in that market decline
      for a period of time. However, only by introducing
      new marketing initiatives can any competitor in a
      market hope to increase its share of sales within
      that market.

      If the statements above are true, then each of the
      following could be true EXCEPT:

      (A)   A company that introduces a new marketing
            initiative does not increase its share of sales
            within that market.
      (B)   A company whose competitor introduces
            a new marketing initiative experiences
            increased sales for a period of time.
      (C)   A company that introduces a new marketing
            initiative experiences an immediate increase
            in its share of sales within that market.
      (D)   A market in which overall sales are not
            declining has been exposed to several new
            marketing initiatives in the recent past.
      (E)   All the competitors in a market experience
            increased sales immediately following the
            introduction of a new marketing initiative by
            one of those competitors.

2. Diagramming Conditional Statements and Contrapositives

A few LSAT args questions require more than just an intuitive handle on the meaning of, and relationship between, the conditional statements they contain. This situation comes up most often with chunks of text that include multiple related conditional statements. Especially if those statements are presented in a counterintuitive order, or in the midst of obscuring language, it can be useful to diagram the statements, making a picture of the argument before you attempt to evaluate the answer choices.

The basic element of diagramming a conditional statement is the arrow: →. As we saw in the previous section on necessary and sufficient conditions, conditional statements only really work in one direction. In a sufficient condition, for example, when the condition is satisfied, we know the result will happen; the reverse, however is not true: the result's happening doesn't tell us anything for certain about whether or not the condition was satisfied. Here's the example we started with:

If I scratch my arm, **then** the crickets will sing.

If we wanted to use an arrow to diagram this, here's how it would look:

scratch arm → crickets sing

The whole point of this diagram is that we *only read it from left to right*. Whenever the thing on the left is true, we know that the thing on the right is.

For our necessary condition, the relationship of the condition to the result was, to use a term loosely, "backwards." In the necessary case, it was the occurrence of the result that allowed us to be sure that the minimum requirement had been met. Here was the initial statement:

Only if a star falls will my baby come home.

The diagram that correctly represents this conditional statement looks like this:

baby comes → star falls

In terms of chronology, this diagram doesn't make much sense. We think of the necessary condition as being something that happens, in time, before the result does. But our diagram isn't a cause-and-effect statement; it simply tells us what we're allowed to conclude, given what we know.

All of this would be a little excessive in an argument where we're primarily working with one conditional statement. But when we get a series of statements that are (or may be) related, it can make our lives a bit easier.

1. If the apple is wormy, then I won't eat it.

2. Anything I won't eat goes in the trash can.

3. Only things that are in the trash can get taken outside.

Here are the diagrams for this series. Look carefully at how we translated statement 3:

1. wormy apple → won't eat

2. won't eat → trash can

3. taken outside → trash can

The first two statements form a chain: wormy apple → won't eat → trash can. When you initially read the three statements together, you might have thought that our wormy apple, which is in the trash can, would also be taken outside. But do our diagrams support that conclusion? Remember that we can only read with the arrows, and notice that the arrow doesn't point from "trash can" to "taken outside." It may not make sense to you that a wormy apple in the trash can wouldn't get taken outside with the garbage, but the statements we have don't exclude that possibility. It's exactly this tendency we have to "forget" that conditional statements only go in one direction that the writers of the LSAT are most fond of exploiting. They especially like to do it in situations where we think the arrow really should point the other way.

Once you have your diagram put together, you can just work with the diagram and forget the initial language of the statement. This is a big help when it comes to combining statements, or when it comes to working with what's called the conditional statement's **contrapositive**. Let's go back to our initial conditional statement for a moment:

If I scratch my arm, **then** the crickets will sing.

We've already talked about the straightforward situation in which we can apply this statement. But there was another situation in which we could use it to reach a conclusion. If the crickets aren't singing, then we could be sure I hadn't scratched my arm. Again, the chronology here gets a little weird, but the conclusion is sound. If I had scratched my arm, the crickets would be singing; but they're not singing; so I must not have scratched my arm. Represented as a diagram, the contrapositive of our initial conditional statement looks like this:

– crickets sing → – scratch arm

The "−" signs here indicate negation. Look at how this diagram relates to the initial diagram we had. We've flipped the order of the statements around the arrow, and negated each of the statements. It probably won't surprise you to know that the contrapositive of our necessary condition—the one about falling stars and my baby coming back home—looks like this when we represent it in a diagram:

$$- \text{ star falls} \rightarrow - \text{ baby comes home}$$

Again, all we did was **flip and negate**. Any time we can correctly translate a conditional statement into a diagram, to find its contrapositive we just flip and negate the statements in the diagram. Let's try out a modified version of our wormy apple example, with a slightly different statement 3:

1. If the apple is wormy, then I won't eat it.

2. Anything I won't eat goes in the trash can.

3. Only things that aren't in the trash can aren't taken outside.

Convoluted enough for you? It's easy enough to do the first two statements. While we're at it, we might as well symbolize their contrapositives, too:

1. wormy apple → won't eat

    will eat → − wormy apple

2. won't eat → trash can

    − trash can → will eat

The first of our contrapositives makes good sense: If this thing is something I'll eat, it must not be a wormy apple. Note that we negated the negative "won't eat" by turning it back into a positive statement. A double-negative is a positive.

The second contrapositive seems a bit stranger: I'll eat anything that isn't in the trash can. The reason this sounds like nonsense isn't that we've somehow flipped and negated wrong; it's a direct consequence of the ridiculous initial statement that anything you won't eat goes straight into the trash can. Hope your television will fit.

Note that the initial chain we made (wormy apple → won't eat → trash can) now has a contrapositive chain as well (trash can → will eat → − wormy apple). We can just flip the order of the whole chain and negate every item in it to form the contrapositive.

Now for our new third statement:

Only things that aren't in the trash can aren't taken outside.

The language here is pretty baffling, but as long we follow the pattern we've established in our previous similar "only" statements, we'll be fine. Every time we've diagrammed one of these things, the "only" statement has gone on the *point* of the arrow. We'll do that again:

$$- \text{ take outside} \rightarrow - \text{ trash can}$$

Its contrapositive is:

$$\text{trash can} \rightarrow \text{take outside}$$

We can see that this really is a different statement from the one we initially saw. With this one, we can now make the chain wormy apple → won't eat → trash can → take outside. What a relief.

As you see, diagramming can be a time-consuming process on args questions. The good news is that very few of the args questions you encounter will require this extreme an approach, so you should always use this method as a last resort; the bad news is that questions that really do require this method can't be reliably worked in any other way.

To assist you in your diagramming, the list below includes the most common phrasings of conditional statements and the diagrams that arise out of them. We've used the generic placeholders A and B to stand for the parts of the statements. Some of the diagrams below may seem a little counterintuitive to you, so it's important to study these carefully if you're going to master the skill.

If **A**, then **B**./**B** if **A**.

All **A** are **B**.

Whenever **A**, **B**.

The only **A** are **B**.

...can all be diagrammed as:

A → B

Note that the phrasing used in the above statements is not the same phrasing used in the "only **A** are **B**" statements below.

B only if **A**./Only if **A**, **B**.

Only **A** are **B**.

...can all be diagrammed as:

B → A

A unless **B**./Unless **A**, **B**.

...is an alternative phrasing of a necessary condition that can be diagrammed:

– A → B

This statement's contrapositive (– **B** → **A**) has the same structure. You can't go wrong on these as long as you negate one, leave the other alone, and put the one you negated at the *origin* of the arrow.

No **A** are **B**.

...can be diagrammed as:

A → – B

Note that this statement and its contrapositive (**B** → – **A**) are very similar. Sentences involving *no* and *none* are the only types of conditionals in which the two parts can be safely switched to form a statement that is both correct and makes sense. In other words, the statement:

No leprechaun is French.

...is in every way equivalent to the statement:

No one who is French is a leprechaun.

Now do the drill on the next page. Answers can be found in Chapter 20.

DRILL #2

1. Samantha's store is having a half-price sale on bicycles this weekend. Anyone who would buy a bicycle at full price would also buy the same bicycle at half price, but no one would buy a bicycle at half price when a bicycle he or she likes better is available at full price.

Which one of the following is best supported by the information in the passage?

(A) Unless all of the bicycles in Samantha's store are included in the half-price sale, she will not sell more bicycles this weekend than she does on any other weekend.

(B) Price is the least important determining factor in a consumer's choice of which bicycle to buy.

(C) If anyone likes any bicycle better than all the other bicycles in Samantha's store, then that person will buy that bicycle, no matter what its price.

(D) No person will buy any bicycle at full price if a bicycle that person likes better is available in Samantha's store at full price.

(E) Given a choice between a bicycle at full price and the same bicycle at half price, a person will choose to buy the half-price bicycle.

2. Auctioneer: Only serious collectors are interested in little-known artworks, and our next auction will contain only little-known artworks. No member of the Chrysanthemum club is an art scholar. Therefore, no member of the Chrysanthemum club will be interested in the artworks contained in our next auction.

Which one of the following, if assumed, would allow the auctioneer's conclusion to be properly drawn?

(A) Every art scholar is a serious collector.

(B) Only art scholars are serious collectors.

(C) Every art scholar is interested in little-known artworks.

(D) Only serious collectors are members of the Chrysanthemum club.

(E) The only art scholars interested in little-known artworks are serious collectors.

3. Roger buys groceries every Thursday. Whenever Roger buys groceries, he walks past my house. Roger walked past my house today. Therefore, today must be Thursday.

Which one of the following commits an error of reasoning most similar to the error of reasoning in the argument above?

(A) The only time Wendy winds her watch is when she is late for work. So Wendy must be late for work, because I just saw her winding her watch.

(B) Sue never plays tennis on Wednesday. Today must not be Wednesday, because I just saw Sue playing tennis.

(C) Rover barks when strangers walk past on the sidewalk, and when Rover barks, our upstairs neighbors call to complain. Our upstairs neighbors just called to complain, so it seems likely that Rover was barking.

(D) Thor always looks up when he does not know what to say, and when Thor does not know what to say, he feels uncomfortable. Thor is looking up. He must be feeling uncomfortable.

(E) Nancy never fails to sign official memos, and she always announces strategic initiatives in the form of official memos. This official memo must be announcing a strategic initiative, because Nancy signed it.

4. Every piece of legislation not supported by the Democrats is supported by the Republicans. If the Democrats support a piece of legislation, then it is extensively debated in committee. If the Republicans support a piece of legislation, then it is vetoed by the President.

The statements above provide the greatest support for which one of the following conclusions?

(A) Any piece of legislation vetoed by the President is not extensively debated in committee.
(B) Any piece of legislation that is extensively debated in committee is not supported by the Republicans.
(C) Only by debating it in committee can a piece of legislation find increased support among the Republicans.
(D) Every piece of legislation is either vetoed by the President, or debated extensively in committee, or both.
(E) Any piece of legislation that is not vetoed by the President is not debated extensively in committee.

5. Only those who understand the theories of quantum physics can fully comprehend chemical bonding. In order to design a practical synthesis of industrial chemicals, a person must have an extensive background in chemistry. No one with an extensive background in chemistry understands the theories of quantum physics.

Which one of the following can be properly inferred from the information above?

(A) No one who can design a practical synthesis of industrial chemicals fully comprehends chemical bonding.
(B) Anyone who fully comprehends chemical bonding must have at least some background in chemistry.
(C) The theories of quantum physics do not apply to the synthesis of industrial chemicals.
(D) If a person has an extensive background in chemistry, that person can design a practical synthesis of industrial chemicals.
(E) No one fully comprehends chemical bonding.

3. All, Most, Some, Few, None

In many LSAT arguments and answer choices, the use of quantity words is extremely important. In drills from previous chapters, we've seen choices that are only one word away from being perfect. The use of extreme language—*all* or *none*—in cases where qualified language—*many* or *few*—is appropriate can turn an otherwise beautiful answer into one that's too strong to be correct. Similarly, a weakly worded choice where strong wording is called for can turn a wonderful answer into one that's second-best.

Some LSAT questions depend entirely on your ability to work with quantity words. In the last section of this chapter, we saw that statements involving *all* and *none* are in fact conditional, and if necessary can be represented in a diagram. Less definite statements of quantity, however—those with *most*, *some*, or *few*—have specific meanings that can't be expressed well in diagrams. It's sometimes worthwhile to think about quantity words in terms of groups, collections, or sets. Here's a brief breakdown of the major quantity words in these terms, along with discussions of what you can—and can't—tell on the basis of them.

All

Every member of one group is also a member of the second group. Take this statement as an example: "All Texans are Americans." We can think about this in conditional terms, of course, but it seems more natural to think of collections of people in analyzing this one. We have a group of Texans, and then a larger group of Americans. Here's a list of what we can conclude:

- Texans are definitely Americans.

- There may be Americans who aren't Texans.

- Anyone who isn't an American definitely isn't a Texan.

It's important to realize that you can't arbitrarily switch the groups in this statement. Although it's true that all Texans are Americans, it would not be correct to conclude that all Americans are Texans.

Most

This word tells us that a majority, though not all, of the members of one group are also members of another. Here's an example: "Most people with strong convictions voted in the last election." This tells us, precisely, that more than half of the people with strong convictions voted, while less than half of them did not vote.

As with "all" statements above, you can't just go around switching the groups. Even if most of the people with strong convictions voted, you can't say that most of the people who voted had strong convictions. You can be assured that some of them did; it's possible that they were a majority of the ones who voted, but without further information, you can't conclude that for certain.

A popular LSAT trick with "most" statements is to mix majorities. If we know that most people with strong convictions voted in the last election, and if we also know that most people with strong convictions have a bumper sticker on their car, then we have two items of information about the group of people with strong convictions: more than half voted, and more than half have a bumper sticker. Because we're dealing with two majorities of the same group, we can be assured that at least one member of the group is a member of both majorities. Somebody who voted in the last election must have a bumper sticker on his or her car. It would be impossible to have all the ones who voted also be ones who don't have bumper stickers.

Some

This is one of the most frequently misinterpreted—and most important—quantity words on the LSAT. "Some" means "at least one." For instance, if we're told that "some rivers are polluted," we know two things:

- There is at least one polluted river.

- At least one of the things in the world that's polluted is a river.

Note that "some" makes no more precise claim about quantity. This statement doesn't contain any information about what relative proportion of the world's rivers is polluted; it might be only a few, but it might also be most of them.

Usually, "some" statements can be reversed without causing problems. If it's true that "some rivers are polluted," it's also true that "some of the polluted things in the world are rivers." We have to be a little careful with the question of whether "some" can mean "all," however. Our statement that some of the rivers are polluted does imply that some of them aren't; however, it leaves open the possibility that the only polluted things in the world are rivers. Whether or not this pitfall can arise is mostly a matter of the language used, and it is hardly ever an important issue. Still, whenever the LSAT wants to play "some"/"all" games, keep an eye out for the phrase *at least* some." When you see it, remember that this statement explicitly includes the meaning "possibly all."

Finally, it's important to note that the word "many," despite its apparent implication, doesn't mean much more than "some" does. "Many" assures us that there's more than one, but it has no more specific meaning.

Few

"Few" is the flipside of "most," and means "less than half." Since the words are so closely related, the LSAT tricks involving "few" resemble those the test will pull with "most." No switching is allowed. The statement "few soldiers are artists" is focused primarily on one group: the group of soldiers. Less than half of soldiers are artists; however, it remains possible that every artist is a soldier. The important question to keep in mind, as always on the LSAT when percentages and proportions are discussed, is "of what?" The test writers love to switch groups on you.

There's a mixed minority trick that's possible with "few" statements, just as the mixed majority trick can come up with "most" statements. If we know that few soldiers are artists, and we also know that few soldiers write home every day, then there's a conclusion we can draw from these two facts. Since "few" must indicate a minority, there must be at least one soldier who both doesn't write home every day and isn't an artist. Even if none of the artist-soldiers are among the ones who write home every day, our two minorities still aren't big enough to cover the whole group of soldiers. Somebody has to fall outside of both groups.

None

As was mentioned in the previous section of this chapter, "none" statements are remarkable in that they can be safely switched. "None of my friends is a knight" is equivalent to saying "no knight is my friend." This is a simple statement that the two groups mentioned have no member in common. As long as you recognize that *none* and *no* have to be treated differently than you'd treat the word *not* in an LSAT argument, you should be fine here.

Now work on the drill below. Answers can be found in Chapter 20.

DRILL #3

1. There can be no justification for any action that results in harm to innocent individuals. Some actions that are presented as being in the nation's interest unavoidably bring harm to innocent individuals. All actions that cannot be justified are considered criminal by international authorities, yet not all actions that are presented as being in the nation's interest are considered criminal by these authorities.

    Which one of the following, if true, best explains the apparent contradiction in the passage above?

    (A) Not all international authorities are effective in the execution of their duties.
    (B) Some harm to innocent individuals is often necessary in order to prevent harm to larger numbers of innocent individuals.
    (C) At least some actions presented as being in the nation's interest can be justified.
    (D) Not all actions that are considered criminal by international authorities result in harm to innocent individuals.
    (E) At least some actions presented as being in the nation's interest result in avoidable harm to innocent individuals.

2. In Vitaville, the capital of our state, most adults own at least one car. Surveys conducted in our state demonstrate that most people who own at least one car spend a significant proportion of their income on automobile maintenance. Therefore, in Vitaville, a majority of adults spend a significant proportion of their income on maintaining their cars.

    The argument's reasoning is questionable because it

    (A) makes equivocal use of a key term in arriving at its conclusion
    (B) draws a conclusion on the basis of a survey without establishing that the results of this survey are consistent with other surveys conducted on the same topic
    (C) relies on supporting evidence that provides stronger evidence for a competing claim
    (D) presupposes the truth of the conclusion that it sets out to prove
    (E) draws a conclusion about an entire group on the basis of evidence that pertains to an unknown proportion of that group

3. Official: Every member of the Education Committee is also a member of the Human Services Committee. Every member of the Finance Committee is also a member of the Budget Committee. There are some members of the Education Committee who are not also members of the Budget Committee, but there are also some members of the Education Committee who are. Nevertheless, there are no members of the Education Committee who are also members of the Finance Committee.

Which one of the following, if known to be true, would allow the official's conclusion to be properly drawn?

(A) No member of the Human Services Committee is also a member of the Finance Committee.
(B) Some members of the Human Services Committee are also members of the Finance Committee.
(C) Every member of the Budget Committee is also a member of the Human Services Committee.
(D) Most members of the Budget Committee are also members of the Human Services Committee.
(E) Few members of the Education Committee are also members of the Budget Committee.

4. Our school has both female and male students. Some of our school's female students are cheerleaders. Some of our school's female students play basketball. Some of our school's cheerleaders play basketball, but no basketball player is also a wrestler.

The statements above, if true, provide the most support for which one of the following conclusions?

(A) Basketball season and wrestling season take place during the same time of year.
(B) Some of our school's female students are not wrestlers.
(C) Some of our school's basketball players are not female students.
(D) All of our school's cheerleaders are female students.
(E) The activities of cheerleading and playing basketball require at least one skill in common with one another.

5. Most professionals involved in customer service have good communication skills. To have good communication skills, an individual must have an intuitive grasp of others' needs. Few professionals involved in customer service have technical expertise in any other area.

If the statements above are true, then which one of the following can be inferred on the basis of them?

(A) Few individuals with an intuitive grasp of others' needs have technical expertise in any other area.
(B) Individuals with better communication skills are more likely to be successful in professions involving customer service.
(C) Some people with an intuitive grasp of others' needs do not have technical expertise in any area other than customer service.
(D) Some people with technical expertise in an area outside of customer service have an intuitive grasp of others' needs.
(E) Few people with technical expertise in areas other than customer service have good communication skills.

4. And, Or, and Nor

When the LSAT uses these common little words in conditional statements, you need to interpret their meanings carefully. Take the following statement as an example:

Soap and water are necessary to wash yourself.

This conditional statement is unlike the ones we've seen so far in that it describes two preconditions for washing: You need soap, and you need water. The connective *and* indicates that both are necessary, but if you're missing either, you're out of luck. Compare this to the statement:

A bathtub or a shower is necessary to wash yourself.

Here, having both together will satisfy the necessary condition, but having either alone will satisfy it as well. In both of these examples, the necessary condition has two parts, but the relationship between them is different. *And* means that both have to be true; *or* means that one or the other has to be true, or possibly both.

Take a look at this statement:

If the time is right, I laugh and shout.

We could diagram this statement. Here's what it would look like:

time right → laugh AND shout

Interpreting this diagram is relatively straightforward, but what about its contrapositive? Under what circumstances could we conclude that the time isn't right? Well, when the time is right, I laugh and shout. So if I'm doing neither—or even if I'm laughing but not shouting, or vice versa—then the time must not be right. In other words, the fact that *either* of the results is missing means that the sufficient condition must not have been met. As a diagram, here's how our statement looks:

– laugh OR – shout → – time right

When we flipped and negated, our "and" statement turned into an "or" statement.
Take a look at this conditional statement:

If I drink tea or coffee, I get anxious.
tea OR coffee → anxious

Think about the contrapositive of this one. If I'm not anxious, then what do we know? Either one of coffee or tea (or both) would've caused me to be anxious, but since I'm not, I must have had neither tea *nor* coffee. Or, in other words, I didn't have tea, *and* I didn't have coffee. Here's the diagram:

– anxious → – tea AND – coffee

Negating our "or" statement turned it into an "and" statement.

Keeping track of "and," "or," and "nor" statements and treating them properly when we negate them is important on many LSAT questions that involve conditional statements. You may never have thought of such tiny words as being things that have specialized meanings on the LSAT, but they do.

It is often helpful to think of *nor* as a contraction of *not-or*. We know that the negation of an "or" statement yields an "and" statement.

Now try the drill on the following page. Answers can be found in Chapter 20.

DRILL #4

1. A military coup that displaces an elected government eventually results in violent unrest among the population or in a brutal and repressive regime.

    Which one of the following instances is LEAST consistent with the principle stated above?

    (A) In Geronia, a past military coup gave rise to violent unrest among the population that eventually resulted in the military government being replaced by an elected government.
    (B) In Apollonia, a recent military coup has given rise both to violent unrest among the population and to a brutal and repressive regime.
    (C) In Ardora, a military coup that displaced an elected government did not result in violent unrest among the population.
    (D) In Diblona, a military coup that displaced an elected government did not give rise to a regime that was repressive, nor did it give rise to violent unrest among the population.
    (E) In Himerna, a military coup that displaced an elected government gave rise to a regime that was neither brutal nor repressive.

2. Every member of the Flight Club enjoys both piloting model airplanes and riding in jumbo jets. Everyone who has considered piloting jumbo jets as a career also enjoys piloting model airplanes, but no one who is prone to motion sickness enjoys riding in jumbo jets.

    If the statements above are true, then which one of the following statements must also be true?

    (A) Anyone who is either not a member of the Flight Club or who has not considered piloting jumbo jets as a career must be prone to motion sickness.
    (B) At least some members of the Flight Club have considered piloting jumbo jets as a career.
    (C) No one who is a member of the Flight Club is prone to motion sickness.
    (D) No one who has considered piloting jumbo jets as a career is prone to motion sickness.
    (E) Someone who enjoys piloting model airplanes has not considered piloting jumbo jets as a career.

3. Vivian: Neither the head coach nor the general manager was present at the planning meeting. The source who leaked news about the team's new acquisition was clearly present at the planning meeting. Therefore, press speculations that the general manager leaked news about the team's new acquisition are unfounded.

    Which one of the following arguments employs a method of reasoning most similar to Vivian's?

    (A) These diamonds cannot have been mined in a conflict zone. Their sale was fully certified by international trade organizations, and these trade organizations never certify the sale of diamonds that are mined in conflict zones or that profit factions in any of the world's many ongoing civil wars.
    (B) Neither sculpture nor painting is an emerging art form. Although some newspaper writers have called George an emerging artist, this characterization cannot be thought of as accurate, because George is a painter.
    (C) Every moment of life is dedicated either to work or to relaxation. Because every person must dedicate at least some time to work, it cannot be true that any person dedicates every moment of his or her life to relaxation.
    (D) True charity is both anonymous and effective. Therefore, it cannot be said that the corporate magnate's contribution to the international health fund is truly an act of charity, since it was widely publicized.
    (E) A responsible news story must be supported either by extensive research or by interviews conducted with at least two named sources. This news story includes only one named source, and recent reports have indicated that its reporter conducted no research beyond interviewing that source. Therefore, the news story in question was irresponsible.

4. Although it was previously believed to have become extinct, recent sightings indicate that the ivory-billed woodpecker still survives in one small pocket of wetlands. Efforts to preserve this tiny population have become some of the most publicized environmental initiatives in the country, but their eventual success is by no means assured. In order to be effective, these initiatives must both protect the ivory-billed woodpecker's native habitat and promote the breeding success of the species.

Which one of the following, if true, casts the greatest doubt on the eventual success of efforts to preserve the population of ivory-billed woodpeckers?

(A) Extensive publicity of some environmental initiatives tends to hamper the success of other environmental initiatives that receive less publicity.

(B) The native habitats of the ivory-billed woodpeckers have been all but destroyed by extensive development over the past century.

(C) Past efforts to preserve wetlands and promote breeding through human intervention have only met with limited success.

(D) The desire of bird-watchers to see the ivory-billed woodpecker before it becomes extinct presents a significant obstacle to increasing the extent of the natural wetlands that are their native habitat.

(E) Certain chemicals from pesticides, fertilizers, and detergents, which cause sterility in ivory-billed woodpeckers, are present in all wetland habitats in high enough concentrations that these chemicals could not be removed without draining the wetlands completely.

5. This university offers majors in several related academic subjects, including finance, economics, and political science. Among the students at this university are some who major in both finance and economics, some who major in both economics and political science, and some who major in both political science and finance. Therefore, among all the students at this university, at least one majors in finance, economics, and political science.

Which one of the following, if true, would provide the strongest support for the argument's conclusion?

(A) The number of students who major in finance is greater than the number of students who major in economics.

(B) This university offers majors in no academic subject other than finance, economics, and political science.

(C) Every student who majors in economics also majors in political science.

(D) No student who majors in political science majors in only one academic subject.

(E) At least one student who majors in political science majors in two other academic subjects as well.

5. Positive Results, Negative Results

Finally, we'll revisit necessary and sufficient conditions to look at them in a slightly different light. After having dealt with the technicalities of diagramming, it's important not to lose your intuitive understanding of what these statements mean. You shouldn't be diagramming many args on the LSAT, but very often you'll need to be able to tell what kind of conclusions a given conditional statement is capable of supporting.

Let's return to the very first sufficient condition we saw in this chapter:

> If I scratch my arm, then the crickets will sing.

The whole idea of a sufficient condition is that, whenever the condition is satisfied, the result is sure to happen. In this case, then, the statement above would allow us to conclude, under some circumstances, that the crickets will sing. But could we ever use this sufficient condition to conclude that the crickets will not sing? No. Even if I don't scratch my arm, it remains possible that the crickets will sing for some other reason, or possibly for no reason at all. In other words, this sufficient condition is capable of supporting the positive result (the crickets will sing), but not the negative result (the crickets won't sing).

Now take a look at our necessary condition from the same section:

> Only if a star falls will my baby come home.

What kind of conclusions can this necessary condition support? Remembering that a necessary condition describes a requirement, not a guarantee, we realize that if a star does fall, this statement doesn't assure us of anything; if, on the other hand, a star does not fall, we can be certain that my baby won't come home. In other words, the necessary condition is capable of supporting the negative result (my baby won't come home), but not the positive one (my baby will come home).

Recognizing when a conclusion involves a positive result and when it involves a negative result can help you eliminate choices rapidly and easily on some pretty tough questions. For instance, a statement that says:

> An action is good only when blah blah blah

...describes a necessary condition. That means it can only support the negative result, something like:

> blah blah blah action is not good.

Let's look at the problem a slightly different way. Suppose you wished to support the following conclusion of an argument:

> Driving stupidly is permitted.

Given two forms of answer choices—*blah blah blah is permitted **if*** versus *blah blah blah is permitted **only if***—it's clear that only the first will do: the sufficient condition. Why? Because the result in our argument is positive, and sufficient conditions support positive results, whereas necessary conditions can't.

A *not* in the conclusion can be a sign that a negative result is needed, but realize that the LSAT writers can tinker with positive and negative in conditional statements, too. For instance, suppose we need to support the conclusion of the mini-argument on the following page.

A criminal action is unfair. Therefore, a criminal action is not justified.

Two forms of conditional statement could conceivably support this judgment. Because of the LSAT writer's habits, you'd be more likely to see:

An action is justified only if it is fair.

As a necessary condition, it can support the negative result. Since a criminal action is unfair, that criminal action wouldn't satisfy the minimum requirement for being justified. On the other hand, this statement of a sufficient condition would also support the conclusion:

If an action is unfair, then that action is not justified.

It does so in a more straightforward way. A criminal action is unfair. Our sufficient condition then is satisfied, and we can support its "positive" result that the action is not justified. The main consideration when you're looking at positive versus negative results is to compare the language of your conditional statement to the language of the conclusion you wish to support. If they're the same, then a sufficient condition is called for; if they're opposite, a necessary condition is appropriate.

Now do the drill on the next page. Answers can be found in Chapter 20.

DRILL #5

1. David: Last week, I bought a computer from this store. When I brought it home and read the owner's manual, I discovered that it is not compatible with software produced by one of the most prominent software makers. The store's sales representative, however, had assured me that the computer was compatible with this particular maker's software. Although I do not own any software produced by this maker, nevertheless the sales representative made a misleading statement to me, and I should be allowed to return the computer for a full refund.

   Alice: On the contrary, you are not entitled to a full refund on the return of your computer. Although it is true that the sales representative made a misleading statement to you, that statement did not lead you to purchase a computer that fails to meet your needs.

   Alice's conclusion is most strongly supported by the principle that David is entitled to a full refund on the return of his computer

   (A) if the statements on the basis of which he initially chose to purchase that computer are subsequently found to have been false

   (B) if the false statements made by the sales representative to him do not have a material effect on whether the computer meets his needs

   (C) only if the false statements on the basis of which he chose to purchase that computer pertain to functions that prevent the computer from meeting his needs

   (D) only if the statements made to him by the store's sales representative are subsequently found to be false on the basis of information contained in the owner's manual

   (E) even if the false statements made to him by the store's sales representative do not pertain to functions that prevent the computer from meeting his needs

2. City council member: The proposed ordinance forbidding drivers from using their mobile phones while they are driving within the city limits should be rejected. It is true that operating a mobile phone while driving has been shown to increase the likelihood of the driver being involved in an accident, but this practice is no less safe than other activities by drivers that we have chosen not to regulate, including operating car stereos and engaging in conversation with passengers.

   Which one of the following, if true, most seriously undermines the city council member's argument?

   (A) Conversation with passengers poses a different safety threat than does conversation via mobile phone, since passengers in a car can see when a potentially unsafe condition is developing and refrain from distracting the driver while that condition remains.

   (B) Every measure that serves to decrease the dangers posed by drivers should be adopted.

   (C) No measure that increases driving safety should be adopted unless it can be shown that this measure increases safety to a greater degree than other similar measures that have been rejected in the past.

   (D) The fines levied on violators of the proposed ordinance would be dedicated to funding other measures that further increase driving safety, including the improvement of traffic signs and increased enforcement of existing laws.

   (E) Studies that measure the safety threat currently posed by those who operate mobile phones while driving do not exclude the possibility that, as more drivers engage in this activity, the safety threat it poses may eventually exceed that posed by any other driver activity.

3. The producers of a local morning news program must schedule one or more guests to interview tomorrow. If they are able to schedule an interview with the governor, the program is sure to be a success, but the program will only be successful as long as some elected government representative is scheduled. Appleby has indicated that she is willing to be interviewed as a government representative, but Appleby was appointed to her office, not elected.

If the statements above are true, then which one of the following can be concluded on the basis of them?

(A) Only if the governor is scheduled for the local morning news program tomorrow will that program be a success.

(B) If some elected government representative other than the governor is scheduled to be interviewed on tomorrow morning's local news program, then that program will be a success.

(C) Everyone who holds government office was either appointed or elected to that office.

(D) If Appleby is interviewed on the news program tomorrow, that program will not be successful.

(E) If the local morning news program is to be a success tomorrow, then at least one government representative other than Appleby must be interviewed on that program.

4. Hargrave: The justification of any response to hostile action must include at least two factors: the actual harm caused by the hostile action, and the likely result of the response being considered. No hostile response to hostile action is justified unless harm was caused by that action, or unless the likely result of failing to respond to that action is future harm. It is clear that Robinson's response to Johnson's hostile action was justified, even though Johnson's hostile action did not cause Robinson any harm at the time.

Which one of the following, if assumed, would allow Hargrave's conclusion to be properly drawn?

(A) It is certain that if Robinson had not responded to Johnson's hostile action, Johnson's future actions would have resulted in harm to Robinson.

(B) The likely result of Robinson's response was to prevent future harm to people other than Robinson, and any action that prevents harm to others is justified.

(C) Every hostile response to a hostile action is justified when the likely result of that response is to prevent future harm.

(D) Johnson's hostile action was not itself a response to an initial hostile action taken by Robinson.

(E) Unless Robinson's response was either not hostile, or not harmful, or both, then that response was not justified.

5. In order to be a direct cause of some event, it must be true that, in the absence of the cause, the event would not have taken place. An ultimate cause is one which itself has no direct causes, but which cannot have failed to give rise to its effects. It must be true, then, that if any event has an ultimate cause, then that event cannot have any other direct cause.

The argument above employs which one of the following principles of reasoning?

(A) If any set of circumstances is sufficient to lead to a result, then that set of circumstances is therefore also necessary to that result.

(B) No set of circumstances exists in which a fact necessary to a result is also sufficient to ensure that result.

(C) If any one fact is by itself sufficient to ensure a result, then no other condition that is not necessary to that fact can be necessary to the result.

(D) If any set of circumstances is sufficient to ensure a result, then no contradictory set of circumstances can be sufficient to ensure that result.

(E) If a result is not ensured when a set of circumstances necessary to that result is satisfied, then some other circumstance necessary to the result must exist.

Practice Section 1: Args

Directions: The questions in this section are based on the reasoning contained in brief statements or passages. For some questions, more than one of the choices could conceivably answer the question. However, you are to choose the best answer; that is, the response that most accurately and completely answers the question. You should not make assumptions that are by commonsense standards implausible, superfluous, or incompatible with the passage. After you have chosen the best answer, blacken the corresponding space on your answer sheet.

1. Representative: By themselves, corporate tax cuts do not cause economic growth; rather, a sudden change in companies' tax burdens results in a decrease in costs, even for companies whose earnings do not grow, making these companies more attractive to investors. Many companies spend their tax savings on new equipment or on the hiring of new employees, making these companies more competitive. Either way, the result is that more capital becomes available in the marketplace. For the same reason, the tax cuts I propose will cause the economy to grow.

Which one of the following, if true, would most strengthen the representative's conclusion?

(A) The tax cuts proposed by the representative do not include a reduction of corporate tax burdens.

(B) Any action that makes more capital available in the marketplace will cause the economy to grow.

(C) The tax cuts proposed by the representative will lead companies to invest in new equipment and employees rather than taking their tax savings as increased profits.

(D) Corporate earnings growth is the most important factor in determining whether or not the overall economy will grow.

(E) Any action that makes some companies more competitive will cause the economy to grow.

2. Any training program that involves extensive periods of cardiovascular exercise is one that will increase the health of those who follow it. Therefore, since some circuit-training programs involve extensive periods of cardiovascular exercise, any person, whatever his or her current level of health, will experience greater health as a result of following a circuit-training program.

A flaw in the reasoning of the argument is that the argument

(A) presupposes that the health benefits associated with cardiovascular exercise are equal for all individuals

(B) draws a more qualified conclusion than the one most properly supported by its premises

(C) concludes that the only means of arriving at a goal is some means that is merely one among many possible ways of achieving that goal

(D) assumes that no individuals are currently following circuit-training programs

(E) draws a conclusion about all cases in a certain class on the basis of information that may not apply to some cases in that class

3. The specific tests employed in this case are capable of determining only whether two individuals share a common ancestor, but more extensive testing is required to tell how they are related. In this case, then, even though Franz is Gregor's father, the only conclusion supported by the evidence is that the two men have some male ancestor in common.

From the statements above, which one of the following can be properly inferred?

(A) The tests employed in this case were properly administered.
(B) The tests employed in this case would have been capable of providing definitive evidence that Franz and Gregor did not have a female ancestor in common.
(C) No evidence in this case excludes the possibility that Franz and Gregor are brothers.
(D) In order for this case to be properly considered, more extensive testing must be conducted.
(E) The full details of Franz's ancestry are not part of the evidence in this case.

4. Tremaine: The contract price agreed upon for my overhaul of the company's computer systems was based on the assumption that this overhaul would require approximately 200 hours of labor. In the end, I only required 100 hours of labor to complete the overhaul, but since the contract specified the amount of money to be paid without stipulations concerning the time required, I am not obligated to repay any of my contract price to the company.

Dinah: On the contrary, if you had required more than the estimate of 200 hours to complete the overhaul of the computer systems, you would undoubtedly have requested additional compensation, and the company would have been forced to agree, even though that compensation exceeded the amount specified in your contract.

Dinah's response functions in which one of the following ways?

(A) It calls into question the principle employed to justify Tremaine's conclusion while reserving judgment about the specific case Tremaine describes.
(B) It makes use of a hypothetical situation in providing further support for Tremaine's conclusion.
(C) It demonstrates that Tremaine's conclusion in this instance is motivated by self-interest, rather than by the uniform application of any ethical principle.
(D) It employs Tremaine's principle in resolving a dilemma Dinah has encountered.
(E) It suggests that the principle that Tremaine employs is not the one most properly suited to situations of the kind that Tremaine describes.

5. It has been shown that subjective Freudian theories of behavior are less reliable at predicting individual responses than are more recent theories based on biochemistry and other objective data. It is also known that therapies for behavioral disorders are most successful when those therapies are based on theoretical principles that reliably predict behavior. Thus we might infer that newer theories are better suited for treating individuals with behavioral disorders than are Freudian theories. Nevertheless, studies show that many more individuals are treated successfully for behavioral disorders using therapies based on Freudian theories than are successfully treated using therapies based on all other alternative theories combined.

Which one of the following, if true, best explains the results of the studies described above?

(A) The expense of obtaining crucial biochemical data in individual cases dictates that the vast majority of people receive therapies based on Freudian theories of behavior, which depend upon information that is much cheaper to collect.

(B) No psychological theory is completely successful at predicting individual responses in any case of behavioral disorder.

(C) When offered a choice between methods of treatment, a majority of patients prefer therapies based on subjective theories.

(D) Freudian theories of behavior have been in existence for far longer than has any alternative objective theory that is more reliable at predicting individual responses.

(E) The rate of success for therapies based on newer, more objective theories of behavior is significantly higher than the historical success rate of therapies based on subjective Freudian theories.

6. April: Most writers wish to express their feelings as clearly as possible. However, instead of adopting a style that engages a reader's imagination by leaving room for interpretation, writers often resort to a provocative style that expresses idiosyncratic views. Because readers prefer writing that is descriptive rather than confrontational, they are most sympathetic to writers who convey experience simply without excessive moralizing. Therefore, adopting a provocative style is unlikely to help readers clearly understand a writer's feelings.

Which one of the following is an assumption on which April's argument depends?

(A) Writers who adopt a provocative style do so because they find most other writing bland and ineffective.

(B) Leaving too much room for interpretation may result in writing that fails to convey the writer's feelings clearly.

(C) Moralizing ideas expressed in a provocative style engage a reader's imagination by prompting either agreement or outrage.

(D) Exposure to idiosyncratic views is not essential to the reader's development of sympathy for a writer.

(E) In order to be understood clearly, a writer's feelings must be idiosyncratic and imaginative.

Questions 7–8

Instability within a culture in transition can result from either a redefinition of social roles or from ambiguity in traditional conceptions of economic class. Therefore, the leaders in a culture experiencing instability during transition could mitigate its effect by actively promoting adaptability as a positive cultural value, since members of that culture are likely to find themselves in situations where their social or economic status relative to other individuals they encounter is unclear.

7. According to the information in the passage above, if the recommendation to promote adaptability is to be successful at decreasing social instability within a culture in transition, then which one of the following must be true?

(A) Adaptability is a value that has not traditionally been viewed as positive within the culture.

(B) Traditional conceptions of economic class are not reflected in the language and daily habits of the culture's members.

(C) Promotion of particular values by the culture's leaders does not represent an unacceptable redefinition of social roles.

(D) At least some instability is inevitable when members of a culture are unclear about their social or economic status relative to other members of that culture.

(E) The new social roles defined within the culture are no more rigidly defined than the traditional social roles they supplanted.

8. Which one of the following most closely parallels the questionable reasoning in the argument above?

(A) A work's original author is less capable of detecting mistakes in that work than are editors or proofreaders. Therefore, a publisher who wishes to prevent as many mistakes as possible from appearing in the works he or she publishes would be well advised to hire both editors and proofreaders.

(B) Since students who participate in extracurricular activities develop either leadership skills or creativity, the administrators in public education systems that are perceived as ineffective should press for additional funding of these activities. A public education system can be perceived as ineffective when its graduates lack either of these qualities.

(C) Naturalists become established either by studying relevant academic subjects in a university or by becoming assiduous observers of their natural surroundings. Therefore, a person who wishes to become an established naturalist would be well advised to follow one of these two paths, since there are many established naturalists who have never studied academic subjects in universities, and many who have never become assiduous observers of their surroundings.

(D) People of both of these tribes value nonviolence as a significant cultural value, but in every case where these tribes have interacted with one another, strife has resulted. Therefore, the international agency would be well advised to open two separate aid stations serving the two tribes separately rather than opening one aid station to serve them both.

(E) Parents should encourage their children to join the school choir. Although both the school choir and the school orchestra offer similar benefits in terms of exposure to high culture, most students enjoy choir more than they enjoy orchestra because choir involves a great deal more social interaction.

9. Journalist: Patient choice in both the physicians they visit and the kind of treatment they receive guarantees that the quality of health care overall is as high as possible. In most countries, however, either private companies or government ministries place limits on the physicians that individuals can visit and the types of treatment that they are permitted to receive. For this reason, the power that such organizations exert over individual patient choices needs to be reduced. Even those who work in these organizations agree in principle that choice in medical care is an important value, yet they continue to limit this choice in the interest of saving their organizations money.

The journalist's argument is structured to lead to which one of the following conclusions?

(A) The quality of health care throughout the world is deteriorating.
(B) Preserving patients' freedom of choice in which physicians they visit and what kind of treatment they receive is crucial.
(C) The control many private and public organizations have over patient choice must be limited.
(D) Monetary interests in health care are responsible for limiting the quality of care all patients receive.
(E) In most countries, either private organizations or public ministries have a virtual monopoly on health care.

10. In a recent experiment, scientists studying burrowing in a species of cloned roundworms altered a single gene believed to be related to this activity. Roundworm clones with unaltered genes were able to burrow both by the use of their mouthparts and by wriggling; roundworm clones with the altered gene were able to burrow by the use of their mouthparts, but not by wriggling. The scientists concluded that roundworms of this species that have been observed to burrow only by the use of their mouthparts and not by wriggling do so because they possess a damaged copy of the studied gene.

Which one of the following is an assumption required by the argument?

(A) The impact of genetics on burrowing behaviors in roundworms is not fully understood.
(B) No gene other than the one studied is required for burrowing by wriggling in this species of roundworm.
(C) At least some members of all species of roundworms are capable of burrowing either by the use of their mouthparts or by wriggling.
(D) No gene found in this species of roundworms is required for both manifestations of the activity of burrowing.
(E) Members of this species of roundworms who have been observed not to burrow by wriggling do so because they live in coarse sands where wriggling is not an effective method of burrowing.

11. The theory of evolution includes a concept known as adaptive radiation, whereby a single population living in an area gradually becomes several different species as subgroups of that population occupy vacant ecological niches in that area. For example, many aquatic mammal species such as manatees and whales are believed to have descended from land animals that lived in herds and fed on plant matter. It is hypothesized that populations living near water found that this environment offered easier access to food and greater protection from predators, and gradually developed adaptations that allowed them to live entirely in an aquatic environment.

Which one of the following facts, if it were known to be true, would most support the hypothesis above concerning the ancestry of many aquatic mammals?

(A) The forefeet of elephants have an unusual skeletal structure found also in the front flippers of manatees but in no other mammals.
(B) A harmless virus commonly found in domestic cattle shares more than 90 percent of its genetic material with another harmless virus found in many species of whale.
(C) The nutritional requirements of dugongs, a grazing aquatic mammal, are similar to those of some species of water buffalo.
(D) Both zebras, which communicate with one another through color changes, and dolphins, which communicate by means of sound, have unusually large vocabularies of signals that are capable of conveying both practical information and the animals' emotional states.
(E) Both American bison and Pacific sea lions have themselves created multiple ecological niches, since both have parasites that live on their skins and both support symbiotic species that feed on these parasites.

12. Advocates of government reform have claimed that a broad consensus believes that the current political system does not effectively address issues important to them and exists only to serve the narrow interests of wealthy individuals and corporations. However, reform advocates are overstating the prevalence of these opinions. In a survey conducted recently by unions of federal and municipal government workers, only 15 percent of respondents indicated that they felt government was not addressing issues important to them, and only 4 percent characterized the government as being controlled by moneyed interests. These results are worthy of serious consideration, since the respondents have much more knowledge of the day-to-day workings of government than does the average citizen.

The reasoning in the argument is flawed because the argument

(A) takes as proof that the government is not in need of reform survey data that merely indicate a majority belief that government is not in need of reform
(B) draws its conclusion based on statements about individual interests rather than on those issues that the population broadly considers to be most important
(C) fails to consider the extent to which the manner in which survey questions are presented to respondents plays a role in what responses those people offer
(D) bases claims concerning a broader consensus on the responses of individuals who are acknowledged by the argument not to be typical of the broader group
(E) presumes without warrant that the interests of wealthy individuals and corporations conflict with the interests of average citizens

13. Hakim: Global warming does not pose a threat of extinction to humans. Geological data indicate that humanity has survived significant climate shifts in the past, including ice ages, and there is no reason to believe that humanity would be less able to survive extremely warm weather than extremely cold weather. In fact, humanity may thrive in higher temperatures: demographic data indicate that birth rates and overall crop yields are much higher today in Earth's warmer regions than they are in its colder regions.

Veronica: While it is true that warmer regions are more fertile than Arctic and tundra regions, at the same time desert and tropical regions are relatively infertile, and crop yields are highest in temperate areas. Climate models and recent data show that global warming would result in smaller temperate areas, the growth of deserts, and the widening of the equatorial tropical band.

The dialogue lends the most support to the claim that Hakim and Veronica disagree on whether

(A) global warming poses a possible danger of extinction to humans

(B) humanity would cope with conditions of global warming as well as it did with past ice ages

(C) global warming is likely to increase the overall land area on Earth that could be considered temperate

(D) the likely result of increasing global temperatures would be a net increase in average crop yields on Earth

(E) there are any possible benefits to humanity offered by an increase in global temperatures

14. Many people now believe that lying to government officials in order to save money on taxes is ethically acceptable. Nothing could be further from the truth, however. It would be true if the individuals being taxed did not have the means available to them to modify tax laws through their elected representatives, but the fact that this assumption is untrue demonstrates unequivocally that the common belief is incorrect.

Which one of the following most accurately describes a reasoning flaw in the argument?

(A) The argument appeals to a particular set of ethical standards in criticizing the behavior of those who may or may not subscribe to the same set of ethical standards.

(B) The argument takes for granted that the fact that people have elected representatives necessarily means that these same people have the means available to them to modify tax laws.

(C) The argument mistakenly assumes that, if the truth of some condition implies the existence of a particular state of affairs, then the fact that this state of affairs does not exist implies that the condition is untrue.

(D) The argument derives from the fact that a practice cannot explicitly be shown to be ethical, so then the conclusion is that this practice must therefore be unethical.

(E) The argument takes for granted that, if the truth of one claim implies the truth of some second claim, then the falsity of the first claim therefore demonstrates the falsity of the second claim.

15. If every mystery story includes a definite resolution of its central question, and this novel is a mystery story, then it follows that this novel includes a definite resolution of its central question. But this novel's resolution of its central question is extremely ambiguous. So either this novel is not a mystery story, or not all mystery stories include definite resolutions of their central questions.

Which one of the following arguments is most similar in its pattern of reasoning to the argument above?

(A) If every city park closes at sundown, and the historic site in the center of downtown is a city park, then it follows that the historic site in the center of downtown closes at sundown. But the historic site in the center of downtown is a state park. So the historic site in the center of downtown does not close at sundown, or not all city parks close at sundown.

(B) If all land in the city that is owned by the railroad is abandoned, and this strip of land downtown is owned by the railroad, then it follows that this strip of land downtown is abandoned. But there is evidence that the railroad continues to make use of this strip of land downtown. So not all land in the city that is owned by the railroad is abandoned, and this strip of land downtown is not owned by the railroad.

(C) If all walking trails in national parks receive adequate maintenance, and this path is a walking trail in a national park, then it follows that this path receives adequate maintenance. But poor maintenance on this path has led to its severe erosion. So not all walking trails in national parks receive adequate maintenance, or this path is not a walking trail in a national park.

(D) If all of the council's requests for new recreational facilities will be granted, and this is a request by the council for new recreational facilities, then it follows that this request will be granted. But this request will not be granted. So this is not a request by the council for new recreational facilities.

(E) If every park in the city is maintained by the state, then it follows that maintenance expenditures related to these parks are included in the state budget and those expenditures are paid for by state taxes. But maintenance expenditures related to this city park are not included in the state budget. So this city park is not maintained by the state, or maintenance expenditures related to this city park are not paid for by state taxes.

16. With decreased production in many oil-producing nations, energy costs across the globe have dramatically increased. Analysts blame the increase on the cartel OPEC, which collectively sets production policy for most of the major oil-exporting nations. With a large proportion of the world's newly produced crude oil under its control, OPEC has control over worldwide prices, and when OPEC announces its intention to decrease production, the market often overreacts.

Which one of the following, if true, would most call into question the analysts' explanation of increased energy costs?

(A) Refiners, who buy crude oil and turn it into the products that have the greatest direct impact on energy costs, typically increase the prices they charge for these products in advance of anticipated increases in crude oil prices, and lower their prices more slowly than crude oil prices fall.

(B) When OPEC announces that it will limit production, corporations and governments that maintain their own crude oil reserves increase those reserves in anticipation of future price increases.

(C) When OPEC limits its production of crude oil, exporters who are not members of OPEC realize increased profits by significantly increasing their own production and export of crude oil.

(D) Some governments of countries whose economies depend upon imported oil keep energy prices in these countries artificially low by subsidizing the increased importation of crude oil in times when the promise of high crude oil prices threatens their economic health.

(E) During times when crude oil prices are high, the cost of energy produced from alternative sources such as coal, natural gas, wind, and solar power also tend to increase.

17. Freddie, who buys and restores classic cars as a hobby, was offered the opportunity to purchase a rare automobile from its original owner, who had been trying to sell it for some time. Because the automobile was no longer operable and was significantly damaged, the owner only asked $2,000 for it, but Freddie knew that with a slightly greater investment in restoration, the car would be worth significantly more. Freddie agreed to pay the asking price for the car, restored it, and later that year sold the restored car for $40,000. The original owner read of the sale in a local newspaper and accused Freddie of having cheated him. Freddie maintained that he had done nothing wrong.

Which one of the following principles, if established, most helps to justify Freddie's contention?

(A) A buyer cannot cheat a seller unless, in the buyer's best judgment, the true market value of the product exchanged is higher than the price the seller asks and receives in exchange for the product.

(B) A seller cannot cheat a buyer unless, in the seller's best judgment, the true market value of the product exchanged is lower than the price the buyer agrees to pay in exchange for the product.

(C) A seller can cheat a buyer only if, in the seller's best judgment, the cost of modifications or improvements that would result in a substantial increase in the value of the product exchanged is at least equal to the cost asked for by the seller and agreed to by the buyer.

(D) A buyer can cheat a seller only if, to the buyer's certain knowledge, some modification or improvement to the product exchanged would result in an immediate increase in its value that is greater than the cost of the modification or improvement made.

(E) A buyer can cheat a seller only if, to the buyer's certain knowledge, there exists some other buyer who would agree to pay a significantly greater price for the product exchanged, without any improvement or modification, than the one asked for and received by the seller.

18. Coffee house owner: It is true that the taste, variety, and overall quality of coffee beverages offered by the large national chain are all excellent, and their prices are slightly lower than those typically found in locally owned coffee houses. Nevertheless, consumers should choose to buy from locally owned coffee houses instead. The chain's purchasing power drives down market prices and has already led to thousands of small coffee farmers losing their livelihoods, and significant environmental damage as others seek to cut costs and maximize production in the struggle to survive. Moreover, the chain store does not pass on the savings it extorts to its customers, but instead takes those savings as increased profits. You may be paying a little more out of your own pocket, but in larger terms a cup of coffee at a locally owned coffee house is a lot less expensive than one from the large national chain.

The claim that the large national chain of coffee shops does not pass on its savings on the market price of coffee to consumers plays which one of the following roles in the argument?

(A) It is the conclusion that the argument attempts to establish.

(B) It suggests that whatever supposed benefits may result from the decision to buy coffee beverages from the large national chain do not accrue primarily to the consumer.

(C) It is a reason notwithstanding which the argument suggests that consumers ought to buy their coffee beverages from locally owned coffee houses.

(D) It is an observation whose accuracy is called into question by other statements offered in support of the argument's conclusion.

(E) It is an overly emotional criticism of the large national chain that applies equally to that chain and to locally owned coffee houses.

19. Therapist: Friendship is defined solely by the capacity for one individual to value another's needs above his or her own; certainly, no true friend can ascribe a greater importance to a mere preference than to a friend's manifest need. It may be pointed out that one friend often overlooks another's most obvious faults not because they do not need to be corrected, but instead because attempting to correct them may cause conflict and discomfort. Some use this fact as evidence that people do not always put their true friends' needs above their own. Yet it is clear that everyone is aware of his or her own most obvious faults because of the negative effects they have on other people, and have done everything possible to correct them. Therefore, _____.

Which one of the following most logically completes the final sentence of the therapist's argument?

(A) a true friend values another's need to have his or her most obvious faults overlooked when they cannot be corrected above the preference to be free of the negative consequences of those faults

(B) no true friend overlooks another friend's most obvious faults unless it is clear that the friend who possesses those faults is either not aware of them, or has not done everything possible to correct them

(C) the statement that true friends sometimes overlook one another's faults without attempting to correct them is false

(D) a true friend may at times value his or her friend's preference to avoid conflict and discomfort over that friend's need to be free of the negative consequences of his or her faults

(E) in any case when a person overlooks another's most obvious faults, either those faults do not need to be corrected, or else the person is not a true friend

20. Health insurance companies generally charge higher premiums to individuals they cover who have increased health risks of some kinds. Although most agree that those who smoke, are obese, or engage in risky behavior ought to pay higher prices for their health insurance, the science of genetics has given rise to controversial questions in this area. Since it will soon be possible to determine on the basis of genetic makeup an individual's predisposition for illnesses such as cancer, diabetes, and depression, there can be no doubt that some individuals will eventually be forced to pay higher premiums because of risk factors over which they have no control.

Which one of the following, if true, most undermines the argument?

(A) The development of genetic therapies holds out the hope that individuals may eventually be able to reduce their genetic risk factors for some serious illnesses.

(B) Although there are increased health risks associated with living in some excessively polluted areas, health insurance companies do not charge higher premiums to individuals who choose to live in these areas.

(C) Although the tests currently available for assessing genetic risk factors for many diseases are reliable, they cannot determine to what degree factors such as diet and environment contribute to the development of disease in any one individual.

(D) Established law forbids health insurance companies from charging higher premiums to individuals on the basis of risks associated with race, national origin, and other factors over which they have no control.

(E) Because it is determined before birth, an individual's genetic makeup is one of the few factors that may give rise to health risks over which the individual has no control.

21. Educator: The majority of successful students are hard workers, and all hard workers are able to manage their time well. However, not all successful students are exceptionally brilliant. It follows that some people who are able to manage their time well are exceptionally brilliant.

The educator's conclusion follows logically if which one of the following is assumed?

(A) Most successful students are able to manage their time well.
(B) Most hard workers are successful students.
(C) Some successful students are not exceptionally brilliant.
(D) All people who are able to manage their time well are hard workers.
(E) Most successful students are exceptionally brilliant.

22. All scientific medical treatments have been rigorously tested and are more effective than a placebo, which is a false treatment whose only healing power stems from the fact that the patient receiving it believes that he or she is receiving effective treatment. Many traditional medical treatments lack both of these characteristics, and no medical treatment is both traditional and scientific. Additionally, although only scientific medical treatments have been conclusively shown to be safe, no medical treatment that is more effective than a placebo should be rejected by medical professionals as a viable treatment option.

If the statements above are true, which one of the following must be true?

(A) No traditional medical treatment that is more effective than a placebo has been rigorously tested.
(B) All medical treatments that have been rigorously tested but are not more effective than a placebo are scientific medical treatments.
(C) No medical treatments that have been conclusively shown to be safe should be rejected by medical professionals as viable treatment options.
(D) All medical treatments that have not been rigorously tested should be rejected by medical professionals as viable treatment options.
(E) All medical treatments that should not be rejected by medical professionals as viable treatment options are scientific medical treatments.

23. Legislator A: It is our responsibility to ensure that the water supply in this country is as free as possible from harmful chemicals. Because my proposed bill to update the country's clean-water standards would require water to be free of all such chemicals, we must approve this bill if we agree that we should act on the question of water quality during this legislative term.

Legislator B: Making certain that the water supply is free of harmful chemicals is not the legislature's only responsibility; we also must ensure the financial viability of companies that provide water to our citizens. The new clean-water standards proposed in your bill would put such a heavy financial burden on water utilities that many if not most of them would cease providing water to our citizens, leading to far worse dangers than those posed by the current level of harmful chemicals.

Which one of the following is an issue about which the two legislators disagree?

(A) The legislature should act on the question of water quality during this legislative term.
(B) It is the legislature's responsibility to ensure the financial viability of companies that provide water to the country's citizens.
(C) The clean-water bill proposed by legislator A would cause a substantial number of water utilities to cease providing water to the country's citizens.
(D) If the legislature is to act on the question of water quality during this legislative term, it must approve the clean-water bill proposed by legislator A.
(E) The clean-water bill proposed by legislator A would require water to be free of all harmful chemicals.

24. Some plants grown in high concentrations of nitrogen gas grow faster than they do in an atmosphere with the usual sea-level mix of gases. This requires that these plants be able to fix nitrogen, and no plant can fix nitrogen unless its roots harbor one of a very few varieties of symbiotic bacteria.

If the statements above are true, each of the following could also be true EXCEPT:

(A) Some plants with roots that harbor one variety of symbiotic bacteria are incapable of fixing nitrogen.
(B) Most plants that grow faster in high concentrations of nitrogen gas have roots that harbor the same variety of symbiotic bacteria.
(C) Many plants that are able to fix nitrogen grow more slowly in high concentrations of nitrogen gas than they do in an atmosphere with the usual sea-level mix of gases.
(D) Some plants that harbor symbiotic bacteria only in their leaves are able to fix nitrogen.
(E) Some plants that do not fix nitrogen grow more quickly in an atmosphere that does not contain the usual sea-level mix of gases.

25. Corn farmer: The use of hydrogen fuel cells to power cars will reduce overall emissions of harmful greenhouse gases and represents a more efficient use of energy than internal-combustion engines powered by ordinary gasoline. The hydrogen to power fuel cells can either be derived in the car itself from liquid hydrogen-containing compounds such as ethanol using a fuel reformer, or else produced from seawater using electrolysis. Since ethanol reformers produce carbon dioxide, a greenhouse gas, as their major waste product, some have argued that we should produce hydrogen at power plants using electrolysis, and then distribute hydrogen in gaseous form to fuel cars. But gaseous hydrogen is an extremely dangerous substance to handle and transport. The moderate difference in carbon dioxide emissions is not sufficient to justify the significantly increased safety risk of using gaseous hydrogen; therefore, ethanol fuel reformers should be used in cars to produce hydrogen for their fuel cells.

Which one of the following, if true, would most weaken the corn farmer's argument?

(A) Liquid ethanol burns at such a high temperature that its flames cannot be seen by the human eye, representing an increased danger of catastrophic fires over ordinary gasoline, which burns at a lower temperature.
(B) Natural gas, which contains much smaller quantities of oxygen than ethanol, can be liquefied under pressure and safely used in cars by a type of fuel reformer whose only major waste product is solid carbon.
(C) Electricity used to convert seawater into gaseous hydrogen and gaseous oxygen through electrolysis would be generated by burning fossil fuels, resulting in increased emission of greenhouse gases worldwide.
(D) Hydrogen fuel cells rely on the chemical reaction between hydrogen and oxygen that forms gaseous water, which is itself a greenhouse gas.
(E) Climatic models suggest that the effects of increased gaseous hydrogen in the atmosphere, an inevitable result of any method of handling and transporting it, may be more harmful than the effect of greenhouse gases currently being emitted into the atmosphere.

ANSWER KEY TO PRACTICE SECTION 1: ARGS

For full answers and explanations, turn to Chapter 21.

1. B
2. E
3. C
4. E
5. A
6. D
7. C
8. B
9. C
10. B
11. A
12. D
13. D
14. E
15. C
16. C
17. E
18. B
19. A
20. D
21. E
22. C
23. D
24. D
25. B

8

Practice Section 2: Args

Directions: The questions in this section are based on the reasoning contained in brief statements or passages. For some questions, more than one of the choices could conceivably answer the question. However, you are to choose the best answer; that is, the response that most accurately and completely answers the question. You should not make assumptions that are by commonsense standards implausible, superfluous, or incompatible with the passage. After you have chosen the best answer, blacken the corresponding space on your answer sheet.

1. Surveys conducted in the lake country indicate that current conservation efforts are actually harming the ecosystems there. The lakes that have been the subject of these efforts for at least a year have smaller fish populations and less underwater vegetation overall than do the other lakes in the region. Since fish and underwater vegetation are essential to maintaining a healthy lake ecosystem, the authorities would be wise to discontinue the current conservation efforts immediately.

    Which one of the following statements, if true, most seriously weakens the argument?

    (A) Data collected in the lake country indicate that lakes would quickly return to their former condition if the current conservation efforts were discontinued immediately.
    (B) The current conservation efforts include the reintroduction of native fish species to lakes where those species have all but died out over the past ten years.
    (C) Projections indicate that the fish populations in some lakes that are the subject of the current conservation efforts will recover within the next five years.
    (D) The reduction in underwater vegetation associated with the current conservation efforts has made the lakes that have been the subject of those efforts more desirable places for fishing and other recreational activities.
    (E) Efforts to restore the lakes' ecosystems are focused on removing a nonnative fish species whose unchecked growth has crowded out native fish and led to an unhealthy proliferation of algae.

Questions 2–3

Joe: Critics of the growing dietary supplement industry object to the fact that these substances may be sold without government regulation or testing. Although the makers of dietary supplements are prohibited from making any claim about their products other than that they contribute to general health, these critics argue that the sellers of dietary supplements routinely make more specific claims concerning their efficacy, thus voiding the exemption. Yet none of these critics would argue that multivitamins, which sellers routinely claim can help prevent maladies from osteoporosis to heart disease, ought to be regulated by the government. The critics are clearly acting in the interest of the pharmaceutical industry, and ought to be ignored.

Sarah: Although the multivitamins themselves have not been shown to prevent disease, the substances they contain have been thoroughly studied, and are known to be safe when taken properly. The dietary supplements that are the subject of the current controversy contain ingredients of questionable efficacy, in amounts that may actually be harmful. Everyone expects the government to control the sale of products that could kill or injure those who use them; dietary supplements should not be the exception to this rule.

2. Which one of the following most accurately describes the point at issue between Joe and Sarah?

    (A) whether the government regulation of dietary supplements is warranted
    (B) whether the government regulation of dietary supplements would serve the interests of the pharmaceutical industry
    (C) whether critics who object to the fact that dietary supplements are not regulated by the government have proof that the supplements' sellers make specific claims concerning their curative powers
    (D) whether claims that multivitamins contribute to general health are justified by sufficient evidence
    (E) whether the government ought to regulate every product that could kill or injure those who use them

3. Sarah responds to Joe's argument in which one of the following ways?

(A) She questions Joe's assumption that all dietary supplements are equally safe.

(B) She agrees with Joe's assessment of critics' motives in recommending the regulation of dietary supplements, but provides an alternate reason why all such supplements ought to be regulated.

(C) She reinforces the critics' objection that the makers of dietary supplements defend the efficacy of their products and insist that they do not require regulation using contradictory claims.

(D) She identifies an internal inconsistency in Joe's argumentation.

(E) She points out a relevant difference between two types of dietary supplements that are treated by Joe's argument as being comparable in every important respect.

4. Video game manufacturer: Parent groups claim that our products, which require quick responses to a rapid succession of vivid images, are harming children by shortening their attention spans, giving rise to attention deficit. The only testimony offered in support of this claim comes from parents whose children both play video games and have been diagnosed with attention deficit. But only a licensed psychiatrist can determine whether or not video games are responsible for a given case of attention deficit, and none of the parents who testified are licensed psychiatrists. Therefore, our video games do not harm children by causing attention deficit.

The reasoning in the video game manufacturer's argument is flawed because the argument

(A) attacks the motives of the parents who testified rather than evaluating the merit of their claims

(B) does not rule out other possible ways in which video games can harm children, such as encouraging obesity and tendencies toward violence

(C) fails to provide a determination from a licensed psychiatrist that video games did not cause attention deficit in the cases mentioned

(D) does not discuss positive impacts video games may have on children, such as improving hand-eye coordination and problem-solving skills

(E) uses the term "harm" in an equivocal fashion

5. In one region inhabited by humans during prehistory, a particularly beautiful and rare type of shell can be found. Evidence exists that in some settlements in this area, the shell was used to make ornamental necklaces that indicated high social status; in others, the shell appears to have been instead used as an early form of currency. Two archaeological sites in the area, called A and B, are known to have been inhabited by prehistoric humans. At site A, the specimens of this type of shell have narrow holes and are well preserved; at site B, the specimens of shell have wider holes and show evidence of having been extensively handled. Archaeologists have determined, however, that the shell did not serve as currency among the inhabitants of either site.

Which one of the following, if true, most helps to explain the archaeologists' conclusion?

(A) When used to make ornamental necklaces, narrow holes were drilled in the shells so they could be strung, whereas when they were used as currency, broader holes were needed so the shells could be stacked and carried on small lengths of polished wood.

(B) Primitive hand drills found at site A have exceptionally narrow points, whereas the hand drills found more commonly throughout the region have broad points.

(C) The settlement at site B is known to have used colored beads crafted out of stone as a medium of exchange instead of shells.

(D) Burial sites found at the settlements indicate that, at site A, socially important individuals were buried along with their ornamental possessions, whereas at site B, their ornamental possessions were passed down from generation to generation.

(E) Some evidence exists that the shells in a few settlements in the area could have been used for ornamental purposes and for currency at different times.

6. Some have argued that codes of polite behavior in a society exist primarily to indicate the subjection of its individuals to the standards of the community, thus perpetuating the community's power. But it is clear that the majority of specific behaviors considered polite in any society exist primarily to reduce conflict among its members and ensure the society's smooth functioning. Indeed, the primacy of this particular goal is exemplified most clearly by the fact that no society, however stringent its codes of behavior are, considers it polite to draw attention in public to impolite behavior by other individuals.

The statements above, if true, most strongly support which one of the following?

(A) In every society, the collection of behaviors considered impolite includes all of those that would tend to create conflict.

(B) In every society, there exist behaviors that create conflict only because they are considered impolite.

(C) In some societies, the perpetuation of the community's power requires that some behaviors intended to demonstrate freedom from that power be overlooked.

(D) In some societies, codes of behavior are so stringent that some individuals may never learn that their behavior does not conform to those codes.

(E) In no society do community standards require individuals to draw attention in public to behavior that violates those standards.

7. Efforts to develop fusion as a viable source of power have thus far failed not because it is impossible to sustain and control a fusion reaction using current technology, but instead because the measures used to do so consume more energy than the resulting reaction produces. Ten years ago, containment of a progressing fusion reaction required nearly 20 percent more power than the reaction produced; today, improvements in reactor technology have reduced this excess energy requirement to below 10 percent. We can be sure that, within the next decade, fusion reactors will be developed that can produce more energy than they consume in their operation.

On which one of the following assumptions does the argument rely?

(A) The pace of improvements to fusion reactor technology does not dictate that the reactors' excess energy requirements are halved every decade.
(B) Any method of generation that produces more energy than it consumes in its operation is a viable source of power.
(C) Improvements in the energy efficiency of fission reactors have been consistent throughout that technology's development.
(D) The future rate of improvement in fusion reactor technology will not differ from that in the recent past.
(E) The power required to sustain fusion reactions is greater than that required to contain those reactions.

8. Reviewer: The famous author of this book advocating environmentally friendly economic practices claims that consumer culture in industrialized nations is causing depletion of the world's resources at an unsustainable rate and destruction of the environment through pollution and development. Yet the author himself lives in an extravagantly large house and drives one of the least fuel-efficient models of automobile in the world. His own spectacular failure to adhere to the practices recommended in his book indicates that they are not to be taken seriously.

The reviewer's reasoning is most vulnerable to criticism on the grounds that

(A) it relies on the questionable assumption that the practices of one individual can have an appreciable impact on the world environment overall
(B) it neglects to consider the fact that, as the world's resources are depleted, the cost of those resources increases, providing an economic incentive to search for alternatives and reduce the use of those resources
(C) it ascribes an economic value to products such as pollution, whose costs cannot be reliably estimated
(D) it fails to establish that the reviewer adheres to the practices recommended in the author's book
(E) it dismisses the author's recommendations by raising objections that are irrelevant to their merit

9. Politician: I gave an extensive interview to a
   prominent reporter when I introduced my last
   bill, instead of holding a press conference as
   I usually do. Because the bill gained broad
   popular support as a result of this interview,
   I should grant an exclusive interview to a
   prominent reporter the next time I introduce a
   bill, so it will also gain broad popular support.

Which one of the following principles, if valid, most
helps to justify the reasoning above?

(A) If a bill gains broad popular support because
     of an exclusive interview with a prominent
     reporter, the next bill introduced by the same
     politician will also gain broad popular support
     if the politician grants an exclusive interview
     to the same reporter.
(B) A bill gains broad popular support only if
     the politician who introduced it grants an
     exclusive interview to a prominent reporter.
(C) If any bill introduced by a politician gains
     broad popular support because of an exclusive
     interview with a prominent reporter, then the
     next bill introduced by the same politician
     will also gain broad popular support as long
     as the politician grants an exclusive interview
     with a prominent reporter.
(D) No factor other than the granting of an
     exclusive interview to a prominent reporter
     played a role in the politician's last bill
     gaining broad popular support.
(E) It is not possible for any politician both to
     grant an exclusive interview on any topic and
     to hold a press conference on that same topic.

10. The introduction of reliable systems in a business
    organization allows its products and services to be
    of more consistent quality and thereby improves its
    competitive position; these systems also reduce the
    dependence on individual worker initiative for the
    business's success. Yet workers are satisfied with
    their jobs only insofar as they believe that their
    initiative is a determining factor in whether or not
    the business succeeds. It can be clearly seen, then,
    that the introduction of reliable systems in a business
    organization _____.

Which one of the following most logically completes
the argument?

(A) does not necessarily increase the quality of the
     business's products and services
(B) will decrease worker satisfaction with their
     jobs unless these systems invite a mistaken
     belief
(C) is ultimately counterproductive
(D) causes problems within that business that did
     not exist prior to the systems' introduction
(E) is opposed by all workers who wish to remain
     in their jobs

11. In order to be secure, a nation must maintain the
    capacity to collect and analyze information about
    its citizens. Expensive improvements in a nation's
    capacity to collect and analyze information about
    its citizens will eventually reward that nation with
    a corresponding increase in security. Therefore, a
    nation that is becoming more secure must at some
    past time have made expensive improvements in its
    capacity to collect and analyze information about its
    citizens.

The reasoning in the argument is flawed because it
overlooks the possibility that

(A) a nation that does not maintain the capacity
     to collect and analyze information about its
     citizens may become more secure
(B) some nations lack the resources required
     to make expensive improvements in their
     capacity to collect and analyze information
     about their citizens
(C) a nation that makes expensive improvements
     in its capacity to collect information about
     its citizens may not experience an increase in
     security
(D) a nation that does not improve its capacity
     to collect and analyze information about its
     citizens may become more secure
(E) some nations are able to make improvements
     in their capacity to collect and analyze
     information about their citizens that are not
     expensive

12. Goldfarb: Tannic acid, a chemical found in high concentrations in tea leaves, is known to help stop the bleeding from open wounds and aid in clotting. Ancient records from China indicate that a traditional poultice used to treat many patients included tea leaves. Tannic acid must have been known, even in ancient times, to help stop bleeding in such cases.

Cho: I find your evidence unconvincing. The poultice you mention also included large amounts of tree ear, a fungus now known to thin the blood and prevent clotting.

Cho counters Goldfarb's argument by

(A) suggesting that the intended effect of the poultice mentioned in Goldfarb's argument differed from its actual effect

(B) casting doubt on ancient knowledge of the individual chemical constituents of any traditional treatment

(C) pointing out that an assumption implicit in Goldfarb's argument is unlikely to be true

(D) calling into question the accuracy of evidence on which Goldfarb's conclusion is based

(E) introducing a different chemical constituent of the poultice that is more likely to have been believed in ancient times to be responsible for the effect cited by Goldfarb

13. The system most often used to pay actors for their contributions to a film is unfair. Although the amounts of money that prominent actors earn for their performances may seem large, most often that amount is fixed and does not depend on the total revenues generated by the film. This diminishes the risk for actors in the event that a film is unsuccessful, but it also deprives them of any share in a successful film's future earnings through at-home viewing sales and many other revenue sources that only arise after the film is no longer being shown in theaters.

Each of the following, if true, supports the reasoning in the argument EXCEPT:

(A) The revenue generated by at-home viewing of a film after it is no longer in theaters most often equals or exceeds the revenue generated by the film in theaters.

(B) The amount paid to actors who contribute to a film is most often based on an estimate of the likely revenues generated by that film while it is being shown in theaters.

(C) Even unsuccessful films generate enough total revenue that compensation on the basis of those revenues would not be substantially less for prominent actors than the amounts they most often earn.

(D) It is unfair for the performers in a film not to receive some payment each time that film generates revenue of any kind.

(E) Film budgets, which are based on the likely total revenues the films will eventually earn, have grown much more rapidly in recent years than have the amounts of money paid to prominent actors for their contributions to those films.

14. Agent: The new law that gives our agency powers to combat organized crime has been found by the courts to be constitutional, and this law requires that each time we place a suspect under special surveillance as part of an organized-crime investigation, we must inform the appropriate legislative committee. Thus far, we have not informed the appropriate committee of any suspect in an organized-crime investigation who has been placed under special surveillance. You may conclude from this fact that we have not yet used the special surveillance powers granted by the new law.

Which one of the following is an assumption required by the argument?

(A) The new law to combat organized crime requires the approval of the appropriate legislative committee in order to place any suspect under special surveillance.

(B) The appropriate legislative committee need not be informed of any suspect being placed under special surveillance unless that surveillance is part of an organized-crime investigation.

(C) The placing of some suspects in an investigation under special surveillance does not violate their constitutional rights.

(D) The powers granted to the agency in the new law do not include the ability to place suspects in an organized-crime investigation under special surveillance before informing the appropriate legislative committee that the agency has done so.

(E) No power other than the ability to place suspects in an organized-crime investigation under special surveillance is included in the new law to combat organized crime.

15. Those who earn college degrees in liberal arts do so not because they believe that a background in liberal arts will be useful in their future jobs, but instead because they see college as an opportunity to pursue their intellectual interests. Yet a survey of successful companies shows that by far the majority of top managers and executives in these companies earned college degrees in liberal arts.

Each of the following, if true, helps to explain the results of the survey EXCEPT:

(A) The pursuit of intellectual interests is not inconsistent with the development of skills that are useful to top managers and executives in a successful company.

(B) The number of those who earn college degrees in liberal arts far exceeds the number of those who earn college degrees in areas that are useful in the workplace.

(C) A greater proportion of those who earn college degrees in technical areas that are useful in their future jobs become top managers and executives than do those who earn college degrees in liberal arts.

(D) The survey included primarily entertainment and media companies, whose top managers and executives require skills that are best developed by the pursuit of intellectual interests in the liberal arts.

(E) The willingness to follow courses of action that do not seem clearly practical is a crucial attribute of the top managers and executives in any successful company.

16. Scientist: Critics of the space agency's increased emphasis on unmanned missions rightly point out that this change is responsible for declining public support for the space agency itself. Public interest in the space program is never higher than when human beings put themselves at risk by accomplishing things that have never been accomplished before. The space agency's purpose, however, is to further human understanding of the nature of the universe beyond our own planet, and for the price of one dramatic manned mission, the agency can send ten less glamorous unmanned missions into space.

The scientist's argument is structured to lead to which one of the following conclusions?

(A) Criticisms of the space agency's increased emphasis on unmanned missions are unfounded.
(B) The scientific value of one manned mission is exceeded by the scientific value of the unmanned missions that could be sent into space for the same price.
(C) Declining public interest in the space agency's work is the result of the agency's increased efforts to accomplish its purpose.
(D) The purpose of the space agency is to further human understanding of the nature of the universe beyond our own planet to the maximum degree possible.
(E) Putting human beings at risk in manned space missions does not significantly further human understanding of the nature of the universe beyond our own planet.

17. Columnist: In the last election, every major environmental group supported the opposition party's anti-industry policies, yet the ruling party won the popular vote. Now these environmental groups allege that the ruling party's policy fails to protect the environment against exploitation by industry, but the only evidence they offer for this contention is the fact that the ruling party consulted its supporters in industry, not environmental groups, when the policy was formulated. Their objection is laughable. Why should any party consult its most ardent enemies in deciding what policy to pursue?

The columnist's argument conforms most closely to which one of the following principles?

(A) In determining policy, no ruling party is obligated to consult with any group unless that group shares at least some interests in common with the party.
(B) The fact that some group formed with a particular interest in mind was not consulted in the formulation of a ruling party's policy does not imply that the ruling party's policy is derelict in its responsibility to protect that interest.
(C) No ruling party is obligated to consult during the process of formulating policy with any group whose interests directly conflict with those of other groups whose support was instrumental in the party's election.
(D) That the ruling party formulated its policy without consulting groups that opposed its election does not constitute proof that the ruling party's policy illegitimately favors its supporters who were consulted and whose interests may be in conflict with those of the groups.
(E) In any case when a ruling party is popularly elected despite the opposition of some groups, those groups cannot reasonably expect to be consulted in the formulation of the ruling party's policy with regard to the groups' interests.

18. The Lariat is a new model of polygraph, a machine that attempts to identify when the subject in an interview is lying. Out of every 100 answers that the subject being interviewed believes to be false, the Lariat will correctly identify 99 as being lies. Out of every 100 answers that the subject does not believe to be false, the Lariat will mistakenly identify only 5 as being lies. Therefore, of all answers given during an interview where the Lariat is used, most if not all of those identified as being lies will be statements that the subject believes to be false.

The conclusion above follows logically if which one of the following is assumed?

(A) Most if not all of the answers given during an interview where the Lariat is used will be statements that the subject does not believe to be false.

(B) No interview will include any answer about whose truth the subject has not formed any particular belief.

(C) The Lariat will not identify as a lie any answer that the subject believes to be true, but which is in fact false.

(D) No answer given by the subject in an interview where the Lariat is used will be one that the subject does not believe to be false.

(E) Every statement made by the subject in an interview where the Lariat is used can be judged to be either true or false.

19. Golf pro: A popular magazine recently compared the six best-selling golf balls and found that Flizerite balls are superior to the others. The magazine asked ten of the top golfers in the world to try all six balls during their practice rounds on some of the most challenging courses in the nation, and all of them found that their shots off the tee were consistently longer when they used Flizerite balls. It's clear that Flizerite is the best choice of ball for every golfer who wants to shoot a better score.

Each of the following describes a flaw in the golf pro's reasoning EXCEPT:

(A) The argument overlooks the possibility that some golf ball is superior to the six best-selling golf balls.

(B) The argument overlooks the possibility that the golf ball that works best for the top golfers in the world will not work best for every golfer.

(C) The argument overlooks the possibility that a golf ball that helps golfers shoot a good score on a few challenging courses may lead to worse scores on the majority of courses.

(D) The argument overlooks the possibility that factors other than the choice of golf ball may be involved in determining a golfer's score.

(E) The argument overlooks the possibility that a golf ball that leads to longer tee shots may be more difficult to control.

20. The pursuit of advanced knowledge in an academic area requires extensive freedom, since such a pursuit is incompatible with a regimented set of requirements that leaves no room for individual interests. But experience shows that a degree of regimentation is needed from the beginning of college study, since without it students do not acquire the broad familiarity with an area that allows the pursuit of advanced knowledge. Thus, college students who lament the restrictions placed on them by their academic programs are reacting to a feature of those programs that will not always apply to them.

Which one of the following is an assumption required by the argument?

(A) No college student attains the degree of academic freedom necessary to pursue advanced knowledge.

(B) The more advanced a student's knowledge in an academic area becomes, the less regimented the set of requirements that pertain to that student becomes.

(C) The need for broad familiarity in an academic area dictates that students' freedom of choice be complete.

(D) High school students cannot engage in the pursuit of advanced knowledge.

(E) No academic program exists in which the pursuit of advanced knowledge in its area requires a breadth of familiarity that cannot be attained by a college student.

21. Investment banker: Professional advice does not help individual investors make more money. Plenty of individuals who have never sought professional investment advice do very well with their investments. Likewise, many individuals who have invested according to the advice of investment professionals have lost substantial sums of money.

Which one of the following, if true, most weakens the argument?

(A) Many of those whose investments perform well without the benefit of professional advice are themselves investment professionals.

(B) Professional advice is necessary for all but a few individuals to minimize the expense of taxes and fees associated with investment activity.

(C) The average return on the investments of individuals who seek professional advice is no lower than the average return on the investments of individuals who do not.

(D) No professional investment advice is more helpful to individual investors than the simple and inexpensive investment advice available through many media outlets.

(E) Investment professionals often do not invest their own money according to the advice they offer their clients.

22. It has long been accepted that, because of diets known to have been low in calories and nutrients, all early humans were smaller and lived substantially shorter lives than do contemporary humans. A recent find, however, has cast doubt on this accepted belief. The remains of a group of hunters found to date to humanity's earliest history exhibit humerus bones as long as those belonging to modern humans, with wear patterns that are consistent with those found in modern individuals in their fifties and sixties.

In evaluating the argument it would be most helpful to know whether

(A) hunters in settlements of early humans are representative of the size of all individuals in those settlements

(B) differences in diet are responsible for differences in size and longevity among modern humans

(C) the strenuous activities associated with hunting could create wear patterns on the humerus bones of young humans that are similar to those found in modern humans in their fifties and sixties

(D) the differing lengths of individuals' humerus bones indicate differences either in the number of calories or in the overall nutritional value of the diet consumed by those individuals

(E) the hunters whose remains were found lived in an area where unusually nutritious food was abundant at the time

23. The violation of a law constitutes an act of civil disobedience if the violation is intended to demonstrate that the law is inherently unjust. But an act of civil disobedience is only justified if the person committing that act does not attempt to escape the punishment mandated for those who break the unjust law.

Which one of the following judgments is best supported by the principles stated above?

(A) Ronaldo violated a law banning smoking in public buildings because he wished to demonstrate that the law was unjust. Because he also wished to demonstrate that the fine levied on those who break the smoking law is excessively harsh, Ronaldo refused to pay it. Therefore, Ronaldo committed two acts of civil disobedience, both of which were justified.

(B) Esmerelda violated a law forbidding citizens from sitting on milk crates on the sidewalk because she did not realize such a law existed. Because she paid her fine promptly and the law she violated was inherently unjust, Esmerelda did not commit an act of civil disobedience, but her violation of the law was justified.

(C) Horace violated a law requiring citizens to obey all police instructions because the instructions he received from a policeman were manifestly unjust. At his trial, Horace was sentenced to perform community service, which he promptly did. Therefore, Horace committed an act of civil disobedience, and that act was justified.

(D) Lucy violated a law forbidding the teaching of evolution in her classroom in order to show that the law was inherently unjust. The punishment handed down in Lucy's case was firing, but because of the media attention she was able to attract to her case, that punishment was not enforced. Therefore, Lucy committed an act of civil disobedience, but that act was not justified.

(E) Gladys violated a law requiring all drivers to maintain insurance on their automobiles to demonstrate that the law was inherently unjust. The punishment mandated for violators of this law was a substantial fine and the revocation of her driver's license. Since Gladys both paid the fine and willingly gave up her driver's license, her violation of the law was an act of civil disobedience, and that act was justified.

24. A theory is neither a fact nor an opinion, since no opinion can be conclusively proven to be false, and no fact can be anything but true.

Which one of the following is most closely parallel in its reasoning to the reasoning in the argument above?

(A) A debate is neither a discussion nor a dispute, since no discussion can be decided by a matter of fact, and no dispute can arise from anything but a difference of opinion.

(B) A mistake is neither a success nor a failure, since no success can result in negative consequences, and no failure can be anything but intentional.

(C) A description is neither an explanation nor a prediction, since no explanation depends upon future events, and no prediction can depend on anything but future events.

(D) An exclamation is neither a statement nor a question, since no statement fails to express an idea, and no question expresses any idea.

(E) A portrait is neither a cartoon nor a snapshot, since no cartoon can be criticized for failing to portray its subject accurately, and no snapshot can do anything but record its subject accurately.

25. Just decisions must be made on the basis of both the relevant facts and applicable ethical principles. It is clear, then, that not all reasonable decisions need be just, since in order to be reasonable, a decision must only be supported by some form of explanation. This is why I believe it is likely that the president's policy decisions, although they are always reasonable, are not always just. Even though I do not know all of the facts relevant to any of the president's policy decisions, I can almost always predict what policy decision the president will make.

If the statements above are true, then which one of the following must also be true?

(A) If any decision can be predicted without the knowledge of all the facts relevant to that decision, then that decision must not be just.

(B) The explanations of unjust decisions sometimes include applicable ethical principles.

(C) A certain knowledge of all the facts relevant to a decision is required in order to evaluate whether or not that decision is just.

(D) It is unlikely that a set of decisions that can be anticipated without knowledge of the facts relevant to each one can all have been made solely on the basis of those facts.

(E) Any decision made only on the basis of applicable ethical principles is reasonable but not just.

ANSWER KEY TO PRACTICE SECTION 2: ARGS

For full answers and explanations, turn to Chapter 21.

1. E
2. A
3. E
4. C
5. D
6. E
7. A
8. E
9. C
10. B
11. D
12. C
13. A
14. D
15. C
16. C
17. D
18. D
19. D
20. E
21. B
22. C
23. D
24. E
25. E

PART ◆ III

Analytical Reasoning

9

Games Strategy

WHAT IS ANALYTICAL REASONING?

The LSAT's Analytical Reasoning ("Games") section consists of 22 to 24 questions distributed among four games—situations subject to sets of conditions. On average, this gives you just short of nine minutes per game to complete the section, although it should be noted that the amount of time required to complete an individual game can vary widely, depending on its difficulty. Few test takers are able to complete all of the questions on a Games section, which makes it imperative that you do the best you can to identify which game or games are the most difficult and leave them for last. It is unlikely that you will perform best on this section by working the questions and games in order of appearance.

The characteristic that distinguishes Games sections from all others on the LSAT is that this is the one place where a proper approach can provide you 100-percent certainty of reaching a correct answer. On RC (Reading Comprehension) and Args, it's unlikely that substantially reducing the number of questions you attempt can improve your performance on the section overall; on games, this is not true. A good pacing rule is that, if you're getting fewer than ten right answers on this section, then you will improve your performance by attempting only two of the four games and guessing on the rest; if you're getting fewer than fifteen right answers on this section, then you will improve by attempting three. Developing the skills and knowledge to get right answers, and then spending the time required to get them when you work sections, are the keys to improving your performance on this section.

Games can require you to do quite different things, but they all look similar in their layout. A game includes an initial paragraph describing the situation or task around which the game is built. The paragraph is followed by a series of conditions or clues that pertain to how the task is to be performed. The basic idea on this section is to find a way to represent the task and the conditions visually and work with them on paper; do *not* try to work games in your head! Every time you encounter a game, you should follow the same six-step process:

1. Diagram and Inventory

2. Symbolize the Clues and Double-Check

3. Look for Links and Size Up the Game

4. Evaluate the Question Task

5. Apply the Strategy

6. Use Process of Elimination (POE)

Now, we'll discuss each of the above steps in detail.

1. Diagram and Inventory

This is the step where you set up the game. Every game's setup includes two basic parts: the diagram, which is a fixed representation of categories, spaces, or positions to be filled; and the inventory, which is the list of mobile elements that are to be placed into the diagram with the help of the clues. Think about these things as board games: Your fixed diagram is the board, and the elements in your inventory are the pieces that can be placed on and possibly moved around within the board.

Sometimes it's easy to identify which parts of the initial paragraph should be the core of your diagram, and which ones should be the elements in your inventory, but sometimes it's more difficult. As we'll see in the following chapters, focusing on what the primary task in the game is can provide a great deal of help; the clues, too, can provide helpful insight.

Keep in mind that you're not allowed to use scratch paper—just your test booklet— on the Games section, and that time is definitely an issue. If possible, you'll want to set the game up in such a way that you don't have to redraw the diagram each time you want to work an example; in cases where that isn't possible, you'll want your diagram to be skeletal and compact so that it's quick to redraw and doesn't take up too much of your valuable space. At the same time, you don't want to be erasing your work from other questions each time you generate a new example; as we'll see, your prior work can be extremely helpful in working some difficult questions quickly.

Situate your diagram in a convenient place. Then list your inventory of elements nearby. The test writers will arrange the game so that you never need to use more than a one-letter or one-number abbreviation for your categories and elements. The goal is to be able to dispense with the text the test writers give you and work the entire game exclusively from your representations of the crucial information.

2. Symbolize the Clues and Double-Check

In order to dispense with the text entirely, you'll also need to represent the clues in a way that's more convenient for you to use. The goal here is to be able to use our symbol, rather than the text of the original clue, when we work the questions. Clues are often wordy and convoluted; your symbol should be visual—a picture of what it looks like to apply the clue in your diagram—rather than verbal.

For example, if a clue in a game asks you to rank seven tennis players from highest to lowest, the clue "Smith has a lower rank than Martinez" may have different symbols, depending how your diagram is set up. If you've listed the ranks 1 through 7 from left to right, with 1 being the highest rank, then this clue should be symbolized "M...S" to indicate that M is to the left of S in your diagram, and there may be any number of spaces between them. Similarly, if you've set up your diagram the other way—with 7 on the left—then the symbol should be "S...M." As long as your symbol is visually consistent with your diagram, you'll be able to use it correctly. The symbol to avoid in this case is one like "S < M"; as you can imagine, this algebraic symbol can be easily misinterpreted in a game where 1 is the highest rank, and 7 the lowest. Algebraic symbols should be generally avoided; mathematical language is just that—a language—and one that people usually speak less well than English. Make a visual symbol for each clue; if you can't, then write a short, simple paraphrase of the clue to serve as your symbol. Make sure your symbol is one you can understand at a glance. As we'll see in the following chapters, there's a small but flexible vocabulary of symbol parts that can be used in every game you'll encounter. If you become comfortable with it, then you'll be able to handle the vast majority of clues without having to resort to paraphrasing.

It is above all important that your symbols be accurate representations of the information in the clues. If you overinterpret an oddly worded clue, or if you simply make an honest mistake in symbolizing it, you will later encounter a question that does not have a correct answer, or that has more than one. In order to avoid this disastrous situation, we'll always double-check our clues before moving on. This is a quick but important part of the second step: Go from your symbols back to the written clues, confirming that you have represented the information correctly. By going against the grain in this way, you'll maximize your chances of noticing whether you've made a mistake. As you finish with each clue, physically check it off in the original clue list. At the end, make sure that all of the clues are checked off; under the timed conditions of the LSAT, it is easy to skip over or miss a clue when you're symbolizing.

3. Look for Links and Size Up the Game

Many games have **deductions** that can be extremely helpful in working the questions. A deduction is something that has to be true all the time because of the ways the clues interact in your diagram. Very often, you'll make deductions by linking the information in two clues: if an element is mentioned in two different clues, or if a particular part of your diagram is mentioned in two of them, you may be able to draw useful conclusions from the combination.

If you can, it's important to represent these conclusions as new clues; by making deductions now, you'll save yourself time on questions later because you'll have more information to work with on every one of them. Some games have so many deductions that there are only a very few ways you can actually satisfy all of their conditions; in those cases, getting the deductions can turn a set of difficult questions into one that takes very little time.

It is important to be a little cautious, though, in what you decide to write down as a deduction. You should avoid deductions of the form "if this happens, then we also know that…" Although they'll be helpful on a few questions, they don't apply all the time, and so aren't worth writing down as deductions. Especially dangerous are pseudodeductions—things that you "deduce" but that really don't have to be true all the time. Keep in mind that there's a difference between a suspicion and a true deduction: You should be able to articulate a relatively simple line of reasoning that leads to a deduction; if you only suspect that something has to be true all the time, keep it in mind but realize that you may not know the whole story yet. When in doubt, suspend judgment; if you later realize that your suspicion is actually correct, at that point you should add it to your list of deductions, but not until you're sure it's true all the time.

There are also games that don't have definite deductions, but that instead are driven by a **key** symbol, clue, or element. The key can take different forms in different games, and you may not be able to identify it at this stage; generally, you're looking for the clue that imposes the most stringent restriction on the game, or alternatively one that is extremely powerful because it applies to multiple elements and multiple areas of your diagram. The key is the place where you'll go first when you're working the questions, and you may not recognize it until you have a question or two under your belt. If you find yourself using the same clue over and over in every question, chances are that this is the key to the game. If you can identify it at this stage, then you'll know where to look first when you work the questions.

It is important not to let this step bog you down. You should always look for deductions and try to anticipate what the key on a game will be, but if you can't, that doesn't necessarily mean you're missing something important. Some games don't have any deductions to speak of, and these games may not have an obvious key. Games like these will take a good deal less time at this step, but you'll need to spend more time answering the questions. Get there as quickly as you can if your search for deductions isn't getting you anywhere.

4. Evaluate the Question Task

A number of ingredients go into a full understanding of what a question requires you to do. We'll look at some of these ingredients individually before we arrive at a three-category classification of the questions.

Some questions impose a **new condition** that applies only for that question. Often these questions begin with the word *if*, but they don't always. They may tell you where an element goes in your diagram, or simply describe a new relationship between the elements that can be symbolized much as you symbolized the original clues.

Some questions do not impose any additional conditions, but merely ask you to deal with the game **as-is**. Very often (but not necessarily), these questions will begin with the word *which*.

Finally, the last question on a game may **change the rules**, either erasing or fundamentally modifying the conditions that you've been using for all the other questions.

No matter what a question does with regard to the clues, the question itself may ask you to deal with the described situations in different ways. A question may ask you to find the choice that **could be true**, **could be false**, **must be true**, or **must be false**. Some questions ask you to find the choice that is a **list of possibilities** for where an element can legally be placed, or which elements can be in a particular part of your diagram. Some questions may ask you to **count the ways** that a particular thing can be done. Each of these tasks requires a slightly different approach to reach the answer most efficiently.

It's important to realize that you're not required to work the questions in the order in which they appear, and that in many cases it's helpful to work them in a different order. Generally speaking, which broad classification a question falls into will determine when you work the question.

When you start on the questions for a game, you should look at the very first question. Sometimes, this question is a **grab-a-rule**, and should definitely be worked first. A grab-a-rule question asks you to identify the answer choice that either does or does not satisfy the rules; this is most often a "which" question, but you'll be able to identify it because the answer choices are complete listings of the elements that occupy every part of your diagram. Partial lists aren't as easy to work with, but a question with complete lists in the answer choices can be worked quickly and easily using POE, since you should simply be able to apply the rules one at a time and reach the correct answer without any further work.

After the grab-a-rule question, if there is one, you'll want to work the **specific questions**: those that involve **new conditions** but don't have complex tasks. A question that adds a rule is a bit easier to work because it gives you additional information with which to start. The only questions of this sort that you'll want to leave for later are those that require you to identify a list of possibilities, or those that ask you to count the ways; these complex tasks are much easier to accomplish once you're more familiar with the game.

Next, you'll want to work **general questions**. These are the ones that leave the game as-is and that involve relatively straightforward answer choices. As before, you may want to leave complex tasks such as listing possibilities or counting the ways for later.

Finally, you'll work the **complex questions**. Now that you have as much experience as possible with the game, hopefully these questions will go more quickly. It is important to note that the rule-changing question, if there is one, should always be worked at the end of this pass. As we'll see in a moment, our past work can sometimes be used to answer general questions, but it's imperative that we only use past work that actually satisfies all the rules. Since your answer on the rule-changing question will not necessarily follow all the original rules, you want to make certain you don't work on this one until you've taken a shot at all the others.

Here's a quick summary of the order in which you'll generally want to work the questions:

- First: grab-a-rule

Specific

- New conditions with straightforward tasks

General

- Game as-is with straightforward tasks

Complex

- Consider whether there are new conditions or not, with tasks such as counting the ways and listing the possibilities
- Last: rule-changer

It is perfectly fine to work general and complex questions together on a second pass, as long as you leave the rule-changing question, if there is one, for last.

5. Apply the Strategy

The best strategy to adopt will depend on the exact combination of ingredients in the question, but there are a few things we can say for certain.

If a question provides a new condition, then you'll need to work with it before moving to the answer choices. First, represent the new information, but if you need to make a new symbol, make sure you put it in a different place from your symbols for the whole game. The new condition in this question will apply *only* to that question, and if you accidentally apply it to others, you may run into trouble. Once you've symbolized the new information, make as many deductions as you can from it. Sometimes you'll be able to fill in your entire diagram, but other times you won't be able to deduce anything at all. Once you're done with your deductions, move on to the answer choices. Don't dawdle at this part of the process, but don't skip over it, either. If possible, we'd like to be able to do work here that allows us to identify the correct answer directly without having to do any additional POE work on these questions.

Questions that ask about the game as-is, unfortunately, don't provide any information for you to start with, so you'll have to go straight to the answer choices on these.

Rule-changing questions may require the most work of all. If the question stem removes a clue that you've relied on in making your original deductions on the game, you'll need to go back and audit those deductions to discover which ones you can still count on, and which ones you don't have anymore. Obviously, this process can be confusing and time-consuming, and these questions can at times be very difficult. Most often, though, the rule-changing part of the question is more of a distraction than anything else; by just moving to the choices and keeping the change in mind, you'll often see that this question is no more difficult than the others.

The only question task in which you have to work the question completely without looking for help in the answer choices is a count-the-ways question. Your deductions are essential here, and once you've reached the end of the line, you'll often have a little more work to do. The thing to look for is an "either-or": something that has to be either one way or the other, with no other possibility, and no way that you could accidentally count one arrangement twice. Once you've drawn a diagram for each of the possibilities in your either-or, you'll usually be able to count up the possibilities in each case, and then add them to determine which answer you should pick. This can take a while, which is one reason why you should leave these questions for later on in the game.

6. Use Process of Elimination

Don't be misled by the name for this step: Your objective on a games question is to either identify the one correct answer, or else to identify the four incorrect answers. But unlike with args and RC, you won't go through the choices on games with intention of doing both. Since games is the section where you can determine for certain whether or not an answer is correct, you'll want to take advantage of this fact: Once you know what the right answer has to be, pick it and move on with confidence.

For questions that give you a new condition, you're hoping to find a choice that your deductions tell you has to be the answer. If you can't, very often your deductions will allow you to identify four that definitely aren't the answer. If all else fails, you'll have to move through the answer choices one at a time.

The question task determines how you have to do POE. On a question that asks you to identify a choice that could be true, what you'll need to do with each answer choice you work is try to **make it true**. If you can, then it's the answer; if not, then you can eliminate it. This is also the method you should use on questions that ask you to identify which choice must be false; in this case, if you can make the answer choice true, then you can eliminate it; if not, then it's the answer. Could-be-true questions and must-be-false questions form a pair, and you should realize that adding an "EXCEPT" or "NOT" to one of these questions turns it into the other one: the answer to a "could-be-true EX-CEPT" question is the choice that must be false.

The other pair of basic questions is "must-be-true" and "could-be-false." The POE objective when you're working an answer choice on one of these questions is to try to **make it false**. Unless you deduce it, you won't be able to directly identify a fact that must in all cases be true; the way you'll have to do it is try to make it untrue. On a must-be-true question, if you can make an answer choice false, you can eliminate it; if you can't, then it has to be true all the time, and it's the answer you want to pick. Similarly, on a could-be-false question, if you can't make the choice false, you can eliminate it; if you can make it false, then it's the answer.

Deductions are also essential on the more complex questions that ask you to find the list of possibilities. Your deductions will provide you an opportunity to eliminate choices that include a possibility you've discovered can't happen. Most often, you'll be down to two or three answer choices if you've done a good job with your deductions, at which point you'll want to examine the differences between or among the remaining choices. Most often, you'll only need to try out one possibility to determine which of the remaining choices is correct, but occasionally you'll need to try two.

On a question that asks you to deal with the game as-is, there are a number of possible strategies that can help. Always remember that you can rely on the game's original clues and any deductions you've made for the game overall for guidance; on a grab-a-rule question, you should be able to arrive at the answer just by using these.

Since a question of this type does not impose any additional restrictions on the game, your prior work can be extremely helpful for POE, as long as you're careful to make sure all your prior work follows the rules. If you should happen to generate an example that doesn't satisfy the rules, make sure you cross it out so that you don't accidentally use it on a later question. Depending on the basic question task, you may be able to use your prior work to eliminate some answer choices or, occasionally, to identify the right answer directly. Be sure to use all this work before you adopt the expedient of working the answer choices one at a time. Most often, if you're doing everything correctly, you'll only need to work one or at most two of the answer choices before you arrive at the answer.

The main thing to understand about POE on games is the overall goal: Do the work that's required to be certain what the right answer is—no more and no less. Don't give up when you're down to two; it's worth your time to do one additional example in order to be certain of your decision. By the same token, when you've done enough work to find out what the answer is, don't keep working on the question. Doing no more than the required work is the key to good performance on the Games section.

10

Basic Tasks

DIAGRAMMING STRATEGIES

Every game is built around a basic task—the thing that you're asked to do with the elements. The task at the heart of a game determines what diagram is most useful for representing it. As we'll see in this chapter, there are four basic tasks a game can be built around, and one of two fundamental diagramming strategies will work for each of them.

The thing to keep in mind with all your games diagrams is that they need to be as compact as possible—both to conserve space on the page and to minimize the time spent drawing them—and they also need to allow you to represent and retain as much useful information as possible. With that in mind, let's look at the two possible diagramming strategies you can use.

MAKE A TABLE

In most ordering and grouping games, all you'll need to do is make an initial header row at the top of your diagram, and then generate successive examples by adding a new row to your table each time. It's smart to reserve the top line of your table to record deductions and those clues that can best be symbolized directly in the diagram, and then to keep this line clean so you can refer back to it. The result will be a table with your header row, the top-line deductions, and then one row apiece for each of the examples you generate.

Since this is the more compact and more easily read of the two diagram styles, any game that can be diagrammed this way should be. However, there are situations in which making a table to hold all of your work for a game will not be appropriate.

MAKE A CHART

Most games that require drawings of the space in which your elements will be placed, or those that require you to determine more than one attribute of your elements, are not most clearly represented in a table. In these cases, a chart is more appropriate.

The way you'll work with your chart is similar to the way you work with a table. First, make an initial master diagram, in which you represent your clues and deductions in much the same way as you did on the top line of a table. Keep your inventory and all your symbols near the master diagram. Then, to generate examples as needed, you'll make a rudimentary copy of your master diagram to work with. It's very important never to erase your completed examples; not only does this waste valuable time, but your prior work contains useful information that you won't want to lose. Keep your copies small, spare, and easy to read. It can be difficult to manage your space on the page in a game you have to diagram this way.

We'll use each of these diagramming strategies as appropriate to work the games in this chapter, which present relatively straightforward examples of the basic tasks— ordering, grouping, spatial arrangement, and organizational arrangement.

1. Ordering

A game involves ordering whenever the categories in your diagram have a simple, relative relationship to one another. Hours in a schedule; ranks from first to last; and positions in a linear arrangement from left to right, east to west, and top to bottom all fit this description. Whenever the clues in a game mention the elements using words such as *before/after, higher/lower,* or *to the left of/to the right of,* you're looking at an ordering game. Many people find games of this type intuitive to diagram, but that doesn't mean that all of them are necessarily easy.

Here are some common clue types found in games that involve ordering, along with symbols for them.

Range:
A occurs at some time before B.   A...B

Block:
A occurs immediately before B. $\boxed{A\ B}$
A occurs either immediately before or
 immediately after B. $\boxed{A\ B}$

Antiblock:
A does not occur either immediately
 before or immediately after B. $\boxed{A\ B}$

Either/or:
Either A or B is first. $\dfrac{1}{A/B}$
 (in diagram)

A is either first or second. $\overset{A}{\underset{1\quad\ 2}{\longleftrightarrow}}$
 (in diagram)

Conditional:
If A is first, then B is second. $A_1 \to B_2$
 (contrapositive) $B_2 \to A_1$
A is first only if B is second. $A_1 \to B_2$
A is not first unless B is second. $A_1 \to B_2$

Try the game on the next page. Answers can be found in Chapter 20.

DRILL #1

A collection contains seven essays, appearing in chapters numbered sequentially 1 through 7 from the beginning of the book to the end, with exactly one essay per chapter. Each essay is written by one of seven authors—F, G, H, J, K, L, or M. No author writes more than one essay in the collection, and the collection contains nothing aside from the seven authors' essays. The content of the chapters conforms to the following conditions:

Either chapter 1 or else chapter 4 contains the essay written by M.

The essays written by H and L are contained in consecutively numbered chapters, whether or not the essay written by H precedes the essay written by L.

The essays written by F and J are contained in consecutively numbered chapters, whether or not the essay written by F precedes the essay written by J.

The essay written by M is contained in an earlier chapter than is the essay written by J.

If the essay written by K is contained in a later chapter than is the essay written by H, then the essay written by K is also contained in an earlier chapter than is the essay written by F.

1. Which one of the following could be a complete and accurate list of the authors whose essays are contained in chapters 1 through 7, listed sequentially in the order in which they appear?

    (A) G, F, J, M, K, L, H
    (B) L, H, G, K, M, F, J
    (C) M, F, J, L, H, K, G
    (D) M, G, J, F, K, H, L
    (E) M, H, K, L, G, J, F

2. Which one of the following is a complete and accurate list of the chapters, any one of which could contain the essay written by K?

    (A) 1, 4, 5
    (B) 4, 5, 6
    (C) 2, 3, 4, 5
    (D) 1, 2, 3, 4, 5
    (E) 2, 4, 5, 6, 7

3. If chapter 4 contains the essay written by G, then which one of the following must be true?

    (A) The essay written by F is contained in a later chapter than is the essay written by H.
    (B) The essay written by H is contained in a later chapter than is the essay written by J.
    (C) The essay written by K is contained in a later chapter than is the essay written by G.
    (D) The essay written by L is contained in a later chapter than is the essay written by G.
    (E) The essay written by M is contained in a later chapter than is the essay written by K.

4. Which one of the following CANNOT be true?

    (A) Chapter 1 contains the essay written by K, and chapter 3 contains the essay written by G.
    (B) Chapter 2 contains the essay written by K, and chapter 7 contains the essay written by G.
    (C) Chapter 3 contains the essay written by K, and chapter 4 contains the essay written by J.
    (D) Chapter 4 contains the essay written by G, and chapter 6 contains the essay written by L.
    (E) Chapter 5 contains the essay written by G, and chapter 6 contains the essay written by F.

5. If the chapter containing the essay written by J immediately precedes the chapter containing the essay written by K, then which one of the following could be true?

    (A) Chapter 2 contains the essay written by J.
    (B) Chapter 3 contains the essay written by L.
    (C) Chapter 4 contains the essay written by M.
    (D) Chapter 5 contains the essay written by G.
    (E) Chapter 6 contains the essay written by J.

6. Which one of the following must be false?

    (A) Chapter 1 contains the essay written by H.
    (B) Chapter 2 contains the essay written by J.
    (C) Chapter 3 contains the essay written by G.
    (D) Chapter 5 contains the essay written by F.
    (E) Chapter 6 contains the essay written by G.

2. Grouping

A game whose main objective is to assign elements to locations where relationships such as before/after or left/right are not relevant is very often a grouping game. Most grouping games have named categories that can accommodate multiple elements, and many of the clues in these games require that elements either be placed in the same group as one another, or in different ones. For such clues, we use the same block and antiblock symbols that we do in ordering games, without any concern for the order in which the elements appear in our symbols. Grouping games also often include conditional clues.

One key type of clue and deduction that applies in grouping games (but not in most ordering games) pertains to the number of elements in each group. Often, the distribution of elements among the groups is restricted but not completely determined by the clues, and this is always a factor to keep in mind while making deductions and working questions. You'll find that you make a lot of headway when you can determine that one or more of the groups in the game is full, and you'll need to know the groups' maximum sizes in order to know when that's happening.

Here's a list of common types of clues found primarily in grouping games.

Element types:
Two adults—F and G—and two
  children—X and Y...
  (in inventory)

A: F G
c: x y

Max/min:
Group 1 contains at most 3 members.
  (in diagram)

There are at least 3 roses in the garden.
  (in inventory)

r r r +

Placeholders:
Each group of 3 contains at least
  1 adult.
  (in diagram)

Group 1 includes either X or Y,
  or both.
  (in diagram)

Movable spaces:
Each of seven people is either in
  group 1 or else in group 2; each
  group includes at least 3 people.

Take a shot at the game on the following page. Answers can be found in Chapter 20.

DRILL #2

Tamika has seven articles remaining to move to her new apartment: two boxes, a chair, a file cabinet, a mattress, a sofa, and a trunk. She moves all of these articles, without unpacking or disassembling any of them, by making exactly two separate trips in her truck. The trips she makes are subject to the following constraints:

On the trip when she moves her sofa, Tamika moves at most two other articles.

Tamika does not move the file cabinet and the mattress on the same trip.

Tamika moves the chair and at least one of the boxes on the same trip.

1. Which one of the following could be a complete and accurate list of the articles Tamika moves on her first trip?

    (A) one box, the chair, and the mattress
    (B) both boxes, the chair, and the file cabinet
    (C) both boxes, the chair, and the trunk
    (D) both boxes, the sofa, and the trunk
    (E) the chair, the file cabinet, the mattress, and the trunk

2. If Tamika moves the sofa on her second trip, then she could also move any one of the following articles on her second trip EXCEPT:

    (A) a box
    (B) the chair
    (C) the file cabinet
    (D) the mattress
    (E) the trunk

3. What is the maximum number of articles that Tamika could move on either trip?

    (A) 2
    (B) 3
    (C) 4
    (D) 5
    (E) 6

4. If Tamika moves at least the sofa and the mattress on her first trip, then how many distinct possible combinations of articles exist for Tamika's second trip?

    (A) 1
    (B) 2
    (C) 3
    (D) 4
    (E) 5

5. If Tamika moves the trunk and both boxes on the same trip, then each one of the following could be true EXCEPT:

    (A) Tamika moves both the chair and the file cabinet on her first trip.
    (B) Tamika moves both the file cabinet and the sofa on her first trip.
    (C) Tamika moves both the trunk and the mattress on her second trip.
    (D) Tamika moves exactly two articles on her first trip.
    (E) Tamika moves exactly four articles on her second trip.

6. If the constraint is added that Tamika must move the mattress and the trunk together on the second trip, but all the other initial constraints remain in effect, then it would be possible to determine precisely which articles must be moved on each trip if which one of the following additional constraints were imposed?

    (A) Tamika must move at least one box on her first trip.
    (B) Tamika must not move the file cabinet and the chair on different trips.
    (C) Tamika cannot move the file cabinet on her second trip.
    (D) Tamika must move at least three articles on her first trip.
    (E) Tamika cannot move fewer than four articles on her second trip.

3. Spatial Arrangement

Although games that only require arrangement in one direction—left to right, north to south, and so on—can be dealt with as basic ordering games, some LSAT games involve more complicated arrangements of your elements. Any game that includes two possible spatial relationships—across from versus next to, to take one example—requires a chart to keep track of these relationships as you place the elements in your diagram. We'll adopt this diagramming method when a game involves spatial arrangement.

Remember that the idea in symbolizing clues is to line them up with your diagram. However you represented above/below versus left/right or north/south versus east/west in your diagram doesn't matter, as long as you're consistent with that diagram in the way you symbolize your clues and interpret the work you do.

Here are some common clues you may encounter on spatial arrangement games, along with good ways of symbolizing them.

Single row/column:
A is on the north side of the street.
B is on the western end of the street.
  (in diagram)

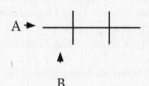

Universal:
No cat can be the same breed as the
  cats in any cage beside it.
No cat can be the same breed as the
  cats in the cages above or below it.
  (multiple breeds of cats in game)

Range:
A appears to the left of both B and C.

A appears above both B and C.

Try the following game on the next page. Answers can be found in Chapter 20.

DRILL #3

Questions 1–6

The television screens in a display window at an electronics store are numbered 1 through 6 and arranged as follows: screens 1, 2, and 3 are adjacent to one another in the bottom row, from left to right; screens 4 and 5 are adjacent to one another in the middle row, from left to right; screen 6 is the only one in the top row. The rows are situated so that screens 6, 4, and 1 form a single column on the left side of the display, from top to bottom; screen 5 in the middle row is immediately above screen 2 in the bottom row, forming the center column of the display; and screen 3 is the only one in the column on the right. On each screen is displayed either a single video game or a single movie, with no two screens displaying the same video game or movie, according to the following conditions:

The movies displayed are *Orange Tree*, *Perspectives*, and *Queen Jane*.

The video games displayed are *Xenophobe*, *Yikes!*, and *Zero Sum*.

No movie is displayed immediately adjacent to any other movie in the same row.

No video game is displayed immediately above or below any other video game in the same column.

Orange Tree is not displayed anywhere in the same column as *Queen Jane*.

Yikes! is not displayed anywhere in the same row as *Zero Sum*.

1. Which one of the following could be true?

    (A) *Orange Tree* is displayed on screen 3.
    (B) *Perspectives* is displayed on screen 5.
    (C) *Xenophobe* is displayed on screen 4.
    (D) *Yikes!* is displayed on screen 6.
    (E) *Zero Sum* is displayed on screen 3.

2. If two video games are displayed adjacent to one another in the same row, then which one of the following must be true?

    (A) *Orange Tree* is displayed somewhere in the same column as either *Perspectives* or else *Yikes!*
    (B) *Perspectives* is displayed somewhere in the same column as either *Yikes!* or else *Zero Sum.*
    (C) *Perspectives* is displayed somewhere in the same row as either *Queen Jane* or else *Xenophobe.*
    (D) *Queen Jane* is displayed somewhere in the same row as either *Orange Tree* or else *Yikes!*
    (E) *Queen Jane* is displayed somewhere in the same row as either *Yikes!* or else *Zero Sum.*

3. If *Perspectives* is displayed somewhere in the same row as *Xenophobe* but not immediately adjacent to it, and somewhere in the same column as *Orange Tree* but not immediately above or below it, then which one of the following could be false?

    (A) *Perspectives* is displayed either immediately below or immediately adjacent to *Zero Sum.*
    (B) *Queen Jane* is displayed either immediately above or immediately adjacent to *Yikes!*
    (C) *Yikes!* is displayed either immediately above or immediately adjacent to *Perspectives.*
    (D) *Zero Sum* is displayed either immediately below or immediately adjacent to *Orange Tree.*
    (E) *Zero Sum* is displayed either immediately below or immediately adjacent to *Queen Jane.*

4. If *Yikes!* is displayed on screen 5, then which one of the following could be true?

    (A) *Orange Tree* is displayed on screen 1.
    (B) *Perspectives* is displayed on screen 2.
    (C) *Queen Jane* is displayed on screen 3.
    (D) *Xenophobe* is displayed on screen 6.
    (E) *Zero Sum* is displayed on screen 1.

5. Which one of the following must be true?

    (A) A movie is displayed on screen 2.
    (B) A movie is displayed on screen 4.
    (C) A movie is displayed on screen 5.
    (D) A video game is displayed on screen 3.
    (E) A video game is displayed on screen 4.

6. Tomorrow, the electronics store will replace the video game *Xenophobe* with the movie *Rabblerouser* without changing the position of any other movie or video game in the display. If tomorrow's display must adhere to the same conditions as today's display, then which one of the following is a complete and accurate list of the screens on which *Orange Tree* could be displayed?

    (A) 1, 6
    (B) 1, 5, 6
    (C) 2, 4, 6
    (D) 2, 5, 6
    (E) 1, 2, 4, 5, 6

4. Organizational Arrangement

The fourth task around which an LSAT game can be built—and the most difficult of all to diagram—is organizational arrangement. Like spatial arrangement games, these games require diagrams that can indicate two different relationships between elements, so a chart is most appropriate for organizing the information in these games. Diagrams on these games usually look very similar to the diagrams of spatial arrangement games.

Most often a game that involves multiple variables—one in which, for example, we have to figure out not only in what order the cars are going through the car wash, but what color each of the cars is and what kind of wash each one receives—is an organizational arrangement game, best worked with a chart. There are certainly others: a game in which the votes of four legislators on three different issues must be tracked; a game in which two artisans work on the same five projects, one project each per day, but the two artisans cannot work on the same project on the same day; a game in which we must determine the members of the junior-varsity and varsity golf teams at two high schools. These are just a few examples, and they are by no means an exhaustive list.

Some organizational arrangement games are all but impossible with standard table diagrams; others can be forced that way, but are quicker and easier with a chart. Some of these games will strike you as needing a chart right away, while others require more experience to recognize. This is the most varied of all the games tasks.

The big idea on these, however, remains the same: to find the core of the game, the thing (or things) that are fixed in place; to devise a chart that lays the fixed information out in front of you, allowing you to place the elements in it using the clues; and to always symbolize the clues with your chart in mind, to minimize the difficulty of using them. Most of all, don't try to work these in your head or muddle through without some kind of diagram. For many of these games, there is no one "right" diagram to use; the only wrong way to go is not to come up with a diagram at all. Answers can be found in Chapter 20.

DRILL #4

In a supplemental draft, two football teams—the Antelopes and the Cheetahs—draft exactly six different rookies: H, K, L, M, O, and P. Each of the rookies drafted plays either quarterback, running back, safety, or tackle, and at least one of the rookies drafted plays each of these positions. No rookie plays more than one position. The rookies drafted and the positions they play are subject to the following conditions:

  Each team drafts exactly three of the six rookies.
  Each team drafts a quarterback, and each team drafts a tackle.
  If the Antelopes draft K, then M plays tackle.
  L and O are not drafted by the same team.
  H plays quarterback.
  P is drafted by the Cheetahs.

1. Which one of the following could be a complete and accurate list of the rookies drafted by the Antelopes and the positions they play?

    (A) H: quarterback; K: running back; L: safety
    (B) H: quarterback; K: safety; M: tackle
    (C) H: quarterback; L: safety; M: tackle
    (D) K: running back; O: quarterback; P: safety
    (E) K: tackle; L: quarterback; M: safety

2. If K is drafted to play quarterback by one team and O is drafted to play tackle by the other team, then each of the following pairs of rookies could play the same position EXCEPT:

    (A) H and K
    (B) L and O
    (C) L and P
    (D) M and O
    (E) O and P

3. If M is drafted by the Antelopes to play safety, then which one of the following must be true?

    (A) H and L are drafted by the same team.
    (B) K and O are drafted by the same team.
    (C) K and P are drafted by the same team.
    (D) L and P are drafted by the same team.
    (E) M and O are drafted by the same team.

4. If L is drafted by the Antelopes to play quarterback, then which one of the following must be true?

    (A) If K plays running back, then P must play safety.
    (B) If K plays safety, then O must play running back.
    (C) If O plays tackle, then P must play safety.
    (D) If P plays running back, then K must play safety.
    (E) If P plays safety, then O must play quarterback.

5. If K and O play tackle and P plays safety, then each of the following must be true EXCEPT:

    (A) The Antelopes draft M to play quarterback.
    (B) The Cheetahs draft K to play tackle.
    (C) The Cheetahs draft L to play quarterback.
    (D) The Antelopes do not draft any rookie who plays safety.
    (E) The Cheetahs do not draft any rookie who plays running back.

6. Which one of the following must be false?

    (A) H is drafted by the Antelopes to play quarterback.
    (B) K is drafted by the Cheetahs to play safety.
    (C) L is drafted by the Antelopes to play tackle.
    (D) M is drafted by the Cheetahs to play running back.
    (E) O is drafted by the Cheetahs to play quarterback.

11

Mixing It Up

VARIATIONS ON THE BASIC TASKS

The primary factor that determines a game's difficulty isn't the task around which it is based. Historically, the LSAT has had easy games, as well as difficult ones, based around each of the tasks. The main difference between easier games and more difficult ones is that the harder ones are constructed with a greater number of complicating factors.

You've already seen some of these factors. Multiple element types, conditional clues, and flexible group sizes all ratchet the difficulty level slightly over and above the difficulty of the most basic versions of these games. In this chapter, we'll look at other factors that have a more significant impact on a game's difficulty. These factors most often concern one of two fundamental features of the game.

ELEMENTS: NOT 1-TO-1

Our last example in the previous chapter introduced us to one possible situation in which the elements and the spaces in your diagram aren't 1-to-1; in other words, although all the elements were used, not all of the spaces were filled, so we had to add blanks to our inventory to represent the full range of information we might require.

Some games offer other variants on the 1-to-1 assumption we usually bring to a game. In some games, the same element may be used more than once; in others, not all of the elements are necessarily used; some games have both of these attributes. In any of these cases, you'll need to be careful how you interpret and use the clues. It's easy to assume too much when you start making deductions.

DIAGRAM: COMPLEX OR COMPOSITE TASKS

The fourth game in the previous chapter provided a good introduction to this situation, and like that game, these tasks most often require a chart to keep track of the important information. Some games may ask you both to group and order the elements; some games may ask you to order elements that have multiple attributes. Different variations on these situations may require slightly different solutions, so you'll need to preview the clues before you finally decide how to diagram the game. In fact, it's always a good idea to examine the clues as part of your process of deciding how to diagram a game.

In this chapter we'll look at four examples that bring in various combinations of these more complicated situations.

1. Tiered Diagrams

These games are fairly common on the LSAT and appear especially often in games that involve an ordering task. One example might be a game that asked you to determine which doctor and which nurse are on duty for each of four days; another might ask you to determine the order in which six books are published, and whether each is a hardcover or a paperback.

The key thing to look for in these cases is two or more element types with a strict separation between them. In the first example above, there is no chance that any slot may be taken up by either a doctor or a nurse, and we know that each of the days has exactly one of each. In this case, what you'll want to do is make a chart with the order across the top (the days) and one row or "tier" each for the separate element types (doctors and nurses). That way, you'll be able to symbolize clues that pertain to which doctors and nurses can serve on the same day (vertical) differently from the way you symbolize clues that relate to adjacent days (horizontal).

Try out the next game, which is best represented using a tiered diagram. Answers can be found in Chapter 20.

DRILL #1

Questions 1–6

During a four-day period, an artist works on four paintings—D, E, G, and H—and four sketches—V, W, X, and Y. The artist works on exactly one painting and one sketch each day, and each day the artist works either in the morning or in the afternoon, but not both. The artist's work schedule is subject to the following conditions:

The artist works on two mornings but does not work in the morning on consecutive days.

The artist works in the afternoon on the second day.

The artist works on W in the afternoon but does not work on Y in the afternoon.

The artist does not work on E and G on consecutive days.

The artist works on G on the day immediately following the day on which the artist works on W.

The artist works on D on the day immediately prior to the day on which the artist works on G.

If the artist works on G on the same day that the artist works on V, then the artist works on H in the afternoon.

1. Which one of the following could be true of the artist's work schedule if the artist works in the afternoon on the fourth day?

   (A) The artist works on G before the artist works on Y.
   (B) The artist works on H before the artist works on G.
   (C) The artist works on W before the artist works on E.
   (D) The artist works on X before the artist works on E.
   (E) The artist works on Y before the artist works on V.

2. Which one of the following must be true of the artist's schedule?

   (A) The artist works on D in the afternoon.
   (B) The artist works on E in the morning.
   (C) The artist works on G in the morning.
   (D) The artist works on E and V on the same day.
   (E) The artist works on H and X on the same day.

3. If the artist works on H on the first day, then which of the following must be true?

   (A) The artist works on D on the second day.
   (B) The artist works on E on the second day.
   (C) The artist works on V on the second day.
   (D) The artist works on X on the second day.
   (E) The artist works on Y on the first day.

4. If the artist works on X on the third day, then each of the following could be true EXCEPT:

   (A) The artist works on E and Y in the morning of the same day.
   (B) The artist works on G and X in the morning of the same day.
   (C) The artist works on G and Y in the morning of the same day.
   (D) The artist works on H and V in the afternoon of the same day.
   (E) The artist works on H and Y in the morning of the same day.

5. Each of the following could be true EXCEPT:

   (A) The artist works on D before the artist works on E.
   (B) The artist works on E before the artist works on Y.
   (C) The artist works on V before the artist works on H.
   (D) The artist works on W before the artist works on V.
   (E) The artist works on W before the artist works on X.

6. If the artist works on V on the third day, then which of the following is a complete and accurate list of the days on which the artist could work on Y?

   (A) 1
   (B) 4
   (C) 1, 2
   (D) 1, 4
   (E) 1, 2, 4

2. The "Out" Column

Games in which not all of the elements are necessarily used can be tough unless you add an "out" column to your diagram and work carefully. The idea of an "out" column is to create a place in your diagram where you can put every element—even those which, in particular cases, you are sure are not used. You should treat your "out" column as a group separate from the other parts of your diagram; when it's full, you'll know that all of the remaining elements are in. It's important to realize, however, that the clues you symbolize for your "in" column—range clues, antiblocks, and so on—may not apply the same way in the "out" part of your diagram. For instance, a clue that tells you A and B may not be used at the same time does not exclude the possibility that both are out together. It's often helpful to separate your "out" column with a double line as a reminder of the fact that your clues may not apply there in the same way they do elsewhere in your diagram.

The basic type of game in which you'll need an "out" column is a pure in/out game: one in which the only task is to determine which elements are used and which are not. These are not always difficult games, although they certainly can be. Keep in mind, though, that ordering games, grouping games, and even the more complicated games can be constructed so that not all of the elements are necessarily used. Any time that happens, you'll need an "out" column to keep track of the ones that aren't.

Try the in/out game in the next example and note the similarities and differences between it and the grouping game you saw in the last chapter. Answers can be found in Chapter 20.

DRILL #2

Questions 1–6

Out of eight possible items at a grocery—fish, juice, limes, milk, onions, pasta, rice, and steak—a shopper purchases exactly five. The shopper selects items for purchase according to the following conditions:

If the shopper purchases pasta, then the shopper does not purchase steak.

If the shopper purchases fish, then the shopper does not purchase onions.

If the shopper does not purchase pasta, then the shopper purchases rice.

If the shopper purchases milk or does not purchase fish, then the shopper purchases steak.

If the shopper purchases both juice and onions, then the shopper also purchases pasta.

1. Which one of the following could be a complete and accurate list of items the shopper purchases?

   (A) fish, juice, limes, milk, and steak
   (B) fish, juice, limes, onions, and pasta
   (C) fish, juice, limes, rice, and steak
   (D) juice, limes, milk, pasta, and rice
   (E) juice, milk, onions, rice, and steak

2. Which of the following could be true?

   (A) The shopper purchases both juice and milk.
   (B) The shopper purchases both juice and onions.
   (C) The shopper purchases both milk and pasta.
   (D) The shopper purchases neither fish nor milk.
   (E) The shopper purchases neither juice nor limes.

3. If the shopper purchases neither fish nor onions, then which one of the following must be true?

   (A) The shopper does not purchase juice.
   (B) The shopper does not purchase rice.
   (C) The shopper does not purchase steak.
   (D) The shopper purchases limes.
   (E) The shopper purchases pasta.

4. If the shopper does not purchase juice, then which one of the following could be true?

   (A) The shopper does not purchase limes.
   (B) The shopper does not purchase milk.
   (C) The shopper does not purchase steak.
   (D) The shopper purchases fish.
   (E) The shopper purchases pasta.

5. Which of the following must be true?

   (A) The shopper purchases limes.
   (B) The shopper purchases rice.
   (C) The shopper purchases steak.
   (D) The shopper does not purchase onions.
   (E) The shopper does not purchase pasta.

6. Each of the following could be true EXCEPT:

   (A) The shopper purchases both fish and pasta.
   (B) The shopper purchases both fish and steak.
   (C) The shopper purchases both juice and limes.
   (D) The shopper purchases both limes and milk.
   (E) The shopper purchases both onions and pasta.

3. Multiple Uses of Elements

When elements in a game can be used more than once, deductions may be more difficult to make. For example, the clue "A cannot be in a group unless B is in that group" means one thing in a grouping game in which all the elements are used exactly once, and a rather different thing when they are all used at least once. In the first case, this clue is simply a complicated way of describing a block: Since A and B both have to be used exactly once, they'll appear together in one of the groups; in the second case, when elements may be used more than once, this clue means that A will appear with B at least once, but B may appear in another group as well, without A.

When elements can be used more than once, be very careful how you interpret the clues. When in doubt, symbolize them as literally as possible, and don't jump to conclusions. A "deduction" that excludes legal possibilities can cause tremendous problems.

Try out this game that requires multiple uses of the elements. Answers can be found in Chapter 20.

DRILL #3

Questions 1–6

A hobby store has four Frankenfighters, a classic toy, in its display case, numbered 1 through 4 from left to right. As originally sold, Frankenfighters came in five different models: Galaxis, Hyperion, Iceage, Klaxxon, and Monstro. The torsos and legs of Frankenfighters are interchangeable so that new toys can be made by combining the torso of one original Frankenfighter with the legs of another. The Frankenfighter toys in the hobby store's case are subject to the following conditions:

At least the torso or the legs of each of the five original Frankenfighters is used in the case's four toys.

The toy with Hyperion's torso is located to the left of the toy with Hyperion's legs, and no other toy includes either Hyperion's torso or legs.

The toy with Monstro's torso is located to the right of the toy with Monstro's legs, and no other toy includes either Monstro's torso or legs.

None of the four toys is composed of any combination of the Frankenfighters Galaxis and Klaxxon.

If any of the four toys includes Klaxxon's torso, then that toy also includes Iceage's legs.

At least one of the toys includes Galaxis's torso.

Exactly one of toy 1 or toy 4 includes Iceage's legs.

1. Which of the following could be the Frankenfighters combined to create toys 1 and 2?

(A) Toy 1: Hyperion's torso and Iceage's legs
Toy 2: Galaxis's torso and Monstro's legs

(B) Toy 1: Hyperion's torso and Klaxxon's legs
Toy 2: Klaxxon's torso and Monstro's legs

(C) Toy 1: Iceage's torso and Hyperion's legs
Toy 2: Iceage's torso and Kaxxon's legs

(D) Toy 1: Iceage's torso and Klaxxon's legs
Toy 2: Galaxis's torso and Monstro's legs

(E) Toy 1: Monstro's torso and Iceage's legs
Toy 2: Klaxxon's torso and Iceage's legs

2. If toy 2 includes Hyperion's legs and toy 3 includes Monstro's legs, then which one of the following must be true of the toys in the hobby store's case?

(A) At least one of toys 1 and 4 includes Galaxis's legs.

(B) At least one of toys 1 and 4 includes Galaxis's torso.

(C) At least one of toys 1 and 4 includes Klaxxon's torso.

(D) At least one of toys 2 and 3 includes Galaxis's torso.

(E) At least one of toys 2 and 3 includes Klaxxon's torso.

3. If toy 2 includes Klaxxon's torso and toy 3 includes Hyperion's torso, then which one of the following must be true of the toys in the hobby store's case?

(A) Toy 1 includes Galaxis's torso.
(B) Toy 1 includes Hyperion's legs.
(C) Toy 1 includes Monstro's legs.
(D) Toy 4 includes Galaxis's torso.
(E) Toy 4 includes Iceage's legs.

4. If toy 3 includes both Galaxis's torso and legs, then which one of the following must be true?

(A) Toy 1 includes either Iceage's torso or legs.
(B) Toy 1 includes either Klaxxon's torso or legs.
(C) Toy 2 includes either Iceage's torso or legs.
(D) Toy 2 includes either Monstro's torso or legs.
(E) Toy 4 includes either Hyperion's torso or legs.

5. Which of the following could be a complete and accurate list of the Frankenfighters whose torsos are included in toys 1 through 4, listed in that order?

(A) Galaxis, Iceage, Monstro, Hyperion
(B) Hyperion, Klaxxon, Iceage, Monstro
(C) Klaxxon, Hyperion, Monstro, Galaxis
(D) Klaxxon, Monstro, Hyperion, Galaxis
(E) Monstro, Hyperion, Galaxis, Klaxxon

6. If every toy that includes any part of Iceage also includes a part of Klaxxon, then which one of the following must be true?

(A) Exactly one toy includes some part of Galaxis.
(B) Exactly one toy includes some part of Iceage.
(C) Exactly two toys include some part of Galaxis.
(D) Exactly two toys include some part of Iceage.
(E) Exactly two toys include some part of Klaxxon.

4. More Than Two Types of Elements

We've already seen games that include two types of elements, and we've used capital and lowercase letters to distinguish between them. When a game has three or more types of elements—or when an upper-/lowercase distinction wouldn't allow you to see the difference between element types easily in your diagrams—you'll need to adopt another method of distinguishing between them. If the game can't be split into tiers to keep the element types separate, the only remaining alternative is to use subscripts to label the elements of different types.

It's important, when you're using subscripts, to use them in symbolizing your clues as well. However, when you're filling in your diagram, there may be cases in which the diagram would become difficult to read if you included the subscripts as well as the elements' names. Let the information you need dictate how fully you label the elements in your diagram, always remembering that you can consult your inventory if you need to refresh your memory.

Try out the ordering game on the next page with three types of elements. Answers can be found in Chapter 20.

DRILL #4

Questions 1–6

Throughout a seven-week period, a bookstore places seven different books on sale, one book each week. Two of the books are in hardback format—J and K; two of the books are in paperback format—Q and R; and three are in the format of trade books—U, V, and W. The schedule of books on sale is subject to the following conditions:

No two books in the same format are on sale in consecutive weeks.

Both hardback books are on sale before any paperback book is on sale.

Q is on sale during the week either immediately before or immediately after the week during which W is on sale.

If J is on sale during an earlier week than U is on sale, then K is on sale during the week immediately before V is on sale.

1. Which one of the following could be a complete and accurate list of books on sale for weeks 1 through 7, listed in that order?

   (A) K, U, J, Q, V, R, W
   (B) K, V, J, Q, W, U, R
   (C) V, J, U, K, Q, W, R
   (D) V, K, U, J, R, W, Q
   (E) W, Q, J, U, K, V, R

2. If Q is on sale during week 4, then which one of the following must be true?

   (A) K is on sale during week 1.
   (B) R is on sale during week 7.
   (C) U is on sale during week 2.
   (D) U is on sale during week 7.
   (E) W is on sale during week 3.

3. Which of the following must be true?

   (A) If J is on sale during week 1, then W is on sale during week 4.
   (B) If J is on sale during week 3, then V is on sale during week 2.
   (C) If K is on sale during week 2, then Q is on sale during week 5.
   (D) If Q is on sale during week 6, then W is on sale during week 7.
   (E) If U is on sale during week 6, then J is on sale during week 3.

4. If U is on sale before V is on sale, then at most how many weeks can occur between the week that U is on sale and the week that V is on sale?

   (A) 2
   (B) 3
   (C) 4
   (D) 5
   (E) 6

5. Which of the following must be false?

   (A) J is on sale during week 3 and V is on sale during week 6.
   (B) K is on sale during week 2 and Q is on sale during week 5.
   (C) Q is on sale during week 7 and V is on sale during week 1.
   (D) R is on sale during week 6 and J is on sale during week 1.
   (E) W is on sale during week 4 and U is on sale during week 2.

6. If J is on sale during week 2, then which of the following could be true?

   (A) Q is on sale during week 6.
   (B) R is on sale during week 7.
   (C) U is on sale during week 4.
   (D) U is on sale during week 6.
   (E) V is on sale during week 1.

12

Difficult Games

WHAT MAKES A GAME DIFFICULT?

A number of factors determine a game's difficulty. Broadly speaking, the amount of time required to complete a game's questions ultimately dictates a game's difficulty. Since it's impossible to identify with 100-percent accuracy when you're facing long questions, you won't be able to anticipate difficulty levels perfectly. However, a game's setup and clues can provide hints as to the level of difficulty to expect.

The factors mentioned in the previous chapter—elements not 1-to-1, multiple element types, a large number of complicated conditionals—tend, when they are combined with one another, to make a game more difficult and time consuming. As we'll see in this chapter, certain telltale signs of distribution deductions are also good indicators of potential difficulty. Above all, there are two main factors that determine how difficult the game will be for you to work.

UNCERTAINTY ABOUT THE DIAGRAM

If, even after considering the clues, you're still not certain how to diagram a game, then that game will be difficult for you. There are cases when you have no choice but to struggle with such a game: If you've worked the other three, and you still have time left, you'll have to dive in and do the best you can. But you should never work a game that you don't know how to diagram when there are other games to work instead.

UNCERTAINTY ABOUT THE CLUES

Sometimes you'll encounter games with a clue that you don't really have a good way of diagramming. If there's just one of these in a game, chances are you'll be able to cope with it by writing a quick paraphrase, in your own words, of what the clue means and working with it carefully. Some games, though, have several of these clues, and often they turn out to be very important in working the game. If you encounter a game with multiple clues that you don't really have a good way of representing, it's best to look elsewhere.

As was mentioned above, there will be times when you have no choice but to work difficult games. The most important thing to do is to be persistent, be patient, don't stop trying to write down the information you have, and—most importantly—make an intentional effort to learn about the game as you work with it. Some games become much clearer once you've worked a concrete example or two, but the only way to get to that point is to struggle with the game at first.

1. Distribution Deductions

"Distribution" is a catchall term that refers generally to restrictions that have to do with numbers and counting. Distribution often plays a role in grouping games, in connection with the group sizes. Imagine a game in which you have five differently colored balls and three boxes, into each of which at least one ball must be placed. In this situation, the distribution of balls to boxes is somewhat flexible, and also somewhat limited. After placing the one required ball in each of the three boxes, there are still two balls left. Those two may go in different boxes or in the same box, giving rise to what we might characterize as two possible distributions: 1-1-3 or 1-2-2. Keep in mind that which group has which number is still completely up in the air; nevertheless, we have made a deduction that will be useful in working the questions, and further clues may limit the range of possibilities even further.

Distribution deductions can arise in connection with the number of uses of the elements as well. Imagine an ordering game in which there are five elements and seven days of the week. Suppose we're told that each element must be used at least once. In this case, using each element once fills five of the slots, leaving two unfilled. We may either fill them with two additional copies of the same element, or with a second copy of two different elements. You might characterize these two distributions as 1-1-1-1-3 or 1-1-1-2-2. Further restrictions might give us an idea of which elements may or may not be used multiple times, narrowing the possibilities.

These are only two relatively simple situations in which making distribution deductions is crucial to an initial understanding of how the game works. Many games have these types of deductions; they're sometimes difficult to make, but they are always useful. Any time you find yourself counting, wanting to do scratch work to outline possibilities, or wishing you knew upper and lower limits on group sizes or the number of uses of your elements, chances are that you need to look for distribution deductions before proceeding to the questions.

Because distribution deductions can be very involved, they're a favorite ingredient of more difficult games. The good news is that a game with many distribution deductions is often very quick to work once you have found the deductions: You'll often learn that the number of possibilities on a game with lots of distribution deductions is extremely limited. The bad news on these games is that, if you don't somehow find the distribution deductions, the questions can be outrageously difficult. So when you encounter a game that has a strong scent of distribution about it, be sure to look for those deductions before you move on, and don't worry if it takes you a while. The time you spend finding them will be amply repaid. Try the following game. Answers can be found in Chapter 20.

DRILL #1

Five writers—Philips, Quo, Reader, Soward, and Thorpe—collaborate on the screenplays of four films—*Fling*, *Gavel*, *Harvey*, and *Junior*. Two writers collaborate on two of these screenplays, and three writers collaborate on the other two. Every writer is a collaborator on at least one of the screenplays. The assignment of screenplays to writers is subject to the following conditions:

Soward collaborates on three of the four screenplays.

There is exactly one screenplay on which Philips and Reader are both collaborators.

There is exactly one screenplay on which Quo and Thorpe are both collaborators.

Quo is a writer on the same number of screenplays as is Thorpe.

Fling has exactly two writers, and *Junior* has exactly three.

There is no screenplay on which Reader and Soward are both collaborators.

1. Which one of the following must be true?

   (A) Exactly two screenwriters collaborate on *Harvey*.
   (B) Exactly three screenwriters collaborate on *Gavel*.
   (C) Philips collaborates on exactly two screenplays.
   (D) Quo collaborates on exactly three screenplays.
   (E) Reader collaborates on exactly two screenplays.

2. Which one of the following could be true?

   (A) Philips and Thorpe, and no other writers, collaborate on *Gavel*.
   (B) Quo and Philips, and no other writers, collaborate on *Fling*.
   (C) Quo and Thorpe, and no other writers, collaborate on *Gavel*.
   (D) Reader and Thorpe, and no other writers, collaborate on *Harvey*.
   (E) Soward and Thorpe, and no other writers, collaborate on *Harvey*.

3. If Philips collaborates on *Gavel* with two other writers, then which of the following must be true?

   (A) Philips is a writer on *Harvey*.
   (B) Philips is a writer on *Junior*.
   (C) Quo is a writer on *Gavel*.
   (D) Reader is a writer on *Fling*.
   (E) Thorpe is a writer on *Junior*.

4. Each of the following could be true EXCEPT:

   (A) There is exactly one screenplay on which Philips and Thorpe are both collaborators.
   (B) There is exactly one screenplay on which Quo and Reader are both collaborators.
   (C) There is exactly one screenplay on which Quo and Soward are both collaborators.
   (D) There are exactly two screenplays on which Philips and Soward are both collaborators.
   (E) There are exactly two screenplays on which Soward and Thorpe are both collaborators.

5. If Philips, Quo, and Reader collaborate on *Harvey*, then which one of the following could be true?

   (A) Philips is a writer on *Fling*.
   (B) Philips is a writer on *Junior*.
   (C) Quo is a writer on *Fling*.
   (D) Quo is a writer on *Gavel*.
   (E) Reader is a writer on *Junior*.

6. If there is exactly one screenplay on which Soward and Thorpe are both collaborators, then which of the following must be true?

   (A) There is exactly one screenplay on which Philips and Quo are both collaborators.
   (B) There is exactly one screenplay on which Philips and Thorpe are both collaborators.
   (C) There is exactly one screenplay on which Quo and Reader are both collaborators.
   (D) There is exactly one screenplay on which Quo and Soward are both collaborators.
   (E) There are exactly two screenplays on which Philips and Soward are both collaborators.

2. Structured "In" Columns

As was mentioned in the previous chapters, one of the ways a game can be made more difficult is to open the possibility that not every element is used. We've already seen a game where the primary task is to determine which elements are used ("in") and which are not, but these are only the most basic versions of an in/out task. Some games not only open the possibility that some elements are not used, but further ask you to order, group, or otherwise arrange the elements that are used.

These games with structured "in" columns can be significantly more difficult than similar-looking straight in/out games or straight ordering/grouping/arrangement games. The main thing to be cautious about on these games, as mentioned before, is to make sure that you interpret the clues correctly, and that you don't make unwarranted deductions. Some of these games can be time-consuming and rather tedious, but as long as you stick to the clues and apply them carefully, you should be able to work your way through these.

Try the game on the following page that combines an in/out task with an ordering task, with a touch of distribution thrown in for good measure. Answers can be found in Chapter 20.

DRILL #2

During one week, a human resources director conducts five interviews for a new job, one interview per day, Monday through Friday. There are six candidates for the job—R, S, T, U, V, and W. No more than two candidates are interviewed more than once. Neither S nor U nor V is interviewed more than once, and no other candidate is interviewed more than twice. The schedule of interviews is subject to the following conditions:

If T is interviewed, then T must be interviewed on both Monday and Friday.

If S is interviewed, then U is also interviewed, with S's interview taking place earlier than U's interview.

If R is interviewed twice, then R's second interview takes place exactly two days after R's first interview.

If V is interviewed, then W is interviewed twice, with V's interview taking place after W's first interview and before W's second interview.

If U is interviewed, then R is also interviewed, with U's interview taking place on a day either immediately before or immediately after a day on which R is interviewed.

1. Which of the following could be a complete and accurate list of candidates the human resources director interviews and the days on which those interviews take place?

    (A) Monday: S; Tuesday: U; Wednesday: R; Thursday: W; Friday: R
    (B) Monday: S; Tuesday: W; Wednesday: R; Thursday: W; Friday: U
    (C) Monday: T; Tuesday: R; Wednesday: S; Thursday: R; Friday: T
    (D) Monday: T; Tuesday: R; Wednesday: W; Thursday: V; Friday: T
    (E) Monday: W; Tuesday: R; Wednesday: V; Thursday: W; Friday: T

2. If V is interviewed on Tuesday, then which one of the following must be true?

    (A) T is interviewed on Friday.
    (B) U is interviewed on Thursday.
    (C) W is interviewed on Friday.
    (D) R is not interviewed.
    (E) S is not interviewed.

3. If W is not interviewed, then which one of the following must be true?

    (A) R is interviewed on Thursday.
    (B) S is interviewed on Tuesday.
    (C) T is interviewed on Monday.
    (D) U is interviewed on Wednesday.
    (E) T is not interviewed.

4. If S is interviewed, then which one of the following could be true?

    (A) S is interviewed on Thursday.
    (B) U is interviewed on Monday.
    (C) V is interviewed on Tuesday.
    (D) W is interviewed on both Tuesday and Wednesday.
    (E) W is interviewed on both Tuesday and Thursday.

5. If neither U nor T is interviewed, then each of the following could be true EXCEPT:

    (A) R is interviewed on Monday.
    (B) R is interviewed on Thursday.
    (C) V is interviewed on Tuesday.
    (D) W is interviewed on Wednesday.
    (E) S is not interviewed.

6. If both U and V are interviewed, then which one of the following is a complete and accurate list of the days on which W could be interviewed?

    (A) Monday, Friday
    (B) Tuesday, Thursday
    (C) Monday, Wednesday, Friday
    (D) Tuesday, Wednesday, Thursday
    (E) Monday, Tuesday, Wednesday, Thursday, Friday

3. Overkill Games

Some games have setups and lists of clues that look difficult at a glance. Gargantuan setups, or those with an enormous number of clues, tend to be intimidating, but that isn't a reason in itself to avoid them. Yes, sometimes these games are quite difficult, but sometimes the fact that you're given so much information to start with can be a benefit. The challenge is finding a good way to organize and work with it.

By now, hopefully you've picked up on the fact that our simple vocabulary of diagrams and symbols can be extremely flexible. By combining and adapting the methods we've seen so far, you can often construct a complex diagram, or a symbol for a massive clue, that is easy to use and very powerful. Remember to take everything in the game one piece at a time, and above all be resourceful and adaptable. As long as you stay calm and work steadily, no matter how many complicating factors a game's designer throws in, you'll always have a way of handling it. There are games whose primary difficulty is in devising a good diagram, and once that's done, you're practically home free. Try the next game. Answers can be found in Chapter 20.

DRILL #3

A basketball coach must decide on her lineup for the first and second quarters of a basketball game. Her lineup must consist of five players: one who plays center, two who play forward, and two who play guard. Her players, along with the positions they can play, are as follows:

    Lewis: guard
    Marte: forward
    O'Shea: guard
    Prince: center
    Shibe: guard
    Tompkins: center, forward
    Vasquez: forward, guard

There are no other players on the team, and none of the players can play any position other than those listed for her. The coach's lineups for the first and second quarters will be consistent with the following conditions:

    To form her lineup for the second quarter, the coach substitutes exactly one player who does not play in the first quarter for one who does play in the first quarter.

    A player who can play more than one position need not play the same position in the first and second quarters.

    Marte and O'Shea will not be in the lineup with each other during either the first or the second quarters.

    If during any quarter Vasquez plays forward, then Shibe is in the lineup for that quarter.

1. Which one of the following could be the guards and forwards, not necessarily listed in that order, in the coach's second-quarter lineup?

    (A) Lewis, Marte, Tompkins, Vasquez
    (B) Lewis, O'Shea, Shibe, Tompkins
    (C) Lewis, O'Shea, Tompkins, Vasquez
    (D) Marte, O'Shea, Shibe, Tompkins
    (E) Marte, Prince, Tompkins, Vasquez

2. If Tompkins plays center in the second quarter but does not play in the first quarter, then which one of the following must be true?

    (A) Marte does not play during the second quarter.
    (B) O'Shea does not play during the first quarter.
    (C) Prince does not play during the first quarter.
    (D) Shibe does not play during the first quarter.
    (E) Vasquez plays guard during the second quarter.

3. If neither Marte nor O'Shea plays during the first quarter, and if Marte does not play during the second quarter, then which one of the following must be true?

    (A) Lewis plays guard during the second quarter.
    (B) Marte plays guard during the second quarter.
    (C) Shibe plays guard during the second quarter.
    (D) Tompkins plays center during the second quarter.
    (E) Vasquez plays guard during the second quarter.

4. Each of the following could be true of the coach's lineups EXCEPT:

    (A) Lewis plays guard in the first quarter but does not play in the second quarter.
    (B) Marte plays forward in both the first and the second quarters.
    (C) O'Shea plays guard in the first quarter, and Marte plays forward in the second quarter.
    (D) Shibe does not play in the first quarter, and O'Shea plays guard in the second quarter.
    (E) Vasquez plays forward in the first quarter and plays guard in the second quarter.

5. Each of the following players must be included in the lineup for the first or second quarters EXCEPT:

    (A) Lewis
    (B) Prince
    (C) Shibe
    (D) Tompkins
    (E) Vasquez

6. If Marte and Vasquez do not play in the same lineup with each other in either quarter, and if Marte plays in the first quarter, then which one of the following must be true?

    (A) Lewis does not play in the second quarter.
    (B) O'Shea plays guard in the second quarter.
    (C) Prince plays center in the second quarter.
    (D) Tompkins plays center in the second quarter.
    (E) Vasquez plays guard in the second quarter.

4. Time-Consuming Questions and Answers

In contrast to the previous game, there are other games that look deceptively simple. They may have few clues and involve a familiar task. Often you can diagram and symbolize them in a way that seems straightforward and quick, and you find few if any deductions, but the real difficulty of the game doesn't rear its head until you start tackling the questions.

Unfortunately, there's not much you can do to make sure you stay out of such situations. What you can do, once you're in them, is above all to remain calm. Remember that the speed with which you got through the diagramming, symbolization, and deduction steps gives you a built-in cushion of time for working the questions. Also remember that LSAT Games sections are designed with the time limit in mind; if one game turns out to be more difficult or time consuming than you'd initially estimated, then it's almost certain that a game you initially identified as being difficult will be quicker than you'd anticipated.

The one thing you must *never* do on a games section is cut and run once you've begun working the questions on a game. Because you've already invested time in the game, it's extraordinarily inefficient to move to a different one unless you're absolutely certain that you'll be able to return to the game. Also, you'll often find that a game that seems very difficult at first becomes easier as you work with it and become more familiar with it. Many times, after working an example or two, you'll find a key deduction or some other insight that allows you to pick up speed significantly once you've fought your way through a question or two. Now try the example on the next page. Answers can be found in Chapter 20.

DRILL #4

Questions 1–6

In an analysis process, a data packet is processed by five units—A, B, C, D, and E—not necessarily in that order. The packet is processed by each of the five units, one at a time. The packet may only by processed by a unit with which it is compatible at the time of processing, and no other unit is involved in processing the data packet. The order of the packet's processing is consistent with the following:

Before it has been processed by any unit, the packet is compatible with any of the five units.

The output of unit A is compatible with units B, C, and D, and with only those units.

The output of unit B is compatible with units A, C, and E, and with only those units.

The output of unit C is compatible with units A and B, and with only those units.

The output of unit D is compatible with units A and E, and with only those units.

The output of unit E is compatible with units B and D, and with only those units.

1. If B is the second unit to process the packet, then which one of the following must be true?

   (A) The first unit to process the packet is either A or C.
   (B) The first unit to process the packet is either A or E.
   (C) The third unit to process the packet is either A or E.
   (D) The fourth unit to process the packet is either A or D.
   (E) The fifth unit to process the packet is either D or E.

2. Which one of the following could be true of the order in which the packet is processed by the five units?

   (A) The first unit to process the packet is A, and the fourth unit to process the packet is C.
   (B) The second unit to process the packet is B, and the third unit to process the packet is D.
   (C) The second unit to process the packet is C, and the fourth unit to process the packet is A.
   (D) The third unit to process the packet is E, and the fifth unit to process the packet is D.
   (E) The fourth unit to process the packet is E, and the fifth unit to process the packet is B.

3. If C is the fifth unit to process the packet, then which one of the following is a complete and accurate list of the units, any one of which could be the second to process the packet?

   (A) D
   (B) D, E
   (C) A, B, D
   (D) A, B, E
   (E) A, B, D, E

4. If B is the third unit to process the packet, then in how many different orders could the packet be processed by the five units?

   (A) 2
   (B) 3
   (C) 4
   (D) 6
   (E) 8

5. Which of the following could be the second and fourth units to process the packet?

   (A) second: A; fourth: C
   (B) second: B; fourth: C
   (C) second: C; fourth: A
   (D) second: C; fourth: B
   (E) second: D; fourth: C

6. If the original conditions are altered so that the output of unit A is compatible only with unit D, and the output of unit B is compatible only with unit E, but if all the other initial conditions for the packet's processing remain in effect, then which one of the following must be true?

   (A) The first unit to process the packet is C.
   (B) The second unit to process the packet is A.
   (C) The third unit to process the packet is E.
   (D) The fourth unit to process the packet is D.
   (E) The fourth unit to process the packet is E.

13

Weird Games

WHAT ARE WEIRD GAMES?

Although the basic strategies of diagramming and symbolization are suitable for all games, a few games require some significant adaptations of those strategies. Weird games—those that require slightly idiosyncratic ways of either diagramming the game or handling the clues—can be intimidating under the LSAT's timed conditions. These games fall into one of two basic categories.

SET TYPES

Pure ordering games, mapping games, and switch-and-mutate games are three particular games types that have appeared at times during the LSAT's history, and which are best handled with set methods that apply specifically to those games. You'll recognize a lot of those methods as extensions or adaptations of things you've already learned, so these should not seem utterly alien. The good thing about these set types is that they are so distinctive that a little experience with them should give you all the tools you need to recognize and handle them.

NONE OF THE ABOVE

LSAT games are built around a task: ordering, grouping, spatial arrangement, or organizational arrangement. The test writers then add and combine complicating factors such as multiple element types, conditional clues, and distribution deductions to give a game its particular character. Although we can't say that most games fall into some simply defined category, nevertheless it's true that nearly all games are composed of familiar pieces that function in familiar ways.

On rare occasions, however, the writers come up with games that seem a step removed from anything they've done before. Yet in more than a decade of exams, there have only been a handful of times when the LSAT has included a game that seems truly alien. In these cases, you'll still want to do everything you can to apply familiar strategies to the game, but above all you'll need to be flexible, stay patient, and keep working. Of course, the best thing to do with these games is avoid them if you don't have an idea of how to represent the information they contain. The good news is that, if you can come up with a good way of diagramming such a game on the spot, it sometimes turns out to be less difficult than it looks.

1. Pure Ordering Games

We come full circle in this chapter by returning to the very first task we examined in talking about games. In that initial example, we saw a type of clue that's found only in games with an ordering task: what we called a "range" clue, which lets us know broadly that one element comes either somewhere before or somewhere after another in the order, with no restriction on how close together or far apart they are in our diagram.

A pure ordering game is one whose clues are all—or nearly all—range clues. Often, a pure ordering game will mention all of the elements in at least one of its clues, creating a web of relationships among all of them, and a large number of deductions. The key on these games is to combine the information contained in all of the range clues in a single symbol, if possible. Take a look at the simplified example below:

Clues:
1) A is ranked higher than both B and C.
2) B is ranked higher than D.
3) E is ranked higher than C.
4) F is ranked higher than A.

Individual symbols:

1) A $\big\langle$ B / C

2) B — D

3) E — C

4) F — A

Combined symbol:

F — A $\big\langle$ B — D / C , E

Reading this symbol can take a little getting used to, but it contains a good deal more information than the individual symbols by themselves do. The idea is that elements along the same branch must appear in a set order; in this case, we must have F...A...B...D in any legal arrangement, and we must also have F...A...C, but we don't know anything about the positions of B and D relative to the position of C. We can also use this clue to draw conclusions that we could never have drawn from the separate symbols. As long as these are the only 6 elements in the game, we can tell that the highest-ranked element must be either E or F; the lowest-ranked must be C or D; B can be at highest third and at lowest fifth; A can be at highest second and at lowest third. This is only a small selection of the information our combined symbol contains.

Try out the pure ordering game in the next drill. Don't be too thrown off by the fact that it takes two combined symbols to represent all the information you need in this one. Answers can be found in Chapter 20.

DRILL #1

Questions 1–6

A food critic rates six restaurants—K, Q, R, S, T, and V. Each restaurant receives a whole number of spoons from 1 to 6, with a 6-spoon rating being the highest and a 1-spoon rating being the lowest. No two restaurants receive the same rating. The food critic's ratings are made in accordance with the following conditions:

S either receives more spoons than Q receives, or it receives more spoons than V receives, but not both.
Both R and T receive more spoons than Q receives.
V receives more spoons than K receives.

1. Which of the following could be a complete and accurate list of the restaurants and the number of spoons they receive?

   (A) 1: K; 2: Q; 3: V; 4: S; 5: T; 6: R
   (B) 1: K; 2: S; 3: Q; 4: V; 5: R; 6: T
   (C) 1: Q; 2: S; 3: R; 4: V; 5: K; 6: T
   (D) 1: Q; 2: S; 3: T; 4: K; 5: R; 6: V
   (E) 1: T; 2: Q; 3: S; 4: K; 5: R; 6: V

2. If V receives a 4-spoon rating, then which one of the following must be true?

   (A) K receives more spoons than Q receives.
   (B) K receives more spoons than S receives.
   (C) Q receives more spoons than S receives.
   (D) R receives more spoons than T receives.
   (E) T receives more spoons than S receives.

3. If K receives more spoons than R receives, then which one of the following could be true?

   (A) K receives a 2-spoon rating.
   (B) K receives a 6-spoon rating.
   (C) R receives a 5-spoon rating.
   (D) S receives a 2-spoon rating.
   (E) V receives a 4-spoon rating.

4. Which one of the following could be true?

   (A) Q receives a 3-spoon rating.
   (B) R receives a 1-spoon rating.
   (C) S receives a 6-spoon rating.
   (D) V receives a 2-spoon rating.
   (E) V receives a 3-spoon rating.

5. If Q receives more spoons than K receives, then each of the following could be true EXCEPT:

   (A) Q receives a 2-spoon rating.
   (B) R receives a 3-spoon rating.
   (C) S receives a 2-spoon rating.
   (D) T receives a 6-spoon rating.
   (E) V receives a 2-spoon rating.

6. If V does not receive more spoons than Q receives, then each of the following must be true EXCEPT:

   (A) K receives a 1-spoon rating.
   (B) Q receives a 4-spoon rating.
   (C) R receives a 5-spoon rating.
   (D) S receives a 3-spoon rating.
   (E) V receives a 2-spoon rating.

2. Switch-and-Mutate Games

In the most general sense, all of the games we've seen so far have the same major ingredients and work in fundamentally the same way: We have a fixed diagram and mobile elements, and the clues tell us how to put the elements into the diagram. What makes switch-and-mutate games unique is that they include not only a fixed diagram and mobile elements, but they also include an initial arrangement of the elements in the diagram. The clues on a switch-and-mutate game, rather than limiting the ways the elements may be placed into the diagram, instead will provide possible ways of either rearranging the elements within the diagram or else changing the elements somehow.

Like all games, switch-and-mutate games can come in a broad range of difficulties. They can be time consuming and require a great deal of legwork, but because they work so differently from other games, some people find that they prefer these games to more ordinary games of comparable difficulty; conversely, some who enjoy making lots of deductions on difficult games find these tedious and slow by comparison, and would rather avoid them. Whichever category you find yourself in, once you've adjusted to the slightly different way this kind of game works, you should find that the methods we've used in earlier games are all applicable to switch-and-mutate games as well.

Take a shot at the following drill. Answers can be found in Chapter 20.

DRILL #2

A puzzle is made up of five colored chips and five buttons. Initially, chip 1 is blue, chip 2 is green, chip 3 is purple, chip 4 is red, and chip 5 is yellow. The buttons, when pressed, cause some chips in the puzzle to change color. The buttons function according to the following:

No button can be pressed more than once in a sequence.
Button 1 causes chip 1 to exchange colors with chip 2.
Button 2 causes chip 1 to exchange colors with chip 3.
Button 3 causes chip 2 to exchange colors with chip 4.
Button 4 causes chip 3 to exchange colors with chip 5.
Button 5 causes chip 4 to exchange colors with chip 5.

1. Which of the following could be the colors of the chips after a sequence in which three buttons are pressed?

    (A) chip 1: green; chip 2: red; chip 3: yellow;
         chip 4: blue; chip 5: purple
    (B) chip 1: purple; chip 2: green; chip 3: yellow;
         chip 4: red; chip 5: blue
    (C) chip 1: red; chip 2: blue; chip 3: purple;
         chip 4: green; chip 5: yellow
    (D) chip 1: yellow; chip 2: blue; chip 3: green; chip
         4: purple; chip 5: red
    (E) chip 1: yellow; chip 2: red; chip 3: green;
         chip 4: blue; chip 5: purple

2. If, after a sequence in which two buttons are pressed, chip 3 is green, then which one of the following must also be true of the puzzle at that time?

    (A) Chip 1 is blue.
    (B) Chip 2 is red.
    (C) Chip 2 is purple.
    (D) Chip 4 is yellow.
    (E) Chip 5 is yellow.

3. If, after a sequence in which four buttons are pressed, chip 1 is purple, chip 2 is yellow, chip 3 is green, chip 4 is blue, and chip 5 is red, then which of the following could have been the colors of the chips after the first two buttons of the sequence were pressed?

    (A) chip 1: blue; chip 2: purple; chip 3: green; chip
         4: yellow; chip 5: red
    (B) chip 1: green; chip 2: blue; chip 3: purple; chip
         4: yellow; chip 5: red
    (C) chip 1: purple; chip 2: red; chip 3: green;
         chip 4: blue; chip 5: yellow
    (D) chip 1: purple; chip 2: yellow; chip 3: red; chip
         4: green; chip 5: blue
    (E) chip 1: yellow; chip 2: purple; chip 3: green;
         chip 4: red; chip 5: blue

4. What is the fewest number of buttons that could be pressed to result in a configuration of the puzzle in which chip 1 is red, chip 3 is blue, and chip 5 is purple?

    (A) 1
    (B) 2
    (C) 3
    (D) 4
    (E) 5

5. For which one of the following sequences of three buttons, listed in the order in which they are pressed, does there exist at least one other sequence of three buttons that results in the same configuration of the puzzle?

    (A) button 1, button 3, button 5
    (B) button 2, button 5, button 4
    (C) button 3, button 1, button 2
    (D) button 4, button 5, button 3
    (E) button 5, button 4, button 2

6. Suppose the condition preventing the same button from being pressed twice in a sequence is removed, but all the other conditions remain in effect. Under these new conditions, if button 1 breaks, then which of the following sequences of buttons could be used to duplicate the effect of pressing button 1?

    (A) button 3, button 5, button 4, button 2, button 4,
         button 5, button 3
    (B) button 4, button 5, button 2, button 3, button 2,
         button 5, button 4
    (C) button 4, button 5, button 3, button 2, button 3,
         button 5, button 4
    (D) button 5, button 4, button 2, button 3, button 2,
         button 3, button 5
    (E) button 5, button 4, button 2, button 3, button 2,
         button 4, button 5

3. Mapping Games

Like switch-and-mutate games, mapping games involve a slightly different way of treating your elements and the diagram. Mapping games most often involve a set of named locations (cities, houses, company departments), and your task is to work with the connections between them. There are several different variants on this type of game, but all of them depend upon assembling your diagram. Start by laying out the locations in a rough circle, and use lines to indicate the connections. You can use this line notation to symbolize any clues, if that's necessary, but there are some map games where the clues simply list all the connections, and then all you'll have to do for the questions is use the map you've assembled.

Sometimes the connections in a mapping game are all completely specified; sometimes there's some variability allowed in the map you'll use. Sometimes the connections themselves are named (train lines, highway numbers). Sometimes the questions will ask you to move along the connections in the diagram (a commuter traveling from point A to point B). Other times, the questions are only concerned with which locations are connected to which. Whatever variation of a mapping game you encounter—if by some remote chance you should encounter one—the key idea is to make your map from the clues and stick with it. If necessary, you may have to draw a new map for some of the questions, but most often a single diagram is all you'll need to zip through the questions.

Try the following mapping game. Answers can be found in Chapter 20.

DRILL #3

Questions 1–6

In a mountainous area, a communications company has five signal towers numbered T-1 through T-5. Each tower can send signals to one or more other towers and can receive signals from one or more other towers, but no tower can both send signals to and receive signals from the same tower. The signal towers are subject to the following conditions:

    T-3 can send signals to exactly three other towers.
    T-1 can send signals to exactly one other tower and can receive signals from exactly one other tower.
    T-4 can send signals to T-5 and receive signals from T-2.
    T-5 cannot receive signals from or send signals to T-2.

1. Which one of the following must be true?

    (A) T-1 can send signals to T-3.
    (B) T-2 can send signals to T-3.
    (C) T-3 can send signals to T-1.
    (D) T-3 can send signals to T-4.
    (E) T-5 can send signals to T-1.

2. If T-3 can send signals to T-5, then at least how many other towers are required to transmit a signal from T-1 to T-4?

    (A) 0
    (B) 1
    (C) 2
    (D) 3
    (E) 4

3. Which of the following is a complete and accurate list of the towers required to transmit a signal from T-4 to T-2?

    (A) T-5
    (B) T-1, T-3
    (C) T-1, T-5
    (D) T-3, T-5
    (E) T-1, T-3, T-5

4. Which one of the following could be true?

    (A) T-1 can receive signals from T-2.
    (B) T-1 can receive signals from T-4.
    (C) T-2 can receive signals from T-1.
    (D) T-3 can receive signals from T-2.
    (E) T-5 can receive signals from T-2.

5. If T-1 can send signals to T-4, then which one of the following is a complete and accurate list of towers that could receive a signal from any tower to which T-3 can send a signal?

    (A) T-1, T-3
    (B) T-1, T-5
    (C) T-4, T-5
    (D) T-2, T-4, T-5
    (E) T-2, T-3, T-4, T-5

6. If a signal originating from T-1 is relayed by other towers and eventually returns to T-1, then at least how many towers, including T-1, must be involved in transmitting the signal?

    (A) 1
    (B) 2
    (C) 3
    (D) 4
    (E) 5

4. None of the Above

As was mentioned in the beginning in the chapter, these games require patience, resourcefulness, and calm under the timed conditions of the LSAT. They are exceptionally rare; in most cases when a game seems strange, a chart of the type we've seen in previous organizational arrangement games will serve to represent the information you need. But sometimes you'll encounter a game where your only real diagramming options are to make lists, draw pictures, or cope with the answers as best you can with only sketchy or partial representations of the information.

Try out the very unusual game on the next page, and remember: Keep working steadily, get the information in front of you on the page, and you should be able to work it out. Answers can be found in Chapter 20.

DRILL #4

<u>Questions 1–6</u>

Four colored flags, a poplar tree, and an ash tree are located in a square field whose edges run north-south and east-west. The colors of the four flags are black, orange, violet, and white. The ash tree is located in the center of the field, dividing it into quadrants I, II, III, and IV as follows: Points in quadrant I are both north and west of the ash tree; points in quadrant II are both north and east of the ash tree; points in quadrant III are both south and east of the ash tree; points in quadrant IV are both south and west of the ash tree. The location of the flags and trees are subject to the following conditions:

   The violet flag is located north of the orange flag and
      south of the black flag.
   The poplar tree is located north of the white flag and
      south of the ash tree.
   The white flag is located east of the violet flag and west
      of the ash tree.
   The poplar tree is located east of the black flag and west
      of the orange flag.
   The violet flag is located both north and west of the
      poplar tree.

1. Which one of the following must be true?

    (A) The poplar tree is located in quadrant III.
    (B) The black flag is located in quadrant I.
    (C) The orange flag is located in quadrant II.
    (D) The violet flag is located in quadrant I.
    (E) The white flag is located in quadrant IV.

2. If the black flag is located in quadrant III, then which one of the following must be true?

    (A) The poplar tree is located in quadrant III.
    (B) The poplar tree is located in quadrant IV.
    (C) The orange flag is located in quadrant II.
    (D) The orange flag is located in quadrant IV.
    (E) The violet flag is located in quadrant I.

3. Each of the following could be true EXCEPT:

    (A) The poplar tree is located to the north of the
         orange flag.
    (B) The violet flag is located to the north of the
         white flag.
    (C) The violet flag is located to the east of the
         orange flag.
    (D) The violet flag is located to the east of the
         black flag.
    (E) The white flag is located to the east of the
         poplar tree.

4. If the orange flag is located in quadrant I, then which of the following is a complete and accurate list of quadrants that cannot contain any of the four flags?

    (A) II
    (B) III
    (C) II, III
    (D) II, IV
    (E) III, IV

5. If quadrant II contains only the orange flag and does not contain the poplar tree, then which one of the following could be true?

    (A) Quadrant I contains exactly one flag and the
         poplar tree.
    (B) Quadrant III contains exactly one flag and does
         not contain the poplar tree.
    (C) Quadrant III contains exactly one flag and the
         poplar tree.
    (D) Quadrant IV contains exactly one flag and the
         poplar tree.
    (E) Quadrant IV contains exactly three flags and
         the poplar tree.

6. If each of the four quadrants contains exactly one flag, then which one of the following must be true?

    (A) The poplar tree is located in quadrant I.
    (B) The poplar tree is located in quadrant III.
    (C) The black flag is located in quadrant I.
    (D) The violet flag is located in quadrant IV.
    (E) The white flag is located to the north of the
         orange flag.

14

Practice Section 3:
Games

SECTION III

Time—35 minutes

24 Questions

<u>Directions:</u> Each group of questions in this section is based on a set of conditions. In answering some of the questions, it may be useful to draw a rough diagram. Choose the response that most accurately and completely answers each question and blacken the corresponding space on your answer sheet.

<u>Questions 1–5</u>

A florist is making two arrangements—1 and 2—that between them must include seven types of flowers—mallow, nasturtium, orchid, peony, saxifrage, trillium, and violet—with no type of flower included in both arrangements. No other type of flower will be included in either arrangement. The arrangements are subject to the following conditions:

Arrangement 1 includes at most five different types of flowers.

If an arrangement includes mallow, it must not include peony.

If an arrangement includes peony, it must not include saxifrage.

If an arrangement includes trillium, it must also include violet.

If arrangement 1 includes nasturtium, it must also include orchid.

1. Which one of the following could be a complete and accurate list of the types of flowers included in arrangement 2?

   (A) mallow, trillium, violet
   (B) mallow, nasturtium, orchid, peony
   (C) nasturtium, peony, trillium, violet
   (D) orchid, peony, trillium, violet
   (E) mallow, nasturtium, orchid, saxifrage, trillium

2. If arrangement 2 includes orchid, then which one of the following must be false?

   (A) Arrangement 1 does not include nasturtium.
   (B) Arrangement 1 does not include peony.
   (C) Arrangement 1 does not include saxifrage.
   (D) Arrangement 1 includes exactly two types of flowers.
   (E) Arrangement 1 includes exactly five types of flowers.

3. If arrangement 1 includes peony along with exactly three other types of flowers, then each of the following must be true EXCEPT:

   (A) Arrangement 1 includes nasturtium.
   (B) Arrangement 1 includes orchid.
   (C) Arrangement 1 includes violet.
   (D) Arrangement 2 includes mallow.
   (E) Arrangement 2 includes saxifrage.

4. Which of the following is the greatest number of other types of flowers that could be included in an arrangement that includes nasturtium?

   (A) two
   (B) three
   (C) four
   (D) five
   (E) six

5. If arrangement 1 includes as many types of flowers as possible, then it must include

   (A) mallow
   (B) nasturtium
   (C) peony
   (D) saxifrage
   (E) trillium

A coffee house offers five espresso-based drinks—E, F, G, J, and K—each of which is made with either a single, a double, or a triple shot of espresso, reflecting the number of espresso shots used to make the drink. Buzz the barrista makes each espresso-based drink once, one drink at a time. The five drinks together require a total of nine shots of espresso, and exactly one of them is made with a triple shot of espresso. The order in which Buzz makes the drinks is subject to the following conditions:

No two consecutive drinks are made with the same number of espresso shots.

Buzz makes G at some time before he makes K.

Buzz makes F either second or fourth.

Buzz makes exactly one drink between J and K, whether or not he makes J before he makes K, and that drink is made with a single shot of espresso.

Buzz makes E with a single shot of espresso.

6. Which of the following is a complete and accurate list of drinks, any one of which Buzz could make third?

(A) G, K
(B) J, K
(C) E, G, J
(D) E, J, K
(E) G, J, K

7. If Buzz makes the second drink with a triple shot of espresso, then which one of the following must be true?

(A) Buzz makes E first.
(B) Buzz makes F fourth.
(C) Buzz makes J third.
(D) Buzz makes the first drink with a single shot of espresso.
(E) Buzz makes the fourth drink with a double shot of espresso.

8. Which one of the following must be true?

(A) If Buzz makes E fifth, then he makes the fourth drink with a double shot of espresso.
(B) If Buzz makes F second, then he makes the fourth drink with a single shot of espresso.
(C) If Buzz makes G second, then he makes the third drink with a double shot of espresso.
(D) If Buzz makes J third, then he makes the fifth drink with a double shot of espresso.
(E) If Buzz makes J fifth, then he makes the first drink with a single shot of espresso.

9. If Buzz makes the fourth drink with a double shot of espresso, then each of the following must be true EXCEPT:

(A) Buzz makes E with a single shot of espresso.
(B) Buzz makes F with a double shot of espresso.
(C) Buzz makes G with a single shot of espresso.
(D) Buzz makes J with a double shot of espresso.
(E) Buzz makes K with a double shot of espresso.

10. Each of the following could be true EXCEPT:

(A) Buzz makes F with a triple shot of espresso.
(B) Buzz makes G with a double shot of espresso.
(C) Buzz makes G with a triple shot of espresso.
(D) Buzz makes J with a single shot of espresso.
(E) Buzz makes K with a double shot of espresso.

11. If Buzz makes as many drinks as possible between the first drink he makes with a double shot of espresso and the second drink he makes with a double shot of espresso, then which one of the following must be true?

(A) Buzz makes E before he makes J.
(B) Buzz makes F before he makes E.
(C) Buzz makes G before he makes E.
(D) Buzz makes J before he makes F.
(E) Buzz makes K before he makes E.

12. If instead of making the five drinks with a total of nine shots of espresso, Buzz makes them with a total of ten shots of espresso, but all the other initial conditions remain in effect, then which one of the following could be true?

(A) Buzz makes E second with a single shot of espresso.
(B) Buzz makes F second with a double shot of espresso.
(C) Buzz makes G fourth with a single shot of espresso.
(D) Buzz makes J third with a triple shot of espresso.
(E) Buzz makes K third with a double shot of espresso.

A computer network has exactly six users—Henman, Kurtz, Moritz, Ngo, Ortiz, and Ponson—each of whom has at least one of the four possible security permissions on the network—administrator, write, read, and guest. Any user with administrator permissions also has permission to read and write; any user with permission to write also has permission to read; no user with guest permissions has permission either to read or write. The assignment of security permissions to the network's users is subject to the following conditions:

Exactly two users have administrator permissions.

Moritz and Ponson do not both have permission to read.

Either Kurtz or else Ortiz has permission to read, but not both.

If Moritz has guest permissions, then Kurtz has permission to write but Henman does not.

If Ngo has guest permissions, then neither Moritz nor Ortiz has permission to write.

If Ponson has guest permissions, then Ngo does not have administrator permissions.

Kurtz has administrator permissions only if either Henman or Moritz also has administrator permissions.

13. Each of the following could be a complete and accurate list of the users with permission to read EXCEPT:

(A) Henman, Moritz, and Kurtz
(B) Henman, Kurtz, Moritz, and Ngo
(C) Henman, Kurtz, Ngo, and Ponson
(D) Henman, Moritz, Ngo, and Ortiz
(E) Henman, Ngo, Ortiz, and Ponson

14. If Ngo has permission to write, then what is the maximum number of users who could have guest permissions?

(A) 1
(B) 2
(C) 3
(D) 4
(E) 5

15. Which one of the following could be true?

(A) Henman has permission to write, and Ponson has permission to read.
(B) Moritz has guest permissions, and Kurtz has administrator permissions.
(C) Ngo has administrator permissions, and Moritz has permission to write.
(D) Ngo has administrator permissions, and Ponson has permission to write.
(E) Ortiz has permission to read, and Ponson has permission to write.

16. If Ortiz does not have guest permissions, then which one of the following must be true?

(A) Henman has guest permissions.
(B) Moritz does not have permission to write.
(C) Ngo has permission to read.
(D) Ortiz has administrator permissions.
(E) Ponson has permission to read.

17. If either Henman or Kurtz has guest permissions, but not both, then which one of the following must be false?

(A) Ngo has guest permissions.
(B) Moritz has guest permissions.
(C) Ortiz has guest permissions.
(D) Exactly three users have permission to write.
(E) Exactly four users have permission to read.

Questions 18–24

In a two-week exhibition of antiquities, a display case contains five figurines individually labeled 1, 2, 3, 4, and 5, which correspond to printed descriptions of each figurine. Two of the figurines are bone—C and D—and three of the figurines are ivory—J, K, and L. After the first week of the exhibition, an error in the labeling of the figurines is discovered, and the labels of one bone figurine and one ivory figurine are switched, but all the other labels remain in place. The labeling of the figurines is consistent with the following:

During each week of the exhibition, two of the ivory figurines have consecutively numbered labels, but at no time do all three of the ivory figurines have consecutively numbered labels.

The bone figurines do not have consecutively numbered labels during either week of the exhibition.

During both weeks of the exhibition, the label for L has a lower number than the label for K.

During neither week of the exhibition is L labeled 1.

During at least the first week of the exhibition, D is labeled 3.

18. Which one of the following could be the list of labels assigned to the figurines during the second week of the exhibition?

   (A) C: 1; D: 3; J: 5; K: 2; L: 4
   (B) C: 1; D: 3; J: 5; K: 4; L: 2
   (C) C: 2; D: 4; J: 1; K: 5; L: 3
   (D) C: 4; D: 1; J: 3; K: 5; L: 2
   (E) C: 4; D: 3; J: 1; K: 5; L: 2

19. If during the second week of the exhibition D is labeled 2, then which one of the following must also be true during that week?

   (A) C and J have consecutively numbered labels.
   (B) K and L have consecutively numbered labels.
   (C) J and L have consecutively numbered labels.
   (D) A bone figurine is labeled 4.
   (E) An ivory figurine is labeled 5.

20. Which one of the following could be true?

   (A) During the first week of the exhibition, C is labeled 4.
   (B) During the first week of the exhibition, K is labeled 2.
   (C) During the second week of the exhibition, L is labeled 5.
   (D) During the first week of the exhibition, a bone figurine is labeled 2.
   (E) During the second week of the exhibition, a bone figurine is labeled 4.

21. Which one of the following is a complete and accurate list of the possible labels for J during the second week of the exhibition?

   (A) 1, 5
   (B) 1, 2, 5
   (C) 1, 2, 3, 5
   (D) 1, 3, 4, 5
   (E) 1, 2, 3, 4, 5

22. If during the second week C is labeled 1, then in how many different ways could labels be assigned to the five figurines during that week?

   (A) two
   (B) three
   (C) four
   (D) five
   (E) six

23. If an ivory figurine is labeled 5 during the first week of the exhibition but not during the second week of the exhibition, then each of the following must be true EXCEPT:

   (A) During the first week of the exhibition, K is labeled 4.
   (B) During the first week of the exhibition, L is labeled 2.
   (C) During the second week of the exhibition, C is labeled 1.
   (D) During the second week of the exhibition, D is labeled 3.
   (E) During the second week of the exhibition, J is labeled 1.

24. Which one of the following must be false?

   (A) During the second week of the exhibition, the number of D's label is one greater than the number of J's label.
   (B) During the second week of the exhibition, the number of D's label is one greater than the number of L's label.
   (C) During the second week of the exhibition, the number of J's label is one greater than the number of C's label.
   (D) During the second week of the exhibition, the number of K's label is one greater than the number of C's label.
   (E) During the second week of the exhibition, the number of L's label is one greater than the number of J's label.

ANSWER KEY TO PRACTICE SECTION 3: GAMES

For full answers and explanations, turn to Chapter 21.

1. C
2. E
3. A
4. D
5. E
6. B
7. D
8. B
9. E
10. D
11. C
12. E
13. E
14. C
15. D
16. C
17. A
18. B
19. B
20. E
21. C
22. C
23. C
24. D

15

Practice Section 4: Games

Directions: Each group of questions in this section is based on a set of conditions. In answering some of the questions, it may be useful to draw a rough diagram. Choose the response that most accurately and completely answers each question and blacken the corresponding space on your answer sheet.

Questions 1–5

Exactly five comedians—Harris, Levin, Moore, Pacheco, and Tan—perform at a comedy club one Saturday night. Each comedian performs exactly once, and no two comedians perform at the same time. The order in which the comedians perform is subject to the following conditions:

Levin is not the first comedian to perform.
Pachecho performs immediately after Harris performs.
If Moore performs at some time before Harris performs, then Harris performs at some time before Tan performs.
If Levin performs at some time before Tan performs, then Levin also performs at some time before Pacheco performs.

1. Which one of the following must be false?

   (A) Harris is the fourth comedian to perform.
   (B) Levin is the fifth comedian to perform.
   (C) Moore is the third comedian to perform.
   (D) Pacheco is the second comedian to perform.
   (E) Tan is the fifth comedian to perform.

2. Which one of the following could be true?

   (A) Levin performs immediately after Pacheco and immediately before Tan.
   (B) Levin performs immediately after Tan and immediately before Moore.
   (C) Moore performs immediately after Levin and immediately before Tan.
   (D) Moore performs immediately after Tan and immediately before Harris.
   (E) Tan performs immediately after Levin and immediately before Moore.

3. Which one of the following, if known, would allow the order in which the comedians perform to be completely determined?

   (A) Harris is the third comedian to perform.
   (B) Levin is the fourth comedian to perform.
   (C) Moore is the third comedian to perform.
   (D) Pacheco is the third comedian to perform.
   (E) Tan is the fourth comedian to perform.

4. Each of the following must be true EXCEPT:

   (A) Levin is not the third comedian to perform.
   (B) Moore is not the first comedian to perform.
   (C) Moore is not the second comedian to perform.
   (D) Pacheco is not the fifth comedian to perform.
   (E) Tan is not the second comedian to perform.

5. If the condition requiring Harris to perform immediately before Pacheco is replaced by a condition requiring as many comedians as possible to perform after Levin and before Harris, but if all the other original conditions remain in effect, then which one of the following must be true?

   (A) Harris is the fifth comedian to perform.
   (B) Levin is the third comedian to perform.
   (C) Moore is the first comedian to perform.
   (D) Pacheco is the third comedian to perform.
   (E) Tan is the fifth comedian to perform.

Questions 6–11

During the three-month period of April, May, and June, five different projects—V, W, X, Y, and Z—will each be worked on by three departments in a corporation—Development, Production, and Sales. Each of the five projects will be worked on by exactly one of the departments during each month, and by the end of the three-month period, each project will have been worked on by each of the three departments. The projects will be worked on in accordance with the following conditions:

During each month of the three-month period, at least one of the five projects is worked on by each of the three departments.

During each month of the three-month period, no department works on project V unless that same department also works on project Z during the same month.

In May and June, project V is worked on by the department that worked on project Y during the previous month.

In the month of May the Production department works on exactly three projects.

6. Which one of the following could be the order in which projects Y and Z are worked on by the three departments?

(A) Y: Production, Development, Sales
Z: Development, Production, Sales
(B) Y: Production, Development, Sales
Z: Sales, Production, Development
(C) Y: Production, Sales, Development
Z: Production, Development, Sales
(D) Y: Sales, Development, Production
Z: Development, Production, Sales
(E) Y: Sales, Development, Production
Z: Production, Sales, Development

7. If during the month of June the Development department works on project Y and exactly one other project, then which one of the following must be true?

(A) The Development department works on project X in May.
(B) The Production department works on project W in June.
(C) The Production department works on project Y in May.
(D) The Sales department works on project V in May.
(E) The Sales department works on project X in April.

8. Which one of the following must be true?

(A) The Development department works on project W and project X in different months.
(B) The Development department works on project W and project Z in different months.
(C) The Production department works on project V and project X in different months.
(D) The Production department works on project W and project X in different months.
(E) The Sales department works on project W and project Y in different months.

9. If the Development department works on project W before it works on project Y but after it works on project X, then each of the following must be true EXCEPT:

(A) V is worked on by the Production department before it is worked on by the Sales department.
(B) W is worked on by the Sales department before it is worked on by the Development department.
(C) X is worked on by the Development department before it is worked on by the Sales department.
(D) Y is worked on by the Production department before it is worked on by the Sales department.
(E) Z is worked on by the Sales department before it is worked on by the Production department.

10. Which one of the following could be true?

(A) The Development department works on exactly two projects in May.
(B) The Development department works on exactly three projects in June.
(C) The Production department works on exactly two projects in April.
(D) The Production department works on exactly two projects in June.
(E) The Sales department works on exactly two projects in May.

11. If the Sales department does not work on either project W or project Z during the month of June, then in how many different orders could the three departments work on project X?

(A) two
(B) three
(C) four
(D) five
(E) six

Questions 12–17

In a soccer league, each team is identified by a square banner that includes exactly four different colors. There are six available colors: green, navy, red, teal, white, and yellow. Each team's banner is divided into four panels of equal size: the upper-left, upper-right, lower-left, and lower-right. Each panel is exactly one color. The composition of the teams' banners is subject to the following conditions:

No team's banner includes both green and red.

If a team's banner includes green, it must also include white.

If a team's banner includes yellow, it must also include navy, with the yellow panel located directly above the navy panel.

If a team's banner includes teal, it must also include navy, with the teal panel located in the upper-left and the navy panel located in the lower-right.

Neither a green panel nor a red panel may be located to the left or right of a yellow panel.

Neither a green panel nor a red panel may be located to the left or right of a teal panel.

12. Which one of the following could be a complete and accurate description of the panel colors in a team's banner?

    (A) upper-left: teal; upper-right: red; lower-left: white; lower-right: navy
    (B) upper-left: teal; upper-right: white; lower-left: green; lower-right: navy
    (C) upper-left: teal; upper-right: white; lower-left: navy; lower-right: red
    (D) upper-left: teal; upper-right: yellow; lower-left: green; lower-right: navy
    (E) upper-left: yellow; upper-right: white; lower-left: green; lower-right: navy

13. If a team's banner does not include a white panel in either the upper-left or the upper-right, then which one of the following must be true?

    (A) The upper-left panel of the team's banner is yellow.
    (B) The upper-right panel of the team's banner is green.
    (C) The lower-left panel of the team's banner is red.
    (D) The lower-left panel of the team's banner is white.
    (E) The lower-right panel of the team's banner is navy.

14. Which one of the following could be true of a team's banner?

    (A) It includes neither green nor navy.
    (B) It includes neither navy nor teal.
    (C) It includes neither red nor teal.
    (D) It includes neither teal nor yellow.
    (E) It includes neither white nor yellow.

15. If a team's banner does not include yellow, then which one of the following must also be true of that team's banner?

    (A) It includes a green panel above a navy panel.
    (B) It includes a teal panel above a green panel.
    (C) It includes a teal panel above a red panel.
    (D) It includes a white panel above a green panel.
    (E) It includes a white panel above a navy panel.

16. If no two teams in the soccer league have exactly the same banner, then at most how many teams may the league include?

    (A) six
    (B) seven
    (C) eight
    (D) nine
    (E) ten

17. Which one of the following must be true of a team's banner?

    (A) It includes navy.
    (B) It includes teal.
    (C) It includes white.
    (D) It includes either green or else red.
    (E) It includes either green or else yellow.

Questions 18–24

Six private investigators—Reed, Thompson, Voss, Williams, Young, and Zeff—are assigned to three cases being investigated by their firm. Two of the investigators are assigned to the Madsen case, three to the Phalanges case, and three to the Quo case. Each of the six investigators is assigned to at least one of the three cases, in accordance with the following conditions:

Reed is not assigned to the same case as Voss, and neither Reed nor Voss is assigned to the same case as Young.

If Voss is assigned to the Phalanges case, then Williams is assigned to the Madsen case.

Reed is not assigned to a case unless Thompson is also assigned to that case.

Thompson and Williams are assigned to the same number of cases.

18. If Thompson is assigned only to the Phalanges case, then which one of the following must be true?

   (A) Williams is assigned to the Phalanges case.
   (B) Young is assigned to the Madsen case.
   (C) Voss is assigned to the Phalanges case.
   (D) Voss is assigned to the Quo case.
   (E) Zeff is assigned to the Madsen case.

19. If Zeff is not assigned to the same case as Thompson and also is not assigned to the same case as Williams, then which one of the following could be true?

   (A) Reed is assigned to the Madsen case.
   (B) Voss is assigned to the Phalanges case.
   (C) Williams is assigned to the Madsen case.
   (D) Young is assigned to the Quo case.
   (E) Zeff is assigned to the Quo case.

20. If Reed is assigned to the Madsen case, then which one of the following must be true?

   (A) Thompson is assigned only to the Madsen case.
   (B) Thompson is assigned to both the Madsen case and the Phalanges case.
   (C) Williams is assigned to both the Phalanges case and the Quo case.
   (D) Young is assigned only to the Quo case.
   (E) Zeff is assigned to both the Phalanges case and the Quo case.

21. If Williams is assigned to the Madsen case, then each of the following could be a complete and accurate list of the investigators assigned to the Quo case EXCEPT:

   (A) Reed, Thompson, Williams
   (B) Thompson, Young, Zeff
   (C) Thompson, Voss, Williams
   (D) Thompson, Voss, Zeff
   (E) Williams, Young, Zeff

22. If Voss is assigned to the Phalanges case, then which one of the following must be true?

   (A) Thompson is assigned to the Phalanges case.
   (B) Williams is assigned to the Phalanges case.
   (C) Williams is assigned to the Quo case.
   (D) Young is assigned to the Quo case.
   (E) Zeff is assigned to the Phalanges case.

23. If Zeff is assigned to as many cases as possible, then each of the following could be true EXCEPT:

   (A) Thompson and Williams are assigned to the same case.
   (B) Thompson and Zeff are assigned to the same case.
   (C) Voss and Williams are assigned to the same case.
   (D) Voss and Zeff are assigned to the same case.
   (E) Williams and Young are assigned to the same case.

24. Each of the following could be true EXCEPT:

   (A) Thompson is assigned to exactly two cases.
   (B) Williams is assigned to exactly one case.
   (C) Williams is assigned to exactly two cases.
   (D) Zeff is assigned to exactly two cases.
   (E) Zeff is assigned to exactly three cases.

ANSWER KEY TO PRACTICE SECTION 4: GAMES

For full answers and explanations, turn to Chapter 21.

1. A
2. B
3. C
4. B
5. D
6. B
7. E
8. D
9. E
10. B
11. B
12. B
13. E
14. C
15. E
16. C
17. A
18. E
19. D
20. C
21. E
22. A
23. A
24. D

PART IV

Reading Comprehension

16
Reading Comprehension
Strategy

WHAT DOES READING COMPREHENSION TEST?

The scored Reading Comprehension ("RC") section of the LSAT consists of 26 to 28 questions associated with four separate passages, giving you an average of a little less than nine minutes per passage. There will be one passage from each of four general subject areas: humanities (art, literature, film, philosophy); social sciences (history, political science, economics, anthropology, psychology); natural sciences (biology, ecology, astronomy, geology, physics, chemistry); and law. Although there are no 100-percent reliable indicators of a passage's difficulty, your familiarity with the subject matter or interest in the area from which it is drawn may have some impact on how easy it is for you to read and understand passage material. Vocabulary, use of jargon or difficult language, and organization are all factors that influence how difficult a passage will be for you. If you can quickly identify one passage as being particularly difficult, it is wise to leave that passage for last, or even skip it altogether. Many test takers will be able to complete the RC section in the time allotted, but many will not. Accuracy is of course important on this section, but it is equally important not to get bogged down in the passage, or to agonize over difficult answer choices.

HOW TO TACKLE RC QUESTIONS

It is important to understand where the passages on RC sections come from, and under what basic assumptions the questions and answer choices are written. RC passages on the LSAT are excerpted from longer published works, but they are edited in such a way that no specialized knowledge is required in order to understand the passage and answer the questions correctly. Usually, RC passages are constructed to present a single main point or main idea that the author wishes to convey. However, the editing of the passage may make this main idea difficult to discern; RC passages often include a great number of details that are not particularly important to discerning the main point of the passage.

RC questions are based entirely on the information presented in the passage. Outside knowledge of the passage topic, in those rare instances when you have it, may actually mislead you if you encounter answer choices that are factually correct but not supported by the passage. RC is fundamentally a section that tests your ability to develop accurate paraphrases of text. You should always try to put passage material, questions, and answer choices in your own words.

On every passage, you should follow the same four-step process:

1. Work the Passage

2. Evaluate the Question Task

3. Apply the Strategy

4. Use POE

1. Work the Passage

The central goal of working the passage is to determine the passage topic, the opinion on that topic that the author wishes to convey (the main point), and a rough notion of how the passage is organized. Many passages are intentionally constructed to make finding the author's main point difficult. Often it is presented in a single sentence somewhere near the beginning or end of the passage, with many details and much factual information surrounding it. Keep in mind that LSAT RC is an open-book test: You'll always be able to return to the passage to obtain more information about particular details. Some respond to the time pressure of the LSAT by thinking that it is a waste of time to return to the passage, and so spend more time reading the passage initially; this course is exactly the wrong one to take. Instead, save time by spending less on an initial reading of the passage, so that you'll have more time to spend working the questions and returning to the passage to find support for the answer you choose.

Some test takers prefer to begin working the passage by skimming the questions quickly. If you do this, look only at the questions, not the answer choices, and don't try to "memorize" the questions as you see them. Instead, look for words or phrases that occur in one or more of the questions. The point of previewing the questions is to give you a provisional notion of the passage's topic, and to help you focus your attention as you read. You must not spend an excessive amount of time previewing the questions, if you elect to do it at all.

When you read the passage, do so actively. You must always evaluate the importance of what you read, and look for the large features while not getting caught up in small things. It may be better to approach what you need to do here as skimming rather than reading. Go through the passage with pencil in hand, picking out important items of big-picture information. Words that indicate value judgments should be marked, and you should always mark the place in the passage, if any, where the author directly expresses his or her main point. It is also helpful to mark structure words: turns in a passage's line of reasoning are often indicated by words such as *however, nevertheless,* or *yet;* words that introduce separate items in a list may help you discern the overall organization of the passage. If you've previewed the questions, you may find places where crucial source material is located, and since you know you'll be returning there, it may be useful to mark these places in the margin.

Above all, do not spend more time than is needed to get a general overview of the passage. When you're done working the passage, you should be able to come up with a simple summary of the content of each paragraph, and an overall statement of the author's opinion. Reading more closely than is needed to get this information is, simply put, a waste of precious time; resist the temptation to read these passages the way you would a textbook.

2. Evaluate the Question Task

There are a wide variety of possible question styles you may encounter, but all of them fall in one of three broad categories, and knowing what kind of question you're answering can help you simplify the approach you take to it.

Specific Questions

A specific question may point you to a particular spot in the passage; it may, alternatively, simply indicate that you'll need to find the one answer choice that is supported by passage material, or the one that isn't. The language of specific questions can differ widely; they may use the word *infer,* or ask you to describe the purpose or role of a particular statement in the passage, but don't be fooled. Your project on these is to find specific support for your answer in the passage without the need for extensive explanation or reasoning.

There are two main ways a question stem can point you to a part of the passage. The clearest way is for a question to use line numbers, since the passages are laid out with line numbers in the left margin. Alternatively, a question stem may include a word or phrase that is used at one particular place in the passage. Other specific questions may simply ask you to identify the statement that is or is not included in the passage. Whichever style of specific question you face, you'll always need to return to the passage at least once in deciding on your answer.

General Questions

A general question asks you to consider the overall point, purpose, or organization of the passage. Again, there are several varieties of these, and each may be worded in various ways, but what these questions have in common is that you should be able to answer them, or at least get very close, on the basis of your initial reading. You may prefer to work these questions after you've worked at least a few specific questions, especially if you've skimmed the passage heavily on your initial pass through it.

A main point question will ask you to identify the author's thesis in the passage. A primary purpose question will ask you to identify the best description of what the author does. A tone or author's attitude question may direct you to a particular paragraph in the passage or an issue the passage addresses, but the main consideration in these questions is what the author's overall point is. Similarly, a question may ask you to describe the purpose or function of one paragraph, but your paragraph-by-paragraph summary of the passage should be all you need to answer these questions. Finally, one of the more challenging types of general questions may ask you to identify the overall structure of the entire passage; your paragraph-by-paragraph summary should help a great deal with these as well.

Complex Questions

Most often, these questions involve reasoning of some sort, and often are phrased in ways that will remind you of args questions. They may ask you to weaken or strengthen a statement in the passage, identify an assumption, pick a principle underlying a statement in the passage, or choose a situation or example that is analogous to one mentioned in the passage.

Like specific questions, complex questions will most often point you to a single place in the passage, and although you'll need to do a little more on these to get ready to answer the question, the first step here will always be to note what clues the question gives you about which specific portion of the passage is important.

3. Apply the Strategy

You will always want to have an idea of what you're looking for when you go to the answer choices, preferably in simple, clear terms. Where you'll need to go to concoct this answer and what precise form it should take depends somewhat on the type of question you're facing.

Specific Questions

In cases when the question points you to a specific place in the passage, you'll need to go back and read the sentences around that place. Stick relatively close to the cited text, not going much more than five lines above or below the citation; you should also try not to go outside the paragraph containing the cited text. Paraphrase the passage material relevant to the question in your own words before moving to the answer choices.

If the question doesn't give you a place to start, but instead only tells you to look for the statement that's consistent with passage text, you'll need to go through the process outlined above with each answer choice, so you won't be able to predict the correct answer nearly as well.

General Questions

The source material for these questions will be your overall summary of the author's perspective and your paragraph-by-paragraph summary of the passage's contents. Using this information, do the best you can to answer the question yourself, always paraphrasing in terms that are as simple as possible.

Complex Questions

You'll need to begin working these in the same way you work specific questions; most of these will depend upon specific statements made in the passage. It is crucial that you first understand what statement you are supposed to weaken or strengthen on a question of this type; on an analogy question, you'll need to understand what the purpose of the cited example or situation is in the passage. Try to resist the temptation to work these questions the same way you would an args question of its related type; there is no need to focus specifically on shifts in language or any aspect of formal logic in answering RC questions of this sort. A solid notion of the relevant passage content should give you the starting point you need for evaluating the answer choices.

4. Use POE

The most important thing to understand about answer choices on the RC section is that they will hardly ever be what you would consider perfect. Answering the question on your own is a key first step to being able to recognize the right answer, but there are many cases in which the answer you pick will be one you don't particularly like. Don't be too demanding; the main thing you want to ask yourself about an answer choice is whether it basically gets the job done. At the same time, don't pick answers that require extensive or complicated justifications; right answers are most often quite directly related to passage text, and shouldn't involve much reasoning. Finally, if you have two or three answer choices remaining after a first pass, as you often will, slow down and look for differences. The basis on which you make your decision will be different on different questions, but you should always look for a rationale for why one of the remaining choices is best, or why the ones you aren't picking are worse.

There are a few specific POE methods that apply to each of the question tasks individually, and which you should always keep in mind when you're working with the answer choices.

Specific Questions

The most important consideration here is to look for choices that basically say the same thing as the passage does in some area near the place you've gone back to. Eliminate choices that contradict the passage or go beyond passage material. Unless a question asks you to think from some other point of view, always prefer answer choices that agree as closely as possible with the author's main point. Don't go outside the immediate area of the cited text to justify your answer choice unless you have no other option. Make sure the language of the choice you pick isn't stronger than the passage's statement is, and avoid choices that are excessively emotional. When you're down to two, look for differences in emphasis; two choices that seem very similar will usually highlight different aspects of the cited texts, and one of them will be a better match with the passage material than the other.

General Questions

Always stay within the scope of the passage: Answer choices that go beyond the specific territory covered by the passage can be tempting but are almost always wrong. Likewise, don't be tempted by answer choices that are too specific, or overemphasize one part of the passage's overall argument. Look for particular words or phrases that don't really resemble anything in the passage, or ones that take a point of view that isn't exactly the author's.

Complex Questions

The most important thing here is to look for an answer choice's impact on or resemblance to passage material. The more direct the impact is, and the closer the resemblance is, the better. Often more than one answer choice will seem to do the job; develop a checklist of everything you want your answer choice to do, based on the passage material, if more than one looks like it has a chance.

17

Just the Facts

WHAT MAKES A PASSAGE DIFFICULT?

The question of what determines the difficulty of a reading comprehension passage can be a complicated one. Clearly, there are two primary areas to look at.

THE PASSAGE

Easier passages concern less intimidating topics, use approachable language, and indicate fairly clearly what the author's opinion is. Often, better passages include multiple paragraphs that help indicate a clear organizational principle, making the author's thesis easier to identify. Individual reactions to passages may vary, however: Even though no specialized knowledge is required for the reading comprehension section, a passage about a familiar topic may be easier for you to read.

THE QUESTIONS

It's impossible to be sure exactly how difficult the questions will be until you get into them. However, a passage that includes several complex questions with long, complicated answers is more likely to be difficult for you, no matter how friendly the passage itself is.

In this chapter, we'll deal with passages whose particular attributes tend to make them easier. This isn't to say that these passages are simple, but they have the advantage of using relatively accessible language and, most importantly, having main points that are relatively easy to identify because they use straightforward methods they use to convey the points.

1. Journalistic Passages

Perhaps as many as 25 percent of reading comprehension passages do not convey any particular opinion of the author's. These "journalistic" passages are primarily concerned with describing a topic rather than stating a position with regard to the topic. Not all journalistic passages are easy, as we'll see in the next chapter, but they have the advantage of not requiring you to adhere to some particular perspective when you answer the questions. As long as you stick to the factual material presented in the passage, you should be fine.

In the drill on the next page, try to keep to the facts. Answers can be found in Chapter 20.

DRILL #1

Among the many enduring mysteries of mathematics, none has attracted more attention than Pierre Fermat's deceptively simple Last theorem.
(5) The idea springs from the Pythagorean theorem, a commonplace of geometry involving right triangles and the equation $x^2 + y^2 = z^2$. There are many sets of integer— that is, whole number— solutions x, y, and z that satisfy the equation. Fermat's Last theorem deals with the related equations $x^n + y^n = z^n$, where n
(10) is greater than 2. Fermat's famous claim, made in a marginal note dating to 1630, is that there are no all-integer solutions to any of these equations; in the same marginal note, Fermat claimed to have discovered a "truly remarkable proof" of this fact.

(15) Nowhere in Fermat's writings has this proof been found, and it seems all but impossible that it was correct. Fermat was not a mathematician by profession, but a lawyer, and published almost none of his work. His usual practice when he made a
(20) discovery was to pose challenge problems to fellow mathematicians, and the only problems Fermat posed in relation to his theorem concerned the cases $n = 3$ and $n = 4$, for which he may have found proofs. It seems likely that a complete proof he believed to be
(25) correct at the time he made his marginal note was found, upon further examination, not to be.

Fermat may have been the first to devise an incorrect proof of his theorem, but he was certainly not the last. The great mathematician Euler, in 1753,
(30) claimed to have discovered a proof for the case $n = 3$; almost twenty years later he published it, and upon review it was shown to be incorrect. In 1847, Cauchy managed the singular feat of making two Last theorem blunders in a single speech, in which he
(35) both lent support to a proof put forward by another mathematician, and then went on to claim that some of his own recent work could also provide a proof. Neither turned out to be correct.

Successful work on the theorem was most often
(40) piecemeal, devoted to particular cases, and carried out by dozens of mathematicians, including such famous names as Gauss and Legendre. Eventually, computers were enlisted in the search for counterexamples, but failure was widely anticipated. What made Fermat's
(45) Last theorem tantalizing was that virtually everyone believed it to be true, and yet a proof of it eluded the planet's best mathematical minds for more than three centuries. Finally, in 1993, Andrew Wiles announced that, as a by-product of work he was doing in a
(50) difficult and esoteric area of mathematics, he had discovered a proof of his own. Given the famous nature of the problem and the history of purported solutions to it, the simultaneous popular acclaim and

professional skepticism Wiles encountered is hardly
(55) surprising. What is surprising is that his solution has withstood the scrutiny it has so far received, and seems almost certain to take its place in history as the first successful proof of Fermat's Last theorem.

1. Which one of the following does the passage identify as a reason why Fermat's Last theorem became one of the best-known mysteries in mathematics?

   (A) Euler's failure to devise a correct proof of it.
   (B) The piecemeal nature of successful work on it.
   (C) The general agreement that it was true.
   (D) Its relationship to the Pythagorean theorem.
   (E) Its application to difficult and esoteric areas of mathematics.

2. Which one of the following most accurately represents the primary function of the description of Fermat's method of presenting his mathematical discoveries (lines 19–21)?

   (A) It provides additional support for the author's claim that Fermat was only an amateur mathematician.
   (B) It demonstrates that Fermat was the first mathematician to discover correct proofs for the cases $n = 3$ and $n = 4$ of his Last theorem.
   (C) It indicates that Fermat's claim to have discovered a "truly remarkable proof" of his Last theorem was most likely correct.
   (D) It helps to explain why other mathematicians after Fermat encountered so much difficulty in discovering a correct proof of his Last theorem.
   (E) It provides information suggesting that Fermat was aware that he had not found a complete and correct proof of his Last theorem.

3. As it is used in the passage, the word "counterexamples" (line 43) most nearly means

    (A) sets of integers demonstrating that Fermat's Last theorem is false
    (B) sets of integers suggesting that Fermat's Last theorem is true
    (C) sets of nonintegers showing that Gauss's partial proof of Fermat's Last theorem is incorrect
    (D) sets of nonintegers showing that Fermat's Last theorem is false
    (E) sets of nonintegers showing that Fermat's Last theorem is true

4. It can most reasonably be inferred from the passage that the author would agree with which one of the following statements?

    (A) Andrew Wiles's proof will most likely cause all work on Fermat's Last theorem to cease.
    (B) Andrew Wiles's proof of Fermat's Last theorem will most likely be seen in the future as less important than his work in other areas of mathematics.
    (C) Andrew Wiles's proof of Fermat's Last theorem will most likely continue to be accepted as correct.
    (D) No mathematician other than Andrew Wiles will most likely attain a full understanding of Fermat's Last theorem.
    (E) Fermat's Last theorem will most likely cease to be one of the most famous problems in the history of mathematics.

5. From the passage it can be most reasonably inferred that which one of the following is true of the famous mathematician Euler?

    (A) Euler's proposed proof of the case $n = 3$ was unnecessary, since that case had already been proven by Fermat.
    (B) The flaw in Euler's proposed proof of the case $n = 3$ was not obvious.
    (C) Euler is best known for the fact that his purported proof of the case $n = 3$ was incorrect.
    (D) Euler was aware that his purported proof of the case $n = 3$ was not entirely correct.
    (E) Euler's work on Fermat's Last theorem, although it was flawed, helped other mathematicians gain a greater understanding of related mathematical concepts.

6. Which one of the following would provide an additional example supporting the author's characterization of successful work on Fermat's Last theorem done before Andrew Wiles's proof?

    (A) In 1832, the well-known mathematician Dirichlet proved Fermat's Last theorem in the case $n = 14$.
    (B) In 1847, the obscure mathematician Lamé proposed a complete proof requiring the unique factorization of complex numbers that was subsequently found to be incorrect.
    (C) Between the years 1908 and 1912, more than 1,000 incorrect proofs of Fermat's Last theorem were published.
    (D) In 1986, it was shown that an obscure mathematical statement known as the Shimura-Taniyama-Weil conjecture was closely related to Fermat's Last theorem.
    (E) Further work published by Euler after the publication of his incorrect proof of Fermat's Last theorem in 1770 can be used to correct the problems with that proof.

7. The primary purpose of the passage is to

    (A) correct an error in a commonly held belief
    (B) resolve a long-standing historical dispute
    (C) trace the development of a crucial area of mathematics
    (D) describe the consequences of a series of mathematical errors
    (E) outline the history of a famous problem

2. Thesis-First Passages

When the author wants to convey a particular point of view or thesis, the most straightforward method is to begin the passage by expressing it. The rest of the passage, then, becomes a support or defense of this thesis. Because the point of view appears so early—most often in the first paragraph, or early in the second—it's difficult to miss, and since it's one of the first things you're exposed to, it's easy to tell how the later paragraphs relate to what the author is trying to say. The earlier part of the passage is definitely one of the places you should focus your attention when you're reading any passage; if the author starts off by expressing the passage's thesis, you want to make sure you identify it.

Try the questions in the drill below. Answers can be found in Chapter 20.

DRILL #2

On the morning of December 29, 1890, on Lakota land near Wounded Knee Creek, white soldiers killed more than 150 Native American men, women, and children. By all accounts, the incident that initiated
(5) this slaughter involved a deaf Sioux warrior called Black Coyote, who refused to give up his rifle. It might be claimed that the massacre at Wounded Knee was caused by a tragic failure of communication, but the root cause of the killing was far deeper.

(10) Two years earlier, a Paiute named Wovoka had experienced a vision while in the grip of fever during a solar eclipse. He saw a cataclysm which cleansed the land of white people and restored it to a pure state. In this millennial paradise, the Native American
(15) dead would return to life, and all tribes would live in harmony forever. The teachings based on this vision were known as the Ghost Dance religion, which advocated abstinence from alcohol, rejection of white technology and ideas, and the unity of Native
(20) Americans.

The Ghost Dance, much to the dismay of U.S. authorities, spread rapidly. It came to be seen as especially threatening when the renowned warrior Sitting Bull adopted the religion. Although not initially
(25) an ideology that advocated armed resistance, the Ghost Dance was reinterpreted by Lakota mystics to confer supernatural powers. A special garment called a Ghost Dance shirt, they believed, would make the wearer impervious to bullets. The perceived danger of
(30) the Ghost Dance led authorities to ban it on all Lakota reservations in 1890; the group at Wounded Knee was gathered together as part of an enforcement of that ban. And it was with the Ghost Dance in mind that a Lakota medicine man advocated resisting the soldiers,
(35) believing that their sacred garments would protect them. The failure of that prediction and the horror at what happened at Wounded Knee all but ended the Ghost Dance, perhaps the most successful pan-tribal identity movement in Native American history.

(40) What made the Ghost Dance so attractive to Native Americans and so threatening to white authorities may have been the same thing: its resemblance to aspects of Christian mysticism. Although fundamentally opposed to white religion, the Ghost Dance included
(45) ideas that would have been familiar, and perhaps appealing, to those Native Americans, or Native American tribes, who had been exposed to Christian missionary teachings: the resurrection of the dead, return to paradise, victory through suffering, the
(50) power of the spiritual over the material. Likewise, the largely Christian authorities of the United States may have seen in the Ghost Dance a threat similar to the one early Christianity posed to ancient Rome. In the historical case, a religion that unified disparate
(55) groups had led to the fall of the most powerful empire in history. Whether or not they were conscious of it, what the soldiers destroyed at Wounded Knee was the burgeoning hope of an entire people.

1. Which one of the following most accurately states the main point of the passage?

    (A) The emergence of the Ghost Dance religion, considered a pan-tribal identity movement by white authorities, led directly to the massacre at Wounded Knee because it advocated armed resistance.

    (B) The massacre at Wounded Knee marked the end of the most successful effort by Native Americans to create a pan-tribal identity that incorporated religious, political, and military elements.

    (C) The violence advocated by Lakota mystics represents an adaptation of religious doctrine teaching resistance to authority first developed by Christian mystics in the ancient Roman Empire.

    (D) The massacre at Wounded Knee was the result of tensions surrounding the Ghost Dance religion, which bears resemblances to early Christian mysticism that may have heightened those tensions.

    (E) White soldiers who massacred Native Americans at Wounded Knee did so in an effort to prevent Native Americans from organizing armed resistance to white authorities.

2. Which one of the following best captures the author's attitude toward the Ghost Dance religion?

    (A) disappointment that the massacre at Wounded Knee ended its ascendancy
    (B) respect for its ingenious incorporation of the teachings of Christian missionaries
    (C) skepticism about the significance of its claim to reject white ideas
    (D) doubt about the most common explanation of its origins
    (E) appreciation of the power of the ideas it espoused

3. The author most likely lists some of the themes and ideas underlying the Ghost Dance religion (lines 48–50) primarily to

    (A) identify specific points of similarity with Christian mysticism
    (B) suggest why the religion would have been appealing to Native Americans of all tribes
    (C) provide further details of Wovoka's vision
    (D) contrast it with the beliefs most commonly held by white authorities
    (E) illustrate the reasons why high government officials considered it a threat

4. Based on the passage, which of the following aspects of the history of Christian mysticism is most similar to that of the Ghost Dance religion?

    (A) A charismatic leader gains both strong adherents and bitter enemies within the same community as the leader spreads a new religion's teachings.
    (B) Despite the fact that followers are persecuted and killed, a religion continues to gain new followers.
    (C) Some early adherents of a religion propose interpretations of that religion that were not originally part of the religion's doctrine.
    (D) Early followers of a religion produce texts that subsequently are considered sacred by other followers of that religion.
    (E) An established authority is converted to and becomes a prominent leader in a religion viewed as being a threat to that authority.

5. Which one of the following, if true, would most challenge the author's explanation of the reasons the Ghost Dance religion was appealing to many Native Americans?

    (A) The return of the land to its pristine state was understood by most of the Ghost Dance religion's followers to be a metaphor for resistance to efforts at imposing white social norms on Native American communities.
    (B) The belief of some Ghost Dance followers that sacred garments associated with the Ghost Dance offered protection from harm was not an interpretation foreseen or intended by Wovoka.
    (C) The Ghost Dance religion spread most rapidly and was most widely accepted by plains tribes whose only contact with white culture was through commercial transactions and armed conflicts.
    (D) The adoption of the Ghost Dance religion by Sitting Bull was a key factor in the rapid growth of the religion's popularity.
    (E) The Ghost Dance religion did not include concepts such as a single omnipotent deity that are central to Christian mysticism.

6. As it is used in the passage, the word "millennial" (line 14) most nearly means

    (A) occurring every thousand years
    (B) supplanting the current imperfect state of being
    (C) enduring for the remainder of recorded history
    (D) representing an ideal but unattainable state
    (E) taking place at the end of a long struggle

7. Based on the passage, which one of the following can most reasonably be inferred about the actions of government authorities on Lakota reservations?

    (A) They primarily involved the use of military force.
    (B) They were not all the result of threats perceived by white authorities.
    (C) They included the provision of food and medicines to the Lakota people.
    (D) They were most often intended to prevent the Lakota from offering armed resistance to white authorities.
    (E) They employed both military and legal means.

3. Thesis-Last Passages

A more difficult way a passage's author can express his or her opinion is to make the passage's thesis explicit in the last paragraph, or close to it. These passages may be more difficult to read because the earlier paragraphs seem to conflict with or in some way contradict one another. Remember that the key thing you're looking for in any reading comprehension passage is the author's perspective; everything else is secondary. If a passage starts off, in its early paragraphs, by describing conflicting opinions or several different aspects of a situation, stay alert in the latter parts of the passage. Chances are that the author will express his or her opinion outright in that portion of the passage.

Now take a shot at the drill on the next page. Answers can be found in Chapter 20.

DRILL #3

Among the many difficult legal issues surrounding
property ownership in the wake of Nazi confiscations
during World War II, none has been more contentious
than the ownership of prominent works of art because,
(5) although individuals may own art, it also has a second
status as the communal property of the culture that
produced it. The case of Maria Altmann and six
paintings by the renowned Austrian artist Gustav
Klimt, including one painting of Altmann's aunt,
(10) Adele Bloch-Bauer, is one in which a conflict in this
dual ownership is made more difficult to resolve by
the manifest and historic injustice of Nazi policies.

The paintings, along with many other artworks,
were confiscated from the Jewish Bloch-Bauer family
(15) after the annexation of Austria in 1938, and remained
in the possession of Austria both during and after the
war. When Ferdinand Bloch-Bauer, Altmann's uncle,
died penniless before the war's end, he unsurprisingly
did not honor his wife's last request to donate the
(20) paintings to the country whose Nazi authorities had
stolen them. After the war, the restitution of stolen
property became the responsibility of the countries
in which the thefts had taken place, and in this regard
Austria's new government had a clear conflict of
(25) interest over the Klimt paintings. Block-Bauer's heirs
had all emigrated to escape the Holocaust, but the
Austrian government was unwilling to allow such
prominent works by a native master to leave the
country. In return for allowing the export of other
(30) valuable items stolen from the Bloch-Bauer heirs,
Austria essentially extorted the donation of the six
Klimt paintings. In 1999, Maria Altmann, the only
living heir of the Bloch-Bauers, sought the return
of the paintings in Austrian courts. Austrian law,
(35) however, requires that anyone seeking the return of
disputed property pay court costs based on its value,
which in Altmann's case amounted to several million
dollars. Despite the government's own findings that it
had illegally profited in the postwar period from Nazi
(40) confiscations of art, the Klimt paintings were objects
of special significance, and the government employed
several strategies to prevent Altmann from being able
to bring her suit.

Altmann, who is a U.S. citizen, has since sought
(45) relief in U.S. courts, which may eventually grant her
compensation for the paintings' value. This would
be a proper remedy. It is unlikely that the court will
return the paintings themselves to her; nor should
they. Although Austria's actions both during and
(50) after the war are unconscionable, this fact should not
be allowed to obscure the central issue of the case.
Altmann's right to her personal property must be
respected, but her radical exercise of that right should

not supersede the right of Austrian citizens to access
(55) their own cultural legacy. To do so, and deny Adele
Bloch-Bauer's last wish that these wonderful paintings
be donated to the people of Austria, is to add to the
litany of wrongs done to the Austrian people by Nazi
occupation, not redress them.

1. Which one of the following most accurately
    expresses the main point of the passage?

    (A) Both during and after World War II, the
        government of Austria behaved in a fashion
        that, either intentionally or unintentionally,
        heightened the injustice done to the Bloch-
        Bauer family by the anti-Semitic policies of
        the Nazis.
    (B) The dual status of prominent artworks as both
        individual and community property dictates
        that, in any case where these two types of
        ownership are at odds, the rights of the
        community must be considered primary.
    (C) The portrait of Adele Bloch-Bauer and other
        prominent artworks by Gustav Klimt that are
        the subject of a current lawsuit should not be
        returned to the sole living heir of the Bloch-
        Bauers.
    (D) Any resolution of the dispute between Austria
        and the heir of the family from which six
        Klimt paintings were stolen by the Nazis
        must be resolved in a fashion that redresses
        the wrong of the theft without perpetrating
        the additional wrong of denying the Austrian
        people access to key pieces of their own
        cultural history.
    (E) Contrary to the position advocated by Maria
        Altmann, the rights of the Austrian state
        to restrict the export of important cultural
        artifacts overrides any right Altmann or
        her family may seek to exercise over those
        artifacts as private property.

2. Which one of the following most accurately describes two main functions of the first sentence of the passage?

(A) It introduces the positions of the two sides in Maria Altmann's dispute with the Austrian government over six paintings by Gustav Klimt and indicates which of the two sides is likely to prevail.

(B) It provides historical background of the events that gave rise to Maria Altmann's dispute with the government of Austria and suggests that no resolution of that dispute will be entirely satisfactory.

(C) It provides a context in which Maria Altmann's dispute with the Austrian government may be placed and introduces the reasons why Altmann's case is one of particular difficulty.

(D) It describes the historical wrong which Maria Altmann's lawsuit against the Austrian government is intended to redress and implies that Altmann's suit is unlikely to be successful.

(E) It outlines the basic principles in the light of which Maria Altmann's lawsuit against the Austrian government must be evaluated and indicates that these principles cannot by themselves determine what the outcome of the suit should be.

3. Which one of the following legal strategies is most closely analogous to the strategy pursued on behalf of Maria Altmann as it is described in the third paragraph of the passage?

(A) A refugee who flees the country of his birth because of persecution brings suit in his new country to resolve a dispute that remained unresolved in his native country's courts at the time he fled.

(B) A woman who does not receive a satisfactory resolution of a dispute with a fellow citizen in the country where she resides brings a second suit against the same person in a second country of which she is also a citizen.

(C) A released prisoner of war who was seriously injured while in the custody of another country brings suit in his home country against the government of the country that harmed him.

(D) The descendent of a former citizen of one country who voluntarily gave up her citizenship brings suit against a company based in his ancestor's former country for the return of land illegally obtained by the company.

(E) A person who has fled his home country because of persecution by a past regime is prevented, because of an amnesty declared by the succeeding regime, from filing suit there against those who persecuted him and instead files suit in the country where he currently resides.

4. It can most reasonably be inferred from the passage that the author views the return of the six Klimt paintings confiscated from the Bloch-Bauer family after the annexation of Austria as

(A) an appropriate remedy
(B) a realistic possibility
(C) a partial but not complete redress for injustice
(D) an excessive exercise of property rights
(E) an unconscionable injustice

5. According to the passage, which one of the following is true of the Austrian legal system?

(A) It imposes excessive restrictions on those who seek the return of disputed property.

(B) It does not always act to redress wrongs identified by the Austrian government.

(C) It serves the interests of those who have profited excessively from wrongs done by previous Austrian governments.

(D) It occasionally renders decisions that are clearly unjust.

(E) It is not always allowed to decide cases that are of importance to the Austrian government's relations with other national governments.

6. Based on the passage, it can be most reasonably inferred that the author would agree with which one of the following statements?

(A) Not all wrongs done by the governments of countries while they were under Nazi occupation should be redressed.

(B) The effects of past confiscations carried out by governments of countries while they were under Nazi occupation were not categorically negative.

(C) No remedy that involves the return of paintings to the families from which they were confiscated by governments of countries under Nazi occupation should be considered.

(D) The fact that property was illegally confiscated by the government of a country under Nazi occupation does not nullify the right of the country's people to access that property if it is culturally significant.

(E) Any party that has profited by the confiscation of property by the government of a country under Nazi occupation has no legitimate right to those profits.

4. The Author Behind the Curtain

Remember in *The Wizard of Oz*, when Toto reveals the person operating the illusion of the great and powerful wizard? The wizard says, "Pay no attention to the man behind the curtain!" Some reading comprehension passages are written to conceal the author behind the curtain, and you'll need to do a little more work to figure out his or her point. There will still be signs of the thesis, but there won't be a particular sentence in any part of the passage where the author comes right out and states it.

Passages in which the author's main point is somewhat concealed are of course a bit more difficult than the passages we've seen so far, but once you've located the author's position, the process of working the questions is fundamentally the same. Use the first question on these passages, which is nearly always a main point question, to help you: Since the answers you pick will need to be consistent with the main point (unless the question itself instructs you to answer from some other point of view), finding out what the question writers believe is the main point of the passage can be immensely helpful on the remainder of the questions.

Now try the drill on the following page. Answers can be found in Chapter 20.

DRILL #4

Beginning in the late 1960s, many visual artists became interested in means of art production other than the traditional methods of painting and sculpture, two pillars of a Modernism that some considered
(5) co-opted by structures of social domination, morally and aesthetically bankrupt. These art forms that would later come to be called "postmodern" served in part to expose the underlying assumptions of art as a cultural production by subverting them, extending outside
(10) the domains delineated for art's interpretation and translation.

One of the most important novel forms was earthwork art: primarily outdoor works, often on a massive scale and carried out in remote locations.
(15) A key attribute that earthwork art shared with other movements of the period, particularly performance art, was its resistance to commodification. Earthworks could not be displayed in a gallery or moved from one place to another. Some earthworks were intended to be
(20) ephemeral—to wear away under the effects of wind, rain, or tide—while others were monumental. Either way, the earthwork served as a counterlandscape, so that instead of capturing land through a medium of external representation, the land became a changing
(25) medium for representation itself. Art dealers found that the only marketable renditions of earthwork art—photographs, films, and drawings—sold for very little because they could be infinitely reproduced, and because they were not the work itself.
(30) Perhaps, though, what makes earthwork art most interesting is its failure to resist the market entirely. Robert Smithson's seminal earthwork "Spiral Jetty," for instance, was erected along a portion of the Great Salt Lake's shoreline that was bequeathed to an arts
(35) center upon his death, much as a traditional painting or sculpture might have been. Although it cannot be physically translated, an earthwork by definition is located in a place that might itself be owned, and therefore raises questions similar to those surrounding
(40) monuments such as Mount Rushmore or the pyramids at Giza, or Native American burial earthworks such as the Great Serpent Mounds. Preservation becomes a paradox with earthwork art, as "Spiral Jetty" again illustrates, since a rise in the water level of the Great
(45) Salt Lake made the work impossible to view some decades after its completion. Either a fundamental aspect of the work—its presence in and connection with an environment—must be compromised in order for it to be experienced, or else the entire experience
(50) must be, at least for a time, lost.

This paradox is one of many that arise around the central paradox of earthwork art. Although many see these works as standing against humanity's long habit of reshaping and exploiting land, the works
(55) themselves are in many cases bold exploitations of it. Few would equate an earthwork artist's activities with strip mining or the clear-cutting of forests, but the works themselves invite such comparisons and leave open the question of whether aesthetic vision alone
(60) can justify one but not the other.

1. Which one of the following most completely and accurately states the main point of the passage?

   (A) Although earthwork art, like other postmodern art forms, was intended to subvert market systems of art and comment on the ownership and use of land, it is most important for the ways in which it did not entirely accomplish these goals.

   (B) Postmodern art was conceived as a response to Modern art, which had been co-opted by the market systems surrounding the visual arts and become a means by which the power structures of the dominant culture perpetuated themselves.

   (C) Earthwork art did not constitute an adequate response to the problems of Modernist visual art, since it was unable to escape commodification and failed to present a positive alternative to humanity's traditional assumptions concerning the reshaping and exploitation of land.

   (D) Earthwork art was primarily interesting because, whether it was intended to be ephemeral or monumental, it recreated the relationship between land and culture implied by such works as the Great Serpent Mounds, Mount Rushmore, and the pyramids at Giza.

   (E) The central paradox of earthwork art is that, although it is often believed to constitute a critique of humanity's long habit of reshaping and exploiting land, its primary means of doing so was by reshaping and exploiting land itself.

2. Based on the passage, the author's attitude toward Robert Smithson's work "Spiral Jetty" is most accurately described as

   (A) ambivalent
   (B) skeptical
   (C) reverent
   (D) admiring
   (E) critical

3. Each of the following statements is consistent with the passage EXCEPT:

  (A) An earthwork that is designed to be eroded over a period of time raises questions about the preservation and permanence of art.
  (B) Performance art is designed to resist the market systems of art because a performance cannot be privately owned or transferred without the consent of the artist.
  (C) Ownership of the land on which an earthwork is located represents a misuse of earthwork art.
  (D) Some earthwork art constitutes a commentary on the tradition of landscape in visual arts.
  (E) Earthwork art is important in part because it subverts traditional notions of the production of art itself.

4. The author most likely uses the word "ephemeral" (line 20) to mean

  (A) small
  (B) of modest importance
  (C) impermanent
  (D) changing through time
  (E) without a definite monetary value

5. Which one of the following most accurately describes the organization of the passage?

  (A) explanation of a general principle; presentation of specific instances of this principle's application; indications that the principle is inadequate to explain these instances fully; discussion of the consequences of the principle's failure
  (B) explanation of an idea that was accepted in the past; presentation of instances in which this idea has been rejected; indications that the rejection of this idea was not complete; discussion of the renewed importance of the idea
  (C) explanation of a new view of an activity; presentation of efforts to manifest this view; indications that these efforts were not entirely successful; discussion of the implications of these efforts
  (D) explanation of the underpinnings of a theory; presentation of a specific effort to expose these underpinnings; indications that the theory is not entirely correct; discussion of the success of the specific effort
  (E) explanation of a situation; presentation of efforts to cope with this situation; indications that the situation cannot satisfactorily be coped with; discussion of the possibility that future efforts to cope with the situation may be more successful

6. The primary purpose of the passage is most likely to

  (A) propose a new theory of visual arts
  (B) introduce a novel form that may completely change visual arts in the future
  (C) describe an effort to overcome inherent limitations in the production of visual arts
  (D) discuss the implications of an attempt to undermine some traditional assumptions of the visual arts
  (E) illustrate the practical impossibility of an effort to reconcile visual arts with postmodern ideals

7. Based on the passage, which one of the following does the author appear to believe about earthwork art's relationship to other uses of land?

  (A) It is ethically preferable to all other uses, although this preference cannot be defended with reference to earthwork art itself.
  (B) It is similar in significant ways to uses of land that are widely considered wasteful and destructive.
  (C) It is ethically defensible only in cases where the earthwork occupies land that is not important or useful for other purposes.
  (D) It is no more ethically defensible than is strip mining or the clear-cutting of forests.
  (E) It represents an imposition of aesthetic vision on land which is considered of inconsequential aesthetic value otherwise.

18

Points of View

HIDDEN POINTS OF VIEW

When reading comprehension passages get more complicated, it's usually because they include several different points of view, in addition to that of the author. Rather than directly present a thesis, the author may express it in terms of differences with other opinions, or even express it about the opinions themselves. Clearly, under the time constraints of the LSAT, it can become a challenge to juggle all these competing points of view at the same time. Therefore, keep the following things in mind.

TRACK AGREEMENTS AND DISAGREEMENTS

Many people, as they read a passage, like to mark specific moments when the author uses value-laden terms in presenting the opinions contained in the passage. A plus or minus sign can very succinctly indicate whether the author expresses agreement or disagreement with that particular point of view.

THE AUTHOR'S VIEW IS YOUR COMPASS

Although the task becomes more complicated in these passages, it remains fundamentally the same: Find the author's opinion, if there is one. Although it may be more difficult to express it in a few words, and it may not be stated outright at any one place, it's the author's point of view that will help you most with the questions. Unless a question specifically asks you to answer from another point of view in the passage, it's the author's point of view that should always be the one that's foremost in your mind when you're looking for a choice that's as consistent as possible with the passage.

The passages in this section illustrate several different ways that reading comprehension passages can incorporate multiple points of view and present conclusions about them.

1. Nobody's Right If Everybody's Wrong

One of the more common, and more confusing, ways a reading comprehension passage can play the point-of-view game is to present alternatives and then conclude that none of them is by itself entirely adequate. It's natural for us, as readers, to expect that the author's purpose in presenting competing points of view is to indicate that one is preferable to the others. It's possible on the LSAT, however, for the author's main point to be that none of the points of view is correct.

An additional difficulty of passages like this is that the author's disagreement can be somewhat nuanced, and isn't necessarily the result of the fact that the author believes some other point of view is correct. Remember that it's possible for some problems discussed in reading comprehension passages to be so difficult that they may have no adequate solution.

Try the drill on the next page. Answers can be found in Chapter 20.

DRILL #1

Advances in computer technology have given individuals affordable access to information and computing power that were unimaginable a century ago. The rapidity of this change has led many
(5) people to speculate about what lies ahead in the next century, and particularly whether computers may become so advanced that they could be considered intelligent. The question is one of interest to cognitive psychologists and many others who are fascinated
(10) with the fundamental question of what intelligence is, and how to identify it.

The earliest accepted standard for artificial intelligence is almost as old as computers themselves. In 1950 Alan Turing, a pioneer in computing,
(15) proposed a standard that has come to be known as the Turing test. A Turing test is conducted by a human investigator interviewing two respondents in text form: one human and one computer. Turing argued that the computer could be considered intelligent if the human
(20) investigator, after conducting five-minute exchanges with each, had no better than a 70 percent likelihood of correctly identifying which was the human, and which the machine.

Ambitious as this goal may seem, there are those
(25) who question whether, even if the likelihood of correct identification could be reduced to its absolute minimum of 50 percent, the machine ought therefore to be considered intelligent. The most famous illustration of this idea is John R. Searle's Chinese
(30) room argument. Searle asks us to imagine a person sitting inside a room with an extensive rulebook. A question written in Chinese, which the person does not understand, is passed through a slot in one wall. The person consults the rulebook, follows its instructions
(35) for concocting a written response in Chinese, and passes the response back out through the slot. Searle's essential objection to the Turing test is that, no matter how sensible the responses may seem to those outside, one cannot say that the person inside the room knows
(40) Chinese. Whatever "intelligence" may be perceived is not a quality of the person at all, but a consequence of the design of the rulebook. Most would agree that it doesn't make sense to say that the rulebook is intelligent: it does not understand the responses it
(45) provides, is not even conscious of them. The Chinese room is a simulacrum of intelligence, so-called weak artificial intelligence, but not intelligence in the sense that humans possess it.

The distinctions this conflict points out are more
(50) than semantic. If one accepts the Turing test as an adequate standard for intelligence, then questions of what role understanding or thought plays in intelligence become at best difficult to answer, and at worst irrelevant. The Turing test makes intelligence
(55) a matter of consensus, and thus in principle arbitrary. On the other hand, Searle's view makes intelligence something that cannot be verified from the outside at all, leaving open the theoretical possibility that not even humans should be considered intelligent.

1. Which one of the following most accurately expresses the main point of the passage?

(A) The consideration of conditions under which programmed artificial constructs may be considered intelligent has led to the realization that there is no adequate standard for deciding whether even human beings are intelligent.

(B) Standards developed for deciding whether or not programmed artificial constructs are intelligent are inadequate for discerning the true nature of intelligence.

(C) The contradictions inherent in any effort to determine whether or not a programmed artificial construct is intelligent lead to the conclusion that cognitive psychologists do not have even a rudimentary understanding of intelligence.

(D) Competing standards for determining whether programmed artificial constructs are intelligent fail to account for the importance of consensus in deciding this question, or else fail to associate activities such as understanding and thought with intelligence.

(E) The consideration of whether some programmed artificial constructs may be called intelligent leads to the conclusion that intelligence consists of some elements that cannot be verified from the outside, but does not consist entirely of those elements.

2. Given the author's argument, which one of the following responses offered by a computer subject during the administration of a Turing test would most help to overcome Searle's objections to a determination that the computer is intelligent?

(A) a response that is precisely identical to the response to the same question offered by the human subject of the test

(B) a response in which the computer claims to believe that it is intelligent

(C) a response that differs from an earlier response offered by the computer to the same question

(D) a humorous response to a question that the human interviewer intended to be rhetorical

(E) a response correcting an earlier statement offered by the computer on the basis of a misunderstanding of one of the human interviewer's questions

3. The discussion in the third paragraph is intended primarily to explain which one of the following?

(A) how a construct that should not be considered truly intelligent might be able to pass a Turing test

(B) how a construct might be able to learn to speak Chinese without being truly intelligent

(C) how a construct that might be considered intelligent by the Turing test in one instance might in some other instance not be considered intelligent by the same standard

(D) why the Chinese room argument places too high a demand on any standard for determining that a given construct is intelligent

(E) why cognitive psychologists' current understanding of human intelligence cannot be applied to constructs that involve nonhuman elements

4. The passage supports each of the following inferences EXCEPT:

(A) It is unlikely that the best computers currently in existence could pass a Turing test.

(B) No set of answers can provide definite verification that the subject answering the questions is engaging in thought.

(C) A set of instructions that is sufficiently well designed can be complex enough to satisfy every standard of intelligence.

(D) At least some people who have studied artificial intelligence would be willing to accept as intelligent a computer that others believe may only constitute a simulation of intelligence.

(E) Under current circumstances, it seems likely that the power and complexity of computers will continue to increase.

5. Which one of the following views can most reasonably be attributed to those who accept the Turing test as the standard by which artificial intelligence should be judged?

(A) A set of instructions that causes a machine to respond to questions in an unpredictable way is sufficient to render that machine intelligent.

(B) A set of instructions that causes a machine to appear intelligent to at least some interviewers is necessary to render that machine intelligent.

(C) Any machine that can be considered intelligent must necessarily possess an extensive set of instructions.

(D) Any machine that can be considered intelligent must necessarily engage in thought and be conscious of the answers it offers.

(E) In order to be considered intelligent, it is sufficient for a machine's responses to be only occasionally indistinguishable from a human's responses to the same questions.

6. Which one of the following, if it were substituted for the rulebook in Searle's Chinese room argument, would LEAST alter the purpose and force of that argument?

(A) a machine that is capable of translating statements back and forth between Chinese and some language the person inside the room can understand

(B) a person who has a partial understanding of written Chinese

(C) a machine that is capable of employing a large range of Chinese characters to produce statements that make sense to those who can read and understand Chinese

(D) a person who can read, write, and understand Chinese but who does not know any language in common with the person inside the room

(E) a machine with extensive programming that allows it to provide comprehensible written responses in Chinese to any question written in Chinese

7. The author's tone in describing Searle's objections to the Turing test can most accurately be described as

(A) dismissive
(B) uncertain
(C) neutral
(D) critical
(E) approving

2. Synthesis

On the other end of the spectrum from the "nobody's right" passage we saw in the prior section is a passage that suggests the possibility that everybody is right. These passages can be difficult to understand because they often involve quite abstract points of view, and the author's presentation of them can seem to change through the passage. Initially, the points of view may be presented as competing; later—usually at or near the end of the passage—the author indicates his or her belief that the two points of view are not actually in conflict, and may both be correct.

This synthesis of views that initially appear to be in conflict can be complex, and even more abstract than the points of view are themselves. Again, though, as long as you're keeping the various points of view straight, and keeping the author's separate from them all, you should be able to deal with these passages effectively.

Take a shot at the drill below. Answers can be found in Chapter 20.

DRILL #2

Of all the fundamental forces of nature, gravity is the one of which physics most consistently seems to overestimate its own understanding. It was Newton, during the Renaissance, who first described how
(5) individual masses attract one another, and into the twentieth century, this was virtually all physics had to say about gravity. That Einstein's theory of general relativity required real changes to the understanding of gravity was seen by many as a problem until Einstein
(10) used relativity to explain the precession of Mercury's perihelion, a long-standing mystery in physics.

Relativity, however, was at odds with the steady-state model of the universe accepted at the time, which held that the universe was neither expanding
(15) nor contracting. Einstein's notion of gravity predicted that, eventually, the universe would shrink inward and perhaps result in a "Big Crunch," in which all the mass in the universe came together. To manufacture agreement with the steady-state
(20) idea, Einstein introduced into his equations what he called a "cosmological constant." The cosmological constant was an invented antigravitational force, a fudge factor not motivated by any experimental data. When later observations revealed that the universe is
(25) in fact expanding, Einstein removed the cosmological constant from his theory, calling it his greatest blunder, and gravitation once again seemed to be well understood.

Around the end of the twentieth century, however,
(30) other observations revealed perhaps the greatest gravitational mystery of them all. According to relativity, the expansion of the universe ought to be slowing down. Incredible as it seemed, though, these new observations showed that the expansion of the
(35) universe was actually speeding up, and physicists have since scrambled to find some way of explaining this bizarre fact.

The most widely held view is that the acceleration of expansion is due to "dark energy," usually
(40) interpreted as a pressure associated with a vacuum. Einstein had been the one to show that mass itself had energy; these new theories go on to say that empty space also has energy, which could counteract gravity's tendency to draw mass together. Certain
(45) results from quantum physics reinforce this idea, and further experiments are being devised in an effort to measure dark energy or observe its gravitational effects.

Others, though, have resisted the idea. One group of
(50) skeptics has sought to explain the acceleration of the universe's expansion by tinkering with the equations of general relativity itself, making adjustments that not only agree with the current state of the universe but also shed light on the problem of the universe's rapid
(55) expansion in the epoch immediately following the Big Bang. Yet although it is presented as an alternative to the dark energy hypothesis, this method certainly does not exclude it. As Einstein's cosmological constant demonstrates, there is a difference between tinkering
(60) with equations and developing physical explanations for phenomena, and it remains possible that this group's tinkering, if it is successful, may in the end only serve to demonstrate that dark energy does, in fact, exist.

1. Which one of the following most accurately states the main point of the passage?

   (A) Although at several times in history physicists believed they had a full understanding of the gravitational force, each time that belief has eventually been shown to be incorrect.

   (B) The mystery of the universe's accelerating expansion indicates that current understandings of gravity are insufficient to explain its nature completely.

   (C) Current theories of dark energy, which have been advanced to explain the accelerating expansion of the universe, will eventually be found to be substantially correct.

   (D) Recent discoveries in physics indicate that Einstein's cosmological constant, which he once characterized as his greatest blunder, in fact provides a correct description of gravity.

   (E) Efforts that have been made to explain the universe's accelerating expansion without reference to dark energy may in fact only constitute adjustments to gravitational equations so that they describe dark energy's effect.

2. Which one of the following does the author use to illustrate the difference between developing physical explanations for phenomena and modifying the equations that describe those phenomena?

   (A) Einstein's cosmological constant
   (B) the accelerating expansion of the universe
   (C) Newton's theory of gravity
   (D) the precession of Mercury's perihelion
   (E) the "Big Crunch"

3. Which one of the following can most properly be inferred from the description of the steady-state model of the universe described in the second paragraph?

   (A) It was widely believed to be a correct description of the universe from the Renaissance through the beginning of the twentieth century.

   (B) Physical explanations devised to account for it were initially rejected, and then later gained wide acceptance.

   (C) It did not predict that the gravitational force might cause all the mass in the universe to be drawn together.

   (D) It was later supported by further astronomical observations.

   (E) Current theories of dark energy have been advanced to explain why it has subsequently been shown to be incorrect.

4. The author's attitude toward the skeptics mentioned in the fifth paragraph can most aptly be described as

   (A) strong admiration for the innovative approach they advocate for explaining the accelerating expansion of the universe

   (B) mild surprise that any theory aside from dark energy would be considered necessary to account for the accelerating expansion of the universe

   (C) reasoned skepticism of the appropriateness of revising the successful theory of general relativity on the basis of no solid experimental data

   (D) legitimate doubt that the skeptics will succeed in their efforts to provide a real alternative to the widely held view that dark energy is responsible for the accelerating expansion of the universe

   (E) scholarly interest in the process of debate among physicists that eventually results in new and better explanations of physical phenomena

5. The passage provides information that answers each of the following questions EXCEPT:

   (A) What development helped convince physicists that Einstein's theory of general relativity provided a fuller explanation of the gravitational force than the Newtonian theory?

   (B) What existing experimental evidence supports the contention that a vacuum may possess energy?

   (C) What discovery eventually led Einstein to conclude that his theory of a cosmological constant was mistaken?

   (D) What advantage, aside from describing the accelerating expansion of the universe, may efforts to alter the equations of general relativity offer?

   (E) What did Einstein's theory of general relativity, after the cosmological constant had been removed from it, predict concerning the rate of the universe's expansion?

6. The primary function of the first three paragraphs is to

(A) describe a theory of a natural force that has long been believed to be correct, but which has been called into question by two new theories of that force

(B) introduce new views of a natural force that provide fuller explanations of the force's operations than the theories of that force that have long been believed to be correct

(C) explain the history of theories of a natural force and provide recent evidence that these theories are incomplete

(D) describe the process by which the current understanding of a natural force has been arrived at and suggest that this process will continue to operate in the future

(E) provide a basis on which past and future theories of a natural force may be evaluated

7. Which one of the following experimental observations would most strongly support the conclusion that the rate of the universe's expansion is increasing?

(A) A distant star observed from Earth at one time is found to be even more distant from Earth at a later time.

(B) A nearby star observed from Earth at one time is observed to be more distant from Earth at a later time.

(C) A distant star observed at one time to be moving away from Earth at one speed is observed at a later time to be moving away from Earth at a lower speed.

(D) A nearby star observed to be moving toward Earth at one time is observed at a later time to be moving away from Earth.

(E) A distant star observed at one time to be moving away from Earth at one speed is observed at a later time to be moving away from Earth at a greater speed.

3. Yes, But. . .

These passages are in some ways similar to the synthesis passages. Sometimes the author's main point is that one or more of the points of view presented in the passage is broadly correct, but requires some extension or slight modification. These can be difficult because the author's correction of the presented idea may or may not indicate outright disagreement with a part of it. It also may or may not indicate agreement with any point of view presented as being in opposition with the point of view that the author prefers.

The difficulty here is primarily one of nuance. You may need to identify specific points of agreement and disagreement with each of the views presented in the passage in order to understand what the main point is exactly. Again, the main thing to do here is to listen for the authorial voice; the good news about a passage like this is that, since the main point can be rather complicated, the author will have to editorialize rather heavily in order to convey it.

Try the following example of this type of passage. The answers can be found in Chapter 20.

DRILL #3

"Critical" legal studies, an effort to accommodate postmodern realities in the practice and understanding of law, have gained some credence in the theory of domestic legal systems but are of little use in practice.
(5) With their focus on the contingency, complexity, and indeterminacy that arise when systems of representation and power interact, they tend to raise more questions than they settle, and seem needlessly circumspect when used in cases to which an agreed-
(10) upon body of law applies. In the area of international law, however, when the substance of many cases involves conflicting interpretations authorized by multiple traditions and systems of belief, the application of critical legal studies seems clearer, and
(15) perhaps more valuable.

The point of origin for a critical view of international law is deconstruction of the positivist ideal, which approaches cases with the goal in mind of discerning universal principles. In practice this
(20) positivist approach involves surveying the panoply of treaties, traditions, and written laws with which a nation is associated in search of evidence that can be offered as "proof" that it has acceded to principles that are advantageous to one party or the other. But
(25) because every nation and culture is a space in which multiple systems operate, some of which compete and some of which constitute incompatible modes of discourse, it seems plain that the positivist method cannot accomplish what it promises: any "universal"
(30) standard can only be an artifact, produced for a purpose and discarded once its use is done. The fact that all such methods of judgment are *ad hoc*, a weakness of the positivist approach and its pretenses to objective truth, is acknowledged by the critical view
(35) and becomes one of its central requirements. Since every party exists at a locus of interaction between several systems of meaning and power, each situation may activate these systems to different degrees and in different ways. In the critical view, a proper resolution
(40) of any dispute takes the full range of operative realities into account and does not privilege any over the others. This approach acknowledges the fractured nature of culture, accepting the fact that a state actor often violates one or more of the standards to which
(45) the state acknowledges itself to be subject.

Yet while it is true that an inclusive view is required to resolve international disputes, the doctrinaire insistence that no mode of discourse be privileged risks deconstructing international law itself along with
(50) positivism. The main value of international treaties, for example, is that their signatories voluntarily privilege the provisions of the treaty and clarify ambiguities in their interests and impulses. Although objective truth may be a fantasy, treaties may be
(55) seen to institute a provisional objective that operates in a limited sphere. Certainly reference to treaties cannot resolve every dispute, and the provisions of treaties themselves may be subject to critical analysis, but insofar as their provisions can be said to apply,
(60) such treaties must serve as the guiding authorities in international law.

1. Which one of the following most accurately states the main idea of the passage?

   (A) International treaties must be considered the sole guiding authority in resolving any international dispute when the parties to the dispute are both signatories of those treaties.

   (B) The positivist ideal, when applied to international disputes, fails because there is no settled body of international law to which all nations can be said to be subject.

   (C) Critical legal studies, when applied to international law, offer an advantage over positivist approaches because the critical view acknowledges that multiple systems of power and modes of discourse may figure in a resolution of the dispute.

   (D) Although a critical view of international legal disputes is required to account for the complex nature of the principles that govern a nation's action, it should not be allowed to undermine the integrity of international agreements into which those nations voluntarily enter.

   (E) Even though a critical view of law has not gained wide use in the analysis and implementation of domestic laws, its usefulness is clear in the case of international laws, which are complex, sometimes conflicting, and not always agreed to by all nations.

2. Based on the passage, which one of the following aspects of a treaty governing international trade would be LEAST likely to be emphasized in a critical view of a dispute concerning that treaty?

(A) traditional views within the nations that are parties to the dispute of the obligations of individuals in fulfilling agreements for the exchange of goods

(B) the doctrines concerning money and trade espoused by a religion that is widely followed by citizens of the countries that are parties to the dispute

(C) the circumstances of past instances in which one or more of the parties to the treaty have violated its explicit terms

(D) the fact that one or more of the countries that are parties to the dispute are experiencing serious economic problems that make the terms of the treaty excessively onerous

(E) the status of the treaty as a binding legal agreement that is subject to fundamental legal principles governing all contracts

3. Which one of the following is the most accurate description of the author's attitude toward the positivist method of deciding international disputes?

(A) concern that the actual practice of this method will eventually undermine the positivist ideal

(B) scorn for the method's reliance on *ad hoc* standards of judgment

(C) disapproval of its lack of regard for the complex and conflicting nature of the multiple traditions that operate in every nation

(D) anger at its willingness to dispense with the binding provisions of treaties that apply to these disputes

(E) disappointment at its simplistic refusal to recognize international agreements as constituting a provisionally objective standard for settling some disputes

4. It can be inferred from the passage that a critical view of international treaties holds a treaty to be

(A) one among many possible modes of discourse that may be used to interpret the actions of a nation

(B) less important than the traditions that are observed within the nations that are signatories to that treaty

(C) equally important to the widely accepted principles of law to which all nations agree that they are subject

(D) void unless the signatories to the treaty have in the past appealed to that treaty to justify their actions

(E) more important than other operative systems of power and discourse within the nations that are signatories to that treaty

5. Which one of the following is LEAST compatible with the author's views, as those views are described in the passage?

(A) Critical legal methods of interpretation are less clearly applicable to domestic disputes than they are to international disputes.

(B) Many international disputes can be satisfactorily resolved with reference to general principles that are present in the body of domestic law in each nation that is a party to the dispute.

(C) The explicit terms of a treaty may have different meanings in different nations that are signatories to that treaty.

(D) The notion of objective truth is not necessarily useful to the resolution of disputes among different nations.

(E) A nation's actions may be interpreted differently by different people within that nation.

6. Which one of the following principles most likely underlies the author's characterization of the role of international treaties in deciding disputes among nations?

(A) Whenever parties have mutually and voluntarily agreed to be bound by a set of requirements, those requirements should be considered of primary importance in any case when they directly apply.

(B) Only those requirements by which a broad consensus of nations have mutually and voluntarily agreed to be bound should be considered of any importance in a case when they directly apply.

(C) Unless the requirements by which parties have mutually and voluntarily agreed to be bound directly apply to a case, those requirements should not be considered of primary importance in that case.

(D) All requirements to which every nation has mutually and voluntarily agreed to be bound should be considered of primary importance in any case when they directly apply.

(E) The requirements to which parties have mutually and voluntarily agreed to be bound should not necessarily be considered of primary importance in a case when they directly apply.

4. Journalistic Passages Redux

We end where we began: with passages that don't express a particular opinion on the author's part. Sometimes the passage includes points of view that are so complicated that the addition of an author's opinion on top of them would make the passage excessively difficult. In this case, the fact that the author does not express a particular opinion may initially pose a challenge; until you understand the points of view being expressed, you may not even be able to tell that the author doesn't have any preference.

In these cases, it's very important to read the questions carefully and make sure you know which point of view you're asked to answer the question from. These questions can be particularly difficult because you may be picking answers that contradict ideas presented in some parts of the passage. Again, the main remedy here is to work carefully. As long as you stick with the material presented and remain mindful of the points of view involved, you should be fine.

Try the journalistic passage below. Answers can be found in Chapter 20.

DRILL #4

Theoretical approaches to the nature of reality and meaning can be seen, at their simplest, as play with the relation between signifier and signified, the word and its "real" referent. Traditional
(5) conceptions of language considered the signifier and signified as belonging to two universes which did not communicate except through a system of mappings between them. Yet the observation that language relations—those that exist entirely among
(10) signifiers—could themselves produce meaning required an extension of the notion of the real into the inaccessible world of the "subject"—thought, belief, personal feeling—which could no longer be seen as strictly separate from language. This breach
(15) in the barrier between universes led to a range of philosophical responses that, at least initially, tended to focus on the ways in which language sought either to obscure reality or else to transcend it. The first was exemplified by such twentieth-century phenomena as
(20) the advent of official euphemism and the transmission of propaganda through mass media; the second found its expression in the abstract and radically stylized art that gained ascendancy through the Modern period.

With the work of Michel Foucault, however, the
(25) capacity of the signifier to create the signified as "real" became a subject of interest. Through his imaginative studies of such social forces as the prison, the medical clinic, and the sexual therapist, Foucault identified the signifier as a primary instrument for the creation and
(30) propagation of real-world power. Technologies for naming transgressions and abnormalities were seen as the means by which social institutions, independent of any individual or collective intention, created the conditions that justified their own existence. Far from
(35) solving such problems as criminal recidivism and sexual perversion, social institutions produced them

and therefore reinforced the urgency of calling upon those institutions to "solve" them. Taken to its logical extreme, this basic tenet of Foucault's can apply to
(40) many commonplaces of organized society. Opinion polls that indicate voting preferences, for instance, can be seen as instruments that produce shifts in opinion, and therefore create the need for further polls to track those shifts.

(45) For Jean Baudrillard, however, Foucault's idea that power even exists is flawed. Baudrillard identifies an evolution in the political economy of signs that has led to the complete collapse of the distinction between signifier and signified, so that both representation
(50) and reality alike have become "simulation." What Foucault calls power, as Baudrillard writes in his work *Forget Foucault*, "is only there to hide the fact that it no longer exists." Reality has become a system of hysterically reproducing signs which are
(55) comprehensible only in terms of prior renditions. The opinion poll, in Baudrillard's view, is remarkable not for the way in which it produces or is produced by power, nor for the way in which it reflects or creates opinion, but instead because it actually *is* opinion.
(60) For Baudrillard, the signifier is at the same time both empty and total, since it has been freed from the burden of signifying anything else.

1. The author mentions "the prison, the medical clinic, and the sexual therapist" (lines 27–28) primarily in order to

   (A) provide examples of social institutions that use language to obscure reality
   (B) indicate situations in which social institutions do not necessarily ameliorate the effects of social problems
   (C) describe instances of new uses of language by some social institutions
   (D) enumerate areas in which the use of language can act to modify reality
   (E) examine actions of social institutions that appear to contradict the purpose normally ascribed to them

2. Which one of the following aspects of the "subject" (line 12) does the author appear to consider most important to the development of theories of language?

   (A) that its existence cannot directly be verified
   (B) that it serves as a bridge between the universes of language and reality
   (C) that representations of it must necessarily be identical to it
   (D) that it indicates why the division between language and reality cannot be maintained
   (E) that it is not, in the strictest sense, real

3. Based on the passage, with which one of the following statements would Baudrillard be most likely to agree?

   (A) Since signifiers such as the word "courage" do not correspond to concrete objects in the real world, they cannot be said to signify anything.
   (B) Even though signifiers such as the word "baseball" correspond to concrete objects in the real world, they cannot be said to signify anything.
   (C) Despite the fact that signifiers such as the word "juggle" correspond to actions rather than concrete objects, they nevertheless signify real things.
   (D) Because signifiers such as the word "ouch" do not correspond to concrete objects in the real world, they must signify other signifiers.
   (E) Although signifiers such as "shoe" correspond to concrete objects in the real world, they can only be understood with reference to other signifiers.

4. According to the passage, which of the following would be LEAST consistent with the philosophical responses described in lines 16–18?

   (A) A novel includes the recurring theme that art is an improvement upon reality.
   (B) A painting depicts its subject engaging in normal bodily functions that most people believe should not be seen or discussed in public.
   (C) A sculpture is composed of objects that can be bought in any electronics store.
   (D) A poem includes quotes from an army's official notice of the death of a soldier in combat.
   (E) A short story portrays a housewife's trip to the corner store using images drawn from an epic poem about a famous hero's journeys.

5. Which one of the following, if true, most supports the author's claim about the application of Foucault's ideas to "many commonplaces of organized society" (line 40)?

   (A) Fashion magazines devote the majority of their articles to new trends in how people dress.
   (B) Pharmaceutical companies fund studies intended to discover new uses for the medicines they manufacture.
   (C) Environmental agencies examine regions with unusual rates of rare diseases in an effort to identify pollution hazards.
   (D) Political candidates adjust the content of their policy speeches based on the least popular features of their opponents' policies.
   (E) Developers of new technologies pay for advertising that describes the new technologies' advantages over earlier technologies.

6. Which one of the following does the author explicitly identify as a characteristic of Baudrillard's philosophy of language?

   (A) It does not consider signifiers to have meaning.
   (B) It makes no distinction between reality and opinion.
   (C) It identifies a change in the function of language over time.
   (D) It dispenses with the idea of objective reality.
   (E) It obscures the way in which language can influence reality.

7. The primary purpose of the passage is to

   (A) describe the development of an idea
   (B) resolve a philosophical dispute
   (C) criticize a controversial theory
   (D) affirm a traditional belief
   (E) exemplify a radical approach

19

Practice Section 5: Reading Comprehension

Directions: Each passage in this section is followed by a group of questions to be answered on the basis of what is <u>stated</u> or <u>implied</u> in the passage. For some of the questions, more than one of the choices could conceivably answer the question. However, you are to choose the <u>best</u> answer; that is, the response that most accurately and completely answers the question, and blacken the corresponding space on your answer sheet.

The ugly legacy of colonial exploitation in Africa is nowhere more evident than in the issue of land reform in Zimbabwe, known as Rhodesia under British rule.
(5) The colony began as a land grab, with Cecil Rhodes's British South Africa Company buying concessions from the British crown and then pushing native Africans off the lands the colonists now "owned" with British military backing. The result was that white colonists, less than 1 percent of the population,
(10) claimed more than 80 percent of the country's arable land, confining Africans to so-called Native Reserves of the poorest and least productive tracts. Rhodesia was ruled by a regime of institutional racism that eventually became unpalatable even to its British
(15) sponsors, and the Lancaster House agreement in 1979 formalized majority rule in the former colony. Robert Mugabe was elected President in 1980, thanks to his Zanu-PF Party, which had been a central force in the long struggle for independence.
(20) Land reform was a main issue in the Lancaster House agreement, which instituted a "willing buyer, willing seller" principle. White landowners who wished to leave Zimbabwe would be bought out by the government, with the help of a fund that was set
(25) up by the British. Reasonable as the idea sounded, its implementation put Mugabe in a situation that negotiators on both sides knew would be impossible. Few white farmers wished to sell their land, some of the most fertile in Africa; the fund for buying it
(30) was of limited size; and Zimbabwe quickly incurred heavy debt to the International Monetary Fund, which imposed structural reforms that weakened Mugabe's government. Inevitably, an alternative method of acquiring land was sought, in the form of
(35) a new constitution put to referendum in 2000, which would have permitted confiscation of land from white farmers without compensation.
The reasons that the new constitution was voted down were another legacy of colonialism. To be sure,
(40) white farmers opposed the constitution, but they could not have affected its defeat by themselves. The blame for its failure belongs with Mugabe himself, and a governing style reminiscent of the repressive and corrupt colonial government he had helped to
(45) overthrow. Redistributed land was disproportionately given to government officials and Mugabe allies, and despite denials it seems clear that land reform

became the foundation of a spoils system designed to reinforce Mugabe's power. There was a plausible
(50) fear that the new constitution would pave the way for Mugabe to become Zimbabwe's dictator for life. Its failure precipitated forced and in many cases violent seizure of land by bands of Zanu-PF war veterans—a seizure that Mugabe made no effort to stop and may
(55) have organized. In response, nervous multinationals withdrew capital, the United States and Britain led the way in imposing sanctions, and within the space of a few years Zimbabwe went from a net exporter of food to a country that no longer produced enough to
(60) feed its own citizens. Land reform ultimately resulted not only in famine and the complete collapse of the country's economy, but also initiated a fatal struggle between Mugabe and his opponents that undermined Zimbabwe's democratic institutions and threatened to
(65) plunge the country into civil war.

1. Which one of the following most accurately expresses the main point of the passage?

(A) In his role as Zimbabwe's president, Robert Mugabe employed governing methods similar to those of the country's colonial rulers by resorting to violence to effect needed land reform.

(B) The issue of land reform in former British colonies in Africa is a complicated one because the descendents of those who seized land aggressively defend their property rights.

(C) The history of land seizure in Zimbabwe, both by British colonists and eventually by those who succeeded the colonial rulers, demonstrates the difficulties of postcolonial government in African countries.

(D) Although Zimbabwe's colonial history is responsible for the difficulty of land reform in that country, Robert Mugabe's use of the land reform effort and his power as president threatens the country's future.

(E) Contrary to the opinions held by those who blame Zimbabwe's difficulties on its past colonial rulers, the blame for that country's difficulties belongs primarily to the failure of that country's democratic systems in the postcolonial period.

2. Based on the information in the passage, with which one of the following statements regarding the Lancaster House agreement would the author be most likely to agree?

(A) Despite its difficulty of implementation, it outlined a reasonable system for redistributing lands seized during the colonial period.

(B) Though the "willing buyer, willing seller" principle respected property rights, it did not go far enough in redressing the historical wrongs of colonization.

(C) It included protections for white landowners whose right to the land they held was of questionable legitimacy.

(D) It was ultimately responsible for the violent seizure of land by Zanu-PF war veterans after the proposed constitution was voted down in 2000.

(E) Its eventual failure to effect a peaceful transfer of land from white landowners to the indigenous residents of Zimbabwe could have been predicted.

3. The author mentions which one of the following in the passage?

(A) a specific example of the racist policies of Rhodesia's colonial government

(B) an example of a way in which land reform in Zimbabwe served some purpose other than to redress historical inequities

(C) an example of the structural reforms imposed on the Zimbabwean government by the International Monetary Fund

(D) the approximate amount of land that was returned to natives of Zimbabwe under the "willing buyer, willing seller" principle

(E) the approximate number of farms seized by Zanu-PF war veterans after the failure of the proposed new constitution in 2000

4. The author's attitude toward the proposed new constitution put to referendum in Zimbabwe in 2000 can most accurately be described as

(A) certainty that at least some of its provisions were necessary to address problems the country faced

(B) approval of the departure from past colonial principles that its provisions represented

(C) surprise at the fact that it was rejected by the country's voting populace

(D) disapproval of the changes to the country's democratic institutions that its provisions would have instituted

(E) outrage at its rejection of the "willing buyer, willing seller" principle

5. In the passage, the author is primarily concerned with

(A) summarizing the history of land reform in Zimbabwe and suggesting why efforts to redistribute land fairly in that country have failed

(B) indicating the historical origins of Zimbabwe's conflict over land and asserting that the country is still not free of the disastrous effects of colonization

(C) illustrating the advantages of allowing difficult domestic issues in Zimbabwe to be resolved with the help of the international community by demonstrating the country's inability to solve those problems peacefully without such help

(D) comparing the difficulty of land reform in Zimbabwe to the other domestic problems that have arisen in the country as a result of its past status as a British colony

(E) discussing the effect of interference of past colonial powers on Zimbabwe's efforts to free itself from the consequences of colonial policies

6. The author's discussion in lines 27–32 is intended primarily to

(A) substantiate the claim that the "willing buyer, willing seller" principle was inadequate to address the historical inequities of land ownership in Zimbabwe

(B) undermine the claim that the "willing buyer, willing seller" principle provided a reasonable method of peacefully solving Zimbabwe's land reform problems

(C) specify the reasons why the "willing buyer, willing seller" principle was eventually superseded in the efforts to redistribute lands seized during Zimbabwe's colonial past

(D) offer evidence that the new Zimbabwean constitution in 2000 represented an improvement upon the "willing buyer, willing seller" principle

(E) foreshadow the violent seizures of land by war veterans in Zimbabwe when the "willing buyer, willing seller" principle failed

7. Which one of the following, if true, would most call into question the author's assertion in the last sentence of the passage?

(A) Most members of Mugabe's Zanu-PF Party are members of one native tribe, while government opponents are primarily members of another native tribe, and these tribes were often engaged in armed conflict during the precolonial period.

(B) U.S. and British sanctions imposed after the forceful seizure of land in Zimbabwe were accompanied by increased funding for humanitarian efforts to distribute food and medicine to the populace.

(C) The constitution of Zimbabwe that took effect in 1980 included provisions that allowed the President to appoint members of the country's highest court without the approval of the legislative assembly.

(D) A decade-long period of drought in many regions of Africa, including Zimbabwe, has led to decreased crop yields and increased food prices throughout the region over this period.

(E) The structural reforms imposed by the International Monetary Fund increased the attractiveness of Zimbabwe to international investors, but they diminished the government's ability to prevent humanitarian disasters in the country.

The Fourth Amendment of the U.S. Constitution states simply that "the right of the people to be secure in their persons, houses, papers, and effects, against unreasonable searches and seizures, shall not

(5) be violated," but the question of how to protect this right is anything but simple. In theory, violations of a defendant's Fourth Amendment rights could be punishable by criminal or civil action, but very few efforts in that direction have ever been successful.

(10) The U.S. Supreme Court has settled, not without vacillation, on a principle known as the exclusionary rule as the only effective means of guaranteeing rights promised by the Fourth Amendment.

One unusual feature of the exclusionary rule is

(15) that it acts at a substantial remove from the conduct it nominally governs. Although its purpose is to prevent illegal searches and seizures, it serves that purpose by dealing with the use of illegally obtained evidence in court. Under a broad interpretation, the exclusionary

(20) rule prevents the introduction of such evidence, and thus ideally deters investigators from violating the Fourth Amendment because it raises the possibility that an illegal search will deprive prosecutors of evidence that is crucial to obtaining a conviction. As

(25) it is applied, however, the exclusionary rule relies on a contingent relation between the illegal search and its consequences that leaves substantial latitude for legal maneuvering. Evidence that arguably would have been obtained without the clues resulting from

(30) an illegal search is not subject to exclusion; evidence obtained by violating a coconspirator or codefendant's Fourth Amendment rights is not subject to exclusion; illegally obtained evidence can be introduced to impeach a defendant's testimony even if it would

(35) have been excluded as proof of guilt. Historically, the exclusionary rule has provided only weak protection against illegal searches.

Popular sentiment in an era of "wars" against terrorism, drugs, and organized crime is heavily

(40) against acquittals on the grounds of perceived technicalities, and this fact has encouraged even further weakening of the exclusionary rule through interpretations that rely on its deterrent effect. These interpretations see the exclusionary rule as applying

(45) to an investigator's knowledge: if an investigator cannot reasonably be said to be aware that a search is illegal, then the exclusionary rule cannot exert its deterrent effect, and thus does not apply. This "good faith" exception means that evidence obtained on the

(50) basis of a warrant that is subsequently found to be flawed is not subject to exclusion as long as the person conducting the search was unaware of the flaw. This exception has been extended to include warrants that are flawed because the laws on which they are based

(55) are subsequently judged to be unconstitutional, with the odd consequence that it becomes possible to obtain a guilty verdict that purportedly does not violate a defendant's rights with the help of a law that does.

Further weakening of Fourth Amendment protections

(60) seems inevitable, as courts have demonstrated an increasing willingness to consider searches conducted without any warrant at all as not being "unreasonable."

8. Which one of the following most accurately states the main point of the passage?

(A) Although the Fourth Amendment of the U.S. Constitution promises citizens protection against "unreasonable searches and seizures," as interpreted by the court this protection applies only to a very few egregious abuses of a defendant's rights.

(B) In the near future, the exclusionary rule will cease to be the main method by which the courts enforce defendants' Fourth Amendment rights under the U.S. Constitution, as searches conducted without a warrant become more common.

(C) The "good faith" exception to the exclusionary rule represents only one example in a long history of efforts by the court to find a way of ensuring the rights guaranteed in the Fourth Amendment of the U.S. Constitution without unduly hampering law enforcement.

(D) Historically, the rights guaranteed by the Fourth Amendment of the U.S. Constitution have been protected by the exclusionary rule, but the application and meaning of that rule have changed throughout its history.

(E) The exclusionary rule provides the only enforceable protection of a defendant's rights under the Fourth Amendment of the U.S. Constitution, but the protection it offers is inadequate, and interpretations of its meaning have tended over time to narrow its scope even further.

9. In lines 28–35, the author lists several exceptions to the exclusionary rule primarily in order to

(A) demonstrate why the exclusionary rule's deterrent effect cannot apply in cases when an investigator acts in good faith

(B) explain the assertion that the exclusionary rule's protection operates at a substantial remove from the conduct it nominally governs

(C) illustrate situations in which the application of the exclusionary rule fails to protect a defendant's Fourth Amendment rights

(D) defend a broader interpretation of the exclusionary rule than the one most often adopted by the courts

(E) provide evidence that the exclusionary rule, as it has been interpreted by courts, does not apply to all evidence that is obtained in a questionable manner

10. Popular sentiment as described in the passage would be most likely to agree with which one of the following statements?

(A) If a defendant cannot be convicted without the use of tainted evidence, then the prosecution should be permitted to introduce that evidence.

(B) If a defendant who is accused of participating in a terrorist plot is acquitted because key evidence was tainted, then the prosecution should be allowed to retry the defendant on the same charges at a later time.

(C) If a defendant is guilty of a serious crime, the prosecution should not be prevented from introducing tainted evidence that is necessary to prove the defendant's guilt.

(D) Only tainted evidence that would tend to exculpate a defendant should be excluded from prosecutions involving drug trafficking, terrorism, or other forms of organized crime.

(E) Only if evidence relevant to a case is tainted should the prosecution be barred from introducing that evidence in its case against the defendant.

11. The information in the passage provides the most support for which one of the following statements about the exclusionary rule?

(A) It has not always been the method courts have prescribed for protecting citizens against unreasonable searches.

(B) Its scope is too narrow because it protects only criminal defendants against unreasonable searches.

(C) It interferes with the prosecution of criminals who commit the most serious of offenses.

(D) It is broadly applied only in cases that do not involve terrorism, drugs, or organized crime.

(E) Its protections are also justified on the basis of a defendant's constitutional protection against self-incrimination.

12. Which one of the following describes a role most similar to that of investigators in the passage who conduct searches on the basis of warrants that are subsequently found to be flawed?

(A) A bank repossesses a car for nonpayment of a loan on the basis of a clerical error made by a bill collection agency and eventually returns the car.

(B) A principal suspends a student for cheating on an exam on the basis of another student's false report and eventually reinstates the student's exam score.

(C) A doctor orders a blood test for a patient because of confusion with another patient's name and eventually finds the cause of the patient's illness because of that test.

(D) A commuter takes an alternate route to work because of a mistaken traffic report and eventually arrives at work fifteen minutes late.

(E) A child obeys a parent's instructions for assembling a new toy and eventually finds that those instructions were faulty, and the toy does not work properly.

13. Which one of the following principles, if established, would most strengthen the position of the courts as it is described in the final sentence of the passage?

(A) A search conducted without a warrant is unreasonable when a warrant could have been obtained for that search without any foreseeable change in the result of the search.

(B) A search conducted without a warrant is reasonable only when a request for a warrant for that search would certainly have resulted in a warrant being issued.

(C) A search conducted without a warrant is reasonable only when the nature of the criminal act being investigated is such that the delay in obtaining a warrant could potentially result in harm to citizens.

(D) A search conducted without a warrant is unreasonable only when there is no reason to believe that the notice of a search being conducted could result in the loss or destruction of relevant evidence.

(E) A search conducted without a warrant is unreasonable even when the evidence obtained in the search provides proof of the commission of a criminal act other than the one for which the investigation is being conducted.

The writings of Franz Kafka have become so
integrated into understandings of contemporary
life that his very name has become a cliché:
"Kafkaesque," referring to the baffling, inhuman, and
(5) alienating experience of an individual acted on by
institutional power. To be sure, the bureaucracies and
totalitarianisms of the twentieth century—whether
they are taken to be actively inimical, as in Stalinist
communism, or to be impersonally labyrinthine, as
(10) in the democracies of the West—have led many to
read Kafka in retrospect as an allegory of developing
social technologies in the government of humanity,
and their corresponding mutilations of the individual.
Yet to read Kafka in this manner is to miss both
(15) the humor and the complexity of his insights into
what it is to live, regardless of government or social
circumstance. In *The Castle*, Kafka's protagonist K.
embarks on an impossible quest to secure a permit
to sleep in the village ruled by the Baron Westwest.
(20) This last of Kafka's works, which like many others
was incomplete at the time of his death, has been read
variously as an allegory of an individual's search for
social acceptance, for religious enlightenment, for
existential justification, or for psychological comfort.
(25) Any such reading, however, obscures the central irony
of the work—or, more to the point, participates in and
duplicates it. *The Castle*, like most of Kafka's work,
concerns a search for meaning in a world that resists
it. To read it with the idea in mind of discerning a
(30) grand truth is to embark on one's own fruitless quest,
seeking admission to a castle that remains forever
shut. K.'s quest is not an allegory of individual
search; it is the search for allegory itself. The reader
who earnestly seeks meaning in the universe Kafka
(35) creates becomes enmeshed in that universe as a direct
reflection of the protagonist.
　　Perhaps the starkest expression of this capacity
of Kafka's work to inscribe the reader's own desire
for understanding is his famous work "In the Penal
(40) Colony." The condemned in the colony do not know
for what crime they are being punished, but their
sentence is to be executed by a machine that writes
the name of their crime in the skin on their backs. The
central image of this machine has been seen by those
(45) who read with a psychological or sociological bent as
a metaphor for paranoia or guilt, or as an expression of
the self-enforcing power of official pronouncements,
but it speaks more broadly to the dangers of ultimate
explanations. The means by which the condemned
(50) approaches knowledge of the reason for his or her
punishment is the instrument of punishment itself;
the moment of realization is the moment of death. In
a similar fashion, the reader who blithely supposes
he or she has found the secret of the penal colony's
(55) meaning—the solution of the existential puzzle
it represents—takes the place of the condemned
prisoner. The folly of the interpreter's search for
ultimate meaning in Kafka's work is inscribed in the
interpretation itself, by the text it seeks to explain.

14. Which one of the following best summarizes the
main idea of the passage?

(A) While many read the works of Franz Kafka
with the intent of discerning its meaning, the
effort is fruitless because Kafka's work is not
intended to convey meaning.

(B) Readers of Franz Kafka's work who seek a
single interpretation of its meaning reenact
the futile and sometimes fatal desires of
Kafka's characters.

(C) The practice of reading texts with the idea in
mind of discerning grand truths represents
a mutilation of those texts, as Franz Kafka's
work illustrates.

(D) Although Franz Kafka's work cannot be said to
convey any single meaning, its success is due
to the fact that it can be interpreted in many
different and sometimes contradictory ways.

(E) No reading of Franz Kafka's work that does
not take into account its resistance to ultimate
meaning can be complete.

15. According to the passage, which one of the
following is true of both psychological and
sociological interpretations of Kafka's work "In the
Penal Colony?"

(A) Although both have merit, neither includes a
satisfactory explanation of the work's text as
allegory.

(B) Both interpret the machine as it is described in
the text as a metaphor for guilt.

(C) Neither involves a proper understanding of the
mechanism of punishment as it is described in
the text.

(D) The text of the work itself suggests that both
are inadequate as explanations of the text.

(E) Neither attempts to put their explanations
in the context of an individual's search for
ultimate meaning.

16. Which one of the following best describes the attitude of the author toward the idea that *The Castle* is an allegory of an individual's quest for social acceptance?

(A) unqualified contempt
(B) cynical indifference
(C) amused dismissal
(D) considered rejection
(E) grudging acceptance

17. Which one of the following best describes the primary purpose of the passage?

(A) providing an extended description of an author's work
(B) defending the controversial assertions of influential critics
(C) detailing the chronological development of a complex theory
(D) examining modern interpretations of a historical personage
(E) analyzing a common shortcoming of several interpretations

18. It can be inferred from the passage that the meaning of the word "Kafkaesque" as illustrated by Kafka's work *The Castle* most nearly means

(A) misunderstood
(B) baffling
(C) alienating
(D) fruitless
(E) existential

19. Which one of the following best describes the organization of the passage?

(A) Several related positions are discussed, and then all of them are subjected to the same criticism.
(B) An interpretive method is described, and then this method is criticized in light of the work it is employed to interpret.
(C) Several positions are outlined, and several different evaluations of these positions are offered.
(D) Examples are given of the inaccuracy of a common belief.
(E) Two theories are rejected through consideration of two separate applications of those theories.

The development of genetic technologies and the ability of companies to patent novel gene combinations in commercially important food crops has led to a new and controversial industry:
(5) the engineering of genetically modified organisms (GMOs). GMOs are produced by taking genetic material from one organism—a bacterium, animal, or plant—and using it to transform the genome of another, perhaps quite different organism to give
(10) it useful properties. *Bt* corn, for instance, involves implanting in corn a gene from the bacterium *Bacillus thuringiensis* that codes for a protein fatal to the corn borer, an insect that can dramatically harm corn crop yields. The protein itself has been used as an
(15) insecticide in organic farming for years and has never been shown to harm any organism aside from corn borers, but it is expensive to apply effectively; *Bt* corn produces the protein in its own cells, obviating the need for external application.
(20) Those who approve of genetic modification of food crops argue that this technique is merely a logical extension of what farmers and scientists have been doing for centuries. Various methods have long been employed to improve food crops' yields, tolerance
(25) for local environmental conditions, and resistance to pests and herbicides. Like conventional breeding, genetic modification is "natural" in the sense that the introduced genes occur in the wild, albeit in different organisms. The benefits offered by such
(30) genetic alterations are not merely commercial: a native resistance to pests allows less use of possibly dangerous insecticides; a food plant better suited to its growing environment requires less fertilizer, a major source of environmental pollution. GMOs also offer
(35) the potential of helping to solve intractable problems in developing countries by incorporating genes that increase a food's nutritional value, or produce compounds that can cure diseases such as malaria that are treatable but nevertheless remain serious
(40) worldwide problems.
Yet those who object to the genetic modification of food crops grown on a global scale have ample reason to mistrust the alliance of science and industry that GMOs represent. Past technologies
(45) that have been adopted too enthusiastically and used too incautiously have led to unforeseen ecological consequences: the use of fossil fuels as a cheap and plentiful energy source has contributed to acid rain and global warming; antibiotics, because of their
(50) indiscriminate use, have led in time to dangerous microbes that modern medicine finds exceptionally difficult to fight. Despite extensive testing and, at least so far, careful use, the technology of genetic modification may have unanticipated effects on
(55) ecologies. Local environmental disasters, such as the explosion of zebra mussels in the Great Lakes region

of the United States, have been precipitated merely by the introduction of naturally occurring organisms into new environments. By allowing individual genes
(60) to propagate independent of the organisms that carry them, genetic modification may be effecting drastic changes that are not yet completely understood. The need for caution in pursuing this technology, however, should not be allowed to stifle its development
(65) entirely. Genetic modification is powerful and, like all power, can be dangerous as well as beneficial. It should never be used lightly. At the same time, to reject utterly a technology that is capable of saving lives and ameliorating serious human problems would
(70) be a deplorable ethical failing.

20. Which one of the following most accurately states the main point of the passage?

(A) Genetically modified organisms offer the opportunity to solve several of the most serious problems in the developing world and must be developed as rapidly as possible.

(B) The alliance of technology and commerce that the growing industry surrounding genetically modified organisms represents poses serious potential environmental problems that science does not fully understand.

(C) Although those who oppose the genetic modification of commercially important organisms are correct to advocate caution in the use of this technology, their objections must not be allowed to prevent its development.

(D) Scientists must mediate between the profit motives of interested corporations and the instinctive mistrust of skeptics in deciding how rapidly the technology of genetic modification should be developed and how widely it should be used.

(E) Genetic modification, which involves the implantation of other organisms' genes into commercially important food crops, will be an important technology in the future growth of the world's food supply.

21. Given the information in the passage, which one of the following best exemplifies the type of danger mentioned in lines 59–62?

(A) The bacteria that occur naturally in the human intestine, after they are exposed to an antibiotic, disproportionately include a gene that confers resistance to that antibiotic; those bacteria may then pass that resistance on to other bacteria with which they come in contact.

(B) Genetically modified corn that has been transformed using a bacterial gene that makes it tolerant to saline soils incorporates that gene in its pollen; these corn plants may then spread this gene to plants in nearby corn fields with less saline soils, harming crop yields there.

(C) Genetically modified tomatoes that have been altered using a gene from salmon to enhance their color produce a protein not normally found in tomatoes that triggers a common allergy; a person who unknowingly consumes food made with a modified tomato may then have an unanticipated allergic reaction to that food.

(D) Genetically modified bacteria that have been altered using a gene from other bacteria in deep ocean trenches that can metabolize sulfur are spread in an area that has been contaminated with sulfur by a chemical spill; after the sulfur in the spill has been metabolized, the bacteria may then die off from lack of food.

(E) Genetically modified potatoes include a marker gene that, in bacteria, causes them to reproduce at substantially increased rates; harmful bacteria living in the soil where these potatoes are grown may then acquire this gene and pose a threat of disease outbreak in the area.

22. Which one of the following is NOT identified by the author as a potential benefit of the genetic modification of organisms?

(A) inclusion of beneficial nutrients in foods that do not normally possess them

(B) increased ability of food plants to inhibit the growth of competing plants in soils where they are planted

(C) enhanced yields of food crops in areas where they do not normally grow well

(D) decreased need for toxic chemicals to control the pests that damage food crops

(E) lessening of the impact of large-scale farming on the local environment

23. The passage suggests which one of the following about *Bt* corn?

(A) The protein that occurs in its cells is not dangerous to people who eat food products made from it.

(B) Some species of harmful insect other than the corn borer may be effectively controlled by its use.

(C) The protein found in its cells does not occur naturally.

(D) By current standards, it can be considered an organic food.

(E) It is now grown by at least as many farmers as conventional forms of unmodified corn are.

24. The reference to zebra mussels in the third paragraph is most likely intended to

(A) indicate why the fact that a change involves natural elements need not imply that the change is not harmful

(B) describe an instance in which the genetic modification of an organism has led to serious environmental consequences

(C) demonstrate that local environmental problems may arise from the global-scale adoption of a technology

(D) illustrate the fact that intentional alterations to a local environment may have unintended harmful consequences

(E) serve as an example of the way in which natural processes may without human intervention lead to environmental disasters

25. Based on the passage, those who object to the genetic modification of organisms would be most likely to respond in which one of the following ways to a proposal to grow a food crop that has been modified to help prevent scurvy, a deficiency in vitamin C, in an area where that deficiency is common?

(A) Food crops that naturally combat scurvy, such as oranges and lemons, should be grown in that area instead.

(B) Instead of growing the modified crops, interested governments and organizations should supply nutritional supplements to the area.

(C) Since many plants not normally grown as food crops contain vitamin C, if any such plants occur naturally in the area and can safely be incorporated in the local diet, they should be grown instead.

(D) Economic development of the area to provide residents the ability to trade for foods that supply vitamin C should be implemented instead.

(E) Since the growth of modified food crops may have unanticipated effects on the local environment, an extensive study of the likely effects of growing the modified crop should be undertaken before planting is begun.

26. Which one of the following most accurately describes the organization of the passage?

(A) The history of the genetic modification of organisms is described, possible future benefits of such modification are discussed, and an evaluation of how likely those benefits are to materialize is offered.

(B) An example of a genetically modified organism is given, the steps undertaken by the developers of that organism to promote its spread are described, and possible reasons for the failure of those who opposed its spread are given.

(C) A new technology is introduced, the possible benefits of that technology are discussed, the reasons why those benefits have so far been insufficient to encourage the wide adoption of the technology are listed, and a revised approach to advocating the technology's use is urged.

(D) One application of a new technology is explained, the current and possible future benefits of this application are described, reasons for caution in pursuing these benefits are indicated, and a balanced approach to using the technology is recommended.

(E) An approach to a controversial problem is described, the advantages of this approach are detailed, the possible drawbacks of this approach are considered, and the approach is ultimately found to be of limited usefulness in addressing the problem.

ANSWER KEY TO PRACTICE SECTION 5: READING COMPREHENSION

For full answers and explanations, turn to Chapter 21.

1. D
2. C
3. B
4. A
5. B
6. C
7. A
8. E
9. E
10. C
11. A
12. C
13. D
14. B
15. D
16. D
17. E
18. C
19. B
20. C
21. E
22. B
23. A
24. A
25. C
26. D

PART V

Answers and Explanations

PART

Answers and
Explanations

20

Answers and Explanations to Drills

CHAPTER 3

DRILL #1

Pages 25 – 28

1. **D** Main Point

A recent study's results seem to show that having two or more pets in the household poses greater health risks to children than owning one pet or no pets. The study, however, included fewer than fifty children. From this fact, the argument concludes that the study's results do not conclusively show that having two or more pets actually does pose a threat. Note that this does not necessarily mean that having two or more pets is safe; the argument is primarily concerned with this particular study, not with whether pets are safe or unsafe.

(A) This answer is too broad. The argument doesn't register an opinion on whether or not pets pose a threat to children; this choice doesn't even mention the argument's main concern: the individual study that involved fewer than fifty children.

(B) Careful! The first part of this one sounds great, but the reason given for why the study isn't convincing doesn't match the one in the argument. The argument mentions the number of children involved in the study; this choice mentions the type of health risk that was studied.

(C) This takes a step beyond the conclusion. The argument's point is that one particular study is not convincing; the argument doesn't offer an opinion on whether or not further studies should be done.

(D) This is the one we want. Its scope includes only "a recent study," and it uses the paraphrase "fails to demonstrate" to convey the idea that this study "cannot be considered convincing." Don't be thrown off by the use of the phrase "causal link." Although this language is not used in the argument, the whole background of the argument is a discussion of whether or not pet ownership poses a risk to children's health—that is, whether or not having multiple pets can cause increased rates of illness.

(E) This one's hypothetical. The argument doesn't tell us what the study would have found if it had included more subjects; the whole point of the argument is that the study didn't include enough, and so we can't be sure what it found.

2. **C** Point at Issue

X's point is that it would make no sense for some other author to have written Shakespeare's famous plays under an assumed name. The reason offered is, in effect, that Shakespeare's plays are good and any famous author who wrote them would wish to have his or her authorship of such good plays known.

Y responds by focusing on X's assumption that some single author was responsible for all of Shakespeare's plays. It is possible, after all, that some group of separate authors, or perhaps a committee working together, wrote them.

When we select an answer here, we want to make sure we pick something about which, at minimum, we can be sure X and Y disagree.

(A) This is very close. The problem with this choice is that it talks about a single playwright having written all of Shakespeare's plays. Although this is definitely the idea that X is arguing against, it isn't precisely the one that Y is arguing in favor of.

(B) Y would definitely agree that this is possible, and it is a large part of the point Y's trying to make. Unfortunately, since this isn't a possibility considered by X's argument, we can't properly say that this is the main point at issue.

(C) This is the best statement of the main point of disagreement between X and Y. X's first sentence states explicitly that it is "ridiculous" to think that anyone other than the historical person named William Shakespeare wrote the plays; Y's main point is that they might not have been written by any individual, but instead were written by a group of authors. X thinks the statement in this answer choice cannot be correct; Y thinks that it can.

(D) Y's argument does not include any mention of wishing to conceal the real authorship of the plays, so this can't be the main point at issue between them.

(E) Careful with this one. X does indeed make the assumption mentioned in this choice, and it is also the one that Y attacks. But, first, X's main point isn't concerned with whether the authorship of the plays is single or multiple; the whole pretext of Y's response is that X doesn't even address this possibility. Second, Y's point is not so strongly stated that we could properly say Y believes that a group of people must have written Shakespeare's plays. Y only argues that this remains a possibility.

3. **A** Main Point

The argument's ultimate concern here is to show that, contrary to most economists' beliefs, government subsidies to food producers are not justified. The reasons offered are that government's obligation is to use its resources in the most efficient manner possible, and that help for consumers when they're struggling would be more efficient overall than ongoing support for producers.

(A) This isn't perfect, but it's the best choice we have to work with. It doesn't mention food subsidies specifically, but it does mention economists, which is definitely part of the argument's main point; note that these "economists" are mentioned twice at key points in the argument.

(B) This is a reason used to support the conclusion, not the main conclusion of the argument.

(C) This is a hypothetical. Remember, on a question like this one you need to pick the exact conclusion that the argument wants you to draw, not something else that seems to be a consequence of what's contained in the argument.

(D) This is certainly something that the argument agrees with, but like (B) it's too narrow. This is a statement that supports the conclusion, but it isn't the conclusion itself.

(E) This is far too general to be the main conclusion of this argument. The scope here isn't the business cycle versus government subsidies generally, but economists' beliefs about government subsidies to food producers specifically.

4. **E** Main Point

This one has tough language. The main point here is that intent matters when it comes to the question of whether or not an individual is responsible for the unintended consequences of an action he or she takes. A person's responsibility for accidental consequences of aggressive and violent actions is offered in support of this statement.

(A) This is close, but it isn't quite specific enough. The argument's main point is focused on intent as it relates to accidental consequences; this choice, however, doesn't mention intent or anything like it.

(B) The argument doesn't say that aggressive and violent actions are the only ones for which the person performing them can be held responsible for unforeseen consequences. This certainly isn't the main thing that the argument is trying to convince us of.

(C) This is a side issue. Remember, the answer to a main point question is the one thing that the argument is constructed to lead us to believe.

(D) This is a logical consequence of information presented in the argument, but once again it isn't the main thing that the argument wants us to know.

(E) This is the one we want. It contains all the pieces we were looking for in the main point: responsibility, accidental consequences, and—most importantly for a comparison with (A)—what the intent of the action was.

5. **B** Point at Issue

Inez argues that there is no reason to refurbish the home to comply with new fire codes. She offers two reasons: First, compliance with the new codes would not have prevented the property damage associated with a recent fire in their home; second, the cost of complying with the codes is greater than the costs in fines associated with not complying.

Jacques responds by focusing the discussion not on property, but on the potential loss of life associated with a fire. Complying with the new codes would make any fire like the recent one less of a threat to their lives. Jacques, then, clearly provides a reason to comply with the new fire codes.

(A)   Careful here. Jacques directly appeals to the reason for the new fire codes, but Inez does not. She mentions property damage and expense, but she never actually says that protecting against property loss is the purpose of the new codes.

(B)   This captures the substance of their disagreement. Inez says there is no reason to refurbish their home; Jacques says there is: providing additional protection to their lives, in the event of a fire.

(C)   Inez states clearly that it isn't, and although we might infer that Jacques believes it is, he never directly says so. In fact, Jacques never registers an explicit opinion on whether or not they should refurbish their home; he simply points out a reason for doing so, responding to Inez's claim that none exists.

(D)   This misses the main substance of their disagreement. Although both make use of the furnace fire last winter to illustrate their points, neither of them is primarily interested in arguing about whether or not it posed a danger.

(E)   The question of whether the protection offered by the new fire codes is "adequate" is never explicitly addressed by either of them. This is a value judgment, and unless the argument explicitly makes such a judgment, it should be avoided when you're picking your answer.

6. **B** Main Point

The point here involves pieces scattered throughout the argument. Put most succinctly, the argument's conclusion is that a person's perception of time changes depending upon his or her motion. The reasons provided state that this must be the case in order for observers moving relative to one another to witness sequences of events that are completely consistent. Abstract as all of this may seem, we want to hang on to the initial sentence of the argument: time is in fact *not* "invariant and objective."

(A)   One of the argument's reasons states that the rules of cause and effect cannot be violated, so it isn't consistent with the argument to say that "time is not governed by predictable laws."

(B)   This is the one we want. Its primary description of the main point is clearly contrary to the argument's opening one. The idea that time is invariant and objective is precisely what the argument is trying to say is untrue. Also, the reasons offered by the argument include one that says "two events perceived by one observer to be simultaneous may not appear simultaneous to an observer moving relative to the first." This is well paraphrased in this choice's statement that "a chronology of events perceived by one observer may not be in all ways identical to a chronology of events perceived by an observer moving relative to the first."

(C)   There is nothing in this argument about "recent discoveries." The argument provides us no way of knowing when or how these ideas about time were initially developed.

(D)   This is an overstatement of a reason offered in the argument. For one thing, the argument's purpose is to make a more general statement about time than this. For another, the argument only says that "two events perceived by one observer to be simultaneous may not appear simultaneous to an observer moving relative to the first." It isn't certain that in all cases they can't be perceived as simultaneous.

(E)   This is a blender answer; it mixes up pieces of the argument in a baffling way. It is easy to reject. The main point is a general statement about perceptions of time; this one is a very specific case involving cause and effect, which, although it is mentioned, is not the primary concern of the argument.

7. **D** Main Point

Don't get too hung up on the details of this one. Basically, the economist is arguing that the report is wrong, and that political concerns played a role in its findings. The premises offer some fairly confusing information from the report to show that one of its conclusions is incorrect.

(A) "In large part" is too much. In fact, the economist uses information from the report itself to refute its conclusion.

(B) It's difficult to say, from the information we have, what assumptions the report makes. This isn't what the economist is attacking.

(C) The notion of "unemployment rate" isn't explicitly mentioned in the argument, and we lack the information we'd need in order to tell what the report is trying to say about it.

(D) This is a nice, safe answer to pick. The economist's argument includes economic data, which the economist does in fact use to call the report's conclusion into question.

(E) Tough. Like (A), though, this choice overstates the case. The economist only states that "the report's findings were politically motivated." It's a rather large jump from there to "merely propaganda." After all, the economist does use information from the report itself to refute its conclusion.

8. **C** The psychoanalyst's main point

The geneticist's conclusion is that the causes of anxiety in humans are not experience or environment, but are instead genetic and biochemical. In support of this, the geneticist offers the fact that the defective gene responsible for a particular disorder in pointers has been found.

The psychoanalyst responds by pointing out two crucial facts about this type of anxiety in pointers: Its symptoms are not the same as the symptoms of the most common type of anxiety found in humans, and the gene that causes this anxiety has no analogous single gene in humans.

Be careful not to go too far when you look for a right answer here. The psychoanalyst's response is intended merely to show that the specific instance of anxiety in pointers isn't particularly relevant to studying and treating anxiety in humans.

(A) This overstates the psychoanalyst's case. The response isn't meant to demonstrate that anxiety in humans categorically isn't caused by heredity and biochemistry; it simply shows that the example of anxiety in pointers isn't really comparable to anxiety in humans.

(B) In fact, the psychoanalyst states that there is no human analogue of the gene that is defective in pointers, so this can't be a correct statement of the psychoanalyst's point.

(C) Again, this choice is a safe and accurate representation of what the psychoanalyst is trying to show. The psychoanalyst points out that (1) the genes of humans and dogs aren't similar in this specific way and (2) the symptoms of anxiety aren't similar, either.

(D) This is hypothetical. Since the psychoanalyst's argument includes the fact that the symptoms of anxiety in pointers are not similar to those found most commonly in humans, the question of what gene defects would give rise to symptoms that are similar is outside the scope of the psychoanalyst's argument.

(E) This may sound nice, but it's far too broad to be a correct statement of the psychoanalyst's argument. The psychoanalyst is talking about what the causes of anxiety in humans are *not*; this answer talks about what the causes are.

Drill #2

Pages 30 – 33

1. D Inference

The passage describes a behavior that is widespread in some species of animals, a reason some people think they exhibit that behavior, and an established rule that explains when and how a behavior becomes widespread within an animal population. It's important to note on an initial pass through the text that the reason some people think the behavior is widespread is not the same as the reason provided by the general rule. In other words, the people who think that some species prey on their own young because it prevents overpopulation are wrong.

(A) This is another blender answer—one that recombines phrases from the passage to form a statement that seems to border on nonsense. In this case, it's easiest to eliminate this choice by noting that the material in the passage allows us to conclude that evolutionary pressure to prevent overpopulation could never encourage any behavior.

(B) Careful! The language here would be perfect except for a pesky "not" planted in the middle of it. The whole upshot of the passage is that the behavior is the result of evolutionary pressure to maximize reproductive success.

(C) Careful here, too! This explains one way in which the behavior might conceivably increase an animal's reproductive success, but remember that the burden here is to pick a choice that must be true. The information provided in the argument isn't explicit enough to allow us to draw any conclusion this specific.

(D) Here's the one we want. The passage lets us know that anyone who thinks a behavior becomes widespread because of any evolutionary pressure other than the one to maximize reproductive success must be wrong. This choice is the only one that gets this idea across.

(E) We don't have anything like the information that we'd need to draw this conclusion. Common sense might suggest that this is true, but we don't have the evidence needed to be sure that it is.

2. C Inference

The argument describes the original rationale for making a business decision, based on predictions of what was likely to happen. What was predicted didn't, in fact, happen, and the result was that company sales went down. We won't be able to predict the exact form or content of the answer, but it seems to make sense that it's going to say something like, "the decision to discontinue our old product line and introduce the new one was really bad."

(A) This is very strong language, and you should always be suspicious of overly strong or emotional language on the LSAT. This choice matches the general idea we're looking for, but we want something that's a little softer.

(B) This is softer than (A), but the language of "a radical response" still seems to come from outside the argument. Besides, once you look at it more closely, you realize that the executive's argument doesn't primarily concern whether the decision was made for the right reasons, but instead whether or not the decision was successful.

(C) Here's the nice, soft language we're looking for. It takes nothing for granted, stipulating "if the goal of our company is to maximize sales" before it goes on to say, in appropriately wishy-washy language, that the decision to change product lines was really bad.

(D) Demotion, firing, blaming individuals—none of this is mentioned in the argument, and it shouldn't appear in our answer, either.

(E) The key term here is "attractive to consumers," and that's enough of a value-laden statement that we should be very suspicious of this choice. Unless we're forced to or the premises of the argument justify it, we shouldn't make the leap from sales to attractiveness to consumers.

3. **E** Inference

You always need to be careful on arguments that involve numbers and percentages. In the last election, 95 percent voted for candidates from the two major parties. In this election, only 90 percent did, and 3,000 fewer votes were cast in this election than in the last one. There is some mention of scandals in the two major parties being responsible for the decline in voting overall. As long as we don't assume too much in picking an answer, we should be fine.

(A) Careful here. Although the passage tells us that the scandals were responsible for the decline in the number of votes cast, we cannot thereby be certain that they were also responsible for the decline in the percentage of cast votes received, no matter how much common sense that conclusion might seem to make.

(B) Careful again. We only know that the number of votes cast this time was 3,000 less than it was last time, and that third-party nominees received 10 percent of the vote this time, as opposed to 5 percent last time. It's possible that 3,000 votes is a substantial portion of the number of votes cast in the last election; as long as it is 50 percent or more, this statement isn't true.

(C) Once again, we see value-laden language here that wasn't included in the original text. We don't know what it means for the parties to be "substantially damaged," so we can safely eliminate this one.

(D) Like (B), this one requires some careful parsing of the language and the numbers. This choice talks about the "percentage of the city's population" that supported third-party candidates, not a percentage of those who chose to vote. Since we really don't know anything about the city's overall population or how it changed, we can't conclude this.

(E) Here we go. The number of votes declined. The percentage of all voters who chose one of the two major-party nominees also declined. That means that the number of votes cast for the major-party nominees has to have declined. This one is definitely true.

4. **A** Disagree

The engineer argues that some place other than the chaotic region should be chosen as the surface probe's landing site. The reasons offered are that the most important factor to consider in selecting a landing site is its likelihood of success, and the chaotic region poses a high risk of not being successful.

The scientist counters that every landing site is at least a little risky, and no other site promises scientific benefits that are at all comparable to those offered by the chaotic region.

We need to pick an answer that describes something we can be absolutely certain the two participants in the conversation would disagree about. Don't jump to conclusions; look for explicit statements that indicate one of the participants would say one thing, and the other participant would say the other.

(A) The engineer would say that this is false: No factor is more important than the likelihood of success. The scientist would say that this is true: Scientific benefit should also be considered in deciding about a landing site.

(B) The scientist would say that this is false: No landing site is completely free of risk. We don't know what the engineer's opinion on this matter would be, however.

(C) We know the scientist would say that this is false, but like (B), we don't know what the engineer would say. The engineer appears not to be interested at all in the scientific benefits of the mission.

(D) Very close. We know that the engineer would say this is false: The success of the mission is the "most important concern." Although the scientist indicates that scientific benefit should also be considered, we don't have strong enough evidence to conclude that the scientist considers this the "most important factor." This is just a tad too strong.

(E) This is actually something they agree on. Landing outside the chaotic region would minimize the risks; landing inside the chaotic region would maximize the scientific benefits. They appear to disagree about which choice should be made between the two, but both accept that it's impossible both to minimize the risk and maximize the benefit.

5. D Inference

A new medication can, it is believed, be used to cure some types of cancer, but only if it is administered at very high dosages. At those dosages, the medication is extremely toxic. The medication was approved for use at the lower dosages, but would not receive approval at the higher dosages required to be effective against cancer. We're looking for something that must be true, given all of these facts.

(A) The only thing we know was "erroneous," according to the information presented in the argument, were the original estimates of the dosages at which the medication would be effective against cancer. We can't conclude from the passage material that any of the studies or trials are incorrect.

(B) We aren't told anything in the passage about any medication other than the new one developed by PharmCorp.

(C) Although this might be something it's useful to investigate when attempting to decide whether or not the medication should be approved for treating cancer, it isn't something we know from the information presented in the passage.

(D) Here's what we want. Either it will be administered at the currently recommended and approved dosage, in which case it won't be effective against cancer; or else it will be administered at a higher dosage, in which case the incidence of toxic side-effects would be administered in a way the approval standard classifies as too dangerous.

(E) No, the relevant difference presented in the passage is that, in order to be effective against cancer, the medication must be administered at a higher dosage than it is when used for other purposes. At the lower dosage, the medication satisfies the safety requirements; at the higher dosage, it does not.

6. B Inference

Whew. Loretta's principle states that she can pick an imperfect home as long as that home fails to be perfect in a smaller number of ways than the other homes she has seen do. Got that? Now, we need to score the three homes that are mentioned in the argument with respect to the four requirements we know Loretta is using. One fails on location but is fine in terms of size and age; one fails on size but is fine for location and age; the last one fails on age but succeeds on location and size. Now we put these facts together with the one provided in the question stem; exactly two of the three homes fail on price. That means one of them fails only one requirement, while the other two fail two requirements. Keep in mind that we don't know all of Loretta's requirements yet; there might be more than just location, price, size, and age. The choice we want will add information that allows us to conclude that Loretta can choose one of the three houses mentioned in the passage.

(A) Watch out for the "not"! If this is true, then all bets are off. There might be any number of further requirements, and the three homes might fail to meet any number of them.

(B) This does it. Before, one home failed on one requirement, and the other two failed on two. This choice introduces another requirement that all of them fail, and more importantly lets us know that this is Loretta's only other requirement. So one home fails on exactly two requirements, and the other two fail on exactly three requirements. Under the principle she is using, then, Loretta can select the home that fails two of her requirements.

(C) This one specifies another home that fails at least two requirements, but remember that the argument didn't specify which other requirements Loretta might have. We can't tell what impact this information has on Loretta's decision.

(D) This goes outside the material presented in the passage. We have no idea how long "eventually" is, and we still don't know about possible other requirements, or what homes Loretta might see other than the three mentioned. This only confuses matters.

(E) Maybe not, but this still doesn't tell us that Loretta is allowed to pick one of the three homes mentioned in the passage. This is irrelevant to the issue at hand.

7. D Inference

There's lots of information here. Basically, the terms being played with are number of roommates and type of room (dormitory, house, or apartment); television viewing; and the use of illegal drugs. The most important thing to do in evaluating the answer choices is not to turn the associations mentioned in the passage into strong statements about *cause*.

(A) Again, the material we're presented doesn't give us any definite information about which one of these tendencies causes any other. We certainly can't infer anything this strong from the information that the lowest rates of illegal drug use occurred among this particular group of students.

(B) Like (A), this one makes a judgment about cause that simply isn't supported by the passage, which only talks about correlations.

(C) Academic problems aren't mentioned anywhere in the passage, so we should avoid this choice.

(D) Here's the one we want. This choice discusses television viewing not being the sole cause of any other behavior talked about in the argument. Since we're told that "drug use occurred among both high-viewing and low-viewing students," we can be sure that this statement is correct.

(E) We don't know anything about "all college students," so let's avoid such a sweeping statement.

8. A Agree

Rex's point is that Earache's music isn't truly original popular music. As a reason, Rex offers the fact that Earache's lyrics are repetitive.

Phil says that originality doesn't require original lyrics, but that it does require a range of style and tempo. Earache appears to fail this alternative requirement, too.

(A) Both Rex and Phil would agree that this statement is false. So they agree about its truth, and this is the answer we want.

(B) Phil would say this statement is true, but we're not certain whether or not Rex considers this a requirement for originality.

(C) We aren't sure whether either Rex or Phil believes that this statement is true.

(D) Rex would say that this statement is true; Phil would say it is false. However, our task on this question is to choose a statement about which they would agree.

(E) We know Phil would say this statement is true. Rex doesn't register an opinion on Earache's range of style and tempo.

9. E Inference

The passage describes two conditions that Center City will have to satisfy in order to retain two of its desirable qualities. These conditions involve three key things: the amount spent on social programs, the amount it collects in taxes this year, and the amount it collected in taxes last year. We'll need to keep these straight as we evaluate the choices.

(A) If Center City collects as much in taxes as it spends for social programs, and if it also spends as much for social programs as it collected in taxes last year, then Center City may be able to remain both socially progressive and fiscally healthy.

(B) Careful! If Center City collects exactly the same amount in taxes this year as it collected last year, and if it spends that amount on social programs, then the facts support the conclusion that Center City may be able to remain both socially progressive and fiscally healthy.

(C) Sources of revenue beyond taxes aren't discussed in this argument, and no fact we're given in the passage allows us to conclude that Center City definitely will remain both socially progressive and fiscally healthy.

(D) We have no information in the passage that would allow us to draw a conclusion about which of the two things—fiscal health or socially progressive policies—is more important, so we shouldn't pick this one.

(E) This is what we want. Center City would have to spend the amount it collects in taxes in order to remain socially progressive, of course, but we know that this statement is true. By collecting the same amount in taxes this year, Center City would remain able to keep its two desirable qualities.

1. **E** ID Reasoning

   The point is that economic problems in Erronia needn't necessarily lead to terrible problems for the country's citizens. The main evidence offered in support of this contention is the city of Nod, which has managed to avoid these problems even as the economy has worsened. The argument uses a specific case to prove that something is possible.

   (A) No economic expert is mentioned in the argument.

   (B) Although this argument does include an opposing position, the aid worker doesn't doubt that the economy in Erronia is declining.

   (C) The aid worker's argument doesn't explain why the situation in Erronia is deteriorating.

   (D) Close, but this isn't as good as (E). The only case that is mentioned here is the city of Nod; we don't actually see an example of economic problems leading to disaster.

   (E) This is better than (D). The general claim is that, given its declining economy, humanitarian disaster in Erronia is inevitable. The counterexample is the city of Nod, in which a declining economy has not led to a humanitarian disaster.

2. **C** Principle

   The senator's conclusion is that violence in popular culture must be dealt with through legislation. There are two main premises offered in support of the conclusion: Any reasonable person would agree, despite the lack of definite proof, that portrayals of violence lead to violent behavior; and the vast majority of people are willing to accept limits on free speech when public safety is at risk, as it is in this case.

   (A) The choice emphasizes making the limits on free speech as minimal as possible. This isn't something that the argument appears to be interested in at all.

   (B) Close, but pay careful attention to what this choice tells us. It says that legislative action is "permissible"; the argument, on the other hand, concludes that the problem "must be addressed by legislation." This choice isn't nearly as strong as the conclusion of the argument.

   (C) Here we go. This matches the argument very closely. People are willing to accept limits to free speech, violence in popular culture is widely considered a threat although there is no definite proof of this fact, and the strength of this principle matches the strength of our conclusion: "legislative action is...required."

   (D) This choice has nothing to do with legislative action. It also brings up a distinction between individuals and the public as a whole that isn't dealt with in the argument.

   (E) This choice deals with circumstances under which legislation is acceptable, but our conclusion talks about legislative action being required. Not only that, but this choice doesn't mention threats to public safety at all.

3. **D** Role of the Statement

The conclusion here is that the recent increase in the panther population doesn't mean that the panthers are no longer in danger. The premises let us know that efforts to protect habitat have succeeded, but the panthers' food supply is still in trouble. The statement mentioned in the question stem is the one that the argument is trying to argue against.

(A) No, it is contrary to the argument's conclusion.
(B) No, if the statement is true, then the argument's conclusion isn't true.
(C) The language here is squishy enough to be appealing, but it doesn't describe the relationship between the statement and the argument's conclusion specifically enough. There is a better answer out there.
(D) Here's the one we want. The whole point of the argument is to demonstrate that the panther population isn't stable.
(E) We don't know whether or not this statement can be "directly verified." Certainly this choice doesn't tell us what function the statement is serving in the argument.

4. **E** ID Reasoning in Mikulski's response

Jackson's point is that geneticists must not understand genes well, since attempts at treating genetic illness using genetic means have been unsuccessful.

Mikulski responds that although the technology used in the treatments doesn't "always" or "reliably" work, the scientific ideas behind them do. As evidence, Mikulski cites the same attempts at treating genetic illness and points out "some participants" in these trials for whom the treatment seems to have worked.

(A) Mikulski doesn't dispute the accuracy of Jackson's evidence. Mikulski doesn't try to claim that the trials were in fact a great success.
(B) Although Jackson seems to make a pretty broad generalization, this is not the feature of Jackson's argument that Mikulski attacks.
(C) Like (A), this choice says that Mikulski somehow claims that Jackson's evidence is incorrect.
(D) Close, but it's a little difficult to say that Mikulski considers any of Jackson's assumptions "unlikely to be true." There is a better choice available here.
(E) The relevant distinction is between the technology of gene therapy and the science of genetics. Since Jackson's conclusion is that the science of genetics is somehow incomplete, this choice is the best description of how Mikulski's argument relates to Jackson's.

5. **C** Flaw

The countries of Titania and Oberon are alike in size, population, and per capita income. Titania is very prosperous, and life there is good. The argument concludes from this fact that life in Oberon must be good in similar ways. Broadly speaking, the argument assumes that two countries that are similar in the three given respects must have similar quality of life.

(A) This is a choice often seen on flaw questions, and it's almost always wrong. An argument that uses circular reasoning, the flaw this choice describes, attempts to support the truth of its conclusion using reasons that rely on the truth of that conclusion. This argument doesn't do that.

(B) It's difficult to determine which things in this argument are identified as causes, and which as effects. We want something that fits our argument better than this.

(C) Here's the one we want. This one points out a gap between per capita income, a similarity mentioned in the premises, and overall prosperity, the similarity projected in the conclusion.

(D) Read this one carefully. This one takes two things presented as evidence of "prosperity" and treats them as if they're indications of "economic health." But the problem with this argument isn't the standards used to assert that Titania is prosperous; the problem is that Oberon's prosperity may not be similar even though its size, population, and per capita income are similar.

(E) Careful! This one overstates the case somewhat. The argument doesn't try to argue that they're "identical in every respect." The conclusion merely states that "Oberon…enjoys similar benefits of…prosperity."

6. **A** ID Reasoning in the journalist's response

The spokesperson's point is that Scrappy, Inc.'s accusations about The Tremendous Corporation's trade practices are false. The evidence offered in support of this claim is that a government investigation has recently issued a report finding no evidence of illegal trade practices by The Tremendous Corporation.

The journalist's central claim is that Scrappy, Inc.'s accusations are true. For evidence, the journalist points to the fact that some members of The Tremendous Corporation have admitted to making illegal campaign contributions, and Scrappy, Inc.'s accusations include charges of official corruption.

The difference here is easy to overlook, but it becomes clearer when you focus on the conclusions of each argument. The spokesperson claims that the accusations "concerning...trade practices" are false; the journalist claims that "the accusations...are in fact true." There's actually no disagreement here; the spokesperson is talking only about the company's trade practices, but the journalist is talking about other issues.

(A) This is it. The spokesperson's statement doesn't say Scrappy, Inc., has no case at all; it simply says that the accusations concerning trade practices are false.

(B) It's a bit of a judgment call to say that the journalist's language is "excessively emotional." But the journalist doesn't actually point out a flaw in the spokesperson's argument, so we can't pick this one.

(C) On the contrary, it does a pretty good job of showing that they are in some part true. The ones that are true just aren't the ones the spokesperson is referring to.

(D) The evidence presented may call the character of The Tremendous Corporation's executives into question, but the journalist doesn't "attack" their character in any illegitimate way.

(E) If you read carefully, you'll find that the consideration presented by the journalist actually isn't relevant to the spokesperson's argument.

7. E Flaw

The language is tough on this one. The conclusion is that some student can secure a place they shouldn't be able to. The reasoning goes like this: If the Registrar had told everyone everything, then nobody would've been able to secure a place they shouldn't be able to; the Registrar, however, didn't tell everyone everything. The key thing to note is the opening sentence: As long as nobody knows more than anyone else, nobody can secure a place they shouldn't be able to. So even though the Registrar didn't tell everybody everything, it's still possible that the Registrar told everybody *the same thing*, in which case nobody can secure a place they shouldn't be able to, and the conclusion is incorrect.

(A)   We're told in the argument that the Registrar didn't tell everything to any student. So we already know that the Registrar didn't tell everything to every student; this is just a consequence of one of the premises, and is completely consistent with the information presented in the argument.

(B)   What the student wishes to do isn't relevant to the argument. This kind of language is never used, and we have no way of determining the impact of this fact on the conclusion.

(C)   What might have happened doesn't represent a particularly strong attack on the argument's conclusion.

(D)   This might explain why the Registrar didn't tell any student everything about them, but it doesn't indicate why the conclusion isn't necessarily correct.

(E)   Here it is. Translated into English, this choice says that every student knows the same things. Under the premises of the argument, then, no student can secure a space he or she shouldn't be able to, and the conclusion is incorrect.

8. B ID Reasoning

The argument concludes that there must be something in the garden other than flowers, trees, and statuary. The reasons given are (1) the order of height of objects within the garden is flowers, statuary, trees, from shortest to tallest, and there's no crossover in the heights of the members of these groups; and (2) there's something in the garden that is too tall to be a statue (or, by extension, a flower) and too short to be a tree. The choices on this one are tough, so we'll have to be careful with the language.

(A)   Not quite. This choice talks about something that possesses an attribute (height) to a greater extent than every member of a group, and concludes that this thing must not belong to any group. Although the conclusion in this choice matches the one drawn in the argument, the reasoning isn't quite the same. It also isn't correct.

(B)   Here we go. Something in the garden ("a member of the collection") is the wrong height to be a flower, statuary, or a tree ("possesses an attribute that is not possessed by any member of all the known groups within the collection"). So we know that there is something in the garden other than flowers, trees, and statuary ("the collection cannot be composed solely of members of the known groups"). Whew.

(C)   The argument doesn't include any two groups that have a member in common. We don't want to pick this one.

(D)   The whole point of our argument is that the collection (the garden) is not composed entirely of known groups. This doesn't match our argument.

(E)   This choice talks about the number of things in the garden, which has nothing to do with our argument.

CHAPTER 4

DRILL #1

Pages 42 – 45

1. D Weaken

Keep an eye on what's supporting what here. The most specific conclusion drawn is that a majority of voters cannot evaluate the truth of economic claims or make informed decisions about economic policies. The only evidence offered in support of this conclusion is that only 25 percent of voters can understand newspaper articles on the subject. It's difficult to tell whether the first sentence is an introductory statement, or whether it's the overall conclusion the editorial wants to draw. Either way, we can see several language shifts taking place here on their way to the conclusions. We want to pick the answer that exploits one of them.

(A) All of the information in the argument is negative: "only 25 percent of voters... understand," "do not know enough...to evaluate," and so forth. Adding the information that even those who do know enough to understand newspaper articles can't evaluate economic claims certainly doesn't hurt this argument; if anything, it strengthens it.

(B) This distinction between voters and the votes they cast is outside the scope of the argument. We also are given nothing in the argument that suggests the goal of voting is to elect economic experts.

(C) This is a gorgeous strengthen. Unfortunately, we're working a weaken question.

(D) Here's the one. This severs the link between understanding newspaper articles and one of the things the argument concludes a majority of voters are unable to do.

(E) This choice concerns a link between the two pieces of the conclusion. A weaken should, if possible, sever a link between the conclusion and one or more of the premises. Even if this is true, it may remain true that not many voters are capable of doing either one.

2. A Assumption

The conclusion is that every sport must institute systems of testing for performance-enhancing drugs in order to protect its financial health. The premises basically let us know that the use of performance-enhancing drugs by some athletes in a sport harms competition and fan interest, and fan interest is important for sales of tickets and merchandise. The missing link in this argument is between "sales of tickets and merchandise" in the premises and "financial health" in the conclusion. We want a choice that connects these two ideas.

(A) Here we go. If this isn't true—if the financial health of a sport doesn't depend at all on sales of tickets and merchandise—then the conclusion is basically unsupported.

(B) Similar effectiveness from sport to sport isn't a requirement of this argument. Even if the systems are more effective for some sports than they are for others, the conclusion may nevertheless be correct.

(C) Even if it does, we have premises in hand that guarantee us the use of performance-enhancing drugs by athletes in every sport harms sales overall. So this isn't required in order for the reasoning in the argument to stand.

(D) We have a premise that talks about the situation in which some athletes use these drugs while others do not. However, what would happen in the case where every athlete used these drugs is not relevant to the conclusion of this particular argument, which concerns testing regimes intended to prevent athletes from using them.

(E) This certainly isn't an assumption required by the argument. It would make a pretty good weaken, but that isn't what we're looking for on this question.

3. C Flaw

The conclusion here is that the legal system in Vigona is not excessively harsh. The premises offered in support of this conclusion at best combine to let us know that, by the standards presented in the argument, Vigona's legal system is just. The missing link is between a just legal system and a legal system that is not excessively harsh.

(A)   There are a couple of problems here. One is that pursuing all offenders "with equal vigor" isn't a requirement of a just legal system; it's something that, if it's true, guarantees that a legal system is just. Besides, it seems at least a decent paraphrase of this idea to say that "no country pursues those accused of crimes more zealously than Vigona does." The best reason to eliminate here, however, is that this isn't the primary flaw with the argument. The conclusion involves the phrase "excessively harsh," and what we really want is a choice that indicates this language comes out of left field.

(B)   The motives of Vigona's critics are never mentioned.

(C)   This is better than (A). The argument shows that Vigona's legal system is consistent, and therefore just. It goes on from there to say that it cannot then be called excessively harsh. In other words, the argument requires that any legal system that can be called excessively harsh must be unjust.

(D)   If you look again, you'll see that the vigor with which offenders are pursued and the meting out of equal punishment are separate criteria; the argument never assumes that they're the same, or that one guarantees the other.

(E)   The argument's conclusion does not concern "every consistent legal system." This isn't what we want.

4. C Strengthen

Here's a connect-the-dots strengthen. The conclusion is that a sea cucumber is not a bivalve. We already have a series of links to work with: Every bivalve must be a mollusk, and every mollusk must have a muscular foot and a visceral mass. Anything that tells us a sea cucumber isn't a mollusk, or that it doesn't have one of the two features associated with mollusks, will give us the conclusion we're trying to support.

(A)   This doesn't involve sea cucumbers at all, and that's the piece we need in order to be able to draw this conclusion.

(B)   Like (A), this leaves out sea cucumbers.

(C)   This is the one. If a sea cucumber doesn't have a visceral mass, then it can't be a mollusk. If it isn't a mollusk, then it can't be a bivalve.

(D)   This has sea cucumbers in it, but it doesn't give us a way of determining that a sea cucumber isn't a mollusk. So this doesn't help.

(E)   Like (A) and (B), this one doesn't have anything to do with sea cucumbers.

5. E Strengthen

The conclusion here is that apartments located higher above the street are more desirable to tenants. The premises all concern a single apartment building, in which otherwise identical apartments appear to become more expensive the higher they are above the street. The missing link here is between the apartments' price and their desirability to tenants.

(A)   Careful! This one offers a reasonable-sounding explanation of why apartments higher up are more expensive, but it doesn't include the all-important information connecting this fact to the idea of desirability.

(B)   If anything, this would weaken the argument.

(C)   Like (A), this has nothing to do with desirability.

(D)   This choice has to do with the desirability of an apartment building's location, rather than the location of an apartment in terms of its height above the street.

(E)   This is the only one that has a chance. It provides a direct link between desirability and price.

6. B Principle

The argument concludes that the particular park discussed should be exempt from the rule that requires pets to be kept on leashes. The premises describe the reasons for this rule and then assert that these reasons do not apply in the case of this park. We want a principle that provides us the ability to conclude that in at least some cases, a rule should *not* apply.

(A)   This principle mentions the benefits associated with a rule, but benefits are never discussed in the argument.

(B)   Here we go. If the rules should apply in only those cases where the reasons for the rule apply, then since the reasons for the rule do not apply in this park, the argument's conclusion that the rule should not apply to this park is justified.

(C)   At best, this principle would tell us that the rule should apply to this particular park. This choice doesn't help the conclusion.

(D)   The argument doesn't try to say that the rule should be completely repealed, so this principle goes a good deal farther than the argument does.

(E)   This principle could only justify instituting a rule in the first place; it wouldn't help the argument's conclusion that the rule shouldn't apply in some particular case.

7. **D** ID Reasoning in Y's response

W argues that poetry no longer serves a useful purpose. The premise on which this conclusion is based is basically that only a few people find the same pleasure in poetry that people used to, whereas the majority of people find that pleasure in popular music instead.

Y mentions other activities that serve a purpose, although only a small number of people participate in them. Y, in other words, attacks the link in W's argument between the number of people who do a thing and the notion of serving a useful purpose.

(A) Nothing stated in Y's argument can really be called a generalization.

(B) W makes an assumption, but it would be too strong to call that a "bias."

(C) Y's objection does have to do with the meaning of the term "useful," but it's a bit much to call that "vague terminology." Instead, Y is questioning what it means for something to serve a useful purpose.

(D) This is what we want. The analogy is between reading poetry and these other activities that few people engage in. The basis of W's judgment is that the number of people who engage in an activity determines whether or not it serves a useful purpose in society.

(E) This choice doesn't make it clear that Y disagrees with W; what does it mean, after all, to say that Y's evidence "sheds new light" on a claim?

8. **E** Assumption

The argument concludes that Smith can be held responsible for his action. The premise offered in support of the conclusion is that a person can't be held responsible for an action if he or she can't distinguish right from wrong, yet recent statements by Smith indicate he knows that what he did was wrong. There are several missing pieces here. First, there is no way for us to know for certain that he can be held responsible; there may be other criteria available that would let us know he isn't responsible. Second, there's a little bit of a problem with time in this argument. One premise talks about a person being "incapable of distinguishing right from wrong," but it isn't clear that the fact that Smith "now knows that what he did was wrong" really demonstrates that he isn't incapable. He may have been incapable at the time he performed the action and only later realized the action was wrong. Our assumption should pertain to one or both of these potential weaknesses.

(A) The question of the cruelty involved in punishing an action, although it is mentioned parenthetically in the argument, isn't part of the reasoning that leads us to the conclusion. This is a side issue.

(B) Again, the question of punishment is a side issue. The conclusion concerns only whether or not Smith can be held responsible, and none of the reasoning that leads up to this conclusion directly involves punishment.

(C) Careful! This sounds good up until the moment when this choice specifies "at the time he took that action." Since our premises only tell us what Smith "now knows," and the rule presented doesn't specify at what time Smith needs to be able to distinguish between right and wrong, this answer doesn't seem to affect the conclusion as strongly as we want our assumption to.

(D) Even if this isn't true, it doesn't seem to make the conclusion definitely incorrect. It makes the rule impossible to apply, but since the rule wasn't sufficient to guarantee the conclusion anyway, this doesn't seem absolutely essential to the conclusion.

(E) Sweeping as this sounds, this assumption is absolutely necessary if the argument's conclusion is to be correct. Suppose it isn't true; then Smith meets some criterion that would prevent him from being held responsible, and the conclusion is definitely wrong. Since this choice has the most direct impact on the conclusion, this is the answer we want.

9. **D** Weaken EXCEPT

The conclusion is that material prosperity prevents real happiness. The premises presented in support of this conclusion are that, in America, over the past fifty years real incomes have increased, and Americans have come to possess more labor-saving appliances and enjoy more luxuries, yet at the same time they have become increasingly dissatisfied with their lives. There's plenty of new stuff in the conclusion here: "material prosperity" is evidently meant to be linked with income, labor-saving appliances, and luxuries; "real happiness" is meant to be linked with the survey's findings that Americans are "dissatisfied with their lives." Any choice that breaks one or the other of these links will weaken the conclusion.

It's worth noting as a general matter that you should be careful on EXCEPT questions on the Args sections of the LSAT. Realize that, fundamentally, a weaken EXCEPT question only guarantees you that four of the answers (the wrong ones) weaken the argument. It makes no promises about what the other one (the right choice) will do. The right answer may strengthen, but it doesn't have to; it may simply be irrelevant to the conclusion. The only thing we definitely know about it is that it *doesn't* weaken.

(A) This weakens by breaking the link between "material prosperity" in the conclusion and income, ownership of labor-saving devices, and enjoyment of luxuries in the premises.

(B) This weakens by breaking the link between "real happiness" in the conclusion and "dissatisfied with their lives" in the premises.

(C) This weakens by suggesting that, although the rates of dissatisfaction have increased over time, nevertheless those who had the least material prosperity exhibited the most dissatisfaction, and so material prosperity may very well lead to real happiness.

(D) Careful with this one. If you want to go this far, you may say that the factors mentioned in this choice relate to real happiness, and the choice tells us directly that they have nothing to do with material prosperity, so this choice strengthens. That may be reaching a bit, but there's no question that this choice fails to weaken the argument; it doesn't break either of the questionable links mentioned above.

(E) This weakens at least by calling into question the argument's link between dissatisfaction and real happiness. The argument depends upon the fact that the reason Americans now indicate that they are unhappy is the material prosperity they enjoy. This choice provides an alternate explanation: They are dissatisfied because of communications media, which prompts them to compare their level of material prosperity with increasingly unrealistic levels of material prosperity. It's tough, but by offering a different explanation for Americans' increasing dissatisfaction, this choice undermines the argument's claim that their own increased material prosperity is responsible for the dissatisfaction.

DRILL #2

Pages 47 – 50

1. E Strengthen

The conclusion here is that people must be willing to accept the dangers associated with nuclear power. The reasons provided are that people are willing to accept the dangers associated with fossil-fuel power, and the wastes produced by nuclear power are less dangerous to the environment than those produced by fossil fuels. The problem here is that a comparison about dangers to the environment posed by the wastes produced by each process is taken to mean something about all of the dangers associated with each process. We need to shore up this link in order to strengthen the argument.

(A) Although lower fuel costs and decreased dependence on foreign oil would be additional advantages of nuclear-power generation, they aren't within the scope of the argument. The conclusion deals only with accepting the dangers associated with each method of power generation, not with benefits of various different fuels that could be used.

(B) At best, this choice is trying to weaken the argument. The question, though, asks us to strengthen it.

(C) Like (A), this choice discusses benefits. The conclusion we're supposed to strengthen has only to do with accepting dangers.

(D) Unfortunately, we have no information that would allow us to determine how this fact would apply to our argument. We don't know which of these technologies represents "an advance in human understanding." Also, this choice has absolutely nothing to do with risk.

(E) This doesn't address every potential problem with the argument, but it's the best one we have to work with. This lets us know that the wastes associated with power generation are the greatest danger they pose. This choice doesn't address the stipulation having to do with dangers "to the environment," but nevertheless it does help the conclusion.

2. B Assumption

The argument's conclusion is that, unless something is done to prevent it, the prison population will continue to grow. The premises describe a chain of causes and effects: Harsher sentencing legislation causes increased prison populations, which results in increased profits for companies that serve the prison industry, which results in greater contributions by these companies to politicians, which results in these companies gaining greater influence over the politicians' decisions. The thing that's needed here is the step that closes the "cycle" mentioned in the conclusion: Influence over the politicians' decisions leads back to harsher sentencing legislation.

(A) Careful! Even if the crime rate does go down, it remains possible for the prison population to continue to rise because of the longer sentences mandated by the law.

(B) If this isn't true—if no corporation makes use of its influence in the manner described—then there is no "cycle" like the one talked about in the conclusion, and the argument falls apart. Since this needs to be true in order for the conclusion to have a chance of being right, this really is an assumption of the argument.

(C) Careful here. Although it's true that the information in this answer choice is related to information in the argument, we have a premise that tells us "as their profits grow, these corporations make ever larger contributions." Since a premise guarantees us that this fact is true, we don't need an additional assumption to tell us that it is.

(D) This is too broad to be an assumption of the argument. Although this would help strengthen the conclusion, it isn't needed in order for the conclusion to be correct.

(E) The question of whether these sentences are justified is irrelevant to the argument's conclusion, so this can't be one of the argument's assumptions.

3. **D** Evaluate

The point here is that the plan contemplated by Maria's parents will actually result in Maria improving her grades, and will allow Maria to earn the money she needs to buy things she wants, as long as she works hard. The plan basically involves paying Maria for every A and B she earns. The argument does guarantee us that Maria's grades are "currently below average," but we don't know anything more about them. It seems as though there are many potential weaknesses to this plan; we want to find an answer that helps us determine whether or not it would actually work.

(A) Close, but this choice brings in "state education standards," which aren't clearly relevant to the conclusion. There's a lot of missing information, actually, about Maria's grades: What does it mean for them to be below average? How many A's and B's would she need to earn in order to improve them? Although this choice seems related to these questions, it wouldn't really help us answer them.

(B) The issue here isn't the grades Mara's friends earn; it's what grades Maria earns.

(C) Although Maria's dissatisfaction with the amount of money she receives is mentioned in the lead-up to the conclusion, the conclusion only makes claims about Maria being able to "afford the things she wants." Whether or not that would prevent her from being dissatisfied isn't directly relevant to whether or not the plan would succeed at achieving its stated goals.

(D) This is the best of the answer choices. Since Maria's grades are currently below average, average grades would represent an improvement. If, however, those average grades would not provide Maria enough money to afford the things she wants, then one benefit predicted in the conclusion wouldn't follow. On the other hand, if an average number of A's and B's would result in the amount Maria needs, we could anticipate that the plan really would provide some incentive. Granted, there may be some difference between the number of A's and B's needed for "improvement" and an improvement to the "below average" grades Maria currently earns, but this is the only choice that goes directly to the incentive that the plan wishes to provide.

(E) Like (B), this choice has something to do with Maria's friends, who aren't really relevant to our conclusion.

4. **C** Flaw

The argument's point is that the transportation authorities have fulfilled their purpose by instituting searches of passengers' luggage and persons. The only real support offered for our conclusion is that the searches described are successful at preventing certain acts of sabotage and terrorism, and that the transportation authorities' purpose is to prevent *all* such acts. We should note the difference between preventing "certain acts" and preventing "all" acts of that type.

(A) The "objections" mentioned in this choice refer to a parenthetical statement in the argument concerning violation of privacy. Since we don't know how these considerations relate to the stated purpose of the transportation authorities, we can't really pick this choice, which portrays the argument as saying such concerns are not "inconsistent" with that purpose.

(B) The premises here do not concern possibility or likelihood, so this isn't what we're looking for.

(C) Here's the choice we want. "One representative type" is certain acts of terrorism and sabotage; "the class of events" is all acts of terrorism and sabotage.

(D) The conclusion doesn't claim that the transportation authorities' policy is "required," only that it fulfills the authorities' purpose.

(E) Although the evidence presented indicates that the authorities may not have fulfilled their purpose completely, we can't say that it provides definite evidence that they have not fulfilled their purpose.

5. **B** Strengthen Mandel

Mandel argues that corporate criminals are responsible for harm to the health and safety of their fellow citizens. The reasons given are that corporate criminals cause a decline in tax revenue, and these tax revenues pay for protecting the health and safety of citizens. There are certainly a lot of holes in this argument, but for now it's only necessary to note the conclusion and the reasoning on which it is based.

Schwartz's point is that all criminals are "responsible" for harm in the indirect ways cited by Mandel, and so violent criminals are definitely more serious offenders than corporate criminals. Schwartz explains that pursuing and prosecuting those who commit crime necessarily results in resources being diverted from activities that might have been used to protect the health and welfare of others. Since both violent and corporate criminals cause diversion of resources, the only relevant difference between these two types of crime is the harm directly posed by the criminal him- or herself in the commission of the crime.

It's difficult to predict what the answer will be here. Broadly, Mandel is trying to say that corporate crime causes indirect harm to health and safety. Schwartz points out that all criminals do so, and so the only difference between violent and corporate crime has to do with the direct threat posed by each. We need something that helps Mandel's conclusion defend against Schwartz's response.

(A) This points out a difference between violent criminals and corporate criminals, but we don't know how this relates to questions of harm to the health or safety of citizens, so it isn't clear how this relates to Mandel's point.

(B) This would definitely help Mandel's point. Diminishing the resources available to protect health and safety is the basis on which Mandel concludes that corporate criminals actually threaten these things. Schwartz tries to argue that all criminals do this because of the "diversion of resources" involved in pursuing and prosecuting them. This choice draws a distinction between "diversion of resources" and an action that decreases the amount of resources available to begin with. This points out a type of harm that corporate criminals do but violent criminals do not, and by Mandel's reasoning this type of harm poses a threat to public health and safety.

(C) This would support Schwartz, not Mandel.

(D) Close, but this isn't as good as (B) because it doesn't mention a direct impact on health or safety. "Harm" isn't specific enough to support Mandel as strongly as (B) does.

(E) This would support an argument that corporate crime has some positive effects. Neither of the participants in the conversation is trying to argue anything this extreme.

6. **B** Assumption

The conclusion here is that chemical imbalances play a different role in causing behavioral disorders than they do in causing physical disorders. Although the premises acknowledge that chemicals are involved in both types of problems, the argument distinguishes between the two types of problems by pointing out that physical disorders cannot be consciously controlled, whereas behavioral disorders can. The language here shifts from a discussion of consciousness to a discussion of cause, so our assumption should link these two things together.

(A) This goes too far. The argument doesn't try to say that chemical imbalances have no role at all in behavioral disorders; it only tries to claim that they have a different role in causing them.

(B) This has the language link we're looking for. It's strongly worded, but if this weren't true— if some behavioral disorder were ultimately caused by a chemical imbalance—then the statement of the conclusion would definitely be incorrect.

(C) Since the scope of this argument concerns only humans, its conclusion can't depend on a comparison between humans and other beings.

(D) This choice goes even further than (A) to talk about every "unconscious factor," which is outside the argument's scope. The argument doesn't try to claim that chemical imbalances play no role at all in behavioral problems.

(E) Since we already have a premise that tells us that "humans...are conscious beings," we don't need any further information to support this fact.

7. **C** Weaken

The conclusion here is that a corporation's choice to donate money to charity is a business decision. The reasons state that the purpose of every business decision is to maximize profit, and then points out that charitable contributions have two benefits for the corporation: a decrease in taxes, and an increase in public exposure similar to that created by advertising. We want to pick something that shows us that these two benefits don't necessarily maximize a company's profits, which would allow us to conclude that a charitable contribution may not necessarily be a business decision.

(A) This concerns a side issue. Even if we were to stretch the scope of this argument quite a bit, this would most likely strengthen, not weaken, what the argument is trying to say.

(B) Oh, so close. This choice tells us, in terms of the increased revenue generated, money is better spent on advertising rather than charitable donations. Unfortunately, this choice fails to consider one of the benefits of charitable donations: tax savings. If the amount of tax savings were greater than the difference in the revenue increases expected from advertising versus a charitable contribution, then it remains possible that making a charitable contribution is actually more profitable than advertising in other ways.

(C) Here's the choice we want. Don't be distracted by the details about capital improvements and so forth. What this choice tells us is that all of the known profit-related benefits associated with a charitable contribution combined are definitely less than the profit-related benefits associated with some other use of that money. Thus, a charitable contribution doesn't appear to maximize profits, which casts doubt on the argument's conclusion.

(D) This actually strengthens the conclusion.

(E) This choice pertains to the standard by which charitable contributions ought to be judged. This goes far beyond the scope of the argument, which has to do with whether or not charitable contributions are, fundamentally, business decisions.

8. **A** Strengthen

The conclusion here is that the judge should disregard the sentencing guidelines in Lewis's case. The argument's major premise states that judges should disregard these guidelines when there are mitigating factors related to the crime. In Lewis's case, her motives were to secure medical treatment for her daughter. One clear assumption here is that this motive constitutes a mitigating circumstance. Hopefully our answer will shore up this assumption, although there are certainly other ways a choice could support this conclusion.

(A) Here's the one we want. Not only was Lewis's motive in committing the crime to supply a necessity to her daughter, but she could not have supplied that necessity in any other way. Although we still don't have a premise that tells us straight out that these are "mitigating circumstances," our understanding of the common meaning of the phrase allows us to see that this definitely does strengthen the conclusion. After all, Lewis's case would be rather different if she could have borrowed the money she needed, or worked a little overtime to earn it.

(B) Don't be distracted by this one. Although the major premise uses both the words "may" and "should," the "may" is only mentioned parenthetically. If you cross that phrase out, you're left with exactly the same argument, in terms of its logical structure.

(C) Oh, this is nasty. Certainly this has to do with what we initially identified as a link relevant to the argument's reasoning, but when we compare this with (A), which choice provides stronger support? This choice only permits the consideration of motives; it doesn't require it, or say that motive is the only determining factor. To get really technical with it, we can note the difference in language between the argument ("primary motive") and this choice ("motives," plural) and recognize that some factor other than securing medical treatment for her daughter was important in her decision to commit the crime. Although this choice is very close, (A) goes further toward establishing that there really are mitigating circumstances in Lewis's case.

(D) This choice involves the value-laden term "unduly harsh," which isn't used in the argument. It also doesn't have a particularly obvious bearing on Lewis's specific case.

(E) This choice refers to the "maximum sentence" for a crime, without giving us any idea of how this relates to the "sentencing guidelines." We can't really tell how this affects the truth of the argument's conclusion.

DRILL #3

Pages 52 – 55

1. D Weaken

We have a double conclusion here: The painters were permitted to enter the apartment, and the owner is not responsible for the loss of property that happened while it was being repainted. Let's take them one at a time. The painters were employees of the owner, who are permitted to enter the apartment to make it ready for future tenants if the current tenants have moved all or part of their property out; this condition is definitely satisfied in this case. The other part is a little less clear: "except in the event of negligence or misconduct,...[the owner] cannot be held responsible for any loss...of property." The thing to take note of here is the "except in the event of negligence or misconduct" part. If there was negligence or misconduct, then this rule doesn't apply to this situation, and the owner cannot use this rule to conclude that he or she is not responsible for the stolen cash. To weaken this argument, then, we need to show that there was negligence or misconduct.

(A) This choice introduces the phrase "intent to abandon the apartment." Under the premises, though, we don't know how to interpret this phrase. This doesn't seem to be relevant to the owner's conclusion.

(B) If this were true, then we couldn't be sure to what degree the premises mentioned apply to this case. This fact might weaken the owner's conclusion, but it might not.

(C) This doesn't appear to be at all relevant to the case in question.

(D) Here's the one we want. It tells us, in no uncertain terms, that the owner was negligent.

(E) Close, but there's a difference between this one and (D). (D) explicitly states that the owner was negligent. Although this choice tells us that misconduct took place, it doesn't assure us that this was misconduct "on the part of me or my employees," as the relevant premise requires. So this doesn't actually weaken the argument, because it doesn't tell us whose misconduct it was.

2. D Flaw

The point here is that the action of inviting the independent auditor to this meeting was a mistake that led to the CEO being forced to resign. The reasons present a chain of dependences: The CEO would not have been forced to resign, ultimately, without the information that was discussed in this meeting having been leaked to the press. Don't get too caught up in the language and details here, however. The argument evidently believes it was the independent auditor who was responsible for this leak, although it never says so. It remains possible that the head of the accounting department, not the independent auditor, was the one responsible for the leak.

(A) This tries to play with the language around the conclusion that calls the CEO's decision a "strategic mistake." But the argument doesn't claim that the result of inviting the auditor was "foreseeable," merely that it was undesirable for the CEO. This also doesn't address the large oversight we've already identified in the argument's reasoning.

(B) Like (A), this is trying to play with cause and effect in this argument. In this case, we can easily eliminate this one by noting that none of the statements in the argument relate to a "sufficient" condition. At all points, the argument says that without the leaks, the scandal, and so forth, the CEO would not have been forced to resign. This is all language associated with a necessary condition, not a sufficient one.

(C) Like the other two, this choice is attacking the cause-and-effect relations in the argument. But the chain of events described is reasonable, and correctly interpreted. The problem with this argument is that it identifies one person as being responsible for them when in fact we can't be certain that that person really was responsible.

(D) "One explanation" is, simply put, that the independent auditor was responsible for the leak. The "potential alternative explanation" is that the head of the accounting department was responsible for it. This is the choice that describes the problem we initially identified.

(E) Alternative courses of action aren't really relevant to the conclusion here.

3. **A** A flaw common to the arguments of Doctor Ellis and Doctor Cho

The language in this one is tough. Doctor Ellis's point is that a particular theory may be rejected. The reasoning depends upon applying a general principle to this theory: The most commonly believed explanation may be rejected when a certain condition is met. The theory in question appears to satisfy the condition, but the problem here is that we don't know this theory provides the "most commonly believed explanation" of the phenomenon described. So we don't have enough information to know whether or not we can apply Doctor Ellis's principle to the theory in this argument.

Doctor Cho's point is that the theory may not be rejected. Like Doctor Ellis, Doctor Cho makes use of a general principle: The theory may not be rejected when it's the only one available that meets a certain requirement. Although Doctor Cho provides evidence that the theory in question meets this requirement, we're never told that it's the only one available that does so.

The two arguments have the same problem: They make use of principles without providing us all of the information we need to be sure that we can apply them. Whew.

(A) This is the one we want. For Doctor Ellis, the relevant feature of other theories is that none of them must provide the "most commonly believed" explanation of the phenomenon. For Doctor Cho, the relevant feature of other theories is that none of them must be consistent with other well-supported explanations of related phenomena. This is the choice that describes both of the flaws we identified.

(B) This is an accurate description of Doctor Cho's flaw, but not Doctor Ellis's.

(C) This choice takes issue with the strength of the language used, but we have no information that would allow us to conclude that they're overinterpreting the available evidence.

(D) This is an accurate description of Doctor Ellis's flaw, but not Doctor Cho's.

(E) Doctor Ellis's appeals to the theory's predictions are a way of showing that the theory is unlikely to be correct, but it appears to do so in a legitimate way. Doctor Cho, however, doesn't deal with the theory's predictions at all, so this can't be a flaw that the two arguments have in common.

4. **C** Parallel flaw

The premises describe conditions that, if satisfied, are sufficient to ensure a particular result. A specific instance is described. The argument concludes that the predicted result can be expected in this specific instance. The problem with the argument is that the specific instance doesn't actually satisfy all of the conditions. One thing that will "ensure a successful party" is "music with wide appeal that creates an upbeat mood." Norm's choice of music for his party is said to "appeal to nearly everyone," but we get no information about it creating an "upbeat mood." We're looking for an argument in one of the answer choices that draws a similar unwarranted conclusion.

(A) This argument seems fine, so it's not the answer we're looking for. Veronica's trip to Paris suits all of the stated requirements to ensure an enjoyable trip.

(B) Tough one. Although it seems quite similar to the original, the difference here is in the types of conditions involved. In the original, the conditions describe "all that is needed to ensure a successful party." In other words, satisfying these conditions guarantees a successful party. In this choice, however, we're told about three things that are required for a movie to be a commercial success. The difference here is important: Satisfying some requirements for a particular result doesn't guarantee that result. Since the conditions presented in this choice are of a different kind from the conditions presented in the original, this choice isn't parallel.

(C) Here's the one that we want. The conditions are, taken together, sufficient to guarantee the result. The specific instance is WorldAuto's new sports car. The problem with the argument is that we're never told that this car has a "sleek" appearance.

(D) There's nothing wrong with this argument, so it can't be parallel to our original.

(E) The conclusion of this argument is not correctly drawn, but it isn't anything like the conclusion in our original, so it can't be parallel.

5. **B** Weaken

The sheriff's conclusion is that Tricia will not be allowed to use her new radar detector. The reasons given are that the model of radar detector she purchased is classified as a type-3 electronic device under Union County ordinances, and state law forbids the use of type-3 electronic devices. Unfortunately, we're missing a good deal of information about where else this particular device is classified as being of type 3, and where Tricia intends to use it.

(A) Whether or not the sale of this device is legal isn't relevant to the conclusion, which concerns only whether or not Tricia is permitted to use it.

(B) This is what we want. If Tricia is going to be spending time outside of Union County, she may very well be permitted to use it, depending upon how the radar detector is classified in those other places.

(C) This strengthens the argument, but the question asks us to weaken it.

(D) There is no such conflict in this argument, so this isn't relevant.

(E) Other models of radar detector aren't relevant to the conclusion in this case, so this is outside the scope of the argument.

6. **B** Assumption

The conclusion is that reorganization of the management division will not hurt morale in Giganticorp. The only real premise offered to support this conclusion is that, in three of the largest departments within the management division, morale could not be any lower. Once you clear aside the garbage in this argument, the gap becomes easier to see: We have no guarantee that the three worst departments are really the ones that are going to be reorganized. There are of course other assumptions here as well; it's possible, for instance, that the reorganization of these three departments might somehow affect morale in other departments within the management division, or possibly within other divisions of Giganticorp. We'll need to keep all these possibilities in mind when we evaluate the choices.

(A) The conclusion most directly involves the effect of reorganization on morale, not whether the reorganization will or can be effective. Since this doesn't seem to pertain to ways that morale might be hurt, this isn't an assumption of the argument.

(B) This seems pretty good. Certainly if this isn't true—if the reorganization doesn't include the three departments mentioned—then the conclusion seems a lot more doubtful.

(C) Although responsiveness to its markets is cited as a purpose of the reorganization, this isn't related to the conclusion of the argument, which concerns morale.

(D) This relates to the conclusion, but it's too strong to be an assumption. For one thing, this choice discusses the reorganization of the three departments being required, whereas reorganizing only one of them seems, by the premises in the argument, to at least make it possible that morale would improve. Second, it talks about "any improvement" to morale requiring this specific reorganization. The conclusion only says that the reorganization will "not hurt employee morale"; it doesn't try to claim that the changes will improve it.

(E) Like (C), this pertains to a side issue, not directly to the conclusion. Even if this choice isn't true—if employee morale has no measurable effect—the conclusion of the argument could still be correct.

7. **E** Weaken

The conclusion is that the distributor lied about the results of its high-voltage testing and shipped components it knew to be defective. The premises on which this conclusion is based are rather involved: The components display carbon scoring, and they also displayed the same amount of carbon scoring when the distributor received them; the components are given the same high-voltage testing by the manufacturer and the distributor, and the manufacturer never ships any defective components to the distributor. The distributor claims that the components passed the high-voltage tests. There are a number of potential gaps here. One is the linkage between passing high-voltage tests and being defective. Another are the gaps between the time the manufacturer tested the components, the time the distributor tested the components, and the time the person making the argument received them. Our weaken will most likely exploit one of these gaps. Remember, we're looking for information that tells us that the distributor was *not* aware that the components were defective when it shipped them out.

(A)   Whatever caused the carbon scoring doesn't seem to be directly relevant to whether or not the distributor knew the components to be defective. The important issues involve whether or not the components failed the tests, and at what point they became defective. It isn't even clear whether the carbon scoring is in any way related to the defects in the components.

(B)   In terms of motives, this seems to indicate that the distributor would have had no cost-related reason to ship components they knew to be defective, whereas the manufacturer would. However, one of the premises of the argument states unequivocally that the manufacturer would never ship a defective component, and there may be motives unrelated to cost that might induce the distributor to ship components they knew to be defective. This is trying to weaken, but because it primarily concerns the distributor's motive, it isn't clearly relevant to the argument's primary focus: the distributor's knowledge.

(C)   Careful here. This choice identifies a possible alternative reason for the defect, but it also links that defect to both carbon scoring and to the failure of high-voltage tests. Since the argument lets us know that the carbon scoring was present when the distributor received the components, this fact would indicate that they must have failed at least some of the tests. So this choice actually strengthens the conclusion.

(D)   The fact that not all of the components were defective doesn't really affect the conclusion, which concerns only the defective components.

(E)   This one's good. It indicates the possibility that the components became defective after they passed the distributor's high-voltage tests. This makes the argument's conclusion substantially less certain.

8. **A** Inference

This is one of those rare inference questions that concerns a passage that is also an argument. The conclusion of this one is that an experimenter's perception of physical laws doesn't depend on the experimenter's constant velocity relative to any fixed point. The reason for this conclusion is a thought experiment that shows a moving experimenter prevented from observing any outside reference point cannot by any known means demonstrate that he or she is moving. This one has a big gap: between perception of physical laws and the known means of demonstrating that the experimenter is moving. This is likely to be the connection described in the correct answer.

(A)   Here's the one. The original passage takes the fact that no known experiment can demonstrate that the experimenter is moving as meaning that there is no difference between the physical laws perceived by that experimenter and those perceived by another experimenter performing the same experiments at a fixed reference point. This can only be correct if every experiment that could demonstrate a difference in the perception of physical laws is known. If there is some not-yet-known experiment that could demonstrate motion, then Einstein's conclusion wouldn't be correct.

(B)   This overstates the facts as we know them. It isn't that perceptions of motion have nothing to do with physical laws, but instead that a particular type of motion results in no difference in the perception of physical laws. Other types of motion may well result in such a difference in perception, depending upon what physical laws govern that motion.

(C)   We don't know from the information in the passage that this would be the only way to verify Einstein's conclusions. This is way too strong.

(D)   See (B). The passage pertains only to a certain kind of motion. We don't have enough information to draw conclusions about different kinds of motion.

(E)   This is speculative. We can't be certain what the consequences would be if Einstein's conclusion turned out to be wrong; certainly we couldn't conclude anything this specific about that hypothetical situation.

CHAPTER 5

DRILL #1

Pages 60 – 63

1. **D** Weaken EXCEPT

   The conclusion is that the new government has taken money away from the provinces to support its own interests in keeping power. The only premise offered in support of this fact is really that international observers are reporting more problems in the provinces than they did before this government took power. This is an EXCEPT question, so we're looking for four choices that would weaken the conclusion by providing another explanation of why things in the provinces appear to have gotten so much worse.

   (A) This weakens by suggesting that the difference in the problems being reported is due not to a change in the actual prevalence of these problems, but instead to an increased ability to observe them.

   (B) This weakens by showing that it isn't the central military government that's taking the resources away, but instead the remnants of the old government in the provinces. Although this doesn't explicitly state that the corruption and corresponding diversion of resources is greater now than it was before, at least it explains some way in which the central government cannot be held directly responsible.

   (C) This answer suggests that all of the countries around Trirene are experiencing the same problems, which makes it seem less likely that the military government's distribution of resources is to blame for the provinces' sorry state.

   (D) This is the one. Remember we're looking for an answer that *does not weaken* the conclusion that the military government is diverting resources to maintain its hold on power. This answer provides further support for the conclusion by explaining a reason why the military government might need to do so. This doesn't weaken, so it's our answer.

   (E) This answer weakens by suggesting that the problem isn't that the government is diverting resources, but instead that there aren't any resources left to spend on anything. Like (B) and (C), this choice identifies a source of the problem in the provinces other than the military government's efforts to keep a hold on power.

2. **E** Assumption

   The conclusion here is that development and growth in the cities isn't causing the loss of the state's wetlands. Two bits of evidence are cited in support: First, all new development in the cities has obeyed a law that requires destroyed wetlands to be replaced by artificially constructed ones elsewhere in the state; second, the biggest losses in wetlands aren't occurring anywhere near the cities. There are a couple of links here that need to be shored up: First, we need to know something more about these artificially constructed wetlands. Are they really good substitutes for the ones that the city developers are draining? Second, we need to know more about the locations in which the wetlands are being lost. Might there be some connection between development in the cities and the losses in the rural farming areas that isn't considered in the argument?

   (A) Careful on the language here—this is a bit too strong to be required by the argument. Although one assumption underlying this argument is that the artificial replacement wetlands required by the law are in relevant respects similar to those that are drained, it isn't necessary that this law "cannot have failed to lead to an increase" in the amount of wetlands. Once you sort out all the negatives, you realize that this choice leaves out a possibility: If obeying the law were able to keep the amount of wetland acreage constant, the conclusion would be correct.

   (B) This strengthens the argument by suggesting a potential alternate cause of the problem, but the argument doesn't require that this be true in order for the conclusion to be correct. This choice is way too specific to be an assumption of the argument.

   (C) This choice does a wonderful job of suggesting how growth in the cities can affect wetlands elsewhere in the state. Unfortunately, this choice weakens the argument; we need to pick an assumption on this one.

   (D) Careful. Although this would strengthen the argument if it were true, it's too much to say this assumption is required by the argument. Even if it isn't true—if the loss in wetlands may be attributable to some cause that isn't near the wetlands—the argument may still be correct in saying that the cause wasn't development in the cities.

(E) This is the best we've got to choose from. If the opposite is true—if the artificial wetlands are completely unsustainable—then development in the city may well be the cause of the loss of wetland acreage. Drained acreage is replaced by artificial wetlands elsewhere, which eventually dry up. This would account for where the greatest losses are taking place and explain how the cities could be responsible for the loss even though developers there are obeying the law.

3. **C** Flaw

The conclusion here is that Billups's novels were influenced by Druiard. The evidence offered in support of this claim is that Druiard's ideas were in part responsible for the novels' critical acclaim, and that Billups has said in interviews she is familiar with Druiard's ideas. The flaw on this one isn't obvious, but it certainly has something to do with the relationship between the conclusion's claim that there was influence and the premises' claim of familiarity.

(A) Although it is said that Druiard's ideas were "propounded...almost a century ago," this isn't the primary piece of evidence for the conclusion, which has to do with the author's familiarity with those ideas.

(B) The only thing that's identified as necessary in this argument is Druiard's ideas: They're said to have been necessary to the success of Billups's novels. Again, though, this doesn't pertain to the key piece of evidence, which is that Billups has indicated she is familiar with Druiard's ideas.

(C) This is the one we want. Although the evidence indicates that Billups is presently familiar with Druiard's ideas, we don't know that she was at the time she actually wrote her novels.

(D) Although the statement about the importance of Druiard's ideas is somewhat hypothetical, this isn't the primary piece of evidence in the argument.

(E) We have no evidence that indicates the premises in this argument are unlikely to be true.

4. **B** Assumption

The conclusion here is that if it raises admission prices, Crazy Land will be able to survive. The premises state that if it continues losing money, Crazy Land will have to close, and that its admission prices are lower, and its operating costs higher, than those of other theme parks in the area. Clearly there are some huge gaps here; basically they all center on the questionable idea that raising admission prices will definitely cause Crazy Land to stop losing money. We want a choice that somehow closes that gap.

(A) Careful! This choice identifies a reason the plan might not work. In other words, it weakens the argument; an assumption, however, must strengthen the argument.

(B) Here's the one we want. Although it's a bit convoluted, this choice eliminates one of the possible ways the plan could fail. If this assumption isn't true—if gains in admission revenues are more than offset by losses in other revenues—then the plan certainly will not work, and so this fact is absolutely necessary to the conclusion.

(C) Careful here. The argument doesn't claim that increasing admission prices is the only way Crazy Land could solve its problems, only that doing so will in fact solve them. Other possible solutions, then, aren't actually relevant to our conclusion.

(D) This one is tempting, but in the end it goes beyond the argument's scope. For one thing, we don't know what role Crazy Land's popularity plays in its problems. Even if this statement isn't true—if the poor repair of its facilities is responsible for declining popularity—it may nevertheless be true that raising admission prices could solve its financial troubles.

(E) Even if they are losing money, it isn't clear what bearing the other theme parks have on our conclusion.

5. A Resolve/explain

The contradiction here is that, although the sting operation has been successful at reducing the number of illegal prescriptions in the city, the pharmacy is continuing to receive ever larger numbers of illegal prescriptions. We want a choice that tells us where these new prescriptions are coming from.

(A) This is the one we want. The pharmacy, although it has reduced the number of illegal prescriptions in the city, is also receiving prescriptions from other places. This explains how the number in the city could be shrinking while the overall number received by the pharmacy is growing at the same time.

(B) This isn't as good an explanation as (A). It does help explain why the pharmacy might continue to receive illegal prescriptions written in the city, but it doesn't explain the difference in numbers, which is the central contradiction here.

(C) Legitimate business isn't relevant to the situation described here.

(D) Close, but this still doesn't explain the situation. We're told that the number of illegal prescriptions written in the city is definitely decreasing, so even if the overall number of people getting prescriptions is increasing at the same time, that still wouldn't explain the larger number of illegal prescriptions received by the pharmacy.

(E) This tries to explain by casting doubt on the truth of the information initially presented. It does so, however, in very weak language that isn't adequate to explain away the contradiction. (A) is still definitely a better answer.

6. C Strengthen

The conclusion here is that quality of instruction has improved. The primary evidence for this claim hinges on test scores. Before the changes, scores were lower than those of "comparable students in other cities." Now, those scores are in line with the national average. The two comparisons are made with regard to different groups, which is one potential source of problems. The other potential source of problems is that the argument only talks about scores in "three important areas." It may be that these areas don't necessarily indicate the quality of instruction. Remember that we want to support the argument's conclusion in the answer we choose.

(A) If anything, this choice weakens the conclusion by indicating one way in which the students' test scores before the change can't be properly compared to test scores after the change.

(B) The main focus of this argument is using the information about test scores as evidence that the quality of instruction has improved. While improved test scores could be the result of other changes, that a specific measure (such as class size) might be responsible for the purported increases isn't really relevant to the argument.

(C) This is the one we want. We initially identified the difference in the two comparison groups as a potential problem with the argument. From the information in the argument, it remained possible that test scores in the city hadn't changed at all, and that the national average was lower than the scores of the comparable students mentioned in the first comparison. This choice closes up that gap by assuring us that the two groups mentioned have similar test scores.

(D) Careful! This is a great weaken, but that isn't what we're asked to do on this argument. We want our choice to strengthen the conclusion.

(E) It isn't clear what impact this would have on the commissioner's conclusion. We don't know whether these tests are the same ones mentioned by the commissioners, or whether they're different ones, or even what impact the change in how quality is measured has on this particular city. In the end, it isn't clear how this could help strengthen the link between the evidence presented and the conclusion the commissioner draws from it.

7. **B** Parallel flaw

Here's the pattern we're looking for: A can cause B. B is happening. So A must be happening. The main flaw here is that one possible cause of a state of affairs is taken to be the only possible cause. We're looking for a choice that makes a similar mistake.

(A) This isn't quite the same. In the initial argument, the result is taken as positive proof that the potential cause must have been present. In this choice, we're told directly that the cause is present: "Emerson is a heavy smoker."

(B) Here's the one we're looking for. Don't be deceived by the fact that the statements here don't occur in precisely the same order as they do in the initial argument. In this case, the effect is present, and the argument concludes that one of its possible causes must also have been present.

(C) This one's conclusion isn't at all similar to the conclusion of the initial argument. Whereas the original concludes that the cause must have been present, this choice asserts that it must not have been.

(D) Like (A), this choice includes as one of its premises a definite statement that the possible cause is present.

(E) Like (C), this one concludes that the cause isn't present. It can't be parallel.

8. **C** Weaken

The conclusion is that the ballot initiative will likely result in destabilizing the government. The evidence offered for this conclusion is that Murray supports the initiative, and that Murray is a member of a political party that seeks to destabilize the government. The links in this argument are pretty tenuous; it assumes that Murray would only ever support something that accomplishes a goal desired by some group of which Murray is a member. Our choice will be a general statement that contradicts this assumption.

(A) This choice has to do with what rights should be extended to individuals, but the argument's conclusion has to do with the likely result of a particular initiative. This choice isn't relevant to the conclusion.

(B) This seems to be pointing in the right direction, but it isn't a very strong attack on the argument's conclusion. Also, it doesn't quite fit with what the conclusion is saying: Although Murray's beliefs are central to the argument's reasoning, the conclusion has to do specifically with the likely results of the ballot initiative, not with Murray.

(C) This is the one we want. The general goal is the violent overthrow of the government; the specific course of action is the ballot initiative; and the argument's conclusion does indeed depend on assuming that the likely result of the initiative will be to further the general goal Murray supports. Since this choice indicates that Murray's support is not sufficient to draw the conclusion the argument does, this is the principle that would weaken it best.

(D) This appears to attack the argument, but there are at least two problems with it. For one, we have no idea whether or not the Renewal Party supports the ballot initiative. Worse, this principle doesn't pertain directly to the conclusion, which involves a prediction about the likely result of passing the initiative. This isn't as good as (C).

(E) It isn't clear how directly this pertains to the conclusion of the argument at all. It's even less clear how this choice would weaken the conclusion.

9. **B** Weaken

The argument attempts to explain the fact that Patrona's paintings are becoming more valuable while Avlov's evidently are not by attributing the difference to a "lasting quality" present in Patrona's paintings, but not in Avlov's. We're looking for a choice that would provide some other explanation for the difference in the prices paid for their paintings.

(A) Careful. Although it's possible to read this one in such a way that you can convince yourself it weakens the argument, realize that the conclusion doesn't specify what "lasting quality" Patrona's paintings may have. With this in mind, we see that this choice actually tends to strengthen, since the "intellectual style" may in fact be the lasting quality.

(B) This is the one we want. This choice suggests that the difference between Patrona and Avlov doesn't have to do with the quality of the paintings themselves, but instead with their availability in the market.

(C) Like (A), this describes a "lasting quality" of Patrona's paintings, and therefore tends to strengthen the conclusion.

(D) Like (A) and (C), this also seems to support the argument's conclusion. Also, its relevance is difficult to ascertain, and vagueness is never a good thing.

(E) This one identifies a reason why Avlov's paintings don't last, and thus tends to support the comparison made in the argument's conclusion.

10. **B** Strengthen

The argument claims that the reason more independent films are attracting large audiences is that technology has made techniques available to independent directors that were previously only available to directors of big-budget movies. The argument goes on to explain that these techniques have made the independent products seem as professional as big-budget movies. We're looking for an answer that further explains how new technologies have leveled the playing field.

(A) This doesn't particularly strengthen the conclusion, since it doesn't have anything to do with a potential difference between independent and big-budget movies.

(B) This helps the argument. One of the results of the new technologies mentioned in the argument is that independent films now seem as professional and polished as big-budget movies do. The argument doesn't explicitly link this professional appearance with commercial success, so this choice does improve the reasoning in the argument.

(C) The primary focus of the argument is technology, but this choice brings in other factors that contribute to commercial success. This choice doesn't appear to help make the argument's conclusion seem more likely. It also focuses on big-budget films rather than independent films.

(D) If anything, this weakens the argument. Remember that we're looking to strengthen the contention that new technology is responsible for the increased popularity and commercial success of independent films.

(E) First of all, the language here is quite weak. Worse, it seems to be trying to weaken the conclusion.

DRILL #2

Pages 65 – 72

1. **E** Flaw

The claim here is that law enforcement's warnings about the crime of identity theft are exaggerated. The main support for this claim is that the number of victims of this crime is relatively small, when compared to other types of fraud. There are a few ways this argument might conceivably be attacked. First, the number used refers to "confirmed cases of identity theft"; it's possible that the crime is much more prevalent, but that it is more difficult to detect or report than other types of fraud. It's also possible that law enforcement's warnings about this crime have had the intended effect of actually preventing it. Hopefully we'll find an answer that refers to one or the other of these weaknesses.

(A) The argument does include verifiable evidence, and the problem with it isn't the rhetoric that's used; the problem is that the evidence may not demonstrate what the argument claims it does.

(B) This one sounds good until the very end, but the main focus of this choice is on applying the same methods to prevent other types of fraud. Our conclusion, however, has to do with a judgment about how serious a threat identity theft really is.

(C) Like (B), half of this one sounds pretty good. Unfortunately, the choice refers to the "ineffectiveness of law enforcement's action," which is precisely the thing that the argument fails to establish.

(D) Close again, but this one is too strongly worded. It isn't necessary to the argument that "all" of those who've been a victim of identity theft are aware of it, only that the reported number of identity theft crimes is a good measure of how many such crimes are actually committed.

(E) Here's the one we want. It's possible that the reason the number of identity thefts is so small is the very campaign that the argument is criticizing.

2. **A** Weaken

The conclusion here is that Jennona's economic problems will be solved by continuing to cut taxes. The main piece of evidence here is that tax cuts stimulate growth in every case where they don't increase debt too much. One gap to note here is between Jennona's economic problems and the idea of long-term growth; one clear assumption here is that long-term growth will solve those problems. Another is that continuing to cut taxes in Jennona won't lead to crippling debt. We'd like to find a choice that exploits one of these weaknesses.

(A) Tough as it may seem, this is the choice we want. This one reinterprets the piece of evidence on which the conclusion is based. The conclusion depends on the fact that tax cuts are the cause of long-term growth, and treat crippling debt as a special case. This choice explains that economic conditions are the fundamental determining factor in what tax policy should be pursued. Countries with healthy economies can cut taxes, whereas those who don't have healthy economies must not, which explains why some countries experience growth as a result of tax cuts, while others don't and wind up with crippling debt.

(B) Although this seems to be trying to weaken, it doesn't necessarily contradict the piece of advice given in the conclusion. Even if Jennona's infrastructure is bad, by the argument's reasoning, cutting taxes may still be able to improve its economy.

(C) If anything, this would tend to strengthen the advice in the conclusion.

(D) It isn't clear what this information has to do with cutting the taxes imposed in Jennona.

(E) The stability of Jennona's economy isn't plainly relevant to whether or not cutting taxes will solve whatever problems it has.

3. **C** Assumption

The conclusion here is that Romans first came to this area more than 2,000 years ago. The main piece of evidence is a cornerstone of the bank, which has been in place for more than 2,600 years and was evidently part of an earlier Roman building. Properly speaking, the assumption of this argument is that the Romans were the ones who first put this stone in place.

(A) This one's pretty nasty. The argument states that chemical analysis indicates that the stone has been in place for "at least" 2,600 years, but it does not specify a precise length of time. Even if an error of more than 600 years occasionally arises, we don't know whether or not this would weaken the conclusion. This fact may well have been taken into account in the estimate presented in the argument.

(B) We don't need to know specifics of the rates of chemical weathering over time in order to evaluate the conclusion. It's entirely possible that the analysis described in the argument took changes in these rates into account.

(C) Here's the one we want. It closes off one possible weakness in the argument: The Romans might conceivably have used stones that were already in place in building the bath.

(D) This is far too specific to be something required by the argument, although it would tend to strengthen the conclusion if we knew it were true.

(E) This is too strong to be an assumption of the argument. Clearly, it's a matter of common sense that the Romans couldn't have built anything before they arrived, but we don't have to know that they began building immediately upon their arrival in order for the argument's reasoning to be all right.

4. **B** Strengthen

The conclusion here is that there was once liquid water on Mars. The main pieces of evidence are that solid water is currently present; that a mineral that forms in the presence of liquid water on Earth is present; and that certain features that could form because of liquid water are also present. Clearly, to strengthen our argument, we need to find ways to shore up one of many possible holes left open by the evidence. For instance, although hematite forms on Earth in the presence of liquid water, we don't know that that's the only way it could form. In fact, the argument states that it forms "almost exclusively" in the presence of liquid water, indicating that it can form without it. Similarly, we don't know that the spherical concretions mentioned could only have formed in the presence of liquid water.

(A) The issue isn't whether there's currently water on Mars; we know there is. This choice only guarantees us that water vapor must once have been present, not that liquid water once was.

(B) This looks pretty good. Although it doesn't shore up either of the gaps mentioned above, it does indicate that the temperature was higher at one time, and the argument says that the reason water currently on Mars remains in solid form is that the surface temperature is too low. This isn't perfect, but it's the best choice we've got.

(C) This might explain where some water in the polar ice caps came from, but it doesn't establish that that water ever existed in liquid form.

(D) This would weaken the conclusion by providing a possible alternative explanation for how the concretions formed.

(E) Since hematite can apparently form on Earth without liquid water being present, this choice doesn't actually deal with the potential weakness mentioned above.

5. **E** Strengthen the pollster against the strategist

The pollster predicts that the Future Party will gain a majority in the upcoming parliamentary elections. The evidence presented in support of this conclusion is a bit complicated: Sixty percent of those surveyed indicate that the Future Party shares their view on the issue they identify as most important. The strategist, in response, points out that while the Future Party is most strongly supported in the cities, the majority of parliament is made up of representatives from rural areas. The strategist predicts that the Future Party will not do as well as the pollster predicts. We're looking for a new item of information that would tend to support the pollster's prediction.

(A) This isn't bad, but it doesn't quite do the job. It doesn't deal with the strategist's primary piece of evidence: that supporters of the Future Party are concentrated in cities, whereas the majority of seats in parliament represent rural districts.

(B) Like (A), this one is trying, but it doesn't answer the primary piece of evidence in the strategist's response. Neither participant in the conversation disputes that the poll is an accurate representation of how many people in the nation overall will vote for Future Party representatives. The strategist's point is that the distribution of this support is the party's problem: If virtually none of the party's supporters vote in rural areas, where the majority of representatives come from, then there is no way the Future Party can become a majority, even if every single person in the cities votes for the party.

(C) Like the two previous answers, this helps the pollster's contention generally but doesn't answer the strategist's objection. We want something that tells us why the imbalance between urban and rural districts won't be a problem for the Future Party.

(D) This is pretty weak. Having a candidate on the ballot in the rural districts doesn't necessarily mean that the Future Party will win.

(E) Here it is. This item of information provides very strong evidence that the Future Party will win, and answers the urban/rural objection by showing that the Future Party is guaranteed to win enough seats in rural districts to assure a majority.

6. **D** Weaken

The conclusion is that the flood stories found in many ancient texts provide accounts of actual historical events. A great deal of specific information is provided in the argument, but the upshot of it is that once there was a massive flood in a specific area where human settlements appear to have existed. We want a choice that provides some other explanation of how the flood stories originated, or demonstrates that the historical flood could not have been the inspiration for those stories.

(A) This strengthens slightly by making it seem more likely that the settlements mentioned were in place at the time of the historical flood. This fact doesn't seem in need of too much support, since those settlements are under water now.

(B) Although this is trying to weaken, it isn't a very serious attack. There's no reason why the story would have to have been originally written down only in places that were near the site of the flood.

(C) Details of the speed with which the flooding took place don't necessarily contradict the fact that the flood stories were inspired by the formation of the Black Sea.

(D) Here's the one we want. This choice points out an inconsistency between the historical event and the accounts in the stories. Whereas the Black Sea filled and did not recede, the stories all describe the flood waters receding.

(E) It's not absolutely clear what effect this answer choice would have on the conclusion. If anything, it seems to strengthen by indicating that the stories were widespread throughout the region.

7. **D** Flaw

The conclusion here is that the accusations that the government participated in the fall of Menae's government are at least in part true. The only evidence offered in support of this fact is that one government official has refused to testify in person to a commission investigating the events surrounding the collapse. The problems here are huge; any of a number of other reasons could explain the minister's behavior.

(A) The argument doesn't really refute any other argument, so this choice doesn't really fit the situation.

(B) Close, but this doesn't get to the heart of the problem, which is that the argument presumes the reason the minister doesn't testify in person is that she has done something wrong.

(C) This argument does at least provide some fact in support of its assertion. That fact doesn't support the conclusion very well, but it's a fact nevertheless.

(D) Here's the one we want. This choice makes an assumption about the purpose of the minister's refusal: to conceal evidence.

(E) The only fact in this argument—that the minister refused to testify in person—is one that doesn't seem to be in further need of establishment.

8. **A** Assumption

This one's a little odd. The conclusion is that interviewers should end any interview with a job candidate if the interviewer has a negative impression of the candidate after one minute; the conclusion's wording says there is "no reason" for such interviews to be extended. The reasons given are that initial impressions are formed in the first minute, and interviewers only rarely are convinced to hire candidates of whom they have a negative impression as a result of other materials not having to do with the interview. Since this is an assumption question, we want something that'll support the conclusion, but the main gap here is between the likelihood of hiring a candidate and there being "no reason" to give them a full interview. Hopefully our answer will have something to do with reasons an interviewer might want to extend an interview with a candidate of whom the interviewer has a negative impression.

(A) After another look at the initial argument, you'll see that this is the one we want. It's important to look at the evidence carefully here: The premise only tells us that it's extremely rare that materials such as personal references and resumes cause interviewers to hire candidates of whom they receive a negative impression, but we don't have any information about what impact the latter portions of the interview have on that decision. If this choice isn't true, then there certainly would be a reason to extend the interview beyond the first minute.

(B) The language here sounds good, but as outlined in (A), the problem with the argument is that it doesn't tell us what impact the rest of the interview has on hiring decisions.

(C) This starts off sounding pretty good, but it brings in the question of being qualified. Since we don't really know what impact this has on our conclusion, we can't pick this one.

(D) Like (C), this choice brings in a concept that isn't clearly relevant to our conclusion.

(E) Although this may appear to be a logical consequence of the information presented in the argument, remember that our task here is to identify an assumption, not infer some new information.

9. **B** Weaken EXCEPT

The conclusion here is basically that people are exercising more. The main evidence for this claim are two items of information: First, new memberships at gyms are growing very quickly; second, surveys have shown that people are feeling healthier. We're looking here for four answers that tell us these facts don't necessarily show that people are exercising more; the remaining choice will be the one we want to pick.

(A) This weakens by showing that the increase in the number of new gym memberships issued is attributable to people who have always exercised changing gyms, not people who haven't historically exercised beginning to do so.

(B) Here's the one we want. Although this does explain why the number of new gym memberships is growing, it doesn't actually tell us that people aren't using them, which is what we'd need to know in order to weaken the argument.

(C) This weakens by providing competing information that people are actually engaging in more sedentary activity than they were before, not less.

(D) This weakens by suggesting that, although people are exercising more at gyms, they're also exercising less in other ways they previously did. Although we can't make a value judgment about which of these activities is better for you, nevertheless this choice tells us that physical activity actually isn't increasing, which is the standard presented by the argument.

(E) This explains the feelings of health presented in the evidence as a result of a change in diet, which isn't mentioned as a factor in increasing health, and as a result of the purchase of gym memberships that aren't actually used. This choice also weakens.

10. **D** Resolve/Explain EXCEPT

The paradox here is that, at the same time that repression has grown in the country, international aid agencies assert that quality of life has also grown. We're looking for four choices that will explain how increasing repression doesn't necessarily decrease quality of life in the country; the remaining choice will be our answer.

(A) This explains by showing that increased repression has been accompanied by decreases to corruption and crime, which presumably are related to quality of life.

(B) This explains by showing that increased repression has been accompanied by other benefits that have improved housing and medical care, which presumably are related to quality of life.

(C) Tough, but this one does actually help to explain. The idea is that repression now isn't excessively high, but that instead it was nonexistent before, and other benefits associated with having effective government have presumably improved quality of life.

(D) Tough, but this is the one we want. Of all of the answers, it's the one that seems to have the least direct connection to the welfare of the country's citizens. International aid agencies paying closer attention to the country doesn't translate as directly to increased quality of life as the other factors mentioned.

(E) This explains by showing that the government's efforts have resulted in increased economic health, which presumably has increased quality of life.

11. C Weaken

The language here is difficult. The conclusion is that the pattern of observed occultations demonstrates the existence of an undiscovered planet in the solar system. The evidence basically explains what occultation is: Some dark stellar object passes between the Earth and a distant star, concealing the star from view for a period of time. We're looking for a piece of evidence that would tell us the observed pattern really isn't due to an undiscovered planet in the solar system.

(A) The argument concludes that this undiscovered planet is "orbiting slowly." It's possible that it orbits so slowly that the next time the occultation recurs, this particular pattern will be far in the future.

(B) Careful. All this choice tells is that several of the distant stars that are part of the pattern may have planets of their own.

(C) This is the one we want. As much as it may seem like a technicality, this provides one explanation of how the astronomers could be wrong: It's not a planet orbiting beyond Pluto, but a comet.

(D) This choice actually strengthens the conclusion quite nicely. Our mission, however, is to weaken it.

(E) This seems to be trying to offer another explanation for the occultations, but the fact that this choice describes a factor that "cannot be predicted" doesn't really explain the pattern described in the initial argument, so this doesn't weaken as well as (C) does.

12. B Evaluate

Sandy asserts that *The Sun* was irresponsible in its reporting of a scandal surrounding Representative Smith. The main evidence offered is that the allegations surrounding Representative Smith haven't been proven true. Pat responds that newspapers are responsible for reporting stories that are part of the public debate, and every other paper is reporting on Representative Smith's situation as well. We're looking for a question whose answer would cause us either to support or reject Sandy's conclusion in light of the information Pat presents.

(A) Knowing more specifics of the disclosure rules wouldn't really help us evaluate Sandy's conclusion, which has to do with *The Sun*'s behavior.

(B) Here's the one we want. Since the allegations aren't proven, it would indeed be irresponsible to report that they were true; on the other hand, if the paper did not represent them as true, then they are indeed merely reporting on a situation of current interest, as Pat claims.

(C) This wouldn't really help us evaluate Sandy's argument. This is a consideration raised by Pat, not Sandy.

(D) The awareness of the public isn't clearly relevant to Sandy's conclusion, which claims that the paper reported irresponsibly.

(E) Close, but this one doesn't really allow us to evaluate Sandy's argument with Pat's objection in mind. Pat states that it's responsible for media to report on unproven allegations in some cases, and this question wouldn't help us to evaluate whether this is one of these cases or not.

13. **B** Resolve/Explain

The apparent contradiction here is between the results of the change in the minimum drinking age and the legislators' claim that the change was both "adequate and successful" as a response to the problem of drinking-related accidents among a certain age group. What we have to explain, essentially, is why the fact that the number of these accidents increased doesn't necessarily mean the legislation failed.

(A) For one thing, this choice mentions harsher penalties, although we don't know that the change in the drinking age involved changing these penalties. For another, the legislators' claim is that the measure really was successful at addressing the problem, so this doesn't explain.

(B) Here we go. A quick consultation of the original passage shows that the increase was in the number of accidents, not the rate of accidents within the age group. If this choice is true, then an increase in the number of accidents could be consistent with a significant reduction in the rate of accidents, since there are so many more people in the age group mentioned.

(C) This doesn't provide particularly direct information that the solution was successful at reducing accidents within the age group of concern.

(D) What other states did doesn't help us explain what happened in this particular state.

(E) This is interesting, but since it has nothing to do with accidents, we definitely shouldn't pick it.

14. **A** Strengthen

The conclusion here is that the ruling party's policies have led to a greater income gap between the country's richest and poorest residents. The main piece of evidence is a comparison between the number of the country's citizens who live below the poverty line now compared to ten years ago. There are a number of gaps here. The biggest is probably between the number below the poverty line and the disparity between rich and poor, which aren't necessarily the same thing; it may be that the entire country became poorer over this span. There are certainly other potential problems here, but we're looking for a choice that reinforces the conclusion.

(A) This is the one we have to pick. While it doesn't directly attribute the change over the past ten years to actions of the ruling party, it does address a potential problem with the conclusion: The fact that more of the country's residents are considered poor doesn't necessarily mean that the gap between rich and poor has widened. This choice provides us with that assurance and thus strengthens the conclusion.

(B) Although this does mention one policy of the ruling party, it doesn't mention any consequence of the policy that shows how it made the income gap worse.

(C) This points in generally the same direction as the passage information, but it doesn't provide any additional support. We already know that half of the country is below the poverty line, so this isn't new information for us.

(D) This actually weakens the argument by suggesting that the gap between rich and poor has probably narrowed, not grown.

(E) So close, but this one has too many holes to be better than (A). The primary problem here is the comparison to "many other countries," which doesn't really allow us to pin down just how much the rich people in this country are making. It could be that the rich were even richer ten years ago, which is why this doesn't really strengthen. Since the conclusion is based on a comparison over time, we need our answer to help that comparison, and this one doesn't.

15. **E** Principle

The conclusion here is that the police were justified in preventing Graves from destroying irreplaceable works of art. The premises are primarily a description of the situation: Graves destroyed the works during a period of mental illness, and once he had recovered he regretted this destruction and thanked the police for stopping him from destroying others. This is the key reason the argument appeals to in contradicting the judgment attributed to the court, which claimed that the intervention wasn't justified. We want a choice that matches the argument's reasoning.

(A)   This agrees with the argument's judgment, but it's missing the piece that lets us know the primary reason the police were justified was that Graves, once he was in his right mind again, would have wanted the police to intervene.

(B)   This doesn't agree with the argument's judgment, which is that the police were justified in stopping Graves.

(C)   This brings in a side issue—one of "collective cultural property"—that isn't raised in the argument. Since we're looking for a principle to which the reasoning conforms, this isn't a good choice.

(D)   Like (C), this brings in a side issue that isn't addressed by the argument.

(E)   Here we go. This is the only choice that mentioned Graves's later regret, which is the fact used by the argument to conclude that the police were justified in their intervention.

CHAPTER 6

DRILL #1

Pages 77 – 79

1. D Flaw

The conclusion here is that Roderick will make the Olympic team as a distance runner. The only evidence offered in support of this claim is that Roderick can run a five-minute mile, and in order to make the team as a distance runner, a competitor has to be able to run a five-minute mile. This one's pretty straightforward: Satisfying the five-minute mile requirement is treated as if by itself that fact can assure Roderick's success.

(A) There is a mention of percentages here, but it isn't really essential to the argument's reasoning. It's Roderick's ability to run a five-minute mile that's being misused here, not his membership in the ten percent of the population that can run a five-minute mile.

(B) Having this information wouldn't make the reasoning in the argument any less abysmal. The problem is that a single requirement is treated as though it were the only requirement.

(C) There's no description of past Olympic teams included in the argument.

(D) Here it is. Once you've parsed the language, you see that this describes what's wrong here: A single requirement that Roderick fits is treated as making it certain that he'll succeed in his bid to join the Olympic team.

(E) The argument never misuses language in this particular way.

2. C Parallel

We have a chain of requirements here. Anyone who has attribute A also has attribute B; anyone with attribute B also has attribute C. So anyone who has attribute A also has attribute C. We're looking for a similar chain in our right answer.

(A) This starts off seeming pretty good, but the clearest problem here is that the conclusion goes in the wrong direction. In order to be parallel, the conclusion here would have to be something like "everyone who can play ice hockey also has superb balance."

(B) This argument has some serious problems. The clearest indication that it isn't parallel is that the two requirements in its premises aren't similar to one another: One is necessary, but the other is sufficient. Compare that to the two premises in the initial argument.

(C) This is the one we want. Here attribute A is "impermanent," attribute B is "must eventually end," and attribute C is "must have begun at some definite time."

(D) The conclusion here isn't at all similar. It has to do with a situation in which someone doesn't have the attributes in question.

(E) Like (B), the premises in this one aren't similar, so this can't be parallel.

3. C Inference

The passage here describes some necessary conditions for life as we know it: In order to support that life, a planet must have a magnetic field, and in order to have a magnetic field, it must have a molten core. We're given information, then, about a planet that does not possess a molten core. We can easily conclude that, because it doesn't fit the initial requirement, it must also not have a magnetic field and thus be incapable of supporting life as we know it.

(A) We don't know anything about the relative spin speeds of planets with and without molten cores. This goes far beyond the passage information.

(B) Careful here. This is a sweeping statement about all life, but the initial passage only specifies that a magnetic field is necessary to life "as we know it."

(C) Here we go. Although the wording is a little strange—it includes the stipulation that life may or may not exist on the surface—this is, basically, a paraphrase of our conclusion that the planet cannot support life as we know it.

(D) This turns our series of requirements—necessary conditions—in the passage into a sufficient condition, which is a no-no.

(E) We don't have information about other factors that might be important to the development of life, so we can't go this far in drawing a conclusion from the passage.

4. **B** Strengthen

The conclusion here is that the program of controlled burning will restore the health of forests. The premises, broadly paraphrased, tell us that forest fires are necessary to the health of forests. As always, the assumption in an argument like this one is that the healthful effects of natural forest fires are the only factors standing in the way of the forests being healthy. We want a choice that tells us this as strongly as possible.

(A) The argument itself lets us know that this program involves burning "without incurring... risks to property and life." Besides, the scope here only has to do with the health of forests, not with whether or not the program is safe for people nearby. This doesn't really help.

(B) Here we go. It doesn't get much stronger than this: As long as we restore these beneficial effects, the forests will be healthy again.

(C) Here's the standard one solution/only solution trick we see on many such questions. The argument only claims that this particular program will work—not that it's the only program that could work. We don't need anything quite this strong to support the conclusion in this case.

(D) This is a simpler paraphrase of our premises. Since this is the fact that we're starting from, stating it again doesn't improve our argument at all.

(E) This explains nicely why there is a problem in the first place, but since it evidently has no impact on the solution proposed in the argument, this can't possibly strengthen.

5. **E** Infer variant: could be true except

There are two basic sides to the passage here. One is that introducing new initiatives inevitably leads to confusion, which leads to a short-term decrease in sales. The other side is that the only way for a company to increase its share of the market is by introducing new initiatives. We can put these together in several different ways, but the upshot is that in order to increase market share, a company has to do something that decreases overall sales in the market for a period of time. It's important to note the distinction between overall sales in the market and the share of that market belonging to one company: One is a raw number, the other is a percentage. It's also important to track what the question is asking us to do: Four of our answers will be possible, given the information in the passage; the fifth will be absolutely impossible, and that'll be our answer.

(A) This could happen. The passage information doesn't guarantee that every new initiative works, just that the only way to increase share is to introduce new initiatives.

(B) This could happen. As with (A), there's no guarantee that a new initiative will increase the market share of the company that introduces it. It remains possible, then, that another company within the market gains so much more market share that, although the overall size of the market is shrinking, that one company's sales increase.

(C) This could happen, too. A successful new initiative could conceivably work right away, so that the company introducing it immediately sees the benefits.

(D) Nasty. Initially this looks all right, although it's somewhat worrisome that the new initiatives are identified as having been introduced "in the recent past." The passage only guarantees us that overall sales decline "for a period of time," leaving just enough wiggle room for this one to be true. It may be that the new initiatives were all introduced long enough ago that overall sales have by now recovered from the confusion the initiatives caused.

(E) Here's the one that's most directly contradicted by our passage information. The thing that makes this better than (D) is that the result of increased overall sales takes place "immediately following" the new initiative. Since the time frame is tighter than the one described in (D), this choice is the one we need to pick.

Drill #2
Pages 83 – 84

1. D Infer

We're given a few facts about Samantha's store here. We can diagram the major ones this way:

buy bike @ full price → buy bike @ half price
buy bike @ half price → – better bike @ full price

We observe that these two conditionals chain together, letting us know that if someone would buy a bike at full price, then no better bike is available at full price. There is also a contrapositive chain here. We're looking for the choice that's consistent with our diagrams.

(A)   This goes rather too far for the information we have. We can't draw good conclusions about the volume of Samantha's sales on any weekend from the material we're given.

(B)   This goes even further than (A). Certainly we don't know anything about factors other than those mentioned in the argument, so we can't definitely conclude that price is the least important factor among all of them.

(C)   Careful here. If someone sees a bike he or she likes better than all the others, then all our information allows us to conclude is that this person would not buy any other bike, no matter what its price. However, we can't be certain that the person would actually buy the bike he or she likes best, so this one goes just a little too far.

(D)   Here we go. If a better bike is available at full price, then our contrapositive chain allows us to conclude that the person would not buy any other bike at full price.

(E)   This may agree with common sense, but it actually isn't supported by the material in the passage. We know that anyone who would buy a bike at full price would also be willing to buy it at half price, but what decision the person would make in the circumstance described in this answer choice isn't something we can tell from the information we have.

2. B Strengthen

This question asks us to supply a missing piece in the reasoning. Here are diagrams representing the conclusion, and then the premises on which it is based:

C: C. Club member → – interested in artworks from auction
P: interested in little-known artworks → serious collector
P: in auction → little-known artworks
P: C. Club member → -art scholar

The missing link here is evidently between the terms "art scholar" and "serious collector." Starting with the premise listed third above, we need to make the highlighted link below in order for the chain of reasoning to work:

C. Club member → **– art scholar** →
   – serious collector →
      – interested in little-known artworks →
         – interested in artworks from auction

Note that we had to use contrapositives of the premises listed first and second above in order to complete the chain. Now all we need to do is find a choice that provides either one of the two following statements:

– art scholar → – serious collector

OR

serious collector → art scholar

(A)   So close, but this one gives us this statement instead: art scholar → serious collector. That's not what we need.

(B)   Here we go. Remembering how we diagram "only" statements, we can see that this one translates as: serious collector → art scholar. That's what we need.

(C)   Since the information we have about the Chrysanthemum Club is that its members are not art scholars, we need information that tells us something about people who aren't art scholars, not people who are. This doesn't supply what we need.

(D) Since the information we have doesn't allow us to draw conclusions about serious collectors, this isn't what we need. We know that only serious collectors would be interested in little-known artworks, but we don't know that all of them would be.

(E) Like (C), this one gives us information about people who are art scholars. What we need to complete the chain of reasoning, though, is information about people who aren't art scholars, since that's the only thing we know about the members of the Chrysanthemum Club.

3. **E** Parallel flaw

Here's the pattern of reasoning the original argument uses:

P1. If Thursday, then Roger buys groceries.
$A \rightarrow B$
P2. If Roger buys groceries, then he walks past the house.
$B \rightarrow C$
P3. Roger walks past the house.   C
C. Today is Thursday.   A

Hopefully we recognize that this is fundamentally a necessary/sufficient problem involving two conditionals chained together. We're looking for a similar pattern in our answer.

(A) There's actually nothing wrong with this argument, which is a good reason to eliminate it. Also, it only involves one conditional statement, which would be another way to get rid of it.

(B) Like (A), this argument is fine, and it also only involves one conditional statement, not a chain of two.

(C) Very close, but the difference here has to do with the parts of the chain that appear in the conclusion. The reasoning here goes: $A \rightarrow B$; $B \rightarrow C$; C. Therefore B. In order to be parallel, this one would have to conclude that a stranger walked past on the sidewalk.

(D) The reasoning in this case is $A \rightarrow B$; $A \rightarrow C$; B. Therefore, C. Like (C), this one has a necessary / sufficient problem, but it isn't precisely the same one that the original argument has.

(E) Here's our answer at last. If there's a strategic initiative announced, then it's announced in an official memo; if it's an official memo, Nancy signs it; Nancy signed this memo. Therefore, this memo announces a strategic initiative. Don't be thrown off by the slight variations in phrasing and by the fact that the statements here aren't in exactly the same order as they were in the original.

4. **D** Infer

Here are diagrams for the conditionals provided in the passage, with their contrapositives:

1. – supported by Dems → supported by Reps

   – supported by Reps → supported by Dems

2. supported by Dems → debated in committee

   – debated in committee → – supported by Dems

3. supported by Reps → vetoed by President

   – vetoed by President → – supported by Reps

We note that there's a chain to be made. Here it is, along with its contrapositive:

– vetoed by President → – supported by Reps → supported by Dems → debated in committee

– debated in committee → – supported by Dems → supported by Reps → vetoed by President

Our right answer will provide a statement that follows the chain correctly.

(A) The chain we have doesn't allow us to conclude anything on the basis of the fact that the legislation is vetoed by the President.

(B) This has the same problem as (A). Our chain doesn't allow us to draw any conclusion about a piece of legislation that is debated in committee.

(C) The concept of "increased support" doesn't really fit anywhere in our chain. Certainly we can't be sure of this, given the information we have.

(D) This is the one we want, although we have to be careful in the way we evaluate it. Look more carefully at the statement listed first in our original diagramming of the passage. It's not possible for a piece of legislation to be supported by neither the Democrats nor the Republicans; if one of the parties doesn't support the legislation, then the other party has to. So at least one of the party-specific results has to happen. It's possible for legislation to be supported by both parties, in which case both of these results happen. It's tough, but this one is the choice that uses our chain correctly.

(E) On the contrary, our chain guarantees us that any piece of legislation not vetoed by the President will be debated extensively in committee.

5. **A** Infer

Here we have two necessary conditions and a "no" statement. The diagrams for these are:

comprehend chemical bonding → understand quantum physics

design practical synthesis → background in chemistry

background in chemistry → – understand quantum physics

Once again, we have three statements that, with their contrapositives, can be used to make a chain. Here's one direction of it:

design practical synthesis → background in chemistry → – understand quantum physics → – comprehend chemical bonding

This one has a contrapositive as well, which involves switching the order of the arrows and negating each statement. Here's what it looks like:

comprehend chemical bonding → understand quantum physics → – background in chemistry → – design practical synthesis

We want a choice that uses our chain correctly.

(A)   Here's the one we want. The diagram for this one is design practical synthesis → – comprehend chemical bonding. That's consistent with our chain.

(B)   With the information given, we can't really evaluate the statement "at least some background in chemistry," since it isn't anywhere in our chain. We don't know this for certain, as much sense as it seems to make.

(C)   Like (B), this choice brings in terms that we don't know how to translate. It's too much to say that these theories "don't apply"; all we know is that those who understand them can't design a practical synthesis of industrial chemicals.

(D)   This is the opposite direction of one statement from our initial argument. This answer choice would be diagrammed: background in chemistry → design practical synthesis. We can't just go around flipping arrows!

(E)   This is actually a possibility left open by our initial passage, but we can't be certain that nobody comprehends chemical bonding fully.

DRILL #3
Pages 86 – 87

1. C Resolve/explain

The thing we're asked to explain here is why not all actions that are presented as being in the nation's interest are considered criminal by international authorities. We have a few items of information about each side of the paradox. Some actions that are presented as being in the nation's interest harm innocent people. Any action that harms innocent people should be considered criminal by international authorities. The only possible explanation here is that some actions that are presented as being in the nation's interest do not harm innocent people. We want a choice that provides this information to us.

(A) The idea of authorities being "effective in the execution of their duties" isn't explicitly contained in the argument. Certainly this choice doesn't provide the explanation we were looking for. In a pinch, we might be forced to choose an answer like this, but we're definitely hoping for something better. In this case, there is a much better answer.

(B) This would explain why some actions that are presented as being in the nation's interest bring harm to people, but that's not the fact we're looking to explain. This choice leaves out international authorities entirely.

(C) Here's the information we want. It isn't exactly the statement we were looking for, but it's equivalent to it. Since some of these actions can be justified, it must be true that some of them don't bring harm to innocent individuals. This explains quite nicely.

(D) This doesn't help explain the paradox in the passage, although this certainly is a possibility left open by it.

(E) This wouldn't really help explain why international authorities don't consider all of the nation's actions criminal. This just makes the paradox worse.

2. E Flaw

We have to look carefully at the two "most" claims in this argument. We're told that most adults own a car, and most who own a car spend a lot on maintaining it. So we're talking about a majority of a majority here; keep in mind that "most" only means "more than half," and it may mean not many more than that. Our majority of a majority, in other words, may be just above 25 percent of the original population—all adults in Vitaville. The argument claims that the proportion is more than 50 percent. There's another potential problem here, which is that the second "most" claim—the one about maintenance costs—applies to the entire state, whereas the conclusion concerns only Vitaville. It may be that, in Vitaville, automobile maintenance costs are somehow different than they are in the rest of the state. Our choice may attack one, or perhaps even both, of these weaknesses.

(A) All the language in the argument appears to be used consistently, at least.

(B) The first half of this sounds promising, but then the choice goes off on the wrong track. We do need to know that the survey is representative of Vitaville, but this choice simply concerns its consistency with other surveys.

(C) It isn't necessarily true that our majority of a majority provides stronger evidence for a different conclusion. It simply doesn't provide strong enough evidence to establish the conclusion that the argument draws.

(D) The argument isn't circular. It definitely uses outside evidence to support its conclusion; it just doesn't use evidence that's strong enough.

(E) This is the best choice we have. We don't know what proportion of adults in Vitaville actually have high maintenance costs. If it's large enough, then the conclusion is warranted, but without further information, we can't be certain.

3. **A** Strengthen

Tough to keep track of who's who in this argument. It's best to think of this with two primary groups in mind: the Human Services Committee and the Budget Committee. Within the Human Services Committee, a smaller group is also on the Education Committee; similarly, within the Budget Committee, a smaller number is on the Finance Committee. With this setup in mind, we add the information that some of the members of the Education Committee—the smaller group within Human Services—are also members of the Budget Committee—the other large group. The conclusion we're looking to support is that none of these people are members of the Finance Committee, too—the smaller group within the Budget Committee.

(A) Here it is! It's a small mercy, but at least the right answer is the first one we get a chance to see. This choice guarantees us that nobody in the large Human Services group is also a member of Finance, the smaller group within Budget. Since everybody on Education is a member of Human Services, the information that nobody in Human Services is a member of Finance is enough to assure us that nobody on Education can be a member of Finance either.

(B) This doesn't really help. Remember that the conclusion we're looking to draw concerns people not being members of Finance. This choice provides us information about people who are.

(C) This doesn't help either. As with (B), we recognize that the general character of this choice isn't going to be able to help us. We're looking to support a conclusion about people not being members of other committees; this doesn't provide us any information like that.

(D) This one talks about relationships between the two large groups. We need at least some new information about one of the smaller groups in order to support the conclusion of this argument.

(E) The conclusion we're looking to support is a definite one, so wishy-washy information like this isn't likely to help us.

4. **B** Infer

The only definite item of information we have here concerns the relationship between the groups of basketball players and wrestlers: They have no members in common. The rest of the passage information just tells us that the groups of female students, cheerleaders, and basketball players all have members in common with one another, although we can't go any further than that. We'll have to be careful in looking for an item of information we can be certain of.

(A) When the seasons of various sports take place is far more information than we have to work with here. We have no information about why none of the basketball players are also wrestlers.

(B) Here it is! Some of the female students play basketball; no basketball player is also a wrestler. So it must be true that there are at least some female students who aren't wrestlers.

(C) We can't be sure of this, actually. We're never provided information that some of the school's basketball players are male students.

(D) We don't know this, either. Although some female students are cheerleaders, this doesn't imply that all of the cheerleaders are female.

(E) This goes pretty far beyond the scope of our original material. There are some who do both, but we don't have the kind of information that would allow us to conclude that the two activities have anything else in common.

5. **C** Infer

We have one definite statement here—everyone with good communication skills has an intuitive grasp of others' needs—and then two statements of quantity. Most customer service professionals have good communication skills, and few of them have technical expertise in any other area. It's difficult to predict how these statements will be combined to give an answer, so we just need to be careful in evaluating the choices.

(A) Keep an eye on which group this statement concerns. It's trying to tell us something about the entire group of those with an intuitive grasp of others' needs, but really we don't know anything for certain about this group, other than the fact that some of these people have good communication skills, and some of those with good communication skills are customer service professionals. This choice contains quantity information about a group whose complete membership isn't known.

(B) This is a comparative claim that we simply can't support with the kind of information we have in the original argument. Steer clear.

(C) This is what we want. Look at the customer-service professionals with good communication skills; we know they're a majority of the group of customer-service professionals overall. We also know that these people have an intuitive grasp of others' needs. We know further that not many customer-service professionals have technical expertise in any other area. So there have to be at least some customer-service professionals who both have good communication skills and don't have technical expertise in any other area. We've just found at least some of the people talked about in this answer choice!

(D) Careful here. The only way we could attempt to use the passage to support this conclusion would be to find customer-service professionals who have both outside technical expertise and good communication skills. The first subgroup contains only a few individuals; the second one contains a lot of them. Unfortunately, we can't be sure that anyone has both attributes. It might be that the customer-service professionals with outside technical expertise are exactly those who don't have good communication skills. We can't be sure that this choice is true.

(E) Like (A), this contains membership information about a much larger group than any we're given definite information about. We can't conclude this.

DRILL #4

Pages 89 – 90

1. **D** Principle except

   The principle we're asked to use is one that describes what happens when a military coup displaces an elected government. Note that the consequence is compounded in two ways: It results in one thing, or another, and the second possible consequence has an "and" in it. We're looking for the choice that definitely doesn't fit this principle.

   (A) This doesn't contradict our principle. Although we don't know anything about the government that the military coup displaced, this choice describes one of the possible results of the displacement of an elected government. If it displaced some other kind of government, then the principle doesn't really apply, so we can't say that this is inconsistent with it. The kind of government that eventually displaces the military government is completely beside the point. There are no direct contradictions here.

   (B) This doesn't contradict our principle. Remember that the "or" in the initial principle indicates that both results are possible, so this would be consistent with the situation in which the new military government displaced an elected one. Like (A), we don't have a notion of whether or not it displaced an elected government, but this doesn't cause any problems with the principle.

   (C) This doesn't contradict our principle. Even though the coup in this case didn't give rise to violent unrest, it remains possible that it resulted in a brutal and repressive regime. We don't have enough information to say for certain that this situation contradicts the principle.

   (D) Here's the one we want. The coup displaced an elected government, but it didn't cause violent unrest. It also didn't give rise to a brutal and repressive regime, since we know that in particular the regime wasn't repressive. Since neither of the two promised results happened, this one contradicts the principle.

   (E) This one is quite similar to (C). It tells us that one of the possible results didn't happen, but since we don't know that the other one didn't happen, we can't say for certain that this contradicts our principle.

2. **C** Infer

   We can diagram this one if we need to. Here are the statements, along with their contrapositives:

   1. member of Flight Club → enjoys piloting models AND enjoys riding in jumbo jets
       – enjoys piloting models OR – enjoys riding in jumbo jets → – member of Flight Club

   2. considered career piloting jumbo jets → enjoys piloting models
       – enjoys piloting models → – considered career piloting jumbo jets

   3. prone to motion sickness → – enjoys riding in jumbo jets
       enjoys riding in jumbo jets → – prone to motion sickness

   There appear to be a couple of separate chains we can make by joining these statements together. Rather than trying to generate them all, let's evaluate the answer choices one at a time.

   (A) This choice draws a conclusion about two kinds of people—those who aren't members of the Flight Club and those who haven't considered a career piloting jumbo jets—about whom our conditional statements don't allow us to draw any certain conclusions. Avoid this one.

   (B) The information we have doesn't allow us to conclude that any specific person has considered piloting jumbo jets as a career. Avoid this one.

   (C) This is the one we want. We can make this chain out of the material we have: member of Flight Club → enjoys riding in jumbo jets → – prone to motion sickness.

   (D) This choice attempts to draw an unwarranted conclusion about those who have considered a career piloting jumbo jets. We do know that these people enjoy piloting model airplanes, but our chain stops there. We can't draw this conclusion from the information we have.

   (E) This choice attempts to put together two kinds of people—those who enjoy piloting model airplanes and those who have not considered a career piloting jumbo jets—about whom our material doesn't allow us to draw definite conclusions. Avoid this one.

3. **A** Parallel

The pattern of the initial argument is a relatively simple one: A key criterion is presented (the leaker was present at the meeting); neither of two specific cases meets the key criterion (neither the head coach nor the general manager was there). The argument concludes that, specifically, one of the two cases cannot have been responsible for the thing that happened (the general manager was not the leaker). We want a choice that follows this pattern as closely as possible.

(A) Here's the one we want, although it's not an incredibly tight match to our original. The key criterion in this case is certification of the sale by international trade organizations. The two kinds of diamonds that don't meet this criterion are identified as conflict diamonds or those that profit factions involved in conflicts. The argument concludes that the certified diamonds cannot have been conflict diamonds.

(B) The major difference here is that the argument contains a language shift from "emerging art form" to "emerging artist." These two terms clearly refer to different things, and no similar shift exists in the original argument.

(C) This argument involves using evidence about one part of an either/or to draw a conclusion about the other part. This isn't similar to the original argument.

(D) Careful here. This argument includes two criteria that an action must meet in order to be truly charitable and one instance in which the criteria aren't satisfied. This is quite different from the original, which involves only a single criterion and two instances in which it isn't met.

(E) This is similar to (D), with the exception that the criterion involved is an either/or. Again, this dissimilarity with the original criterion is a reason to avoid the choice.

4. **E** Weaken

The conclusion here is that, in order to work, initiatives to save the ivory-billed woodpecker must meet two requirements: They have to protect the birds' native habitat, and they have to promote their breeding success. We're looking for the strongest indication that these efforts will not work.

(A) Other environmental initiatives are not within the scope of this argument. We're only concerned with the ivory-billed woodpecker.

(B) This helps explain why the bird has gotten into such bad trouble, but it doesn't really give any definite information about the likelihood that efforts to preserve it will succeed.

(C) Past attempts aren't strictly relevant to future attempts, which is what the question asks to work with.

(D) Careful here. The argument only requires us to "preserve" the woodpeckers' habitat, not to increase its extent. This choice doesn't pertain to the information given in the argument.

(E) This is the choice we want. It weakens by showing that efforts to save the ivory-billed woodpecker face an impossible dilemma. In order to promote their future breeding success, we have to destroy their habitat. This makes it seem unlikely that the initiatives will succeed.

5. **C** Strengthen

The conclusion is that there is at least one student who majors in all three of the areas mentioned. The evidence offered is that there are students who major in each of the possible pairings of these areas. Clearly the evidence needs a good deal of help on this one.

(A) It isn't clear how knowing the numbers in two of the groups would allow us to be certain that somebody majors in all three.

(B) Other academic subjects aren't relevant to the conclusion here.

(C) This does it. If everyone who majors in economics majors in political science, and since we're told that some people who major in economics also major in finance, there must be some people who major in economics, political science, and finance.

(D) This seems similar to (C), but it has several holes. First of all, there's a possibility that the school offers majors in subjects not mentioned. Even if it doesn't, it may be true that the political science majors each also study exactly one of finance or economics, and that none of them study both.

(E) Again, since we don't know about potential other majors available at the school, this doesn't provide us strong enough information to justify the conclusion.

DRILL #5

Pages 93 – 94

1. **C** Alice's principle

    We need to keep a good deal of information straight here. Most important of all is the conclusion we're asked to support: Alice contends that David is not entitled to a full refund. The situation is that David was misled by a sales representative about the capabilities of his computer; David, however, does not need to use these capabilities. David keys on the fact that he was misled to justify his conclusion; Alice keys on the fact that the capabilities in question were immaterial to David's use of or need for the computer. First of all, we need to note that the conclusion we're supporting is negative: David is not entitled to a refund. Second, the phrasing of the question stem and the answer choices is important. The question gives us the beginning of a sentence: "David is entitled to a full refund...." Because we want to support the opposite of this statement, an "only-if" principle is the suitable choice to look for.

    (A) This is David's principle. It wouldn't help support Alice's conclusion.
    (B) Careful. Remember that the statement begins "David is entitled to a full refund...." This principle supports the opposite of Alice's conclusion.
    (C) This is the answer we want. It tells us that the only circumstances under which David should receive a full refund are those in which the misleading statement causes him to buy a computer that doesn't work for him. Since David's purchase does not fit this criterion, this principle would tell us that he isn't entitled to a full refund.
    (D) This principle, although it includes an "only if," doesn't support Alice's conclusion. At best, it would allow us to conclude that David may in fact be entitled to a full refund.
    (E) Like (A) and (B), the only conclusion this principle could support would be one that tells us David is entitled to a refund. Since that isn't Alice's conclusion, we should avoid this one.

2. **B** Weaken

    The conclusion here is that the ban on driving while using a cell phone should not be adopted. The primary piece of evidence for this claim is that, although dangerous, the practice is no more dangerous than other activities that the council has chosen not to forbid. We're looking for a fact that casts as much doubt as possible on the recommendation to reject the ban.

    (A) Careful. Although this does identify a difference between talking on cell phones and another of the dangers the council has chosen not to regulate, we have a premise in hand that tells us this activity is "no less safe" than the others. Nothing can trump that fact; this choice doesn't weaken the argument.
    (B) This is our answer. Although the practice of talking on cell phones is no less dangerous than other activities, this choice directly asserts that we should ban it nonetheless, because doing so would decrease the overall danger. This is as strong an attack on the conclusion as you'll ever see.
    (C) This is the thinking that underlies the original argument, but we want to weaken our conclusion, not strengthen or explain it.
    (D) There's no reason to believe that this fact changes matters. This doesn't draw any clear distinction between the measure to ban cell phones and other conceivable measures that would ban the other activities that are identified as being equally dangerous.
    (E) What may eventually happen is an extremely weak basis on which to try to draw a distinction. This choice isn't nearly as strong an attack as (B).

3. E Infer

We have a description of a situation here, and then a sentence that tells us specifically about Appleby. Here's the situation: In order for the program to be successful, it is necessary to have an elected representative on; having the governor on is sufficient to ensure success. What we know about Appleby is that she is not an elected representative. We want to pick a conclusion that's consistent with these facts; one leaps to mind rather quickly: If Appleby is the only guest on the program, it won't be a success.

(A) We know that having the governor does ensure success, but we can't be certain that this is the only way the program could be successful. This is too strong a conclusion to be drawn from the information we have.

(B) We know that, if the program has an elected official other than the governor, the program has a chance at success, since it will then satisfy the necessary condition. But the necessary condition doesn't guarantee success. Like (A), this is too strong a conclusion to be drawn from the information we're given.

(C) Although we do have a statement that says Appleby was "appointed…, not elected," we can't be certain that these are the only two choices.

(D) Careful! Having Appleby isn't by itself enough to conclude that the program won't be a success. After all, the program could interview both Appleby and the governor, in which case it definitely would be a success.

(E) This is it. If Appleby is the only government representative, then the program is sure to fail. If the program additionally includes an elected government representative, however, then it has a chance of success.

4. B Strengthen

We need to support the conclusion that Robinson's response to Johnson's hostile action was justified. The support given in the argument itself is rather iffy. We're given a rather complicated rule that covers "hostile response to hostile action," but we need to note that the conclusion doesn't state that Robinson's response was hostile. We're going to need to work through the choices pretty carefully on this one, with the idea in mind that we're always looking to support the conclusion that Robinson's response was justified.

(A) This sounds good, but we have to look more carefully. First of all, we have the troublesome problem that we don't know Robinson's response was hostile. Worse still, the rules given for justifying hostile responses say that no such response is justified unless the condition is met. Since this is a necessary condition, not a sufficient one, this rule can never definitely justify a hostile response. We need more than this to support the conclusion.

(B) Here it is. We're told in the opening statement that the justification for a response to hostile action must include two factors: the harm caused by the hostile action, and the likely result of the chosen response. This choice tells us something about the likely result of Robinson's response, and goes on to give us a new rule that doesn't conflict with the information given, and that definitely justifies Robinson's response. This is a very strong answer.

(C) The problem with applying this to our situation, though, is that we don't know Robinson's response was hostile, and so we can't be sure that this choice applies to the given situation.

(D) This just complicates matters by going even further into the past. We're looking to justify Robinson's response, not cast doubt on the situation that forced a response in the first place.

(E) This choice, complicated as it sounds, could never support a conclusion that Robinson's response was justified. It's a necessary condition, not a sufficient one.

5. **C** ID reasoning

The conclusion is that an event with an ultimate cause has no other direct cause. The language on this one is tough. Paraphrased, the premises here basically tell us that a direct cause is one that is necessary in order for the effect to take place. An ultimate cause is not only sufficient to have given rise to the effect, but its own occurrence also doesn't depend on any other cause. A closer examination of the reasoning shows why our conclusion works. If an event has an ultimate cause, then nothing could have stopped the event from happening other than preventing the ultimate cause itself. So there can't be any other factor that, if it were absent, would have prevented the effect. Whew. We're looking for something that matches this reasoning as closely as possible.

(A) Not only is this bad reasoning, it isn't the reasoning we're working with here. Certainly an ultimate cause is sufficient to lead to its effect, but the conclusion of our argument is that nothing else can be necessary to that effect. This choice doesn't match our argument.

(B) This doesn't match our argument's conclusion closely at all. This choice talks about things not being sufficient to ensure a result; our argument certainly does involve a sufficient condition.

(C) This doesn't capture all of the argument's reasoning perfectly, but it gets the key parts and is the closest of all our choices. Certainly an ultimate cause is sufficient to ensure its effect; the conclusion is, as this choice indicates, that nothing else can be necessary to the effect—namely, that the event has no other direct cause. What it leaves out is the stipulation in the argument that an ultimate cause is not itself dependent upon another necessary condition for its existence. Still, this matches our conclusion very closely, and is the best of the choices we have.

(D) Our argument isn't talking about two potential ultimate causes here, so this isn't similar to the argument at all.

(E) Our argument includes some discussion of ultimate causes—sufficient conditions— but this choice mentions only necessary conditions. This doesn't match our argument closely at all.

CHAPTER 10

DRILL #1

Page 136

Note: All explanations in this section appear in the order in which you should have tackled the questions, based on difficulty level.

F G H J K L M

	1	2	3	4	5	6	7
3.	M	H/L	L/H	G	K	F/J	J/F
5.	M						
2i	K	L	H	M	G	J	F
2ii	M	K	F	J	G	H	L
4A	K		G	M			
6A	H	L	G	M	K	F/J	J/F
6B	M	J	F	K	H/L	L/H	G
6D	M	H/L	L/H	K	F	J	G

Setting it up: This one is pretty straightforward. We can combine clues 3 and 4 into one symbol, and of course we want to note that M, which is at the front of this combined clue, has to be either first or fourth. If you wish, you can note the deduction that neither F nor J can be first. It's important not to think that clue 5 means more than it really does; although H…K…F and F…K…H are two of the possibilities here, K may appear before *both* F and H without violating this rule. Finally, we can expand clue 5 by noting that both H and F are in the two blocks in clues 2 and 3.

1. **D** Grab-a-rule

   (A) has J before M; (B) has M fifth; (C) has H before K but doesn't have K before F; (E) separates H and L. (D) is the only choice that follows all the rules.

3. **C** If G is in 4, then what has to be true?

   G in 4 means M has to be in 1. Now look at what we have left: the HL block, the FJ block, and K; we have to follow the conditional clue. One of these blocks must go before G in 2 and 3, while the other must go toward the end of the diagram, in 5 through 7. If we look at the conditional clue, however, we realize that no matter which of the two blocks goes first, K has to be in 5. The only choice that's consistent with our deductions is (C).

5. **D** If J is immediately before K, then what could be true?

With J before K, F has to go immediately before J. M goes someplace before this three-element block. Look at the conditional now: F is definitely before K, so K has to go before the HL block. Now we have one large range clue that involves every element in the game except for G. M definitely goes in 1; G can go in 2, 5, or 7. The only choice that's consistent with our deductions is (D).

2. **D** Where could K be located?

This is a tough one. In our previous examples, we've seen K in 4 and 5. Unfortunately, these two are contained in all of the answer choices! From the setup discussion above, it seems like K could go in 1, and this would help us eliminate several answer choices if we try it. As it turns out, we can have K in 1, which eliminates (B), (C), and (E). The only decision left is whether K can go in 2 and 3. If we try one of these, we see that can work also, which leaves us with (D) as the right answer.

4. **A** Which can't be true?

This is another tough one. None of these seems like a blatant violation of the rules, so it's best to try the choices starting at (A). In that case, if we have K in 1 and G in 3, then we know M has to be in 4. But now we have the two blocks left to place, but the open spaces are 2 and 5 through 7. There's no way we can fit the blocks into these, so this is the choice we want.

6. **E** Which can't be true?

Again, there are no obvious violations here. Not only that, but we haven't seen any of these situations in our previous examples. Again, we'll start trying choices with (A). That one works; it also eliminates answer choice (C). Now we try (B). It works, but we have to keep going. Now we try (D). It works, too, leaving us with (E) as the only remaining option.

b b c f m s t

	1	2
0i	s f/m	c b m/f _
0ii	c b m/f _	s f/m
	_ _ _	_ _ _
4i	s m	c b f b t
4ii	s m b/t	c b f t/b
5i	c b m/f b t	s f/m
5ii	s f/m	c b m/f b t
6B	c b f b	s m t

Setting it up: The trick here is that none of the clues refers to the trips by name, so unless a question gives us further information, the identities of the groups are going to be interchangeable. Even so, there are things we can deduce. Since the group with s in it can contain at most two other elements, and since one of those elements has to be either f or m, we know that the cb-block must be in a different group from s. The s-group contains either two or three elements; the cb-group contains either five or four.

2. **B** If s is in 2, then which can't be in 2 with it?

From our deductions, we know that s and c have to be in different groups. Sure enough, the chair is choice (B), our answer.

4. **C** If s and m and possibly more are in 1, then how many different sets of elements could be in 2?

This is a tough question. s and m in 1 forces c, b, and f into 2. From there, we have two basic possibilities. Either there are two articles on trip 1, or else there are three articles. In the first case, the remaining two elements—t and the other b—go in 2: that makes one possibility. In the second, we split t and the other b between the two groups: that gives us two more possibilities. The total number of possibilities, then, is three: answer choice (C).

5. **E** If we have t and both b's in the same group, then what can't be true?

To have both b's in the same group, they'll have to go in the group with c. The question doesn't allow us to tie them down into one group or the other, but we know one of the groups will contain c, both b's, t, and either m or f; the other group, then, will have to contain just s and the other of f or m. The only thing that isn't consistent with our deductions is (E), which is the answer we want.

6. **B** If m and t are both in 2, then which item of information would allow us to know the location of all the elements?

The main obstacle here is that we don't know which of the two groups has s, and which has c. We do know that f has to be in 1. We have to consider the choices one at a time, hoping to find that information and anything else we need. (A) doesn't do it; trip 1 could contain either s or c under this condition. (B) does the job: With c and f in the same trip, we know the cb-block has to be in 1; that forces s into 2, and that group is then full, which forces the remaining element—the second b—into 1, and everyone is placed. Just to consider the other choices for a moment, we see that (C) and (D) are things we know from the condition in the question. (E) is the only tricky one left: It does tell us that the cb-block has to go in 2, and s has to go in 1; unfortunately, it leaves unanswered the question of where the second b goes: It could still be in either group. (B) is the answer here.

1. **B** Which could be a correct listing of group 1?

With our template in hand, this one should be easy. (A) doesn't do it because the c-group has to have at least four elements; (B) does fit our template; (C) would force m and f to be in the same group; (D) has too many elements in the s-group; (E) has m and f together. We definitely want (B) here.

3. **D** What's the largest number of elements we could have in either group?

The c-group could contain as many as five elements, whether it's first or second. The answer we want here is (D).

DRILL #3

Page 141

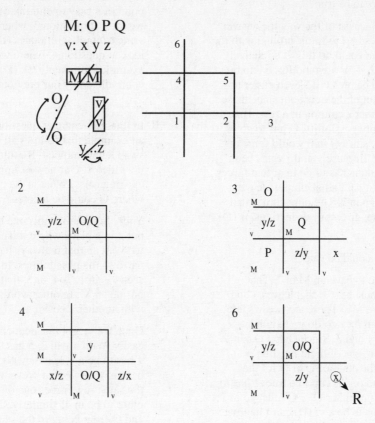

M: O P Q
v: x y z

Setting it up: The main challenge here is to correctly interpret the initial paragraph when putting your diagram together. As it turns out, there are two deductions in this game that can be helpful; you may or may not be able to get them at this stage of the game, however. We're going to proceed under the assumption that you don't find them.

2. **B** If we have two v's side-by-side, what has to be true?

The main question is where we can do this without violating the rules. Our choices are 1 and 2, 2 and 3, or 4 and 5. If we try 1 and 2, we run into a problem: Since v's can't be above v's, we're forced to make both 4 and 5 M's, and that violates another rule. We can see that a similar problem arises if we try to make 4 and 5 both v's. The only way we can do this, then, is to have 2 and 3 both be v's. Since 2 is a v, that means 5 must be an M. Since 5 is an M, 4 must be a v. Then both 1 and 6 must be M's. Additionally, since y and z can't be in the same row, one of them must be in 4; similarly, since O and Q can't be in the same column, one of them must be in 5.

The question wants to know what has to be true. (A) doesn't: we could easily put O in 5, P in 1, and y in 4. (B) does: P has to go in either 1 or 6, which forces it into the same column with 4, which must be either y or z. As for the others, (C) doesn't have to be true: We could easily put P in 6, which doesn't put it in the same row as anything else. Similarly, we could put Q in 6, which would make both (D) and (E) untrue. (B) is the choice we want.

3. **D** If P is in the same row with x and the same column with O but isn't immediately next to either of them, then what doesn't have to be true?

This is a tough one. Because of the way the answer choices are written, it's best to fiddle around with the diagram to see how we could do this. It's relatively easy to see why P in 2, 4, or 5 would force P to be immediately above or below O; it's even easier to see why 3 and 6 are out of the question, since these spaces are alone in either a column or a row. That leaves P in 1 as the only possibility. O has to go in 6, so Q has to go in 5, since Q in 3 would force one v to be above another. Because y and z can't be in the same row, one of them has to go in 4; that forces x into 3 to make sure it isn't adjacent to P, leaving the other of z or y to go in 2. The only choice that doesn't have to be true, given our deductions, is (D).

4. **E** If y is in 5, then what could be true?

With a v in 5, we have to have an M in 2. That means both 1 and 3 must be v's; that leaves 4 and 6 as the remaining two M's. There are two v's left to place—x and z—but they could go in either arrangement in spots 1 and 3. Since O and Q can't be in the same column, one of them must be in 2. That leaves P and the other of Q or O for the remaining spots: 4 and 6. (A) can't be true: 1 has to be a v; (B) can't be true: either O or Q must go in 2; (C) can't be true: 3 has to be a v; (D) can't be true: 6 has to be an M. That leaves (E) as the only choice that's consistent with our deductions.

1. **E** What could be true?

Thanks to the order in which we worked the questions, we lucked out on this one. We saw one possibility that put z in 3 in our diagram for question 4, so (E) is definitely the answer here.

If you didn't have that diagram in hand, you'd have to find the two major deductions of the game to make this question go quickly: 3 has to be a v, and 6 has to be an M. That would get rid of (A) and (D). To eliminate (B), you have to see that in any case where 5 is an M, it has to be one of O or Q; otherwise, they wind up in the same column. To eliminate (C), you have to see that in any case where 4 is a v, it has to be either y or z; otherwise, they wind up in the same row. (E) is the only one that's possible.

5. **D** What must be true?

If you have some examples under your belt at this point, it's easy to eliminate here. To eliminate (A), we look at question 3, where we had a v in 2; the same example eliminates (B). To eliminate (C), we look at question 4, where we had a v in 5; the same example eliminates (E). (D) is the only one not contradicted by our previous examples.

6. **B** In this rule-changer question, we're going to take an example that follows all the initial rules and then swap a new movie—R—into the space occupied by the video x. Our new example has to follow all the existing rules. What is the complete list of places where O could be located?

Yuck. In order for this one to work, we'll have to put x in a place where it isn't beside any M. By now we've seen that 6 always has to be an M, which narrows the possibilities. In all the cases when we've seen v's in 1, 2, 4, or 5, that v has always had to be beside an M. In other words, we have to put x in 3, with another v beside it.

Once we've got this deduction, the rest flow more easily. With a v in 2, 5 has to be an M; that means 4 has to be a v, leaving M's to go in 1 and 6. As before, the rule that prevents y and z from being in the same row forces one of them to be in 2 and the other to be in 4; similarly, the rule that prevents O and Q from being in the same column forces one of them to be in 5. The upshot of all this is that the only places where we could put O are the M-spots 1, 5, or 6, but any of these could be made to work. That's answer choice (B).

Drill #4

Page 142

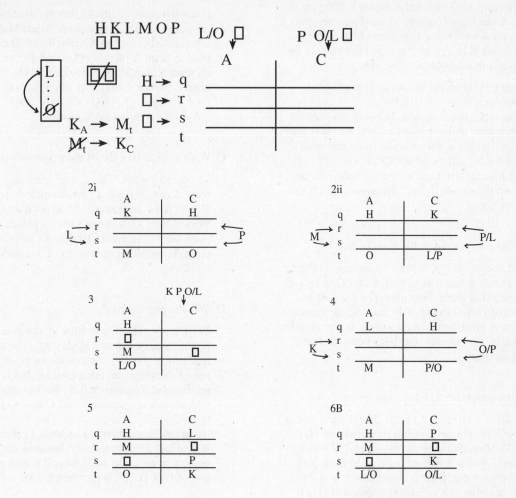

Note: More than one arrangement is possible.

Setting it up: We need to make a chart with the teams (A and C) along one side and the positions (q, r, s, and t) along the other. Our inventory only includes six elements, and since our chart has eight spots, we'll add two blanks to the inventory to make the numbers match. It's worth paraphrasing the LO-antiblock by indicating that exactly one of the two will be on each team. That way, we see that team A already has two elements committed to it (L or O and one blank) and team C already has three elements committed to it (P, O or L, and the other blank). We'll want to keep careful track of when one team or the other is full.

2. **C** If K plays q and O plays t on a different team from K, then which pair couldn't play the same position?

This one's tough. It's best to look at these in terms of two basic options: Either K plays on team A, or K plays on team C.

Try the first case: K on team A means several things: O plays t on team C, and M also plays t, which means M must be on team A; since H must play q, H must be on team C. L has to play on team A because O is on team C. So team A has K at q, M at t, and L playing either r or s; team C has H at q, O at t, and P at the position of r or s that L doesn't play.

Try the second case: K on team C means several things: Since H must play q, H is on team A; O must play t on team A. O on team A means L plays on team C. Since team C is full, M must play on team A. So team A has H at q, O at t, and M at either r or s; team C has K at q, L or P at t, and the other at the one of r or s that M doesn't play. Whew.

Eliminate (A): H and K always have to play the same position; eliminate (B): In case ii, L and O can both play t; (C) is the answer: In case i, they are on different teams, and one plays r while the other plays s, whereas in case ii, they have to be on the same team. As for the others, M and O have to both play t in case i, so (D) isn't our answer; in case ii, O and P can both play t, so (E) isn't the answer. (C) is the choice we want.

3. **C** If M plays s on team A, what must be true?

Since M doesn't play t, K must be on team C. Now team C is full: It consists of K, P, either O or L, and one blank. That forces H to play q on team A, and the other of L or O to play t on team A; the blank on team A is at position r, and on team C it is at position s. Choice (C) is the only one that's consistent with our deductions.

4. **D** If L plays q on team A, what must be true?

L at position q on team A means that H must play q on team C. Now team C is full: It consists of H, P, and O. The remaining elements—K and M—must be on team A. Since K is on team A, M must play t, which means that team A consists of L at q, M at t, and K at either r or s. Team C consists of H at q, either P or O at t, and the other at the position of r or s that K doesn't play.

(A) doesn't work: The player on team C must play safety, but we don't know whether it's O or P. (B) doesn't work for basically the same reason. (C) doesn't work: If O plays t, P may play either r or s. (D) does the trick: P at r (on team C) forces O to play t and K to play s (on team A). (E) can't work at all, since it has O playing q. Choice (D) is definitely the one we want.

5. **A** If K and O are at t and P is at s, then what doesn't have to be true?

P at s (on team C) means that our blanks appear at r on team C and at s on team A. Since M doesn't play t, K has to be on team C (playing t). That means O is on team A (playing t), which forces L to play on team C; L plays q. That forces H to play q on team A, which means that M goes in the remaining spot: r on team A. (A) is the only choice that isn't consistent with our deductions.

1. **C** Which could be a list of the players on team A?

(A) doesn't work: This doesn't have anybody on team A at t. (B) doesn't work either: It forces L and O both to be on team C. (C) looks fine. (D) doesn't work: Like (A), it doesn't have a player at t, and P is on the wrong team. (E) doesn't work: It has K on team A, but M isn't playing t. (C) is the only one that works.

6. **D** Which can't be true?

With many examples to look at, this one should be pretty easy. We saw H playing q on team A in question 5, so (A) isn't the one we want. We haven't seen K playing s on team C so far, but it's easy to generate an example of this. We've seen L playing t on team A in question 3 and O able to play q on team C in the same question. That leaves (D). If we try to put M at position r on team C, then we know K also has to be on team C. But now there are too many players on team C: M and K along with P and one of L or O. (D) is the choice we want.

CHAPTER 11

Drill #1

Page 145

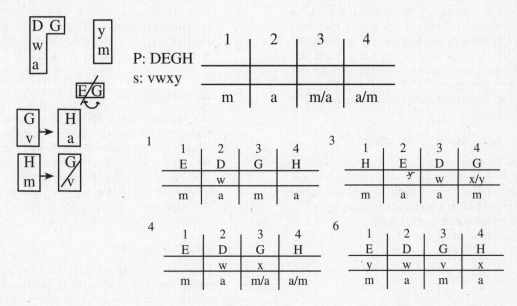

P: DEGH
s: vwxy

	1	2	3	4
	m	a	m/a	a/m

1

	1	2	3	4
	E	D	G	H
		w		
	m	a	m	a

3

	1	2	3	4
	H	E	D	G
		y̶	w	x/y
	m	a	a	m

4

	1	2	3	4
	E	D	G	H
		w	x	
	m	a	m/a	a/m

6

	1	2	3	4
	E	D	G	H
	y	w	v	x
	m	a	m	a

Setting it up: We'll put the days 1 through 4 across the top, then use a separate row for each of the things we have to decide about the days: the painting, the sketch, and morning/afternoon. Clues 3, 5, and 6 combine to give us a large L-shaped block. Clue 1, combined with the fact that day 2's work takes place in the afternoon, tells us that the artist must work in the morning on day 1; otherwise, the artist would have to work in the morning on both days 3 and 4. So our block can only go in days 2 through 3 or 3 through 4.

1. **E** If day 4 is an afternoon workday, then what could be true?

Day 4 being an afternoon workday means that day 3 must be a morning workday. The only place our big block will fit is on days 2 through 3. In order to keep E and G from being on adjacent days, E must go on day 1, which forces H into day 4. y can't go on day 4, but otherwise a number of arrangements remain possible. The only choice that doesn't contradict our deductions, however, is (E), which makes it the answer we want to pick.

3. **B** If H is on day 1, then what must be true?

H on day 1 means that H is worked on in the morning, so G can't go with v. More importantly, we know the block can't go in 2 through 3, because that would force G to come right before E. So the big block goes in 3 through 4, which means day 3 is an afternoon workday, which makes day 4 a morning workday. E, the only painting remaining, has to be on day 2. G is on the same day as x or y. v and the other of y or x go in the first two days, with the only restriction being that y can't be on day 2. The only choice that's consistent with our deductions is (B).

4. **C** If x is on day 3, then what can't be true?

x on day 3 means that the big block must go in 2 through 3. To keep E away from G, we have to put E in 1 and H in 4. There are still several possibilities from here, and all of our choices turn out to be possible, given our diagram, except for (C). That's the choice we want.

6. **A** If v is on day 3, then in which places could y go?

v in 3 means that the big block must go in 2 through 3. That forces E into 1 to keep it away from G, leaving H to go in 4. Since G is with v, H is worked on in the afternoon, which means day 3 is a morning workday. Since y has to be worked on in the morning, it goes in day 1, while x goes in day 4. Our diagram is completely filled out, with y in 1. That makes (A) the answer we want.

2. **A** What must be true?

(A), our answer, is a deduction we made initially in combining the clues to form our large block. All the others are contradicted by work we've done so far: We saw a counterexample for (B) in question 3, for (C) in question 4, for (D) most directly in question 6, and for (E) in question 4. (A) is definitely the one to pick here.

5. **A** What can't be true?

Let's see if we can use our prior work to help us on this one. We've seen (B) in question 3 among others; we've seen (C) in question 6; we've seen (D) in question 6; we've seen (E) in question 6. (A) is definitely the choice we want here, and it's pretty easy to see why. If we were to try putting D before E, then our block would have to go before E. Since E and G can't go next to one another, that would force us to put H as a buffer between the block and E; but that would force us to put the block in 1-2, which we know can't happen. (A) is definitely it.

DRILL #2

Page 146

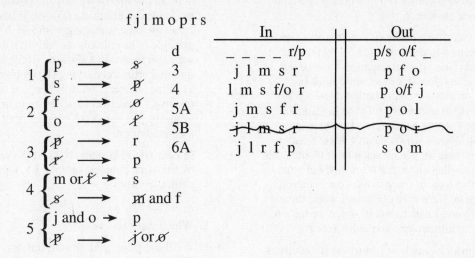

```
            f j l m o p r s
                          d        In                Out
  ┌ p  ──→   s̶            3    ─ ─ ─ ─ r/p      p/s  o/f ─
1 ┤                                             
  └ s  ──→   p̶            4    j l m s r            p f o
  ┌ f  ──→   o̶            5A   l m s f/o r          p o/f j
2 ┤                                             
  └ o  ──→   f̶            5B   j m s f r            p o l
  ┌ p̶  ──→   r            6A   j̶ l m s r            p o r
3 ┤                            j l r f p            s o m
  └ r̶  ──→   p
  ┌ m or f̶ ─→ s
4 ┤
  └ s̶  ──→   m̶ and f
  ┌ j and o ─→ p
5 ┤
  └ p̶  ──→   j̶ or o̶
```

Setting it up: We'll make an "in" column with 5 slots and an "out" column with 3. Clue 1 guarantees us that at least one of p or s is out, so we can reserve a place in the "out" column. Clue 2 guarantees us that at least one of f or o is out, so we can reserve another place. Either p or r must be in, so we can reserve a space on the "in" side; keep in mind you'll need to watch for interactions between this placeholder and your p/s placeholder on the "out" side. Note that l is unrestricted, and therefore will always be available to fill in spaces when you're done satisfying the clues.

1. **C** Grab-a-rule

   (A) violates rule 3 with p out but r not in. (B) violates rule 2 with f and o both in. (D) violates rule 4 with m in but s out. (E) violates rule 5 with j and o in but p out. (C) is the only choice that doesn't contradict a rule.

3. **D** If f and o are both out, then what must be true?

   With both f and o out, our "out" column is full. Everyone not appearing in our diagram so far—j, l, and m—must be in. m in means that s must be in (clue 4). s in means p must be out (clue 1). p out means r must be in (clue 3). Our diagram is complete. (D) is the only choice that's consistent with it.

4. **D** If j is out, then what could be true?

   Since j isn't in either of our "out" placeholders, putting it out fills the "out" column. Everyone not appearing in our diagram so far—l and m—must be in. m in means s is in (clue 4). s in means p is out (clue 1). p out means r is in (clue 3). We're left with one open space on the "in" side, and either o or f out. Checking the rules, we see that there's nothing that forces us to put o or f in either place. (D) is the only choice that's possible.

2. **A** What could be true?

As it happens, we lucked out on this one. We saw an example of answer choice (A) in working question 3, so that's our answer.

As for the others, here's why (B) can't work: j and o both in means p must be in (clue 5); p in means s must be out (clue 1); s out means m must be out and f must be in (clue 4); f in means o must be out (clue 2), which is a contradiction. Here's why (C) can't work: m in means s must be in (clue 4), but p in means s must be out (clue 1), which is a contradiction. Here's why (D) can't work: f out means s is in (clue 4); s in means p must be out (clue 1); p out means that either j or o must be out (clue 5), but there's no more space in our "out" column for one of them. Here's why (E) can't work: there's no space for j and l both to be out, since we have to hold places for either p or s and either o or f.

Finding the prior example or just trying it directly is clearly the best way to arrive at (A).

5. **B** What must be true?

Prior work, unfortunately, can only help us a little here. In question 4 we saw the possibility of o being in, so we can eliminate (D). We'll have to try to break the others, starting with (A). It turns out to be possible to have l out, and unfortunately the example we generate doesn't allow us to eliminate any of the others. Fortunately, trying (B) by putting r out gets us to the answer: r out fills the "out" column, which means j, l, and m must all be in. m in means s is in; s in means p is out. p out means r must be in, which is a contradiction.

In case you're curious, (C) and (E) can be eliminated by the same counterexample: f, j, l, p, r. (B) is the choice we want.

6. **E** Which can't be true?

We'll use prior work to start this one: We've seen (B) in question 4, (C) in question 3, and (D) in question 3. We try (A) and realize it's possible. The remaining answer can't work because p in means s is out (clue 1), s out means m is out and f is in (clue 4), and f in means o is out (clue 2), which generates a contradiction. (E) is the correct choice here.

DRILL #3

Pages 147 – 148

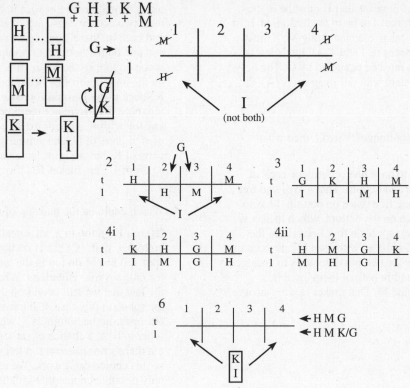

Setting it up: This is an organizational arrangement with toys 1 through 4 from left to right, with torsos in the top tier of the chart and legs in the bottom tier. Except for the range clues (the second and third), there's not much in the way of deductions here. H can't be on bottom in 1 or on top in 4; similarly, M can't be on top in 1 or on bottom in 4.

2. **D** If H is in the bottom of 2 and M is in the bottom of 3, then what must be true?

H in the bottom of 2 means H must be in the top of 1, because of the range clue; the same type of deduction shows that M must be in the top of 4. Aside from that, all we know is that G must be in the top of either 2 or 3, and I must be in the bottom of either 1 or 4, but not both. K, the only element remaining, can't be in the open slots in 2 and 3. It needs to fill at least one of the open places, but aside from that, there are plenty of possible arrangements. (D) is the only choice that's consistent with our deductions.

3. **A** If K is in the top of 2 and H is in the top of 3, then what must be true?

    K in the top of 2 means that I must be in the bottom of 2. H in the top of 3 means that H must be in the bottom of 4. That forces I to be in the bottom of 1. In order to satisfy the range clue involving M, it must occupy the open spaces in 3 and 4. All that's left is the top of 1, which must be occupied by G. The only choice that's consistent with our diagram is (A), the answer we want.

4. **D** If both the top and bottom of 3 are G, then what must be true?

    We know we need to have one occurrence each of H and M in the top and bottom. That leaves one free space on top and one free space on bottom. I has to go in the open space on the bottom, which means K has to go in the open space on top. Because of the conditional clue, K must go with I, and I has to go in either 1 or 4. There are two possible ways to arrange things from here, and in both of them toy 2 is a combination of H and M. That makes (D) the answer we want to pick.

6. **B** If every toy with a part of I has K as its other part, what must be true?

    We have to use I on the bottom at one end or the other; K will be on top with it. Since we have to have two occurrences each of H and M on the top and bottom, there's one space remaining on the top and one on the bottom. G occupies the remaining space on top, so the top is full. The remaining space on the bottom must be occupied by either G or else K, since using I would force us to use K with it on top; note that we're not required to use I on top for any toy with K on bottom. So we have either 1 or 2 uses of parts of G, and similarly either 1 or 2 uses of parts of K, but we must have only 1 toy that includes a part of I. That makes (B) the choice we want.

1. **A** Which could be the makeup of toys 1 and 2?

    (B) has K on top in 2 but something other than I on bottom with it. (C) has H on bottom in the leftmost spot. (E) has M on top in the leftmost spot. So much for obvious rule violations. What makes (D) fail is the fact that we still need I on the bottom in one of the spots; in this case, it'll have to be 4. The only slot left open on the bottom is 3, which has to be H in order to have a chance of satisfying the range clue, but there's no space on top left open for H before 3, so this choice can't work. We're left with (A) as the only possible choice that satisfies the rules.

5. **C** Which could be a list of the elements on top from 1 to 4?

    (A) has H on top in 4. (B) doesn't have G listed. (D) has K on top in 1, which means I must go on bottom with it; the next element to appear on top is M, but M needs to be on bottom before it can go on top. (E) has M on top in 1. (C) is the only choice remaining, and the one we want to pick.

DRILL #4

Page 149

h: J K
p: Q R
t: U V W

	1	2	3	4	5	6	7
2	K_h	U/V_t	J_h	Q_p	W_t	R_p	V/U_t
6	U_t	J_h	V_t	K_h	Q/R_p	W_t	R/Q_p
3A	J_h	U_t	K_h	V_t	Q/R_p	W_t	R/Q_p
3C	U/V_t	K_h	V/U_t	J_h	Q/R_p	W_t	R/Q_p
3D	K_h	V/U_t	J_h	R_p	t	Q_p	t
5A	K_h	U_t	J_h	W_t	Q_p	V_t	R_p

Setting it up: The diagram is a standard 1 through 7 ordered table, and as long as we organize it by element type, the inventory is fairly normal. The big deduction here comes from looking at the first two clues together: Since both h's have to be used before the p's are, we have a pretty big range clue, but it gets even better. Since the h's can't be back-to-back, there has to be at least one element between them; moreover, the element in between can't be a p, so it has to be a t. Even better, since t's can't go back-to-back, the h's must be in an hth-block; for similar reasons, the p's must be in a ptp-block. That leaves only one t that can go either before the first block, in between the blocks, or after the later block—namely in positions 1, 4, or 7. We'll want to keep track of these three possibilities, and slide in the element-specific clues as we learn more about specific cases.

1. **D** Grab-a-rule

(A) separates Q and W. (B) has trade books W and U back-to-back. (C) has J before U but separates K and V. (E) has paperback Q before any of the hardbacks. (D) is the only one left, and is the choice we should pick.

2. **A** If Q is in 4, then what must be true?

Since Q is a paperback, we know the order has to be h t h p t p t. The only place W can go to remain next to Q is in 5; R, the remaining paperback, goes in 6. The next deduction is a little tricky: We have to watch out for the relative positions of J and U; if J comes before U, then the only place K can go immediately before V is in 1 through 2. It's pretty evident that putting J in 1 would cause a contradiction, so we have to put J in the only remaining hardback spot—3—which forces K to go in 1. Note that V and U could still go either way in the remaining slots 2 and 7: Either arrangement satisfies the conditional clue. The only choice that has to be true, given our deductions, is (A).

4. **C** If U comes before V, then what is the greatest number of weeks we can put between U and V?

Although it's dangerous to be too aggressive about using prior work on an "if" question, it's clear in this case that one of the examples we generated in question 2 satisfies the condition in this question, and there are 4 weeks between U and V. The only possible way to put more space between them would be to put them at opposite ends of the diagram, but our deductions about the possible ordering of the element types make it clear that this can never happen. We have to pick (C).

6. **B** If J is in 2, then what could be true?

J is a hardback, so putting it in 2 forces us into the order t <u>h t h</u> <u>p t p</u>. K, the other hardback, has to go in 4. We see that having K immediately before V is impossible, so U has to go before J—namely, in spot 1. In order to have a chance of putting Q and W together, W has to go in 6. That leaves V, the remaining trade book, to go in 3. Q and R can go in either order in the remaining spots—5 and 7. The only choice that's consistent with our deductions is (B), the choice we want to pick.

3. **E** What must be true?

Because of the form of the answer choices, we pretty much have to go through this question one choice at a time.

In (A), putting J in 1 means that J will definitely go before U, which means we have to have K immediately before V. That has to happen in weeks 3 through 4, which contradicts the result predicted in the choice. There are further deductions that have a chance of being helpful later, so you may want to complete the diagram.

For (B), we've actually already seen a case in which J is in 3 but V doesn't have to be in 2: question 2.

In (C), putting K in 2 forces us into the order t <u>h t h</u> <u>p t p</u>. Then J is in 4, and in order to have a chance of being next to Q, W has to go in 6. U and V can go in 1 and 3 in either order; a similar thing is true for Q and R in 5 and 7. Alas, we haven't found our answer yet.

In (D), putting Q in 6 forces us into the order <u>h t h</u> <u>p t p</u> t. That forces R into 4, the other paperback spot. We can stop here, as it's pretty clear that nothing prevents us from putting W in either 5 or 7. If you like, you can make a deduction similar to the one in question 2 here: putting J in 1 would make K V both necessary and impossible, so J must go in 3, which puts K in 1. At this point, though, you're at the end of the line with no further information about where W has to go.

(E) is the only choice left. It's probably fine to just pick it and run, but if you have any doubts, here's how it goes: U in 6 means the last three slots have to be the ptp-block. In order to have Q and W together, Q has to go in 5, W in 4, and R in 7. J is definitely going to wind up in front of U, so we have to put K right in front of V. That forces K into 1, V into 2, and J into 3, which is the result predicted in the choice. (E) is the right one.

5. **D** Which can't be true?

Prior work offers a little help here. We've seen an instance of (B) in question number 3C; we've seen an instance of (C) in the same example. Aside from that, we need to try the choices. We find pretty quickly that (A) works. Thankfully, that example also provides an instance of (E), which leaves (D) as the only choice we haven't eliminated.

If you're curious why (D) can't happen, it's pretty easy to see. R in 6 and J in 1 means the order has to be <u>h t h</u> <u>p t p</u> t. K has to be in 3 with a paperback, Q, in 4, but J has to be somewhere before U, which is a contradiction. We definitely want to pick (D).

CHAPTER 12

DRILL #1

Page 154

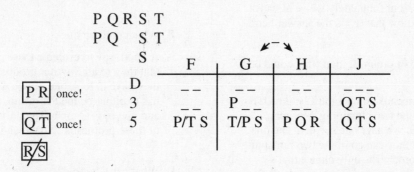

```
        P Q R S T
        P Q   S T
            S
                    F         G         H         J
              D    ___       ___       ___       ___
  [P R] once! 3    ___       P__       ___       Q T S
  [Q T] once! 5   P/T S     T/P S     P Q R     Q T S
  [R/S]
```

Setting it up: We'll use a standard grouping diagram, but the question arises of which should be our elements, and which our groups. The clues provide a good deal of help: Clues 2, 3, and 6 are all most easily represented with the writers as elements; the other clues can be represented in those terms without any problems. We know that group F will have 2 elements in it, and group J will have 3; each of the remaining two groups will have at least 2 elements, with one element left over to be distributed to one or the other.

The real fun here is trying to determine how many times each of the elements can be used. We know S is used 3 times; since R can't go with S, R is used only 1 time. So far we have exactly 3 uses of S, exactly 1 use of R, and at least one use of each of P, Q, and T, for a grand total of 7 slots filled. We have 10 slots to fill altogether, leaving us 3 open. Since the number of uses of Q has to be equal to the number of uses of T, one possibility that springs immediately to mind is that we can use P, Q, and T each exactly once more, for a grand total of 2 uses each. The only other way we could try it would be to have P in all 4 groups. It's pretty difficult to see why this can't work: If we use P 4 times, then P is in a group with Q and T, which maxes out that group, forcing S to go in all 3 of the others. But then we're forced to put R in one of the groups with S, since the only group that doesn't contain it is already full. This is a violation, so we can't use P 4 times.

So the upshot of all this is that R is used exactly 1 time; P, Q, and T are all used exactly 2 times; and S is used exactly 3 times. Note that we did all this without making any reference to which groups any of the elements are actually in! We can actually go a little further by noting a few things. Since R is used once, its single use will be in a group with P. Whatever group that is has to be the one group that doesn't contain S, which means in particular that one of our three-writer groups has to contain Q, T, and S. Looking to locate the QTS group will be important in working specific examples.

3. **E** If P is in group G with two other elements, then what must be true?

P in group G with 2 others allows us to lock the QTS block down into group J. From here there are several different possibilities—group G might or might not be the PR group—but fortunately we've already done enough to know that (E) is the answer here.

5. **A** If P, Q, and R are in group H, then what could be true?

PQR in group H means group J must be the QTS group. S goes in the two remaining 2-writer groups—F and G. We have one use of T and one use of P left, and they can go in the two remaining groups in either order. The only choice that's consistent with our diagram is (A), and that's the choice we want to pick.

6. **B** If S and T appear together only once, then what must be true?

The one place when S and T appear together is going to have to be in our QTS group. We have to keep the second use of T away from the other 2 uses of S; the only group where we can do this is the one where R appears, so our other 3-writer group has to be PRT. S appears in both of the 2-writer groups, and we have one use of Q and one use of P left for them. Without knowing which groups they are, we at least know what the 2-writer and 3-writer groups are going to look like: QTS; PRT; QS; PS. The only choice that's consistent with these deductions is (B), the answer we want.

1. **C** What must be true?

This is a straight deduction. (A) and (B) could be true, but don't have to be; (D) and (E) can't ever be true. The one that has to be true is (C), the answer we want.

2. **E** What could be true?

A good way to evaluate these choices is to realize that they're all 2-writer groups, and we know that they have to look one of two ways: A 2-writer group has to either be the PR-group, or it has to involve S and one of P, Q, or T. The only choice that fits either of these profiles is (E), which is the answer we want.

4. **D** What can't be true?

We don't have much in the way of prior work at this point—only questions 5 and 6—but we should still try to eliminate what we can; fortunately, the answer choices are general enough that they should be pretty easy to evaluate. We saw (A) in question 6; we saw (B) in question 5; we saw (C) in question 5 as well; we saw (E) in question 5, also. That only leaves one choice, and you should feel free to pick it and run.

As for why (D) can't be true, it's actually fairly easy to see. P is used twice, and one of those uses has to be with R; in order to make this choice true, then, we'd have to put R in the same group with S, which is a no-no. (D) is definitely the choice we want to pick.

DRILL #2

Page 156

R̸ S T U V̸ W̸

		M	T	W	H	F		OUT
* = repeater	D	V̸			8̸	8̸	V̸	_ (_ _)
max 2 *								
2 uses of each *	2	W*	V					T S
	3	T*				T*		W V R̸
T → T_M and T_F	4	U̸						V T/W_{not both}
S → S...U	5							U T S
R* → R* _ R*	6							S T
V → W*...V...W*								
U → U R								

Setting it up: The diagram, at least to start with, isn't too complicated. We need the days across the top as in a standard ordering diagram, with an "out" column added to accommodate the element(s) that aren't used. There'll be at least one of them. The main difficulty here is finding a good way to symbolize clues about the repeater(s), which we'll use an asterisk to mark. When in doubt, you'll need to come up with short, clear paraphrases of clues that are too difficult to represent visually. The main deduction of note here is that if we have the largest possible number of repeaters—2—then we're going to force 2 more elements out. At least 1 has to be out because of the sheer numbers; we may, though, have as many as 3 out.

There are a couple of element-specific deductions in this game. Since putting V in forces us to put it between the two occurrences of W, V can never be on Monday or on Friday. Also, since putting S in forces us to put at least 2 other elements after it, that means S can never go on Thursday or Friday.

Finally, we note that just because we haven't written symbols for the contrapositives of these difficult conditional clues, that doesn't mean they don't have contrapositives. It's just that the symbols, if you simply flip and negate, border on nonsense. When a conditional is complicated, it's best to give some thought to how we might use its contrapositive. Take the V-clue, for instance (question 4). Its contrapositive might be activated in a lot of different ways: if W is not repeated, if V is on Monday or on Friday, or if the second use of W is on Tuesday, or if the first use of W is on Thursday. Since there are so many ways to falsify the statement on the end of this conditional, we'll simply need to keep an eye out for specific situations that have an impact on it.

1. **A** Grab-a-rule

    (B) uses U but doesn't have R immediately before or after it; (C) uses S but doesn't have U at some time after it; (D) uses V but doesn't use W twice; (E) uses T but doesn't use it on Monday. (A), the only choice remaining, is the one we want to pick; it doesn't violate any rules.

2. **E** If V is on Tuesday, then what has to be true?

    V on Tuesday triggers the W*...V...W* clue; the first occurrence of W must be on Monday. Since T can't now go on Monday, it must be out; the second occurrence of W goes on one of the three remaining days. The deduction that gets us to the answer on this one is a bit difficult: Putting S in forces us to put U in, and putting U in forces us to put R in. But then there'd be no space for the second occurrence of W. That means we have to put S out, which is choice (E), the one we want to pick.

3. **C** If W is out, then what must be true?

W out means V must be out. We have R, S, T, and U to decide about. The next deduction on this one is pretty tricky: We still have one "out" slot to work with, but remember that having 3 elements out relies on our being able to repeat 2 elements. That means that if we try to put either R or T out in this case, we're going to run into a problem: We'll only have one element left "in" that can be repeated, and we won't be able to fill all five slots. In other words, R and T both have to be in. T in means it has to go on both Monday and Friday; there are two basic possible scenarios from here, depending upon whether or not we repeat R, but either way we've already made the deduction we need: (C) is the answer on this one.

4. **D** If S is in, then what could be true?

S in means U is in, with S appearing before U; U in means R is in, with U next to R. With 3 spaces already taken up on the "in" side, there's no way we could satisfy the clue that requires us to put W*…V…W* whenever V is in; that means V must be out. There's still enough room to put T in or W in, but not both; that means at least one of them must be out. At least one of them must be in, however, because if we try to put them both out, then we won't be able to fill all five spaces. R may or may not be repeated.

(A), we know, can't happen; putting S on Thursday wouldn't leave us enough room to satisfy the range clue. (B) has a similar problem. We know V must be out, so we can't do (C). (E) makes it impossible to put U next to R. (D) is the choice we want here.

5. **D** If U and T are both out, then what can't be true?

U out means S must be out. With S, T, and U all out, we know everybody else—R, V, and W—must be in. We're repeating both W and R, with the two R's one space away from one another. There are several ways we could do this, but we know V can't be first or last. The answer here turns out to be a slightly trickier deduction: If we try (D), then V and the other W have to occupy either Tuesday-Monday or Thursday-Friday. Either way, there's no space to fit the R _ R block. That makes (D) the answer here.

6. **C** If U and V are both in, then where could W go?

U in means R is in, with U next to R; V in means W*…V…W*. That fills up all five of our "in" spots, so S and T are both definitely out, and W is our only repeater. The possible positions here depend on the placement of the flippable UR-block. If it's in Monday-Tuesday, then W will be on Wednesday and Friday: eliminate (A), (B), and (D). That's nice: Now all we have to decide is whether W could go on Tuesday or on Thursday. If we try Tuesday, then we discover that V and W must occupy 2 of the slots out of Wednesday through Friday; that would leave us nowhere to put the UR-block. So we want to pick (C).

DRILL #3

Page 158

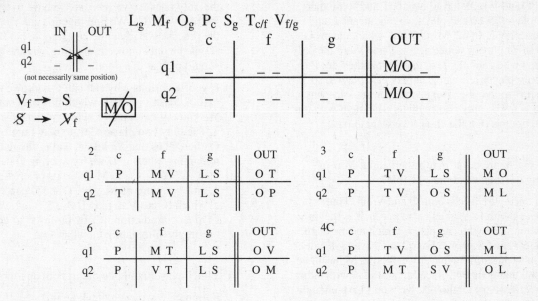

Setting it up: This is a tough diagram. We'll start with the q1 lineup: We need one slot for a c, 2 slots for f's, and 2 slots for g's; that leaves 2 players out. The q2 lineup looks the same; to organize the information well, we'll stack the two quarters' lineups on top of one another. We'll need to improvise as visual a representation as possible of the quarter-switch rule. We'll use subscripts to indicate which players can play which positions. It's worth noting that there are 2 players who can play c, 3 who can play f, and 4 who can play g. We'll want to keep a close eye on our "out" column, and especially on the fact that either M or O (or possibly both) is out every quarter.

2. **B** If T is out in q1 and plays c in q2, then what must be true?

T out in q1 means that P must play c, since P is the only other player that can. The only remaining players who can play f in q1 are M and V; V playing f means S must be in, and S can only play g. M in means O is out, so the last player—L—must be in.

In q2, T comes in; P, then, has to go out, since T is the only other player who can play c. Everybody else stays where they are, since we can't swap anyone between g and f, and only one player can cross the in/out line between quarters. The only choice that's consistent with our deductions is (B), the choice we want.

3. **C** If M and O are both out in q1, and M is out for q2, then what must be true?

In q1, with M and O both out, we have to put L, P, S, T, and V in. P has to play c. T and V are the only players who can play f, so that means L and S must play g. In q2, M stays out, which means O goes in. O plays g. Once again, T and V are the only players who can play f, so that's what they do; P is the only player left who can play c. V plays f, so S stays in—playing g. The odd player out—L—has to go out. The only choice that's consistent with our deductions is (C), the choice we want to pick.

6. **C** If M and V are never in together, and if M is in during q1, then what must be true?

M in during q1 forces both O and V out. That leaves us with L, P, S, and T to put in. T is the only remaining one who can play f, which means that P plays c. L and S play g. For q2, we have to decide whom to put in. Whichever we choose, M has to be the one that goes out, since M can't play with either O or V. If we try O, though, we won't have enough players who play f. So V comes in and replaces M; everybody else stays put. The only choice that's consistent with our deductions is (C), the choice we want.

1. **A** Which could be the players who play g and f in q2?

(D) has M and O together, so we can eliminate that one. (B) lists three players who can only play g; eliminate that one. (E) has P playing either g or f; eliminate that one. Only (A) and (C) are left. (C) only has two players who play f—T and V; with V playing f, S would have to play g, but S is not listed, so we can eliminate that one. (A) is the only choice left.

4. **D** What can't be true?

Use prior work first, if you can. We've seen (A) in question 3. We've seen (B) in question 2. Those are the only ones we've seen, so we have to try choices starting with (C). We find that this can work, and in the process you generate an example of (E) as well. (D) is the only choice remaining, and the one we should pick at this point.

If you're curious why (D) can't work, we can look at that. S doesn't play q1, which fills the "out" column. We know V can't play f, which means V must play g. The only two players left to play f are M and T; O, then, goes out. P plays c, and L, the only player remaining, plays g. If we try to bring O in for q2, then we have to send M out in its place. So L, O, P, T, and V are our q2 players. L and O can only play g, which forces V to play f. But S is out, which leads us to a contradiction. It's by far faster to get to (D) by simply eliminating the other four.

5. **A** Which player could be out in both quarters?

Fortunately, we get a break on this one. If we bothered to generate the complete example for 4(C), we found a case in which L is out in both quarters. That gets us answer choice (A).

DRILL #4

Page 160

A B C D E		1	2	3	4	5
A B/C/D	1A	E	B	C	A	D
B A/C/E	1B	C	B	E	D	A
C A/B	3i	~~E~~	A	~~D~~	B	~~C~~
D A/E	3ii	D/B	E	B/D	A	C
E B/D	4ia	D	E	B	A	C
	4ib			B	A	D
	4ii	D	E	B	C	A
	4iii	A/C	C/A	B	E	D

Setting it up: The diagram here is simple ordering, and all the clues are pretty much the same: blocks with one element and the 2-3 possible choices that could come after them. There are of course several ways we could symbolize these, but whichever we choose, there aren't a lot of deductions that we're likely to be able to make at this stage. It's probably best to charge ahead to the questions and do what we can with them.

1. **D** If B is in 2, then what must be true?

   Since B has three possible options that could follow it, this one is pretty tough to do from the front. The form of the answer choices offers some hope: We'll be able to eliminate if we can find any element other than the two listed that could go in the spot mentioned.

   Try (A): A, C, and E are the only elements that could go immediately before B; in order to attempt to eliminate this choice, we'll try E in 1. We see that there may be more than one way of making E be first, but all we have to do is make the easier one, which has C in 3. That eliminates not only (A), but (C) as well.

   Try (B): To eliminate this one, we'll try C in 1. Again, we may have some options for 3, but all we have to do is make the easier one, which puts E there. That eliminates (B) and also, fortunately, (E).

   At this point, we've eliminated everything but (D), which is the choice we should stick with. Showing why this is true involves trying both C and E in spot 4 and discovering that we simply can't do it. It's much better to trust our work on the other choices and pick (D).

3. **B** If C is in 5, then what's the complete list of elements that could go in 2?

   It's tough to do this one from straight deductions, so we should pick something to try, based on the lists in the choices. A, B, D, or E would all be good choices, since they all appear in 3 of the answer choices. We'll assume you try A first. The only elements that can go immediately before C are A or B; since A's already used, we have to have B in 4. The only remaining element that could go after A is D, so it has to go in 3. Since D can't go immediately before B, A can't go second. We eliminate choices (C), (D), and (E).

   Now all we have to do is decide whether or not E can go in 2. E in 2 may be followed by either B or else D in 3; C in 5 may be preceded by either A or else B in 4. The only legal combinations of 3 and 4 are, respectively, B A or D A. Either B or D may go before E, so it turns out that there are two ways we can have E second. Either way, (B) is the choice we definitely want to pick.

4. **C** If B is in 3, then how many different orders could we have?

Unfortunately, we have to do this one from straight deductions. To make matters worse, we see that all three of the elements A, C, and E could go either before or after B. A good method to use to try out all these possibilities is to try these three elements one at a time in slot 4 (or slot 2—as long as you pick one or the other, it doesn't really matter). We'll try these three in slot 4.

With A in 4, we see that the possibilities split again. Either C or D could go after A, and either C or E could go before. Again, pick one spot and pursue the two options: Let's try the two options in 5. With C in 5, we've placed B A C in the last 3 spots; now E has to go before B, and the only element remaining for slot 1 is D. This follows all the rules. Now we try D in 5. This gives us B A D in the last 3 spots. C and E go in the first two spots, but neither of these can work; C cannot appear before E, and E cannot appear before C. We're finished with the possibility of A in 4: there's only one arrangement there.

With C in 4, we see that the only remaining element that could follow it is A; it has to go in 5. That leaves D and E for the first 2 spots; either could go before the other, but only E can go before B. We're finished with the possibility of C in 4; there's only one arrangement there.

If you're feeling clever, you may check something that you've probably figured out by now: Every element can be preceded by exactly the same elements that can follow it. In other words, any legal example can always have its order reversed to produce another legal example, and since the condition here is that B is third, we may suspect that if we look at the possibility of E in 4, we're going to find two more arrangements: the reverse orders of the two arrangements we've already found.

If you don't make this observation, you have to finish this one by brute force. With E in 4, we see that the only remaining element that could follow E is D; it has to go in 5. That leaves A and C for slots 1 and 2; either could go before the other, and either could also go before B. So A and C can go in the first two slots in either order. We're finished with the possibility of E in 4; there are two arrangements there.

The grand total, then, is four possible arrangements. That's (C), the answer we finally get to pick.

2. **E** What could be true?

You might want to look at all this prior work we've done in an effort to luck out of this question. Unfortunately, we haven't made an example of any of these things. We'll have to try the choices one at a time.

Try (A): A is in 1, and C is in 4. The elements before and after C have to be A and B, in either order. But A is already used, so we can't fill both spots. This one can't work.

Try (B): This one's easy: B can't go before D.

Try (C): It has a similar problem to (A). The elements before and after C have to be A and B, but A is already used elsewhere.

Try (D): It has a similar problem to (A) and (C). E has to have D on one side of it, but D is already used elsewhere.

That leaves us with (E). Pick it and run.

5. **E** Which could be second and fourth, respectively?

No, we haven't made an example of any of these, either. We'll have to work the choices one at a time.

Try (A): C has to have A on one side of it and B on the other. But A is used elsewhere in the diagram, so we can't do this.

Try (B): C has to have A on one side of it and B on the other. But B is used elsewhere in the diagram, so we can't do this.

Try (C): This is the same choice as (A).

Try (D): This is the same choice as (B).

We're left with (E). Pick it and run.

6. **A** If we change the rules so that A can only go before D and B can only go before E, then what must be true?

You may see the big deduction on this one right away, but you may not. If not, then you may have to try an example before you realize that the rule changes have taken away the only two elements that could appear before C. So any legal arrangement—there are two of them—has to have C in 1. That's choice (A), the one we want to pick.

CHAPTER 13

DRILL #1

Page 164

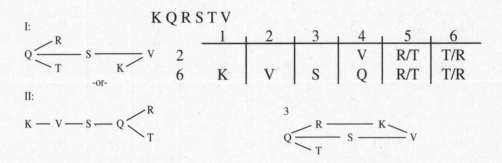

K Q R S T V

	1	2	3	4	5	6
2				V	R/T	T/R
6	K	V	S	Q	R/T	T/R

Setting it up: This is a standard 1-6 ordering diagram; you may want to note that the right-hand side of the diagram contains the higher-rated restaurants. The first clue gives us two possibilities for the game: Q…S…V or V…S…Q. These will form the backbone of our two combined diagrams; we can tack the remaining elements and their range clues onto these backbones. Every element appears in our combined clues; we'll have to use the information in the questions to tell which scenario applies.

1. **D** Grab-a-rule

   (A) has S ranked higher than both Q and V; (B) has S ranked lower than both Q and V; (C) has K with more spoons than V; (E) has Q with more spoons than T. (D) is the only choice that satisfies all the clues, and that's the answer we want to pick.

2. **E** If V is in 4, then what must be true?

   V can only be in 4 in scenario I. That forces R and T into 5 and 6, in either order. 1-3 are Q…S and K; there are three possible orders from there. The only choice that's consistent with our deductions is (E), which is the choice we want.

3. **D** If K is ranked higher than R, then what could be true?

   K can only be ranked higher than R in scenario I. That forces Q to be the lowest-ranked; either V or T could be the highest, but there are several possibilities that work. We'll have to take the choices one at a time. (A) can't happen: Both Q and R have to be ranked lower than K; (B) can't happen either: V must be ranked higher than K; (C) can't happen: R must be ranked lower than both K and V; (E) can't work: At least Q, S, R, and K all have to be ranked lower than V. (D) is the only one that can work, and that's the choice we want.

5. **C** If Q is ranked higher than K, then what can't be true?

   Q can be ranked higher than K in either scenario. Scenario II is pretty straightforward: K is in 1, V in 2, S in 3, and Q in 4; in scenario I, in order for Q to rank higher than K, K has to be in 1 and Q has to be in 2. (A) can happen in scenario II; (B) can happen in scenario I; (D) can happen in either scenario; (E) can happen in scenario II. Since slot 2 has to be either V or Q, depending on which scenario applies, we can see that (C) is the choice that doesn't work here.

6. **C** If V is ranked lower than Q, then which doesn't have to be true?

   "V lower than Q" is scenario II. The only elements that aren't set in this scenario are R and T, so we'll pick the answer that involves one of them. Since R could be in either 5 or 6, we want to pick (C).

4. **D** Which could be true?

   (D) works in scenario II, and if you've just worked questions 5 and 6, this one may jump off the page at you. If not, it's easy enough to eliminate the others.

   (A): In scenario I, the highest Q can be is in 2; in scenario II, it has to be in 4. (B): In scenario I, the lowest R can be is in 2; in scenario II, it has to be in either 5 or 6. (C): In scenario I, the highest S can be is 5; in scenario II, it has to be in 3. (E): In scenario I, the lowest V can be is 4; in scenario II, it has to be in 2.

   Either way, (D) is the choice we want.

DRILL #2

Page 166

```
                              b g p r y      1      2      3      4      5
                                        ┌──────┬──────┬──────┬──────┬──────┐
at most 1 use of each button       I:   │  b   │  g   │  p   │  r   │  y   │
                                   2I    │  b   │  g   │  p   │  r   │  y   │
b1:  1   2   3   4   5              b1    │  g   │  b   │  p   │  r   │  y   │
           ⋎                       b2    │  p   │  b   │  g   │  r   │  y   │
                                   4I    │  b   │  g   │  p   │  r   │  y   │
b2:  1   2   3   4   5              b5    │  b   │  g   │  p   │  y   │  r   │
             ⋎⋎                    b4    │  b   │  g   │  r   │  y   │  p   │
                                   b2    │  r   │  g   │  b   │  y   │  p   │
b3:  1   2   3   4   5
               ⋎⋎

b4:  1   2   3   4   5
                 ⋎⋎

b5:  1   2   3   4   5
                   ⋎
```

Setting it up: The diagram on this one is pretty easy: buttons 1 through 5 across the top, with the initial arrangement of the colors indicated in the top line of the diagram. The clues are all relatively simple to represent. It's worth noting that each change affects only two chips, and that the moves are all completely reversible. It's important to note that a button can only be pressed once in each sequence. It's best to get right to the questions on this one.

2. **E** After two buttons are used, 3 is green; what must also be true of the puzzle then?

The initial arrangement has g in 2. In order to get to chip 3, g has to go to one end or the other. If we're to do it in two presses, then g has to go to the end on the first press, and then go to chip 3 on the second. So the sequence of buttons is 1, then 2. The only choice that's consistent with our deductions is (E).

3. **B** After a sequence of four buttons, the sequence is p y g b r; what could the sequence have been after two presses?

We can evaluate our choices from two ends: whether the initial order could get there in two presses, and whether we could get from there to the four-button order in two presses. We pretty much have to go with the choices on these.

Try (A): As we saw in the previous question, the only way to get g to chip 3 in two presses is to do 1 then 2; this isn't an arrangement we can get to in two presses.

Try (B): We can definitely get here from the initial arrangement: Any order of buttons 1 and 5 will work. To get from here to our target arrangement, all we have to do is switch g and p, and switch b and y. Any combination of buttons 2 and 3 will do.

If you're curious about the others, here's the info about them: (C) has the same problem as (A); for (D), we can make a similar deduction with it as we did with g to eliminate (A) and (C), and thus see that two presses can't get us to this arrangement; (E) has the same problem (A) and (C) did. We definitely want to stick with (B).

1. **A** Which could be the result of a three-button sequence?

    We'll have to try these one at a time. In (A), we note that p and y have switched places; that suggests that button 4 was part of the sequence. If we back up from that press, we're looking for a two-button sequence resulting in g r p b y. r seems to have moved to 2 by having button 3 pressed; if we back up from that press, we're looking for one button that could result in g b p r y. That's button 1. We breathe a sigh of relief for having found the answer on our first try, and pick (A).

    If you're really concerned about the others, here are ways to eliminate them: (B) has both g and r in the same places they started, and although this arrangement works with button 2, then button 4, there's no way we can add a third button press without disturbing the position of either g or r. (C) has a similar problem: We can make this arrangement with button 3, then button 1, but adding any other will disturb either p or y. To make (D) work, we have to move y from one end to the other, which involves using button 4 then button 2, but in order to arrive at this arrangement, we have to add button 1 before button 2 and button 5 after it, which is four presses. Finally, (E) also has y in chip 1, which means we have to use button 4 then button 2, but in order to arrive at this arrangement, we have to use button 1 before we press button 2, and button 3 after we press button 1, which is four presses.

    Hopefully, you realized (A) works before you ventured into the other choices.

4. **C** What's the shortest way we could get r in chip 1, b in chip 3, and p in chip 5?

    The easiest way to get p from 3 to 5 is with button 4; the easiest way to get b from 1 to 3 is with button 2. Assuming we use these two buttons, we see that it's relatively easy to get r to position 1 if we just switch y and r (button 5) before we start. So the sequence of buttons 5, 4, 2 will do the job. Is there a sequence with fewer presses? Well, the absolute shortest way to get r from 5 to 1 involves two presses—3, then 1—but that doesn't change the position of p at all. Three presses is the shortest sequence we're going to be able to find, and that's choice (C).

5. **B** Which 3-button sequence has another 3-button sequence with the same result?

    This one can be really tough. A good way of working these choices is to look at the chips that each move affects; if any choice has adjacent button presses that don't affect the same chips, then the order of those presses can be reversed without changing the outcome. Let's try that:

    (A): Button 1 affects chips 1 and 2; button 3 affects chips 2 and 4; button 5 affects chips 4 and 5. Each consecutive pair has a chip in common, so we can't reverse the order of any of these moves.

    (B): Button 2 affects chips 1 and 3; button 5 affects chips 4 and 5; button 4 affects chips 3 and 5. By our reasoning above, we should be able to reverse the order of button 5 and button 2 without changing the outcome. Both, it turns out, result in the same arrangement: p g r y b.

    We can check the others if you're skeptical: The sequence for (C) is 2 and 4, 1 and 2, 1 and 3; the sequence for (D) is 3 and 5, 4 and 5, 2 and 4; the sequence for (E) is 4 and 5, 3 and 5, 1 and 3. (B) is definitely the only one in which two adjacent presses don't affect any of the same chips, and is the choice we want to pick.

6. **A** Which sequence using buttons 2–5, if repeats are allowed, would result in the same arrangement as a single press of button 1?

    Yuck. A good way to evaluate these is to focus on just one of the chips and see where it goes. b, for example, should move from chip 1 to chip 2 as a result of the correct sequence. In (A), b lands at 2; it remains a possibility. In (B), b lands at 1; eliminate it. In (C), b lands at 5; eliminate it. In (D), b lands at 1; eliminate it. In (E), b lands at 1; eliminate it. Pick (A) and run. If you're a glutton for punishment, you can verify that it actually works.

DRILL #3

Page 168

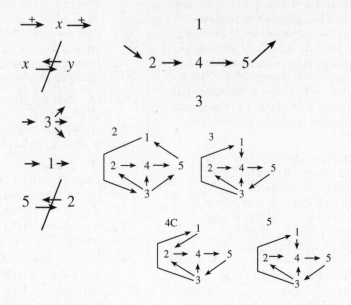

Setting it up: We can't settle on one complete map before going to the questions on this one. The good news is that we can make an axis for our diagram: the 2 → 4 → 5 clue contains a lot of information. 2 has to receive from some other tower; 5 has to send to some other tower. The clue involving 3 is useful as well; it'll send to three of the other towers and receive from the fourth, which means that in one way or another it has to be connected to all of the other towers. Finally, 1 has to receive from exactly one and send to exactly one, and one of these connections has to be to 3. It seems as though there may be several ways to satisfy the clues on this one, and there may be deductions out there waiting to be had, but it's going to be time-consuming to find them at this stage. We go to the questions looking to learn a bit more about the game as we work.

2. **B** If 3 sends to 5, then how many others must be in the chain to send signals from 1 to 4?

We update our diagram: 3 sends to 5. Now we have to watch out for several things: 2 needs to receive, 5 needs to send, and they can't be connected to each other; also, 1 can only have one of each type of connection, and must be somehow connected to 3. Think about who 5 can send to: 2, 3, and 4 are all out of the question. That only leaves 1, so 5 sends to 1. 1 has to send to somebody and also has to be connected to 3. That means 1 sends to 3. 3, then, must send to everybody else. We've arrived at our complete diagram: No other connections are possible.

The shortest route from 1 to 4 in this diagram is 1 → 3 → 4. That involves one other tower, which makes (B) the answer we want.

5. **C** If 1 sends to 4, then which is a list of the towers that could be the second to receive a signal starting from 3?

1 sends to 4; that means 3 must send to 1. 5 needs to send, and 2 needs to receive; their only remaining options for doing these things is, in both cases, 3. So 5 sends to 3, and both 2 and 4 receive from 3. Our diagram is done.

A signal starting from 3 can travel to 1, 2, or 4; take these options one at a time. From 1, a signal can go only to 4: eliminate choices (A) and (B); from 2, a signal can go only to 4; from 4, a signal can go only to 5. Since our diagram is a complete specification of what has to happen when 1 sends to 4, we can confidently say that towers 4 and 5 are the only possibilities, so we pick (C) and move on.

6. **C** What's the minimum number of towers, including 1, that are required to transmit a signal from 1 back to 1?

A signal can't travel to just one tower and then right back, and since our choices also count tower 1, choices (A) and (B) make no sense. In question 2, we saw an arrangement that would allow us to make the circuit $1 \rightarrow 3 \rightarrow 5 \rightarrow 1$. That's three towers, the next smallest number available in the answer choices, so we pick (C) and keep going.

1. **D** What must be true?

We'll use our prior work to eliminate. We saw a counterexample for (A) in question 3. We saw a counterexample for (B) in 3. We saw a counterexample for (C) in question 2. We saw a counterexample for (E) in 3. That leaves (D), the choice we want to pick. You may want to add this deduction to your master diagram.

3. **D** Which is a list of other towers required to transmit a signal from 4 to 2?

This is a tricky one. We've already seen a couple different arrangements, and our answer choices will include only those that are required—that is, in all cases necessary—to get the signal from 4 to 2. In question 2, we needed 5, 1, and 3 in that order. In question 3, however, we were able to do it just with 5 and 3. Eliminate (B), (C), and (E). The only thing left to decide is whether we could somehow do this without needing 3.

Our remaining choices guarantee us that we have to go through 5. The question, then, is whether we could get from 5 to 2 without going through 3. The only chance of doing this would be to go through 1, but then 1 wouldn't be connected to 3 at all, which would violate our clue about 3. It looks like both 3 and 5 are required, which is answer choice (D).

4. **C** What could be true?

We can check our prior work, but we haven't seen an example of any of these yet. Check (A): 2 sending to 1 means 1 must send to 3; 3, then, sends to everybody else. In this case, 5 can't send to 1, 2, 3, or 4. This doesn't work. Now check (B): 4 sending to 1 means 1 must send to 3; 3, then, sends to everybody else, and we have the same problem we saw in (A). Check (C): 1 sending to 2 means 1 must receive from 3. 5 still isn't sending to anyone, and 3 is the only remaining option. So 5 sends to 3, and 3 sends to both 2 and 4. This follows the rules, so we can pick it and be done.

If you're interested, check out the reasons why the other two choices don't work. Here's (D): 2 sending to 3 means that 3 sends to everybody else. Now 5 can't send to 1 (it's already being sent to), 2, 3, or 4. That can't work. (E) directly contradicts the last clue in the game. (C) is the only one that works.

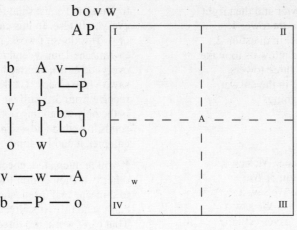

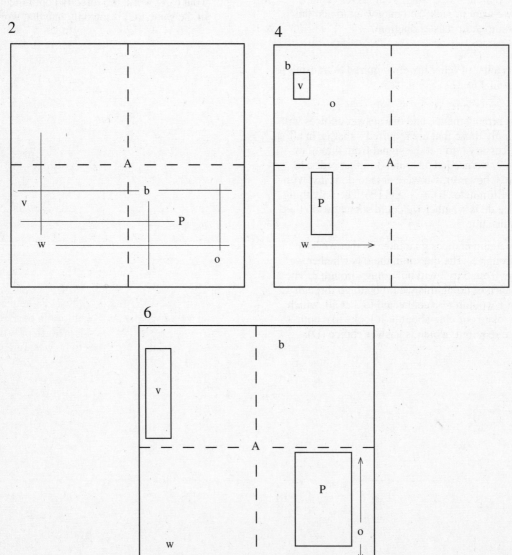

Setting it up: At least the diagram on this one isn't too tough: a square, with A in the middle. You probably want to label the north, south, east, and west sides of the field, and also label the four quadrants. The clues are basically range clues, with the added complication that we're essentially ordering in two directions at the same time. We can make some deductions to start with: w is both south and west of A, so w is in quadrant IV. Also, b is both north and west of o, so we can add that symbol. P goes south of A but north of w; v goes west of w. Once we have those deductions represented, it's time to tackle the questions.

2. **A** If b is in quadrant III, then what must be true?

b has to be northwest of o, so o is even further south and east in quadrant III. P is between b and o in the east-west direction and has to be north of w. v has to be north of P and south of b; the only thing we don't really know here is whether w is north or south of o. Let's try the choices: (A) looks good; since P has to be south of A, it's either in III or IV, but it also has to be east of b, which places it definitely in III.

If you're curious about the others, the reasoning above shows why (B) isn't true. (C) and (D) aren't right: o has to be in III. v has to be south of b (either III or IV), and it also has to be west of w, which forces it into IV.

(A) is the one we want.

4. **C** If o is in I, then which quadrants must not have flags in them?

o is in I, which means b must be even further north and west in I. We know that P must be between b and o in east-west terms, and it also must be south of A, so P is definitely in IV, north of w. v has to be between b and o in north-south terms, and has to be west of both P and w, so v is definitely in I. So b is definitely in I, o of course is in I, v is in I, and w is in IV. II and III can't contain anything; that makes (C) the answer.

5. **D** If o is in II but nothing else is in II, then what could be true?

w is definitely in IV. b has to be north and west of o but not in II, so it must be in I. P has to be between b and o in east-west terms but has to be south of A, so P is either in III or IV. v is west of w and has to be between b and o in north-south terms, so it's definitely in I. (A) can't be true: I has to contain at least 2 flags (b and v). (B) can't be true: III can't contain any of the flags. (C) is wrong for the same reason. (D) looks like it could work: IV can contain the poplar tree, and it also must contain w. (E) isn't right: IV can't have any flag other than w. (D) is the one we want.

6. **B** If each quadrant has exactly one flag, then what must be true?

IV has to contain w, so that one's done. v has to appear west of w, so it has to go in I. b has to be north and west of o, so b goes in II and o goes in III. The big remaining question is where P can go. It has to be between b and o in east-west terms; it also has to be between A and w in north-south terms. It's definitely in III, and there are no issues with v being northwest of P. The only choice that's consistent with our deductions is (B). Everything else listed must be false except for (E), which could be true but certainly doesn't have to be. Choose (B).

1. **E** What must be true?

This is a straight deduction. We deduced that w must be in IV, and sure enough there it is: (E).

3. **C** Which can't be true?

We have some prior work that can help here. (A) can be true: We saw this possibility in 6. (B) has to be true (v is north of P, and P is north of w). There's no way (C) can work: v has to be west of P, and P has to be west of o. As for the others, we've seen (D) in question 4; we've also seen (E) in 4. (C) is clearly the choice we want.

CHAPTER 17

DRILL #1

Pages 193 – 194

The passage:

The passage describes the history of Fermat's Last theorem and various attempts to prove it. The first paragraph describes what it is and Fermat's note indicating he had proven it. The second paragraph indicates why it is unlikely that Fermat's proof was correct. The third paragraph describes other unsuccessful efforts by famous mathematicians to prove the theorem in whole or in part. The final paragraph describes successful efforts to prove parts of the theorem, and then finally a relatively recent proof that is likely to be correct.

1. **C** Specific: Why was Fermat's Last theorem so well known?

There is not much in the passage that pertains to this fact; the closest it seems to come is a statement in the last paragraph about what made it so "tantalizing." Although all of the answer choices provide correct facts about it, only (C) relates to a stated reason why the problem was so famous. That's the choice we want.

2. **E** Specific: Why does the passage mention Fermat's method of presenting his mathematical discoveries?

The referenced test indicates that Fermat posed, as challenge problems, those theorems for which he believed he had complete and correct proofs. Since he never posed the full statement of his Last theorem as a challenge problem, but instead elected only to pose the more restricted cases as problems, the passage concludes that Fermat never found a proof that he could be satisfied was both complete and correct. (A) is a statement that is made in the paragraph, but the purpose of this description is not to impugn Fermat's ability as a mathematician. (B) is also mentioned in the paragraph, but this is not the primary purpose of the discussion. (C) is the opposite of the paragraph's purpose. (D) does not pertain to the discussion in the cited paragraph. (E) is the choice we want; it's the one that best describes the role this evidence plays in the claim presented in this paragraph.

3. **A** Specific: What does the word "counterexamples" mean?

The reference is to the final paragraph and the discussion of computers' role in working on Fermat's Last theorem. The word "counterexample" generally means a single instance that proves a general statement is untrue. In the context of Fermat's Last theorem, which claims that no integer solutions to a particular equation exist, a counterexample would be a solution to the equation. (A) is the correct statement of this idea.

4. **C** Specific: With which one of the statements would the author agree?

(A)   This might seem reasonable at a glance, but this is not said in the passage. Also, since it seems that not everyone is sure Wiles's proof is correct, it seems likely that some work on it actually will continue to go on.

(B)   The passage mentions Wiles's work in other areas of mathematics, but not how important it will be judged to be in comparison to his solution to this famous problem.

(C)   This is consistent with the last sentence of the passage.

(D)   This seems unlikely, given that Wiles has now proven it.

(E)   Although the problem is no longer unsolved, there's no passage material that supports the conclusion that it will be entirely forgotten.

Answer choice (C) is most clearly supported by statements in the passage.

5. **B** Specific: What is true about Euler?

Euler is mentioned in the passage's third paragraph, in connection with a published proof of one part of Fermat's Last theorem that turned out to be incorrect. (A) might be argued for, but it isn't directly supported by the passage material. (C) overstates the importance of Euler's mistake, since we don't know what else he might be known for. (D) is in fact not supported by the passage, since he published his proof. (E) might be true, but it certainly isn't said in the passage. (B) seems a reasonable inference from the material, since the passage says that Euler published the proof some time after he claimed to have found it. Euler would certainly have found an obvious error in that amount of time.

6. **A** Complex: Which would be another example of successful work on Fermat's Last theorem?

In the final paragraph, successful work is characterized as "piecemeal"—that is, accomplished one piece at a time. (B) and (C) both concern incorrect proofs, which can hardly be called successful. (E) talks about a subsequent correction to an incorrect proof, which is along the right lines but not the best choice we have. (D) is also along the right lines but doesn't talk about any actual progress on the Last theorem itself. (A) is the clearest example here of someone correctly proving a piece of Fermat's Last theorem.

7. **E** General: What is the passage's primary purpose?

The purpose is to describe Fermat's Last theorem and the long history of work on it. Eliminate (A) because the passage does not include a "commonly held belief"; eliminate (B) because no "historical dispute" is mentioned in the passage. (C) has a chance, but this passage is about a particular theorem, not about an entire area of mathematics, and we have no idea how "crucial" this work really is. (D) sounds decent because it mentions "mathematical errors," which are certainly described in the passage, but this leaves out any mention of the problem the mathematicians were attempting to solve, as well as the fact that the problem was eventually solved. (E) is pretty straightforward, and matches the description of the passage's contents.

Drill #2

Page 195 – 196

The passage:

The massacre at Wounded Knee was the result of the spread of the Ghost Dance religion among Native Americans and white authorities' fear of the religion. The first paragraph introduces the Wounded Knee massacre and says that its apparent cause was not the true reason it happened. The second paragraph describes the origin and teachings of the Ghost Dance religion. The third paragraph describes how the Ghost Dance spread among native tribes, and how it came to be interpreted to advocate resistance to white rule. The final paragraph attempts to describe both why the Ghost Dance might have been so popular among Native Americans and why white authorities would have seen it as a serious threat in terms of the religion's resemblance to Christian mysticism.

1. **D** General: What is the main point of the passage?

As stated above, the main point concerns the fact that the Ghost Dance religion was in some sense responsible for the massacre at Wounded Knee. (A) seems close, but it's probably too much to say it led "directly" to the massacre, and the passage indicates that its initial teachings did not advocate armed resistance. (B) has the wrong emphasis; although the passage does state that the Ghost Dance religion was a very successful pan-tribal identity movement, the passage is concerned with explaining the reasons for the Wounded Knee massacre, and what was so important about the Ghost Dance religion. (C) mixes parts of the passage together, but it doesn't mention anything about Wounded Knee or the threat that white authorities felt. (E) focuses too exclusively on the motives of white authorities without describing the Ghost Dance religion itself. (D) is the best of the choices we have to work with here.

2. **E** General: What is the author's attitude toward the Ghost Dance religion?

The only thing in the passage resembling a value judgment about the Ghost Dance is a statement in the third paragraph that called its efforts to unite Native American tribes "successful." Although obviously the passage doesn't celebrate the massacre, it's too much to say that the passage openly expresses "disappointment" at what its result was, in terms of the religion itself; eliminate (A). The passage does draw similarities between the Ghost Dance religion and Christian teachings, but to say it involved the "incorporation" of those teachings is a bit much; eliminate (B). No skepticism toward the religion itself is ever expressed: eliminate (C). No doubts are expressed about the religion's origins: eliminate (D). (E) is the closest statement of the attitude revealed in the passage.

3. **A** Specific: What is the purpose of the cited text in the final paragraph?

The final paragraph describes similarities between the Ghost Dance religion and early Christian mysticism; the cited text describes common themes present in both. (C) is clearly not right; Wovoka is mentioned in the second paragraph, not here. No contrast is indicated in the passage, so we can eliminate (D). (E) is in this paragraph, but it's the similarity to the history of Rome that's cited to indicate this point. (A) and (B) both seem close. Although one major purpose of this paragraph is to suggest why the Ghost Dance religion might have been appealing to Native Americans, the passage's qualification that these were "perhaps" reasons why should steer us away from (B). Certainly these are cited as similarities between Christian teachings and the Ghost Dance religion, so (A) is the safer answer here.

4. **C** Specific: Which is a similarity between the history of Christian mysticism and the history of the Ghost Dance religion?

The main similarity, as the history of Christian mysticism is described in the final paragraph, seems to be that both united "disparate groups." (A) refers to a "charismatic leader," which is not a key aspect of the Ghost Dance religion as it is presented in the passage. Although persecution may be indicated in the passage by implication, it is the killing at Wounded Knee that is identified as the end of the Ghost Dance religion's spread, so we should avoid (B). No texts of the Ghost Dance religion are mentioned, so we should eliminate (D). The conversion of an established authority is nowhere in this passage, so we shouldn't pick (E). (C) wasn't the answer choice we were looking for, but there is an instance in the Ghost Dance religion that parallels this development: the interpretations of the Lakota mystics mentioned in the third paragraph. (C) is the best choice here.

5. **C** Complex: Weaken the author's explanation of why the Ghost Dance religion was appealing to many Native Americans.

The statement of this explanation is in the last paragraph, where the teachings of the religion are described as being "familiar, and perhaps appealing, to those who had been exposed to Christian missionary teachings." Eliminate (A): Whether the return to paradise was literal or figurative doesn't seem to weaken the author's claims. Eliminate (B): How the religion's teachings were adapted or changed doesn't seem to relate to the reasons for its popularity. Eliminate (D): The fact that a popular figure's adoption of the religion hastened its spread doesn't necessarily weaken the author's explanation of why it was appealing. Eliminate (E): The passage doesn't insist that the Ghost Dance religion was similar to Christianity in every respect. (C) is the best answer here; it indicates that the religion was most popular among those who did not have contact with Christian missionaries, casting significant doubt on the author's explanation of why it was appealing.

6. **B** Specific: What does the word "millennial" mean?

The word is used in the passage in connection with the word "paradise," which comes after a cataclysm that cleanses the land. No specific amount of time is mentioned, nor is the idea of regular recurrence; eliminate (A). "Recorded history" does not appear to directly relate to the matters discussed; eliminate (C). There is no mention that the state involved was unattainable; eliminate (D). A "cataclysm" indicates a sudden development, not a long struggle, and moreover the word "millenial" contains no implication of how the state is to be attained; eliminate (E). Since the "paradise" is identified as replacing the current order and returning the land to pure state, (B) is the best choice here.

7. **E** Specific: What does the passage tell us about the actions of government authorities on Lakota reservations?

We are told in the third paragraph that the Wounded Knee massacre happened as a result of the government's efforts to enforce a ban against the Ghost Dance religion on Lakota reservations. (A) goes too far; we aren't told in the passage that military means were the main ones used by the government. (B) and (C) might be true, but we have no direct evidence for these choices in the passage. Like (A), (D) tries to characterize all of the government's efforts, but we don't have enough information to conclude this. (E) is the best choice we have; certainly military means were employed at Wounded Knee, and the fact that they were there to enforce a "ban" against the Ghost Dance religion indicates that the authorities' actions included ones that they, at least, would have called "legal."

DRILL #3

Pages 198 – 199

The passage:

Maria Altmann's suit to recover paintings confiscated from her family under Nazi occupation should respect her property rights but not involve returning the paintings to her personal possession. The first paragraph asserts the dual status of art as both private and cultural property, and introduces the Altmann case as one in which obvious injustice complicates this status. The second paragraph outlines the history of the paintings both during and after World War II. The final paragraph describes Altmann's efforts to recover them and asserts that returning them to her would worsen the injustice of the situation.

1. **D** General: What is the passage's main point?

   We definitely want an answer that includes the passage's contention that the Klimt paintings should not be returned to Maria Altmann. (A) definitely does not include this idea. (B) does, indirectly, but it doesn't mention Altmann's case specifically. (C) is a decent statement of the passage's position with regard to the artworks, but it leaves out the other issues of cultural ownership that are important to the passage's argument. (E) defends the actions of the Austrian government, which is definitely not part of the passage's purpose. (D) is the clearest and most complete statement of what the passage is trying to say; it is a good capsule summary of the last paragraph.

2. **C** Specific: What are two functions of the first sentence?

   The sentence in question sets the stage for the dispute over the Klimt paintings by indicating the injustice of Nazi confiscations on one hand and the tension between collective and private rights to cultural property on the other. Eliminate (A): This sentence doesn't indicate at all who is likely to win in the Altmann case. (B) is close, but this particular sentence doesn't go so far as to say that no resolution will be satisfactory. Eliminate (D): Like (A), this choice tries to say that this sentence includes some statement of which side is likely to win. (E) has a very similar problem. (C) is the best summary of the material contained in this sentence.

3. **E** Complex: Which situation is most similar to Maria Altmann's efforts to recover paintings from the Austrian government by bringing suit in a U.S. court?

   Altmann's case is one in which efforts to resolve a dispute over events that took place in one country cannot be satisfactorily resolved in that country, so efforts are instead pursued in the country where that person is currently a citizen. (A) seems close, but the analogy is not exact: In Altmann's case, her attempts to bring suit in Austria were unsuccessful, not merely unresolved. (B) talks about bringing suit first in the country where "she resides"; Altmann, however, first attempted to bring suit in Austria. Like (A), (C) seems close, but it doesn't talk about trying first to bring suit in the offending country. (D) includes no mention of where this suit is being brought. (E) is closest; since the person who has been harmed is prevented from bringing suit in the country itself, he brings suit in the country where he resides.

4. **D** Specific: What would the author's opinion be on returning the paintings to the family?

Simply put, the author is opposed to it. (A) is out. (E) is too strong; the author acknowledges that the family does have some right to be compensated for the lost property. The passage indicates that this isn't likely to happen, so we don't want (B). (C) has the wrong emphasis; this choice makes it seem as if the author is demanding more in terms of compensation than just the return of the paintings, and this is certainly not consistent with the passage. (D) is the one we want; the author describes Altmann's demand for the paintings' return as "radical."

5. **B** Specific: What is true of the Austrian legal system?

Not much is said about it, except that a suit to recover property requires that the person seeking its return must put up an amount of money determined by the property's value. (A) is a bit too harsh: The author never indicates a belief that this practice is "excessive." (C) goes too far as well; to say that it "serves their interests" is to ascribe bad faith in a way that the author does not. (D) also is harsh; it's too much to say that its decision in this case is "clearly unjust." Relations with other nations are beyond the scope of the passage, so we can toss (E). Since in the second paragraph the author mentions a report by the Austrian government itself indicating that it has profited from Nazi confiscations, and since in at least one case the courts did not act to redress such a wrong, (B) is the right strength and is consistent with passage material.

6. **D** Specific: With which one of the statements would the author agree?

We're looking for passage support for the choice we pick. (A) is going a bit far; the author doesn't argue that the Bloch-Bauer family shouldn't be compensated at all, only that the particular remedy being sought is not really just. (B) certainly isn't like anything in the passage. (C) is too strong; although this is the author's opinion in this specific case, we can't draw conclusions about the author's opinion in other cases. (E) might or might not be a statement the author agrees with; it's sweeping enough that we can't really decide. (D) is a great statement of the reason why the author says the paintings shouldn't be returned to Altmann, and is the answer we want to pick.

Pages 201 – 202

The passage:

Earthwork art represented an attempt to subvert or escape from certain cultural assumptions about art, but is most interesting because it did not entirely succeed in doing so. The first paragraph explains the reasons why alternative methods of producing art were sought, and what their practitioners hoped to accomplish. The second paragraph describes earthwork art specifically, and how it attempted to accomplish that goal by resisting efforts to make it marketable. The third paragraph describes ways in which earthwork art is in fact subject to the market, and therefore doesn't entirely succeed. The final paragraph goes beyond this paradox of earthwork art to indicate a larger paradox of which its failed attempt to escape marketability is one aspect.

1. **A** General: What is the passage's main point?

   (B) is far too general; it doesn't even mention earthwork art! (C) characterizes earthwork art as a complete failure, which is not really the passage's intention. (D) is too specific; it doesn't talk about earthwork art in terms of the market. (E) has the same problem. (A), however, has it all: earthwork art, other postmodern forms, market forces, use of land, and a nuanced description of why it is interesting. This is the one we want.

2. **D** Specific: What is the author's attitude toward "Spiral Jetty"?

   The author characterizes it as a "seminal earthwork," and also uses it as an illustration of two reasons why earthwork art is interesting. We want something positive, so we can eliminate (A), (B), and (E). "Reverent" is too far to the positive side on this one. (D) is the safest choice here.

3. **C** Specific: Which isn't in the passage?

   (A) concerns one of the paradoxes or questions described in the third paragraph. (B) concerns a purpose of novel forms mentioned in the first paragraph, although performance art itself is discussed in the second paragraph. (D) is consistent with the statement in the second paragraph that earthwork art can be seen as "counterlandscape." (E) is consistent with statements in the first paragraph. (C) is an overstatement of earthwork art's relationship to land and ownership, and is the choice we want here.

4. **C** Specific: What is the meaning of the word "ephemeral"?

   In the passage, it is opposed to "monumental," and attached to works that are worn away by natural forces. In other words, these works do not last. (C) and (D) are both along the right lines, although nothing else is. Specifically, though, the point here is that the works don't last, not that they change, so we want to pick (C).

318 ■ LSAT WORKOUT

5. **C** General: What is the organization of the passage?

(A) is close, but for one thing the use of the word "principle" to explain efforts to produce art in new ways is a little strange, and for another this choice overstates the passage's attitude toward earthwork art by characterizing it as a "failure." (B) includes a past versus present ingredient that isn't in the passage, not to mention that it gets the last paragraph's point very much wrong. (D) talks about efforts to expose the underpinnings of a theory, which isn't really like anything in the passage, and goes on to say that these efforts were successful. (E) talks about trying to solve a problem, which again isn't really what earthwork art is trying to do, as it's described in the passage. (C) is nice: The new view of an activity is the attempt to produce art outside of conventional power structures; earthworks are efforts to manifest the view; they were indeed not entirely successful; the passage goes on to discuss the larger implications of earthwork art. (C) is the one we have to pick here.

6. **D** General: What is the primary purpose of the passage?

The passage discusses and evaluates one new approach to producing art. It's not so much about presenting a theory, however; eliminate (A). No projection about what earthwork art will do to future art is offered; eliminate (B). Nothing is said about limitations in visual arts being "inherent"; eliminate (C). "Practical impossibility" is putting it rather strongly; eliminate (E). (D) is the right strength and is the choice we want to pick.

7. **B** Specific: What is the author's opinion of earthwork art's relationship to other uses of land?

This pertains to the last paragraph. The author says that, although many people think earthwork art is opposed to environmental exploitation, it is also itself an exploitation of the environment. The author compares earthwork art to strip mining and clear-cutting. (A) is a bit strong; we can't say that the passage prefers earthwork art to "all other uses." (C) brings in things not mentioned in the passage; possible other uses of the specific land on which earthworks are made is not anywhere in the text. (D) is putting the comparison too strongly; the passage acknowledges that few think that the two activities are in every way equivalent. (E) goes very far in being critical of aesthetic vision, but the passage isn't this critical. (B) is nice and soft, and mostly just indicates that there is some comparison between them. This is the choice we want.

CHAPTER 18

DRILL #1

Pages 205 – 206

The passage:

The Turing test and Searle's Chinese room argument both depend upon notions of what constitutes intelligence, but neither is entirely adequate to describe what intelligence is. The first paragraph introduces the possibility of artificial intelligence, and why questions of whether it is possible and how to decide when it has arisen are of interest to cognitive psychologists. The second paragraph describes the Turing test, a proposed method for determining when an artificial construct can be considered intelligent. The third paragraph describes Searle's Chinese room argument and demonstrates his belief that even a machine that would pass such a test should not be considered truly intelligent. The final paragraph indicates problems with each of these two views of what intelligence really is.

1. **E** General: What is the main point of the passage?

Neither Turing nor Searle presents complete views of what intelligence really is. (A) is strong when it claims that there is "no adequate standard," and then becomes a bit ridiculous when it indicates that there is some question as to whether or not humans actually are intelligent. (B) is certainly consistent with the passage, but it's a bit too specific; Searle's Chinese room argument isn't a standard for deciding whether an artificial construct is intelligent, but instead an argument showing that it may be impossible to know whether any construct is intelligent. (C) goes too far by saying that psychologists do not even have a "rudimentary understanding of intelligence." (D) goes beyond passage material by trying to characterize the failures of all such standards. (E) is the closest statement we have to the gist of this passage: Turing's completely external notion of intelligence isn't perfect, but neither is Searle's entirely internal one.

2. **E** Complex: What answer given by a computer would best address Searle's objections?

Searle's objection is, in short form, that intelligence implies thought, understanding, and consciousness. We're looking for a choice that somehow indicates one or more of these things. The similarity mentioned in (A) might be convincing in Turing's view, but it isn't necessarily in Searle's. (B) comes close, but again it can't overcome Searle's objection that the machine may have been programmed to respond in this way. (C) seems to be trying as well, but inconsistency or randomness might also be programmed features of a machine's responses. Since we can't know that the response was intended to be humorous, (D) doesn't quite do it. (E) is as close as we can get: The computer's "misunderstanding" of the question suggests that understanding is possible, and the fact that the computer later corrects it indicates that thought is probably taking place.

3. **A** Specific: What is the purpose of the third paragraph?

The third paragraph of the passage concerns Searle's Chinese room argument and the objection it represents to the notion of intelligence implicit in the Turing test. Since the whole point of the Chinese Room argument is that the rulebook can't really speak Chinese, we should eliminate (B). (C) refers to inconsistency in the results of Turing tests, which is not part of Searle's objection. (D) is not an idea mentioned in this paragraph. (E) is a distinction that isn't made anywhere in the passage. (A) is a nice summary of the contents of this paragraph, and is the answer we should pick.

4. **C** Specific: Which isn't anywhere in the passage?

(A) is in there; the passage describes the Turing test's standard as "ambitious." (B) comes from Searle's objections, and from the author's agreement that a weakness of the Turing test is that it makes intelligence completely a matter of "consensus." (D) is there: A machine that the Turing test would accept as intelligent would not be accepted by Searle. (E) is a good inference from the first paragraph. (C) actually seems to contradict the passage; no matter how complex its instructions, a computer could never be accepted as truly intelligent in Searle's view.

5. **B** Specific: Which statement agrees with the point of view associated with the Turing test?

(A) isn't really right; a machine that merely responds in an unpredictable fashion might nevertheless be quite different from a human respondent. (C) might seem likely, but we don't really know how complex a set of instructions has to be in order to give the machine a chance of appearing intelligent. (D) describes Searle's view, not Turing's. (E) is extremely specific; nobody says that a Turing test must involve posing the same exact questions to the human and computer respondents. (B), however, is completely consistent with the passage; if a computer can't convince at least some people, then it could never pass a Turing test.

6. **E** Complex: Which could be used in the Chinese room argument instead of the rulebook?

The point of the rulebook is that it's the source of the room's responses, and it definitely isn't intelligent. We want to find something else that fits that description. (A) doesn't do the job; now the intelligent person is the one who's providing the responses. (B) has a similar problem; it's introducing real human intelligence into the process. (D) has the same problem; there's no requirement that the person in the room be able to communicate with the source of the answers. (C) and (E) are the only real possibilities, and (E) is by far the better one. (C) only says the machine can make sentences, not that it can actually interpret questions and provide sensible responses. (E) is definitely the choice we want here.

7. **D** General: What is the author's attitude toward Searle's objections to the Turing test?

There's no one place where it's explicitly stated, but we know what the main point of the passage is: Searle points out something about intelligence that the Turing test can't measure, but he also makes intelligence something that can never be externally verified, which isn't ideal. We're looking for a similarly balanced answer choice. (A) and (E) are both too categorical. (B) is never the answer to a question like this on the LSAT. (C) is too—well—neutral; the author does have an opinion on the subject, it just isn't entirely positive or entirely negative. (D) is a good, middle-of-the-road answer here, and is the one we should pick.

DRILL #2

Pages 207 – 209

The passage:

Two efforts to explain the accelerating expansion of the universe—one hypothesizing the existence of "dark energy," the other tinkering with the equations of general relativity directly—do not necessarily disagree. The first paragraph outlines the history of understanding of the gravitational force, up to Einstein's theory of general relativity. The second paragraph describes the history of the cosmological constant in general relativity, which was Einstein's effort to tinker with his own equations so they would agree with models of the universe accepted at the time, but those models were eventually found to be incorrect. The third paragraph describes a recent discovery that current theories of gravity cannot explain: the acceleration of the universe's expansion. The fourth paragraph describes the "dark energy" hypothesis, an effort to describe the cause of this acceleration. The final paragraph describes an effort to correct general relativity without reference to dark energy, and presents the author's assertion that this method of explaining the acceleration does not necessarily exclude the dark energy explanation.

1. **E** General: What is the main point of the passage?

   (A) emphasizes the fact that gravitational theories have been repeatedly found to be wrong, and although this is mentioned in the passage, its purpose is to place the author's opinion in context; eliminate (A). (B) is also consistent with the passage, but it makes no specific reference to efforts to explain the mystery; eliminate it. (C) is not a prediction that the passage makes. As for (D), although the passage does relate the current debate to Einstein's cosmological constant, the passage doesn't go so far as to say that it was correct. (E) is specific, but is the only choice that contains the opinion expressed by the author, and is the choice we should pick.

2. **A** Specific: Which is an illustration of the difference between developing physical explanations and merely changing equations?

   This question pertains to the two methods of solving the mystery of the universe's accelerating expansion. "Dark energy" is presented as a physical explanation, whereas the alternative hypothesis is presented as merely tinkering with equations. In the second case, Einstein's cosmological constant is cited as a previous example of this method. We want to pick (A).

3. **C** Specific: What does the passage tell us about the steady-state model of the universe?

   In the second paragraph, we learn the following things about the steady-state model: (1) it predicted that the universe was not expanding or contracting; (2) it was at odds with predictions from Einstein's theory of general relativity; (3) it turned out to be incorrect.

   (A) makes reference to the amount of time this view was held, but the passage doesn't make any specific statement of this sort. (B) seems to be describing the cosmological constant, and while it wasn't a "physical explanation devised to account for it," there's nothing in the passage that tells us it was ever accepted again. (D) is precisely the opposite of what the passage says; it was eventually rejected because of experimental observations. (E) mistakenly identifies the dark energy hypothesis as an effort to explain why it isn't right; according to the passage, however, it had been rejected long before experimental observations required the consideration of dark energy.

   (C) is a correct paraphrase of item 1 in the explanation above, and is the answer we should pick.

4. **D** Specific: What does the author think about the scientists mentioned in the fifth paragraph?

The scientists in question are those who reject the dark energy hypothesis and instead wish to modify the equations of general relativity. The passage says that their efforts do not constitute a true alternative to the dark energy hypothesis, since they make no effort at a physical explanation of the reasons why the universe's expansion is accelerating.

(A) has the wrong attitude: The author doesn't appear to admire this approach much. (B) is rather emotional; the author doesn't believe these scientists are right, but it's a bit much to say the author is surprised by them. (C) is out of line with the passage; general relativity is not entirely correct, so the author agrees that some adjustment to gravitational theory is required. (E) is too neutral; the author has a definite opinion on the matter.

(D) is the best summary of the author's statements about the approach described in the final paragraph, and is the answer we should pick.

5. **B** Specific: Which one is not supported by the passage?

The question in (A) is answered in the first paragraph: the explanation of the precession of Mercury's perihelion. The question in (C) is answered in the second paragraph: The universe was discovered to be expanding, so the steady-state theory had to be incorrect. (D) is answered in the final paragraph: These efforts also may explain the rapid expansion of the universe after the Big Bang. (E) is answered in the third paragraph: The universe's expansion ought to be slowing down, according to general relativity.

(B) is not answered in the passage. Although the fourth paragraph mentions that certain results from quantum physics reinforce the idea, no specific experimental result is mentioned.

6. **C** Specific: What is the function of the first three paragraphs?

Taken together, they describe the history of theories of gravitation and present the recent observation that indicates current understandings of gravity are not complete. (C) is about as close to that paraphrase as you can get.

7. **E** Complex: Which observation supports the conclusion that the rate of the universe's expansion is increasing?

(A) only supports the conclusion that the universe is expanding. (B) supports the same conclusion, although it does so only weakly. (C) supports the conclusion that the expansion of the universe is slowing down. (D) doesn't clearly tell us what's happening in terms of the universe's expansion or contraction. (E) is the choice we want: If it's moving away at an ever faster speed, the expansion of the universe is accelerating.

DRILL #3
Pages 210 – 211

The passage:

Although a critical legal approach to resolving international disputes is necessary to take into account the complexity of such cases, it should not be taken so far that international treaties and agreements are seen as being of equal or lesser value to other possible means of deciding the dispute. The first paragraph indicates that critical approaches have been of limited practical value in domestic cases, but that they are better suited to the kinds of disagreements that arise in international cases. The second paragraph describes the idea of a critical approach to law by contrast with the traditional positivist approach. A positivist approach searches for "universal" principles but cannot succeed; a critical approach acknowledges complexity and accommodates many different views. The final paragraph asserts that the desire not to privilege any one principle artificially should not be allowed to undermine the principles to which parties in a dispute have explicitly agreed in the form of an international treaty.

1. **D** General: What is the main point of the passage?

   (A) isn't bad, but the phrase "sole guiding authority" is rather strong, and no mention of critical legal approaches is included in this choice. (B) focuses exclusively on the positivist approach. (C) focuses exclusively on critical legal approaches without any mention of the author's main point, which is that they shouldn't be allowed to extend too far. (E) has a similar problem. (D) is the only one that mentions the kernel of the author's idea, which is that critical legal studies are great for deciding international legal disputes but shouldn't be carried too far. This is the choice we want.

2. **E** Complex: Which provisions of a treaty would be least important in a critical view of a dispute about the treaty?

   A critical view recognizes that there are multiple traditions and systems of representation at work within each country and culture. (A) definitely fits that description. So does (B). (C) and (D) both refer to circumstances not covered by the treaty that may nevertheless be relevant to how its provisions should be enforced. (E) is the odd choice out on this one: Its reference to "fundamental legal principles" is more in line with a positivist approach, so this is the choice we should pick.

3. **C** Specific: What is the author's attitude toward the positivist approach?

   The author doesn't like it. Although the point of the passage is that critical approaches shouldn't be allowed to go too far, the author doesn't subscribe to the positivist ideal at all. (A) is certainly not right. (B) uses an emotional word—*scorn*—that we don't often see in right answers on the LSAT; moreover, the objection to the positivist ideal isn't that it relies on *ad hoc* methods of judgment, but instead that it pretends not to. (D) isn't a criticism leveled against positivism; this choice is an emotional overstatement of the author's attitude toward critical approaches. (E) contains a reference to the approach the author recommends, but the author never really complains about the positivists' reaction to the idea; in fact, we're not really sure what their reaction to this idea would be. (C) is a good paraphrase of the reason the author considers critical approaches more applicable to international disputes than positivist ones, and is the choice we want to pick.

4. **A** Specific: What is the critical view of international treaties?

The passage indicates that a critical view considers a treaty to be one of possibly many sources of authoritative guidance in deciding an international dispute, with none preferred over the others. (B) is an overstatement; the author never accuses critical approaches of making treaties less important than other sources. (C)'s mention of widely accepted principles of law is a reference to the positivist idea, not the critical one. (D) is not something that's mentioned anywhere in the passage. (E) is the author's opinion, roughly, but it's not one that a pure critical approach suggests. (A) is the best summary of a critical legal approach to international agreements, as that approach is described in the passage.

5. **B** Specific: With which statement would the author be most likely to disagree?

(A) is a statement made in the passage. (C) is suggested in the final paragraph, when the author acknowledges that the provisions of a treaty may themselves be subject to critical analysis. (D) is right in line with the author's dismissal of positivist approaches. (E) is in line with the author's broad agreement with a critical approach toward international disputes. (B), with its dependence upon "general principles," sounds very much like a positivist idea, with which the author would not agree. This is the choice we want.

6. **A** Complex: What principle underlies the author's opinion about international treaties?

The author believes that, when they apply, they should be the primary guiding authority, since the parties to the treaty have agreed to accept that authority. (A) is a good, direct statement of that idea. (B) sounds more like a positivist idea, but, even worse, it basically says that agreements entered into by only a few countries shouldn't matter in deciding disputes. (C) talks about trying to apply treaties in cases when they don't directly apply, which isn't really like anything the author is advocating. (D) talks about "every" nation agreeing to something; this isn't necessarily the case for all treaties and agreements, and the author wants any treaty that's applicable to be the primary source of legal authority for deciding a relevant case. (E) is the critical idea, not the author's. (A) is by far the best answer here.

DRILL #4

Pages 212 – 213

The passage:

The first paragraph introduces theoretical approaches to meaning in terms of the relationship between "signifier"—language—and "signified"—reality. It goes on to explain that the fact that this distinction is not strict has led to a range of responses. The second paragraph describes Foucault's response: that language can in part create reality, especially as seen in certain social institutions. The third paragraph describes Baudrillard's response: that language has entirely displaced reality.

1. **D** Specific: What is the purpose of the passage's mention of the prison, the medical clinic, and the sexual therapist?

   These are presented as three institutions studied by Foucault, demonstrating the ability of language to create and perpetuate real-world power by producing the problems they exist to "solve." (A) includes the idea of obscuring reality, which is mentioned in the first paragraph, not in the one describing Foucault. (C)'s mention of "new uses of language" isn't quite on-point; Foucault's idea isn't that these mechanisms are new, although Foucault did advocate a new approach to studying them. (B), (D), and (E) all seem approximately in line with the passage. Another look at the sentence referred to shows that these are primarily, in terms of the passage, used to demonstrate the ability of language to create real things. Since both (B) and (E) have something to do with the efficacy of these institutions, neither is as good as (D), which is more in line with the main purpose of the passage. (D) is the choice we want.

2. **D** Specific: What does the passage tell us about the "subject" in relation to theories of language?

   This part of the first paragraph explains how the domains of reality and language cannot be strictly separated from one another. Several of the choices are consistent with passage material, but only (D) includes this idea, and it's the answer we want.

3. **E** Specific: Which statement is consistent with Baudrillard's ideas?

   We're looking for something that comes out of the final paragraph. (A) takes a very limited and concrete view of what is "real," which is definitely not what the passage tells us about Baudrillard. (B) characterizes words as being meaningless, which is not really consistent with what we're told about Baudrillard. (C) has to do with a distinction between an action and an object, which isn't really addressed anywhere in the passage. (D) again maintains the distinction between language and reality, which according to the passage is not a distinction Baudrillard recognizes. (E) is a paraphrase of the passage's statement about "signs which are comprehensible only in terms of prior renditions." Choose (E).

4. **C** Complex: Which is not consistent with the responses described in the first paragraph?

   The referenced text talks about ways in which language can either obscure or else transcend reality. (A) is an example of language transcending reality. (B), although it has to do with a visual art, describes an artwork representing something that is obscured in the customary use of language. (D) is a reference to official euphemism, one example cited in the passage of language obscuring reality. (E) is an example of transcendence in language. (C) doesn't appear to have any explicit connection to the idea of either transcending reality or obscuring it, and is the best choice here.

5. **A** Complex: Which is an example of Foucault's idea of how social institutions operate?

The example cited in the text after this reference is the opinion poll, which in part serves to perpetuate society's need for opinion polls. We'd like to find another choice that's an example of this idea. (A) isn't perfect by any stretch, but it seems decent: The fashion magazine creates new trends, which perpetuates the need for fashion magazines. (B) doesn't seem to show anything perpetuating a need for itself. (C) describes a social institution uncovering a real problem, not creating a problem that it exists to solve. (D) talks about a change of opinions in response to other opinions, which doesn't seem to perpetuate any sort of need. (E) is very similar to (B). Although it isn't wonderful, (A) is the best choice we have to work with here.

6. **C** Specific: What does the passage say about Baudrillard?

(A) is, in a way, the opposite of what the passage says about Baudrillard: Signifiers are not only meaning, but reality itself. "Opinion" is a difficult word to evaluate in light of the information in this paragraph, so we should avoid (B) if we can. (E) actually isn't consistent with passage material; in Baudrillard's opinion, language has gone past the ability to influence reality and instead has become reality. (D) is difficult to evaluate. On the one hand, it seems similar to the ideas presented in the passage; on the other hand, it's difficult to say that the idea that language has become reality actually means that Baudrillard thinks reality doesn't exist. We should pick (C) because it is definitely mentioned in the passage: In the third paragraph, we learn that "Baudrillard identifies an evolution in the political economy of signs."

7. **A** General: What is the passage's primary purpose?

(A) is tough to pick here because it's difficult to call the passage material all an example of a single idea, but on the other hand you might argue that the whole thing is about the nature of language. (B) is definitely not it: Nothing is resolved in this passage. (C) also isn't it: The author doesn't step forward and criticize any of these ideas. There are no traditional beliefs affirmed here, so we should avoid (D). If it's hard to pick (A) because it seems to be talking only about one thing, then it's even harder to pick (E), since there are examples in the passage of more than one "radical approach." (A) is the best answer of the group, and is the one we have to pick.

21

Answers and Explanations to Practice Sections

CHAPTER 7

PRACTICE SECTION 1: ARGS

Page 96

1. **B** Strengthen

The point here is that the representative's proposed tax cuts will cause the economy to grow. The premises on which the conclusion is based are a little difficult to interpret. Basically, they boil down to a description of how corporate tax cuts result in economic growth. The upshot is that these tax cuts make more capital available in the marketplace. Keep in mind that the tax cuts mentioned in the conclusion aren't described as corporate tax cuts, although they are said to make more capital available in the marketplace. We'd like to strengthen the connection between the proposed tax cuts in the conclusion and the information given in the premises about how corporate tax cuts stimulate growth.

(A) This doesn't really help. Remember that we're looking to connect the tax cuts mentioned in the conclusion with what's known about how corporate tax cuts stimulate growth.

(B) Here's a pretty good answer. The original argument lets us know that the proposed cuts will make more capital available in the marketplace. This choice strengthens the connection between that result and the promised result of economic growth.

(C) Careful here. The original argument doesn't explicitly make a link between increased availability of capital and economic growth. Although this choice lets us know that the proposed cuts really would make more capital available, we're still missing the connection between that and the promised result.

(D) Since we don't know what kind of tax cuts are being proposed in the argument, this doesn't really help us support the conclusion.

(E) Again, since we can't be sure that the result of the particular cuts proposed will be to make companies more competitive, this doesn't really help the conclusion.

2. **E** Flaw

The conclusion here is that any person would benefit from a circuit-training program. We're told that any person would benefit from a training program that involves extensive periods of cardiovascular exercise, and that some circuit-training programs involve this kind of exercise. The problem with the argument is that the word "some" seems to get lost between the premises and the conclusion; although we're told that only some programs involve cardiovascular exercise, the argument concludes that all people would benefit from following any of them.

(A) The argument doesn't go this far. It doesn't claim that everyone will benefit to the same degree, just that everyone will benefit.

(B) This is exactly the opposite of the problem this argument has. It draws a more sweeping conclusion than the premises justify.

(C) The argument doesn't try to claim that this is the only way people can improve their health, just that everyone will benefit from following this sort of a program.

(D) Under the premises given in the argument, this actually isn't a problem. We're told that extensive periods of cardiovascular exercise will "increase the health of those who follow it." Since there's no qualification here that excludes people who are already following training programs from this benefit, this choice isn't a problem with the argument.

(E) Here's the answer we want. The "class" mentioned refers to circuit-training programs; the argument draws a conclusion about all of them on the basis of information that only applies to some of them.

3. **C** Infer

The passage material here concerns a test that's only capable of determining whether two people have a common ancestor. We're also told that Franz is Gregor's father, although the test is not capable of determining this fact. We want to choose an answer that has to be true, given this information.

(A)   We don't have enough information to be sure that this is true. In fact, we have no real basis on which to judge what it means for this test to be "properly administered."

(B)   We can't be sure that this is true. Although the information in the passage indicates that the test is able to determine that these two men had a male ancestor in common, it may not be able to make this specific conclusion.

(C)   This is the one we want. Certainly brothers have a male ancestor in common, and the passage indicates that the evidence in the case only supports the conclusion that the two men have a male ancestor in common.

(D)   We can't be certain that the information that Franz is Gregor's father is necessary in order for the case to be "properly considered," so we can't draw this conclusion.

(E)   Careful! Franz is the father out of the pair. It remains possible that Franz's full ancestry is included in the case, and yet the only conclusion supported by the evidence is that the two men have a male ancestor in common, since Gregor is not one of Franz's ancestors.

4. **E** ID Reasoning in Dinah's response

Tremaine's point is that he is not obligated to return any portion of his contract fee. He bases his conclusion on the fact that a fixed fee was agreed to without any requirement concerning the number of hours the project would take, and so it's irrelevant that he spent half as long as he'd initially estimated to complete the project. Dinah disagrees, and shows that, if the project had taken more time than his initial estimate, then he certainly would have asked for and received a higher fee. Evidently, Dinah intends to argue that Tremaine would not have relied on the same principle to justify his actions if the error had not been in his favor.

(A)   This is close, but the more you look at it, the worse it gets. It isn't the principle so much as Tremaine's likely consistency in using it that Dinah calls into question. Moreover, it doesn't appear that Dinah reserves judgment in Tremaine's specific case. She seems to think that he does need to return at least some portion of the money.

(B)   Dinah does make use of a hypothetical situation, but it doesn't support Tremaine's conclusion.

(C)   Like (A), this one seems decent, but it still is a little off. For one thing, Dinah never explicitly identifies the real reason Tremaine reaches the conclusion he does, and although she certainly shows that the principle he appeals to is not one he would likely apply in all cases, it isn't clear that Dinah is recommending that Tremaine follow some "ethical principle" instead.

(D)   Dinah does not resolve any of her own dilemmas in this one.

(E)   This is the closest available description of what Dinah is really saying. She isn't suggesting an alternative principle; she's saying that the one Tremaine is using isn't a good one to use in cases where the initial estimate of time involved for work is significantly different than the actual time involved.

5. **A** Resolve/Explain

The paradox here is that, although newer theories predict behavior better than Freudian ones, and the most successful therapies are based on theories that predict behavior well, nevertheless more individuals are successfully treated using therapies based on Freudian theories than on alternative theories. We want some explanation of why it is that the inferior theory is responsible for a greater number of successful cures.

(A) This does the job nicely. Even though the Freudian therapies may not be as successful, so many more people receive them that it isn't surprising they result in more cures than all other theories do.

(B) The fact that all theories are at least somewhat unreliable doesn't really explain why the less reliable of the unreliable theories should be responsible for more cures.

(C) This seems similar to (A), but it has more holes in it. For one thing, there may be subjective theories other than Freudian theories. For another, we don't know how many patients actually get a chance to select the treatment they receive. Finally, "a majority" isn't by itself enough to explain why so many more cures can be attributed to Freudian treatment. Any of these reasons is good enough to eliminate the choice.

(D) Again, this one seems to be pushing in the right direction, but it doesn't come right out and say the thing (A) does: that a lot more people get treatment based on Freudian theory.

(E) This choice just makes the paradox worse, and it doesn't give us base numbers. Avoid it.

6. **D** Assumption

The conclusion here is that a provocative style won't help readers understand a writer's feelings clearly. We have a pretty tangled mess of premises here. Basically, the support for the conclusion comes from the fact that readers are "most sympathetic" to writers who "convey experience simply." We want something that makes the link between these ideas in the premises and the conclusion's language of clearly understanding a writer's feelings.

(A) This goes far beyond the argument. The conclusion has to do with the effect of style on readers, not with any other personal reasons that a writer adopts a particular style.

(B) Close, but keep in mind that the conclusion concerns specifically the "provocative style" mentioned in the argument. The style mentioned in this choice is a side issue.

(C) This seems to be making some attempt at weakening the argument. Since our mission here is to identify an assumption, we should stay away from this one.

(D) Here's the one we have to pick. If we negate this one, it becomes a little easier to see why: If it's necessary for a reader to be exposed to idiosyncratic views in order for him or her to have sympathy for the writer, then the argument's reasoning breaks down. Certainly there's nothing else among the choices that's both within the scope of the argument and pointing in the right direction to be an assumption.

(E) This doesn't help the argument at all; best to avoid this one.

The point here is that leaders in a culture experiencing instability during transition would improve matters if they promoted adaptability as a value. As nonsensical as this sounds, we can at least look at its language in terms of the reasons supporting it, which say that instability can result from either changing social roles or ambiguity in economic class. The argument also includes a reason that explains why the idea of "adaptability" may be needed by individuals to address these potential sources of the problem. We'll need to focus on the language in working these questions.

7.　**C**　Assumption

We're looking for something that pertains to a gap between the possible causes of the instability (social or class confusion) and the idea that adaptability would help.

(A)　Since the conclusion pertains specifically to what the leaders should do, this one is somewhat close but not, most likely, close enough. After all, even if this choice isn't true, and adaptability has been traditionally viewed as a positive value, there could conceivably be some additional benefit to the leaders explicitly supporting that value. We want something that pertains more closely to the conclusion.

(B)　Even if this isn't true, and those things are reflected in language or daily habits, it nevertheless remains possible that there would be some benefit to the leaders promoting adaptability.

(C)　Here's the best choice of the group. If this isn't true—if having the leaders promote any value, including adaptability, represents an unacceptable redefinition of social roles—then the action recommended in this argument seems likely to increase instability, not decrease it. In order for the proposed solution to work, this choice definitely has to be true.

(D)　The argument doesn't specify that this solution can never be completely successful, so although the conclusion only talks about a course of action that could "mitigate" the effects of instability, it doesn't require the assumption that those effects could never be completely removed.

(E)　The nature of the new social roles that replace the old ones doesn't seem to apply directly to the conclusion. If you think hard, you can probably come up with a pretty involved defense of this choice but it is not clearly within the scope of the argument. Adaptability is required to handle the change from one system of social roles to the other, but the argument doesn't depend upon the new system of social roles being somehow looser than the old one. It might conceivably be more rigid, and yet adaptability could nevertheless be required for the transition.

8.　**B**　Parallel Flaw

We're looking for something that talks about two potential sources of a problem and proposes a single solution to handle the problem. It's worth looking more closely at what the flaw in the original actually is, and it can be difficult to pick out. A review of the language makes it clearer: The initial premise describes two ways a problem "can" arise, without stating that these are the only two ways it can arise. The argument then proposes a solution that could conceivably help deal with these possible sources, but may not deal with other potential sources of the same problem.

(A)　This one isn't parallel. The conclusion here doesn't propose a single way to deal with two potential sources of a problem; it proposes two separate ones.

(B)　This is the one we want; don't be thrown off by the fact that the order of statements here is different from that in the original. The two possible sources of a problem (perception of a school system as being ineffective) are identified: lack of creativity or leadership skills. One thing (extracurricular activities) can help deal with those two problems, so a leader should advocate for it. This is very close to the original, and does make the same mistake of leaving out other possible sources of the problem.

(C)　The pattern here isn't at all similar. Two possible solutions are presented, and the conclusion recommends adopting one or the other of them.

(D)　The pattern here is quite different. There doesn't appear to be much wrong with this argument, actually.

(E)　This one recommends one of two possible solutions in preference to the other. That isn't at all similar to the original argument.

9. **C** Main Point

We need to pick out the single thing that the argument is recommending. In this case, it's that the power that private companies and government ministries exert over health care choices needs to be reduced. The reasoning behind this recommendation, basically, is that increasing choice increases the quality of health care, and these organizations exert their power to limit choice. We want something that states the argument's main recommendation as clearly as possible.

(A) This doesn't have anything to do with limiting the power of organizations.

(B) This is certainly part of the argument's reasoning, but, like (A), it doesn't recommend limiting the power of organizations.

(C) Perfect. This is the best paraphrase of the argument's third sentence, which is the most direct statement of its main point.

(D) Again, this one doesn't mention limiting the power of organizations.

(E) This is far too strong, and it doesn't include any explicit statement of what the argument is recommending.

10. **B** Assumption

The conclusion here is that the reason some roundworms of this species do not burrow by wriggling is that they have a damaged version of the studied gene. The support for this contention is, basically, that roundworms with a damaged version of the gene are incapable of burrowing by wriggling. We want something that addresses the main possible weakness of this argument, which is that there may conceivably be other reasons the roundworms in question do not wriggle.

(A) If anything, this weakens the argument. That means it can't be an assumption.

(B) This is it. If there is some other gene that plays a key role in this behavior, then the argument's conclusion is no longer well supported.

(C) "All species of roundworms" are far beyond the scope of this argument, which concerns only one species.

(D) Careful. This seems similar to (B), but the difference has to do with the precise scope of the argument. The conclusion here talks about worms that use one kind of burrowing but not the other; even if one gene is required for both, it may nevertheless be true that those worms that can do one kind of burrowing but not the other do so because they have a problem with a gene that only controls one of the two kinds.

(E) This is a beautiful weaken. Unfortunately, the question asks us to identify an assumption.

11. **A** Strengthen

The point here is that many aquatic mammals descended from land mammals that grazed near water and gradually adapted to a marine environment. We're looking for a choice that provides further support for this explanation.

(A) This is a good answer. It presents one specific instance in which the evidence strongly suggests that an aquatic mammal and a land mammal are closely related. It doesn't give us a definite sense of which descended from which, and of course it remains possible that this is a stunning coincidence, so the evidence could be stronger. Still, it's the best of the group.

(B) This is much less direct evidence than (A). It leaves open the possibility that one of the viruses is descended from the other, but that the animals themselves are not closely related.

(C) This is much less direct evidence than (A). Nutritional requirements may conceivably be quite similar in animals that are not closely related.

(D) This is much less direct evidence than (A). In fact, these means of communication may be more remarkable for their differences than for their similarities.

(E) This is a similarity that has nothing, really, to do with whether the animals are directly related.

12. **D** Flaw

The conclusion here is that government reform advocates' statements about the prevalence of two beliefs about government are exaggerated. The evidence for this claim is a recent survey, which indicated that a minority of those surveyed held the beliefs. The most glaring problem here is that the group surveyed—members of unions that represent government workers—is definitely not representative of the population about which the conclusion is drawn. Hopefully we'll find a choice that talks about this problem.

(A) The problem with the argument is that the survey data don't necessarily represent the majority belief.

(B) Even the meaning of this one seems a little unclear. Certainly the problem isn't which of the survey questions the argument focuses on, but instead the nature of the survey group itself.

(C) The argument does fail to consider this fact, but this isn't the thing the argument does most conspicuously wrong.

(D) This is perfect. The argument itself says that its sample group isn't representative of the whole.

(E) It isn't clear that the argument really does assume this. More importantly, this doesn't address the identified problem with the survey group, whereas another of our answer choices does.

13. **D** Disagree

Hakim's point is that global warming doesn't pose a danger of extinction to humans. Among the many pieces of evidence offered in support of this claim are that humans have survived extreme climate change in the past, and the suggestion that overall warmer temperatures may benefit humans. Veronica's answer relates to Hakim's statement concerning crop yields. She indicates that, contrary to Hakim's suggestion, global warming is unlikely to lead to more fertile farming. We're looking for a choice that sticks as closely as possible to this precise disagreement between the two.

(A) Veronica doesn't register an explicit opinion on this question.

(B) Veronica doesn't register an explicit opinion on this question.

(C) Hakim doesn't register an explicit opinion on this question.

(D) This is the most exact statement of the substance of their disagreement. Hakim indicates that he believes global warming would increase crop yields; Veronica indicates that she believes it would not.

(E) Veronica doesn't claim that there would be no benefits to increased global temperatures, only that one specific benefit suggested by Hakim would not apply.

14. E Flaw

The point here is that lying to the government to save money on taxes is not ethically acceptable. The reasoning here is a little tricky: It describes one condition under which lying to the government for this purpose would be acceptable, then asserts that this condition does not apply. The argument leaves out a consideration of what other conditions might conceivably justify lying to the government to save money on taxes.

(A) Although the argument does mention ethics, the question here isn't what standard is applied, but whether the standards mentioned in the reasons actually lead to the conclusion. We're looking for a problem with the argument's reasoning.

(B) One of the argument's premises is that people do have the means available to them to modify tax laws through their elected representatives. Since it's a stated fact on which the conclusion is based, we can't argue with it.

(C) Close, but not quite. The argument does have, as one of its premises, a statement telling us that if some condition applies, then a certain state of affairs does exist. But the argument goes on to tell us that the condition doesn't apply, and concludes from that fact that the state of affairs doesn't exist. This answer choice reverses these two things in describing the argument's pattern.

(D) No, the argument doesn't demand that any ethical behavior must be conclusively shown to be so. We'd like a very specific statement of the argument's problem, which is that it leaves out a consideration of what other circumstances might allow the behavior in question to be considered ethical.

(E) This matches the pattern in the argument and also identifies its main problem. The argument concludes that, since one condition that would justify the behavior doesn't obtain, then the behavior is not justified.

15. C Parallel

This is a tough one. The core of the argument is simple: If every thing of type A has quality B, and if thing C is of type A, then thing C must have quality B. Thing C, however, doesn't have quality B. The conclusion of the argument is that one of the original premises must not hold: Either not every thing of type A has quality B, or thing C is not of type A. We're looking for another argument that's based around a simple argument, and whose conclusion is that one of that argument's premises must be false.

(A) One key premise in the original is that thing C doesn't have quality B. This choice includes instead a statement that tells us thing C (the historic site) isn't of type A (city park). This isn't parallel.

(B) The conclusion here isn't similar. Our original argument properly concludes that one or the other of the initial premises must be untrue; this choice concludes that both of them are untrue.

(C) This one is parallel. Type A is "walking trails in national parks," quality B is "receive adequate maintenance," and thing C is "this path."

(D) The conclusion here isn't similar. Our original argument properly concludes that one or the other of the initial premises must be untrue; this choice identifies one initial premise that must be untrue.

(E) The initial argument in this one isn't similar. It identifies two qualities that things of type A must have; our original only identifies one.

16. C Weaken

The conclusion here is that OPEC is to blame for the recent increase in energy costs. Basically, we're looking for some item of information that would tell us something other than OPEC and its ability to set market prices is to blame for increased energy costs.

(A) This actually strengthens the argument by showing one of the ways in which the market, as the argument says, "overreacts." Increases in crude oil prices, which the argument attributes to OPEC, are tied closely to increases in overall energy costs by this choice.

(B) This strengthens the argument by describing one way in which the market, as it says, "overreacts." The promise of increasing prices causes an increased demand.

(C) This is the best of the choices we have. It's the only one that indicates one way in which OPEC's decision to limit production is offset by the response of other participants in the market.

(D) This describes one way in which the market, as it says, "overreacts" by artificially keeping prices down, without saying who's responsible.

(E) This is very indirect, since it doesn't make any reference to OPEC's decision. It's too ambiguous to prove anything.

17. E Principle

We're asked to justify the judgment that Freddie didn't cheat the person from whom he bought a car. The basic story is that he purchased a significantly damaged rare car for a low price, invested some of his own money in restoring it, and then sold the restored car at a substantial profit.

(A) Careful. This one starts off sounding good because it talks about a buyer not cheating a seller, but we don't really know whether the condition talked about in this choice applies. It mentions the "true market value" of the product exchanged, but we don't know anything about the value of the car before it was restored.

(B) This one talks about a seller cheating a buyer. Nobody is accusing the seller of the car of cheating anyone in this case.

(C) Like (B), this one talks about a seller cheating a buyer. This isn't at all similar to the situation we're dealing with.

(D) Under this principle, the only conclusion we could draw is that Freddie might have cheated the person from whom he bought the car. That isn't consistent with the judgment in this case.

(E) Here it is. Since we do not know that Freddie had certain knowledge of another buyer who would have paid significantly more, Freddie did not cheat the person from whom he bought the car. This one justifies the argument's judgment.

18. **B** Role of the Statement

The point here is that people should buy their coffee from a locally owned coffee house rather than the large national chain. The reasoning that backs this up is a little involved. Basically, the chain uses its power to drive down market prices for coffee, which has negative consequences in itself, but the savings that result from this practice only increase the chain's profits, and aren't passed on as savings to the consumer. This last statement is the one whose role we're asked to identify; it's one of many reasons provided in support of the conclusion.

(A) The conclusion of the argument is that consumers shouldn't buy from the national chain.

(B) This is good. Although the choice doesn't specify that this is a reason not to buy from the national chain, it describes more specifically what the statement means: The chain's behavior in the market benefits the chain itself, not the consumer.

(C) This choice makes it sound like the statement in question might be seen as a reason why people should buy from the chain. It definitely isn't that.

(D) The fact that the national chain's coffee is a little cheaper doesn't really contradict the fact that their substantial savings on coffee prices contribute primarily to the chain's profits.

(E) "Overly emotional" is a judgment call that we shouldn't be too comfortable with, and we don't know that this statement also applies to locally owned coffee houses. Let's avoid this one.

19. **A** Fill-In

This is a tough argument. We have a rule: Friendship means putting a friend's needs above one's own, and putting one's preferences above a friend's need is definitely not friendship. The argument then raises the issue of one friend who doesn't attempt to address a friend's most obvious flaws. Although some believe that this is an example of a time when friends put their own comfort over a friend's need, the therapist evidently does not agree. We're looking for a statement that, hopefully, explains how the instance in question really is an illustration of friendship, according to the rule presented at the beginning of the argument.

(A) This does it, although the syntax is a bit tough. This does demonstrate how one friend overlooking another friend's most obvious faults is an illustration of the initial rule, which involves putting a friend's needs above one's own needs and preferences.

(B) This is backwards. This choice describes two instances in which a true friend, according to the rule specified in the argument, actually should try to help a friend overcome his or her faults.

(C) This isn't nearly as good as (A). After all, the argument indicates that one friend overlooking another's faults is not an instance in which the initial definition of friendship is broken. The argument definitely acknowledges that there can be cases in which one friend can overlook another's most obvious faults.

(D) The problem here is that the initial rule doesn't provide us any way of comparing a friend's preferences to the individual's needs. This isn't as well supported by the information in the argument as (A) is.

(E) The argument never states that a friend's most obvious faults don't need to be corrected—quite the opposite, in fact. It does say that some of these faults can't be corrected, and this is the key distinction that makes (A) the best answer here.

20. D Weaken

The conclusion here is that some people will eventually be forced to pay higher health insurance premiums because of risk factors over which they have no control. The premise here is that soon there will be tests that can identify genetic risk factors for illness. There are two major assumptions here: that people have no control over their own genes (which seems pretty reasonable as assumptions go), and that the health insurance companies will actually force people to pay in this instance. We're looking for something that casts doubt on the prediction.

(A)   This is extremely weak. One good way to eliminate this is to realize that, since the time frame in which this might be possible is indefinite, it remains possible that people will be forced to pay on the basis of their risk factors for all of the intervening time between when the tests can identify these factors and treatments can "reduce" them. Of course, "reduce" isn't the same thing as "eliminate," which is another reason to avoid this one.

(B)   This choice indicates that health insurers now don't necessarily charge higher premiums due to risk factors over which people do have control; it isn't certain what impact this has on the prediction that they may someday charge for risk factors that people cannot control.

(C)   This is nice, but it's irrelevant. The conclusion has to do with general risk; it doesn't pretend that health insurers need to be able to predict the precise likelihood of any individual developing disease.

(D)   This is good. Although it doesn't address genetics directly, it does indicate quite strongly that people currently aren't expected to pay higher premiums for things they can't control, and that companies are forbidden from making people pay higher premiums because of them. It seems reasonable, given these examples, that similar thinking would prevent companies from charging higher premiums because of genetics.

(E)   This solidifies the argument's assumption that people can't control their own genetics; this strengthens the argument, but the question asks us to weaken it.

21. E Strengthen

The conclusion is that some people who manage their time well are exceptionally brilliant. The question assures us that we need an additional item of information to make this conclusion work, but we have to look at our premises carefully to tell what's missing. We have one definite statement: hard worker $\rightarrow$ manage time well. We have two quantity statements: most successful students are hard workers (and thus manage their time well); some successful students are not exceptionally brilliant. Since the only statement we have that involves "exceptionally brilliant" is this last one, and the phrase also appears in the conclusion, we know our link is going to need to pertain to successful students somehow, in order to complete the chain from exceptionally brilliant people to those who can manage time well.

(A)   This is already a consequence of material we're given in the premises. Restating it doesn't help us reach the conclusion.

(B)   This gives us further information about the larger group of hard workers. Unfortunately, this still doesn't provide the needed link to "exceptionally brilliant."

(C)   This is already a consequence of material we're given in the premises. Restating it doesn't help us reach the conclusion.

(D)   This gives us further information that allows us to conclude, along with information in the premises, that the group of hard workers is identical to the group of those who manage their time well. Unfortunately, this still doesn't provide the needed link to those who are "exceptionally brilliant."

(E)   Here it is. This doesn't contradict information in the premises—even if most successful students are exceptionally brilliant, it remains true that some of them aren't. What it does do is let us know that, since most successful students are exceptionally brilliant, and most of them are hard workers, then there must be some people who are both exceptionally brilliant and hard workers. Since hard workers all manage their time well, we know there are some people who are exceptionally brilliant and who manage their time well. This does what we need it to do.

22. **C** Infer

We have many definite statements here, and one that is qualified. Here are the definite ones:

scientific medical treatment → rigorously tested and more effective than placebo

scientific medical treatment → – traditional medical treatment

shown to be safe → scientific medical treatment

more effective than placebo → – rejected as viable treatment

The qualified statement is that many traditional medical treatments both have not been rigorously tested and are not more effective than a placebo. It's important to note that this means there may be some traditional treatments that have both of these qualities, or either one of them alone. There are a lot of possible inferences here; we're looking for the one that's not only consistent with all of our statements, but can be definitely concluded from them.

(A) We only know that "many" traditional medical treatments lack both of the attributes; it remains possible that some traditional medical treatments both have been rigorously tested and are more effective than a placebo.

(B) This contradicts passage material. All scientific medical treatments are more effective than a placebo.

(C) This does the trick. Following the conditionals in the passage, we can see that a medical treatment that has been conclusively shown to be safe must be a scientific medical treatment; being a scientific medical treatment, we know that it's more effective than a placebo; since it's more effective than a placebo, it shouldn't be rejected as a viable treatment option. This is completely consistent with the passage.

(D) It remains possible that some traditional medical treatments that haven't been rigorously tested are more effective than a placebo, and therefore should not be rejected as viable treatment options.

(E) It remains possible that some traditional medical treatments are more effective than a placebo, and therefore shouldn't be rejected as viable treatment options.

23. **D** Disagree

Legislator A's point is that, assuming the legislature should act on the question, legislator A's bill should be approved. The reason for this is that the legislature has a responsibility to ensure water is free of harmful chemicals, and the bill in question would do that. Don't forget the stipulation in legislator A's conclusion. Legislator B invokes a second responsibility of the legislature, and uses it to defend the contention that legislator A's bill should not be approved. We want a choice that describes something about which these two definitely disagree.

(A) Neither participant in the conversation—not even A—registers a definite opinion on whether or not the legislature should act on this question during this term.

(B) Keep in mind that, although the two legislators refer to different responsibilities, neither claims that this is their only responsibility. We don't know for certain what A thinks about the responsibility mentioned here, which is the one B employs.

(C) We know B thinks this would happen, but we don't know what A would say about it.

(D) Here's our answer. A agrees with this statement; B disagrees with it.

(E) Nobody appears to disagree with this statement.

24. D Infer Variant: Could Be True Except

We have a description of a type of plant, and a chain of two necessary conditions. Some plants, we're told, grow more quickly in high-nitrogen environments. The necessary condition for this is that they fix nitrogen. The necessary condition for fixing nitrogen is having one of a few varieties of symbiotic bacteria. We're looking for four choices that could be true under these circumstances, and one that definitely could not.

(A) This could be true. Since the conditions involved are necessary ones, it remains possible that a plant with symbiotic bacteria in its roots is incapable of fixing nitrogen.

(B) This could be true. Although the passage lets us know that a few varieties of symbiotic bacteria will do, it may be that the majority of plants that can fix nitrogen have the same kind of bacteria.

(C) This could be true. Again, since the conditions described are all necessary ones, it's possible that a nitrogen-fixing plant may grow more slowly in a high-nitrogen environment. All we know is that all the plants that grow more quickly must be able to fix nitrogen.

(D) Here's our answer. One of our necessary conditions is that the plant must harbor these bacteria in its roots; if it harbors them only in its leaves, then it can't fix nitrogen.

(E) Since the alternative mix isn't specified, this could be true. The only possibility we could exclude is that the plants mentioned in this choice grow more quickly in the high-nitrogen environments mentioned in the passage; other mixes of gases aren't discussed.

25. B Weaken

The conclusion here is that ethanol fuel reformers should be used to make hydrogen for fuel cells. Basically, the reasoning describes two basic methods of making hydrogen: either producing it from liquid compounds (including, but not limited to, ethanol) with a reformer in the car itself, or else producing it from seawater in power plants and then distributing hydrogen in gaseous form. Doing it through electrolysis, however, is more dangerous. The only apparent hole in this argument isn't an obvious one; there is a difference between the explanation in the premises of what materials can be used in a fuel reformer and the conclusion that ethanol must be used. Hopefully, our right answer will present another alternative.

(A) This identifies a greater risk of using liquid ethanol compared to gasoline, but it doesn't give us information about its risk relative to gaseous hydrogen. Since the argument relies on the fact that gaseous hydrogen is more dangerous than ethanol, this doesn't tell us enough to weaken that contention.

(B) This does the trick. It doesn't try to show that gaseous hydrogen would be a better choice than ethanol reformers; instead, it cites another possibility that doesn't have the drawback ethanol reformers do and is safe.

(C) All this does is make electrolysis seem like even less of a good idea. This doesn't weaken the conclusion.

(D) This goes far beyond the issue in the argument, which is what method to use in making hydrogen for fuel cells. Whether fuel cells themselves are a good idea is not the question here.

(E) Like (C), this one just runs down electrolysis. We want to weaken the argument, not strengthen it.

CHAPTER 8

PRACTICE SECTION 2: ARGS
Page 110

1. **E** Weaken

    The conclusion here is that conservation efforts should be halted because they are harming ecosystems. The main evidence of this claim is that lakes where conservation efforts have been in effect have fewer fish and less vegetation than lakes where they have not. We're looking for a choice that tells us that these changes aren't necessarily bad things that must be stopped.

    (A) This doesn't give us information one way or the other about whether the change in the lakes' condition is bad. At best, this answer choice would strengthen the conclusion by showing that the proposed solution would solve the perceived problem.

    (B) Although this gives us further information about what the conservation efforts are doing, it doesn't indicate one way or the other whether the conservation efforts are doing harm.

    (C) This is a very weak weaken. It indicates that the fish situation, in at least some cases, is temporary. We're hoping for something that attacks the conclusion more strongly.

    (D) Fishing and recreational activities are nice, but they don't pertain directly to the health of the ecosystems in question.

    (E) This is the one we want. It explains that the evidence provided actually indicates that the conservation efforts are helping, not hurting. This weakens the conclusion.

Questions 2–3

Joe's conclusion is that critics of the dietary supplement industry ought to be ignored because they are acting in the interest of the pharmaceutical industry. It's unclear in Joe's reasoning how the pharmaceutical companies come in, but the rest of Joe's reasoning involves a comparison of dietary supplements to multivitamins, and the fact that the critics' objections apply equally to them, and yet the critics do not object to the way they are regulated.

Sarah responds that supplements ought to be regulated because they, unlike multivitamins, may be harmful. She raises a relevant difference between the two cases that are treated by Joe as being similar.

2. **A** Point-at-Issue

    There are two questions on which Joe and Sarah definitely disagree: whether multivitamins and dietary supplements are similar in all important respects, and whether dietary supplements ought to be regulated. We're looking for something relating to these disagreements.

    (A) Here it is. Joe believes that government regulation isn't warranted; Sarah believes that it is.

    (B) Sarah never registers an opinion on this subject.

    (C) Sarah certainly never registers an opinion on this subject, and it's not clear that Joe does, either.

    (D) Joe doesn't argue for the efficacy of the products, and Sarah only indicates that they may not be effective. We don't have direct-enough statements in the arguments to be sure that they disagree on this question.

    (E) Joe offers no statement that has anything to do with this question.

3. **E** ID Sarah's reasoning

As mentioned above, Sarah's response identifies a difference between multivitamins and dietary supplements, while Joe's argument relies on the assumption that they are similar in relevant ways.

(A) This is not an assumption of Joe's argument; safety isn't an issue for Joe at all.

(B) Sarah never registers an opinion on Joe's claim that the critics are serving the interests of the pharmaceutical industry.

(C) Tough to parse, but this certainly isn't what Sarah does; she doesn't attribute any contradictory claims to the makers of dietary supplements.

(D) It's too strong to say that what Sarah is identifying is "an internal inconsistency." She merely indicates that one of Joe's key assumptions is false.

(E) This is the one we want. You may have to consult the original arguments to verify that Sarah treats multivitamins and "the dietary supplements that are the subject of the current controversy" as both being dietary supplements, but this turns out to be an accurate enough reflection of her argument.

4. **C** Flaw

The conclusion is that video games do not cause attention deficit. The only real support for this claim is that only a licensed psychiatrist can tell whether or not a video game has caused attention deficit in a given case, and no licensed psychiatrist has testified. This is an absence-of-evidence problem: Just because, by the argument's standard, the opponents haven't proven that the video games caused attention deficit in the cases discussed, it concludes that the video games must not have caused it.

(A) The motives of the parents are never mentioned.

(B) Other harmful effects of video games aren't relevant to the conclusion, so this isn't a problem.

(C) This is the answer. A closer inspection of the premises reveals why: Not only does the argument have an absence-of-evidence problem, but its own standard insists that only a licensed psychiatrist can determine "whether or not" video games are responsible; since the argument doesn't include a determination by a licensed psychiatrist that the video games were *not* responsible, the conclusion isn't supported.

(D) Other positive effects of video games aren't relevant to the conclusion.

(E) This word appears to be used consistently throughout the argument.

5. **D** Resolve/Explain

The paradox here is that, although the shells at sites A and B exhibit differences that might be the result of different ways the shells were used, the archaeologists have concluded that the shells at both sites were not used as currency. The only alternative use described for the shells is for making ornamental necklaces that indicated high social status, although it's conceivable that the shells might have been used in some way that isn't described.

(A) This makes the paradox worse, not better. This fact would seem to indicate that the shells at site B likely were used as currency.

(B) This would explain the difference in the size of the holes in each, but since it doesn't relate to the way the shells were used, this doesn't really help explain the paradox we've identified.

(C) This helps with the archaeologists' conclusions about site B, but it doesn't pertain to site A. We want something better.

(D) This is the best answer we have. Although it doesn't address the different sizes of the holes, it does explain away the main fact that seems to suggest the shells were used as ornaments at site A but currency at site B, which is the amount of wear and tear on the shells themselves. This answer choice indicates very strongly that the shells were used for ornamental purposes at both sites.

(E) This choice doesn't have any clear relevance to the two sites described, so we should avoid it.

6. **E** Infer

This is a fairly intricate one. It basically concerns two potential explanations of why codes of polite behavior exist: either to indicate subjection to community standards, or else to reduce conflict and ensure the society's smooth functioning. The passage identifies the second as the true reason and supplies the example of drawing attention to impolite behavior to reinforce this conclusion. Remember that, since this is an inference question, we have to treat all of these statements as absolute truth, and find a statement that follows from them.

(A) This is too strong. Although the purpose of polite behavior is to minimize conflict, the passage doesn't insist that absolutely every behavior that might create conflict is considered impolite.

(B) This is a blender answer. If anything, this would seem to contradict certain claims in the original passage.

(C) This seems to take the wrong point of view about polite behaviors. Indicating subjection to community power is not the purpose that the passage identifies as primary in explaining codes of polite behavior.

(D) This is another very strong statement. We certainly don't have enough evidence in hand to conclude this.

(E) Here's the one we want. This is a strong statement, but the key difference is that it's supported by strong statements in the passage. We're told that drawing attention to impolite behavior isn't considered polite in any society, and it's a reasonable paraphrase of passage information to relate "polite behavior" to "community standards." This is the best answer we have to work with.

7. **A** Assumption

The conclusion here is that, within the next decade, fusion reactors will be able to produce more energy than their operation consumes. The evidence for this conclusion relies on two points in time: Ten years ago, the energy demands for containing a fusion reaction were nearly 20 percent; now, it's less than 10 percent. There are two major gaps here. First, the argument neglects energy requirements other than those associated with containment of the reaction; second, it assumes that the pace of future progress will be similar to that over the past ten years. We want a choice that relates to either of these problems.

(A) Here's the right one, although it can be a little difficult to interpret. Suppose this isn't true, and the excess energy requirement *is* halved every decade. Then, in another ten years, the excess energy requirement will still be 5 percent, and the conclusion would be untrue.

(B) The argument doesn't claim that fusion will become a "viable source of power" in ten years, so this isn't relevant to the conclusion.

(C) This choice pertains to fission reactors, not fusion reactors, and therefore isn't clearly relevant.

(D) Careful! This sounds good, but on a second look it insists on a little too much. If the future rate of improvement does "differ" from the past rate, then it's only a problem for the conclusion if that difference slows improvement. If the rate of improvement differs by speeding up, then the conclusion would still be correct.

(E) This choice relates to the gap mentioned above: that the argument's evidence only deals with the energy required to contain the reaction. We need to remember, though, that this is an assumption question, and assumptions always help the conclusion. This choice certainly does not, so we shouldn't pick it.

8. **E** Flaw

This is a classic *ad hominem* argument. The conclusion is that the book's recommendations aren't to be taken seriously, and the support for this claim is that the book's author doesn't appear to be following them. This argument attacks the individual making an argument without considering the argument itself.

(A) The argument here isn't trying to say that the author by himself is responsible for environmental disaster, only that the author's behavior should lead us to reject his recommendations.

(B) This is far beyond the scope of the argument, which only has to do with the author and his behavior.

(C) Like (B), this one goes far outside the scope of the argument.

(D) This reduplicates the problem of the argument itself by trying to attack the critic personally. It's funny, but it definitely isn't right.

(E) Here's the best choice. What the author himself does is not relevant to the validity of his recommendations.

9. **C** Principle

The conclusion here is that the politician should grant an exclusive interview to a prominent reporter for the next bill, so that the bill gains broad popular support. The only evidence offered in support of this request is that the politician did the same thing on the last bill the politician introduced, and as a result the bill gained broad popular support. We're looking for something that supports the conclusion.

(A) Close, but this one specifies that it needs to be the "same reporter." This isn't exactly consistent with the conclusion.

(B) This necessary condition would indicate a way to provide the possibility that the bill will gain broad popular support, but it can't provide a guarantee. This doesn't support a conclusion as strong as this argument's conclusion.

(C) Here's the right answer. This matches the argument as closely as possible.

(D) Actually, this is a fact already assumed by the premises in the argument, so stating it again doesn't provide any further support.

(E) This is a side issue, and since it doesn't have anything to do with the support a bill gains, it's certainly not as good as other choices we have to work with.

10. **B** Fill-In

We're given two basic facts to combine here: (1) reliable business systems both increase a business's success and reduce reliance on individual initiative; (2) worker satisfaction depends on the perception that individual initiative is essential to a business's success. Clearly, the thing we're looking for here is some statement that reliable business systems decrease worker satisfaction.

(A) This directly contradicts one of the premises we're given to work with.

(B) Here it is. This is even better than what we were looking for, because it includes the possibility that workers might be led to believe that their individual initiative is more important to the business's success than it actually is.

(C) "Counterproductive" is a value judgment that isn't strictly supported by the information we have to work with, so let's avoid this one.

(D) This seems more or less in line with the material in the argument, but given the other choices we have here, it seems a bit too specific. We don't know that whatever problems are associated with decreased worker satisfaction "did not exist" before.

(E) This is far too strong a statement to be supported by the information we have to work with.

11. **D** Flaw

The conclusion is that a nation whose security is improving must have made expensive improvements in its capacity to collect and analyze information about its citizens. The main reason that supposedly supports this conclusion is that any time a nation does make such improvements, its security increases. This is a classic misinterpretation of a sufficient condition; although these improvements definitely result in an increase in security, they may not be the *only* way in which such increases can be accomplished. We need to throw into the mix the argument's opening statement, which indicates it is necessary to "maintain" information-gathering capacity to be secure. This isn't very strongly related to the conclusion, but it is information we may need to consult in evaluating the choices.

(A) Given the information in the argument's premises, this isn't possible, so it can't be a problem with the argument.

(B) Whether it's possible for every nation to make the expensive improvements mentioned isn't relevant to the conclusion in this argument.

(C) Given the information in the argument's premises, this isn't possible, so it can't be a problem with the argument.

(D) This is the one that points to the gap we identified. Just because expensive improvements definitely improve security, we can't conclude that this is the only way to improve security.

(E) Inexpensive improvements are not explicitly covered by the premises or mentioned in the conclusion, so we can't really determine the impact of this fact on the argument.

12. **C** ID Cho's reasoning

Goldfarb's conclusion is that tannic acid must have been known in ancient times to stop bleeding. The only evidence offered in support of this fact is that an ancient and widely used poultice included tea leaves, which contain tannic acid. There are a lot of holes here. Cho attacks one of Goldfarb's assumptions by identifying a different ingredient of the poultice that actually makes it harder to stop bleeding. Since Goldfarb's interpretation of the evidence relies on the idea that this poultice's purpose was to stop bleeding, Cho's evidence casts a good deal of doubt on Goldfarb's conclusion.

(A) Careful! Cho doesn't even concede that the intended effect of the poultice was to stop bleeding; in fact, it makes it seem less likely that this was the poultice's intended purpose.

(B) This certainly would have been a great way to attack Goldfarb's argument, but it's not the one Cho uses.

(C) Here's the one we want. The assumption in question is that the poultice served to stop bleeding.

(D) Cho never claims that Goldfarb is mistaken in saying that tea leaves were an ingredient in the poultice, which is the only real evidence Goldfarb offers.

(E) Cho's mention of tree ear isn't intended to identify a constituent that was believed to have been responsible for the poultice's clotting effect; it casts doubt on the fact that the poultice's purpose was to stop bleeding.

13. **A** Strengthen EXCEPT

The point here is that the system used to pay prominent film actors is unfair. The system in question is one which pays an actor a fixed amount for working in a film but does not give actors a set share of the film's total earnings. The argument points out that successful films earn substantial revenues after they have left theaters. One major assumption we'll have to keep track of here is that the fixed compensation actors usually receive doesn't take those future earnings into account. We're looking for four choices that reinforce the conclusion.

(A) This is the one we should pick. All five of the answer choices seem to be trying to strengthen, but this is the worst of the group. As was mentioned above, the argument never guarantees us that current compensation of actors doesn't take future earnings into account. This is the only choice that doesn't address that assumption in any way.

(B) This strengthens by indicating that these other future revenues are actually not taken into account in deciding how much to pay actors.

(C) This strengthens by showing that the risks to actors associated with paying them on the basis of the film's overall revenue would be small.

(D) This strengthens by directly stating the unfairness of the fact that the payment is fixed. If this is true, then actors definitely should receive a share of revenues.

(E) This strengthens by showing that the current compensation system is indeed unfair; over time, actors have been paid a smaller and smaller share of the film's total revenues.

14. **D** Assumption

The point here is that the agency has not yet used the special surveillance powers contained in the new law. There are two main premises here: The law requires the agency to inform a legislative committee when these powers are used, and the agency has not informed the legislative committee of any such use. The main assumption here appears to be that the agency has followed the law's requirements, although there may conceivably be others.

(A) This choice mentions approval, but the only thing we know about the law is that it requires the agency to inform the legislative committee. This goes beyond the material in the argument.

(B) Suspects in other investigations are not within the scope of this argument.

(C) We're told in the argument that this law has been found to be constitutional, so we wouldn't need further reinforcement of this fact even if it were relevant to the conclusion, which it isn't.

(D) Here's the right one. An assumption of the argument we didn't initially identify concerns the time at which the agency must inform the legislative committee. All we know is that they must do so "each time." But there's no guarantee that they have to do so *before* the surveillance actually commences.

(E) Other powers granted in the same law aren't relevant to the conclusion.

15. **C** Resolve/Explain EXCEPT

We're asked to explain why, even though most people don't pursue liberal arts degrees with professional goals in mind, the top managers and executives at successful companies covered by a particular survey showed an overwhelming majority of people with degrees in liberal arts. Four of the choices will explain this fact; the other one is our answer.

(A) This explains well enough. Even though their intent in pursuing a liberal arts degree is not preparation for a profession, that turns out to be a fringe benefit of doing so.

(B) This explains by showing that the overwhelming majority among managers and executives is consistent with an overwhelming majority in the population overall.

(C) Here's our answer. This actually makes the paradox worse; it makes it seem even less likely that there should be so many people with liberal arts degrees in the survey group.

(D) This explains a feature of the survey that would explain why so many people with liberal arts backgrounds should be found in the top levels of the surveyed companies.

(E) This explains by demonstrating that the characteristics of those who pursue liberal arts degrees are also the characteristics that are required to succeed in the companies surveyed.

16. **C** Main point

The scientist's argument basically turns on two facts: First, public support for the space agency is greatest when the space agency mounts manned missions; second, the space agency's primary purpose is discovery, and for a given amount of money, the space agency can mount many more unmanned missions than manned missions. The point here is that, although public support for the space agency is declining, this decline is the result of the space agency's effort to fulfill its primary purpose. We want a choice that's consistent with this.

(A)   This is an overstatement. The argument says that the critics are right.

(B)   This is the reverse of the evident reasoning in the argument. It certainly isn't the point the argument is trying to convey.

(C)   Here it is. This is the choice that puts together all the major pieces of the argument in a way that's consistent with the original.

(D)   This is related to a principle the argument uses, but it isn't the conclusion that the argument draws.

(E)   This isn't a judgment the argument makes; it simply points out that unmanned missions are cheaper than manned missions.

17. **D** Principle

The point here is that the environmental groups' criticisms are ridiculous. Environmental groups opposed the ruling party, whereas industry supported it. It is only natural, according to the argument, that the ruling party would consult its allies, not its enemies, in formulating policy. We're looking for something that's broadly consistent with this reasoning.

(A)   The standard employed by the argument is one that has to do with support or opposition, not whether or not they share interests in common. This doesn't really match the argument.

(B)   This is close, but it doesn't include any mention of support or opposition. We'd like something better if it's available.

(C)   This is pretty good. The thing that seems a little off about this one is the idea of groups whose interests "directly conflict," which we're not really sure about. Also, no mention is made of whether the new policy formulated could be valid. If there's nothing better, though, this wouldn't be a bad answer.

(D)   This is even better than (C). This includes both the ideas of support and opposition, it includes a softer statement of the conflicting interests between the groups, and by using the word "illegitimately," it gets back to the main point of the argument: that environmental groups' claims don't prove that the ruling party has done anything wrong. This is the closest available answer.

(E)   This one is broadly consistent with the argument. But it includes no mention of supporters and no explicit mention of whether or not the ruling party's actions were legitimate. Like (C), no mention is made of whether the new policy formulated could be valid. And, like (C), it's close but not as good as another choice we have.

18. **D** Strengthen

The conclusion here is that the majority of statements identified as lies by the Lariat will be statements the subject believes to be false. There are two main reasons for this: The Lariat correctly identifies 99 percent of statements the subject believes to be false as lies; the Lariat incorrectly identifies only 5 percent of statements the subject does not believe to be false as lies. In order for this conclusion to be correct, we need to know something about the number of statements of each kind the subject makes in the interview. After all, if a subject makes 100 statements, all of which the subject does not believe to be false, then this conclusion would not be correct; it would identify 5 statements as lies, when in fact none of them are. We need a choice that tells us the subject will tell enough lies to guarantee that the conclusion works.

(A) This is exactly backwards. If this is true, then the conclusion becomes less likely to be correct.

(B) It's difficult to tell how this fact would impact the conclusion. It seems that these would be considered statements that the subject does not believe to be false; although that helps the conclusion a little bit, its impact is very weak.

(C) Whether the statements are actually true or false isn't at all relevant to the argument, which deals only with the subject's beliefs about the falsehood of statements.

(D) This is the one we want. It's extreme, but it certainly would guarantee the truth of the conclusion; if every statement is a lie, then it's completely certain that all the answers the Lariat identifies as lies will in fact be lies.

(E) Like (C), this choice has to do with actual truth or falsehood, which isn't relevant to the argument.

19. **D** Flaw EXCEPT

The conclusion here is that Flizerite balls are best for every golfer who wants to shoot a better score. This conclusion is based on one extremely specific item of information: Ten top golfers playing very tough courses hit longer tee shots with Flizerite balls. There are a lot of potential holes here, having to do with the skill of the golfers, the difficulty of the courses, and the connection between tee shots and scores. We're looking for four choices that exploit these holes; the remaining one will be our answer.

(A) Here's one we didn't identify above, but it's definitely a flaw. Even if we accept that the survey demonstrates what the golf pro thinks it does, it's still possible that some ball is better than any of the six balls that were used in the survey.

(B) This identifies the gap between the top golfers and every golfer.

(C) This identifies the gap between challenging courses and all other courses.

(D) Here's our answer. The argument doesn't mention other factors, but it doesn't try to say that the choice of golf ball is the only important factor; it merely asserts that Flizerite is the best choice of golf ball for improving scores.

(E) This identifies the gap between long tee shots and overall golf score.

20. E Assumption

The conclusion here is that college students who complain their programs are too regimented need not worry because that regimentation won't always apply to their college study. The reasons behind this are, basically, that pursuit of advanced knowledge requires freedom, but before you can pursue advanced knowledge, you have to acquire a broad familiarity that can't be obtained without at least some regimentation. The argument actually seems pretty good, so we want to focus on the fact that the argument makes a prediction and see if we can find a choice that relates to that prediction specifically.

(A) Since an assumption must always help the argument's conclusion, this one doesn't even have a chance.

(B) The argument says that pursuit of advanced knowledge requires freedom, but it doesn't make a strict demand that increases in knowledge always be accompanied by increases in freedom step-by-step. This one's a bit too specific for this argument.

(C) This is backwards from one of the premises of the argument, which says that in order to gain broad familiarity, a student's freedom must be somewhat limited.

(D) High school students aren't relevant to this argument.

(E) Here's our answer. If there's some academic area where the learning task is too great for a college student, then the conclusion of the argument isn't right; there may be some college students whose programs are always regimented. This has a direct impact on the argument's prediction.

21. B Weaken

The conclusion here is that professional advice doesn't help individual investors make more money. The premises basically show that it's possible to make lots of money without professional advice, and that it's possible to lose lots of money with it. There are lots of potential problems here. For one thing, the conclusion is a comparative statement ("more money"), whereas the premises all talk about raw amounts, not comparisons. Also, there's a real question about how many people make lots of money on their own, and how many people lose money with the advice. The argument is so bad that there might conceivably be other weaknesses not mentioned here.

(A) This is not a very strong attack. If "many" are professionals themselves, then there are still some who aren't, and the force of the evidence is only a little reduced. We'd like a stronger answer.

(B) This is the right answer, although it isn't a weakness we initially identified. This choice relies on things that are left out of the reasoning. For one thing, making "more money" depends not only on the return on the investment, but also on costs associated with that return. In fact, the initial argument includes a language shift—"professional advice" in the conclusion, "investment professionals" in the premises—that shows us professionals such as accountants or tax advisors are also covered by the conclusion. The best thing about this choice, though, is that it is comparative: It uses the word "minimize."

(C) "No lower" is a very weak statement. We'd like to find a stronger attack.

(D) If anything, this strengthens the argument.

(E) It isn't clear what impact this has. If it has one, it marginally strengthens the conclusion.

22. **C** Evaluate

The conclusion is that these recent finds contradict the widely held belief that ancient humans were smaller and did not live as long as modern humans. These finds show some ancient hunters who had arm bones that are as long as modern humans' arm bones, and show wear patterns similar to those associated with elderly humans in modern times. The answers all involve a "whether": If the statement goes one way, it should weaken the conclusion; if it goes the other way, it should strengthen.

(A)   The conclusion doesn't really concern all humans in those settlements; it merely says that this evidence shows that not all ancient humans were smaller and lived shorter lives than modern humans do.

(B)   Diet is a bit of a red herring here. Although this is identified as a reason why ancient humans were smaller and did not live as long, the real focus of this argument is what the find of arm bones tells us.

(C)   Here's the best answer. If they could create such wear patterns, then the evidence isn't nearly as good as the argument believes; if they couldn't, then the conclusion would be strengthened.

(D)   Like (B), this one sends us off down the diet road. The main focus here is the archaeological find and what it tells us about the size and longevity of the humans whose bones were found.

(E)   Like (B) and (D), this one deals with diet. The argument concerns the connection between the bones and the size and age of the individuals whose bones they were.

23. **D** Principle

There are two principles working here: First, we get one that provides a condition that's sufficient to show that a violation of the law constitutes an act of civil disobedience; second, we get a condition that's necessary in order for an act of civil disobedience to be justified. We're looking for the choice that correctly uses each of these conditions.

(A)   Under our principle, there is at least one act of civil disobedience here, and possibly two. The question is irrelevant, though, since Ronaldo's failure to pay the fine associated with his first violation of the law fails the requirement for an act of civil disobedience to be justified.

(B)   This is a blender answer. For one thing, we don't have a principle that could tell us a given violation of the law *isn't* an act of civil disobedience; for another, we don't have a principle that would allow us to conclude that any violation of the law is justified.

(C)   Careful! For one thing, Horace's violation of the law doesn't fit the condition sufficient to call it civil disobedience. Even more importantly, realize that our necessary condition will never allow us to conclude that an act of civil disobedience is justified: It's only a minimum requirement, which means that the only conclusion we can draw is that an act isn't justified when it doesn't fit the requirement.

(D)   This is the one we want. Lucy did commit an act of civil disobedience: She violated the law to demonstrate that it was unjust. Lucy did attempt to escape the punishment mandated for her act; therefore, her act of civil disobedience was not justified. This uses both principles correctly.

(E)   Like (C), this one concludes that an act of civil disobedience was justified. Since our necessary condition can never allow us to draw such a conclusion, this one isn't supported by the principles we have to work with.

24. **E** Parallel

This is a tough one. The conclusion here is that a theory is not a fact, and it's not an opinion; the reasons are that no opinion can be shown to be false, and no fact can be false at all. In other words, the whole reasoning depends on the fact that a theory may be proven false. We're looking for a choice that's similar: one with a double conclusion that relies on a single fact about the term or idea in question.

(A) It seems close, but this doesn't quite get it. You might say that the central fact here is "a debate can be decided by a matter of fact," but this doesn't closely match our second premise—that disputes arise from differences of opinion. The difference between "be decided by" and "arise from" is enough to disqualify this one.

(B) If we try to put together the central fact here—a mistake can result in negative consequences—once again we encounter problems with the second premise, which involves the idea of intention.

(C) This one is nonsense. Although both premises have to do with future events, it isn't clear at all what relationship a description can or cannot have with future events. We'd like something much closer than this.

(D) If we try to put together the central fact here—an exclamation may not express an idea—then we see that this doesn't necessarily create a conflict in the second premise. With this central fact in mind, it remains possible that an exclamation is a question.

(E) Here, at last, is our answer. The central fact here is that a portrait can be criticized for failing to portray its subject accurately. That means it isn't a cartoon, and since it's impossible for a snapshot not to portray its subject accurately in the first place, it isn't a snapshot either. This is the best of the five choices we have.

25. **E** Infer

Lots of pieces at play here. We have information about what makes a decision just (made on the basis of both relevant facts and ethical principles), versus what makes it reasonable (supported by some form of explanation). This information is applied to the president's policy decisions: They are always reasonable, but not always just. These decisions can be predicted very often without knowing all of the facts relevant to them. Remember that, even though this sounds like an argument, we're working an inference question; for the purposes of this question, we must accept every one of these statements as true.

(A) This is a bit too strong. It's true that this is along the lines of the passage's reasoning, but it identifies a particular decision as being unjust. The passage merely says that, out of a group of decisions, it's likely that at least some of them are not just.

(B) This might be true, but we don't know it for certain.

(C) Like (A), this one goes a bit far. The passage talks about evaluating decisions as a group, and about the likelihood that at least some of the decisions are unjust. This one presents an absolute standard.

(D) Oh, careful! This seems very much like the argument, but once again we have some strong language here. The passage talks about just decisions needing to be made both on the basis of facts and on the basis of ethical principles; this choice talks about decisions made "solely on the basis of [relevant] facts." This is just a tad too strong.

(E) This is the one we should pick. It deals just with the opening statements—the characterizations of reasonable versus just decisions. A decision made on the basis only of ethical principles is definitely not just; however, since those principles serve as an explanation of the decision, the decision is reasonable. This is entirely consistent with the passage.

CHAPTER 14

PRACTICE SECTION 3: GAMES

Page 172

Note: All explanations in this section appear in the order in which you should have tackled the questions, based on difficulty level.

<u>Game 1</u>

m n o p s t v

		1	2
[m s]	D	m/p _ _ _ _ _ (or less)	p/m _ (or more)
[t v]	2	m/p _ _ _	p/m o n
$n_1 \rightarrow o_1$	3	p t v o	m s n
$o_2 \rightarrow n_2$	4	p	m s n o t v
	5i	p t v n o	m s
	5ii	m s t v o	p n

Setting it up: This is a straightforward two-group diagram, with our seven types of flowers as the elements. Don't be fooled by the conditional phrasing of clues 2 through 4; since each of them applies to the two groups equally, each can be symbolized as either a block or an antiblock. Only clue 5 is a true conditional. Since m and p can't be together, we can reserve one space in each group. Since both m and s can't go with p, m and s must be together. Since there are only two groups, the contrapositive of clue 5 can be rewritten in a more useful way, since if o isn't in 1, it must be in 2.

The familiarity of the diagram and clues for this game make it seem extremely likely that this is the easiest one on the section.

2. **E** If o is in 2, what can't be true?

o in 2 means n is also in 2. Since either m or p has to be in 1, there are at least three elements in 2, which means there are at most four in 1. The only choice that, from our deductions, clearly can't be true is (E), and that's the choice we want to pick.

3. **A** If p is in 1 with exactly three other elements, what doesn't have to be true?

p in 1 means the ms-block is in 2. Four elements in 1 means there are three in 2. The tv-block won't fit in 2, so it has to go in 1. There's one space open in each of the remaining groups; in order to keep from running afoul of the conditional clue, we have to put o in 1 and n in 2. The only choice not consistent with our deductions is (A), the choice we want.

4. **D** If n is in a group, then at most how many other elements can be in a group with it?

It seems reasonable to try n in 2, since that's the group that doesn't have an imposed maximum size. To make 1 as small as possible, we'd put p there; then the ms-block, the tv-block, and o could all go in 2 along with n. This arrangement doesn't violate any rules, and reflects a group with five other types of flowers in the group with n; since each group has to have at least one element in it because of mp, we can't do any better than this, and definitely want to pick (D).

5. **E** If 1 is as large as possible, which type of flower must be in 1?

The maximum group size for 1 is five; that puts two elements in 2. We first try putting the ms-block in 2 and everybody else in 1. That eliminates choices (A) and (D). The only alternative method to try is putting p in 2. That forces the ms-block into 1, and since there's only one slot open in 2, the tv-block must go in 1 as well. Now we have only one slot open in each of the groups; to prevent a conflict with the conditional clue, we put o in 1 and n in 2. That eliminates two of the remaining answer choices, leaving us with (E) as the answer we want.

1. **C** Which could be the elements in 2?

(A) puts m in a group without s, which would force a violation of clue 3. (B) has a similar problem, and additionally violates clue 2 by putting m and p together. (D) has o in 2 without n, which is a violation of clue 5. (E) separates t and v, violating clue 4. (C) is the one we want here.

Game 2

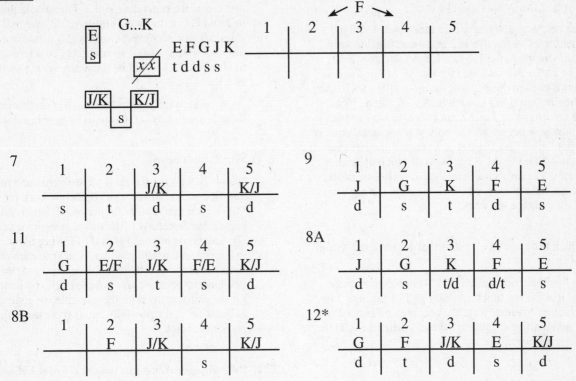

7

1	2	3	4	5
		J/K		K/J
s	t	d	s	d

11

1	2	3	4	5
G	E/F	J/K	F/E	K/J
d	s	t		d

8B

1	2	3	4	5
	F	J/K		K/J
			s	

9

1	2	3	4	5
J	G	K	F	E
d	s	t	d	s

8A

1	2	3	4	5
J	G	K	F	E
d	s	t/d	d/t	s

12*

1	2	3	4	5
G	F	J/K	E	K/J
d	t	d	s	d

Setting it up: We have a two-tiered ordering diagram with the drinks along the top row and the number of shots along the bottom row. We can make a deduction that helps us with the bottom row: Since the five drinks together use nine shots, and since there's exactly one triple, that means the remaining four drinks must between them include six shots, with none of them a triple. The only way we can do this is to have two doubles and two singles. Clue 2 assures us that K can't be first, and G can't be last. There's a very nice deduction here that you might not get immediately: Initially, it seems that the big block can occupy any of the three possible chunks 1 through 3, 2 through 4, or 3 through 5. But putting it in 2 through 4 would occupy both 2 and 4 on the top tier, leaving no room for F. So the big block goes either in 1 through 3 or 3 through 5. Realize that E might go in the middle of this block on the top tier, but it doesn't have to.

This seems like a somewhat complicated game. As we'll see upon consideration of the next two games, it probably isn't the hardest one, but it certainly doesn't seem easy at a first glance either.

7. D If 2 is a t, then what has to be true?

If 2 is a t, then the big block must go in 3 through 5; that makes 4 an s, and J and K have to go into 3 and 5, but we don't know in what order. On the bottom tier, since 4 is an s, that means 3 and 5 can't be; 1, then, must be an s. The two remaining spots of the bottom tier—3 and 5—must both be d's. We can't learn more about the top tier, but if we go to the choices, we'll see that we've already made a deduction that's listed. (D) is the choice we want here.

9. E If 4 is a d, then which doesn't have to be true?

4 being a d means that the big block must go in 1 through 3. That makes 2 an s, and we know that, on the top tier, J must be in 1, K in 3, and G in 2 in order to satisfy clue 2. That forces F into 4 and E into 5. 5 must be the other s; 3 is between an s and a d, so it has to be the t; the remaining slot, 1, must be d. We've deduced everything in the answer choices except for (E), the choice we want.

11. **C** If there's as much space between the two d's as possible, then what has to be true?

The first way to try here is to make both 1 and 5 d's. That forces us to put s in 2 and 4 and t in 3 to keep from violating clue 1. Since E has to be an s, F has to be either in 2 or 4, and the two s's are in 2 and 4, then E goes in one of those spaces and F goes in the other, but we don't know which goes where. Now we have to place J and K, and we also have to put G somewhere before K. The only way we can do this is to put G in 1 and J and K in 3 and 5, although again we don't know which has to go in which of these spaces. The only choice that's definitely true in all of the possible placements of elements in the top tier is (C), the choice we want.

6. **B** Which is the list of elements that could be in the top tier in 3?

By this time, hopefully you've stumbled across the fact that the big block can only go in 1 through 3 or 3 through 5; either way, 3 is occupied by either J or K, and nothing else can go there. That makes (B) the choice we want.

8. **B** What must be true?

Yuck. We'll have to take the choices here one at a time.

Try (A): E in 5 means E is s; that forces the big block to go in 1-3 to keep two s's from appearing next to one another. In order to allow G space to go in front of K, we have to have J in 1, G in 2, and K in 3. That leaves F for 4. In order to keep d's from appearing next to one another, we have to put one of them in 1; the t and the remaining d go in either order in 3 and 4, but this isn't consistent with the rest of the choice. We'll have to keep going.

Try (B): F in 2 doesn't appear to tell us much until we look at the big block. There's no way we could put it in 1-3, since this would make it impossible to have G before K. So the big block goes in 3-5, which means that 4 is an s. We're pretty much at the end of the road on deductions, but we've already deduced the thing in the remainder of the answer choice, so we want to pick this one and run.

Certainly only an insane person would try any of the remaining choices under test conditions. If you're curious, we've already made a potential counterexample for (C) in the example we generated while working on (A). A slight adjustment to the example we generated in (B) shows why (D) can't be true: If we put the t in 5 in this choice and consider the case when J is in 3, it seems clear that

we can still follow all the rules by putting d's in 1 and 3, and the remaining s in 2. That would put G in 1 and E in 4, but we'd still have followed all the rules, and the predicted result in (D) would not be true. All we have to do to adapt this counterexample to eliminate (E) would be to switch the positions of J and K.

As we said, once you find the answer on this one, there is absolutely no reason to keep going. Pick (B).

10. **D** Which can't be true?

We've seen (A) in the example we generated for question 8 (A). We've seen (B) in our work for 11. We've seen potential examples of (E) in several places, but hopefully by this time answer choice (D) jumps out at you: J is part of the big block, so making it an s would put two s's next to each other. If you observe this, then you're done; if not, then you have to generate an example of (C) by hand—I'd suggest starting with the example we generated in question 7. It's possible, and (D) is clearly the choice we want.

12. **E** Rule-changer: What can be true if instead of making the drinks with a total of nine shots, Buzz makes the drinks with a total of ten shots?

It's annoying, but we'll have to revisit the initial distribution deductions we made. Since we can still only have one t, we have four drinks left and seven shots to distribute. The only way we can do this is to have one s and three d's. Since there's only one s, then E has to go in the middle of the big block. That means the block has to occupy 3 through 5; otherwise, we wouldn't be able to place G before K. We still don't know where J and K go specifically, but F has to go in 2, which leaves G in 1. Look at the bottom tier. In order to place three d's, without putting two next to each other, we have to place them in 1, 3, and 5. That leaves t in 2. (A) can't be true: E has to be in 4. (B) can't be true: F has to be a t. (C) can't be true: G has to be in 1. (D) can't be true: J has to be a d, whether it goes in 3 or in 5. (E)'s the only one that could work, and is the choice we want. Whew.

Game 3

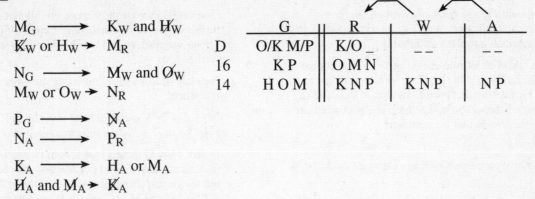

$M_G \longrightarrow K_W$ and H_W

K_W or $H_W \rightarrow M_R$

$N_G \longrightarrow M_W$ and O_W

M_W or $O_W \rightarrow N_R$

$P_G \longrightarrow N_A$

$N_A \longrightarrow P_R$

$K_A \longrightarrow H_A$ or M_A

H_A and $M_A \rightarrow K_A$

	G	R	W	A
D	O/K M/P	K/O _	_ _	_ _
16	K P	O M N		
14	H O M	K N P	K N P	N P

Setting it up: This is an odd one. Every element either is in group G, or else is in group R, and the elements in group R may also be in W and/or A. Everybody in A is definitely in W, and everybody in W is definitely in R. In other words, this is basically a modified in/out game, with group G serving as the "out" side, and some structure to the "in" side. We can do some things with the clues that'll make this one a bit easier to deal with. Since M and P can't both be in R, at least one of them has to be in G; we can reserve a space there. The clue involving K and O is even better: We can reserve one space in G for one of them, and one space in R for the other. As if all this weren't enough, we have four conditional clues, three of which are relatively complicated.

Because it's so odd, and because the clues look like they're going to work out to be difficult to use, it's pretty safe to rate this one as likely the hardest game on the section—a good one to leave for last.

16. **C** If O is in R, what must be true?

Since 14 looks like an awfully tough question to start the game with, it's smarter to skip past it.

O in R means K must be in G. In particular, then, this means that K isn't in W; that means M is in R. M in R means P must be in G. Take a look at the elements left who could be in A: H, M, and O are the only possibilities. If N is in G, then we're going to lose two of these—M and O—since after all if they aren't in W, they can't be in A. So N must, at the very least, be in R. Thankfully, this rather difficult last deduction is the one in the answer choices. Pick (C) and move on.

17. **A** If either H or K is in G but the other one is in R, then what can't be true?

It's a tough call whether this or the other remaining "if" question is tougher, but this one seems to have more straightforward answer choices. Rather than try the two possibilities suggested by the question stem, it's probably more efficient to work on the choices.

Try to make (A) true. If N is in G, then M and O can't be in W, which means they are both no longer possibilities for A. There are only three left: H, K, or P. Putting K there would require us to put H there, but don't forget the condition in the question: Exactly one of H or K is in G. So we have to put K in G and make H and P the two elements in A. H and P, then, both have to be in W and in R; P in R means that M has to be in G, while K in G means that O has to be in R. We've found a contradiction: M in G means that H can't be in W, but as we saw, we have no choice but to put it there. This is the answer, thankfully, and there's no need to suffer through the other choices.

For your reference, in case you were unable to see why the answer you picked can be true, here are arrangements that would allow us to eliminate the other choices:

(B), (C), and (D) all fall to this example:

G: H O M

R: K P N

W: K P N

A: P N

(E) falls to this one:

G: K P

R: H M N O

W: H M

A: H M

(A) is certainly the one we want on this question.

13. **E** Which can't be the list of elements in R?

This wouldn't have been an awful one to have worked first, but since it isn't quite a grab-a-rule, it's also reasonable to work at this stage.

It can take a bit of rule-checking to find the choice that doesn't work. In (E), if we look at who has to be in G, we note that both K and M are there; M in G means K has to be in W, which is a contradiction. (E) is the choice that we want here.

14. **C** If N is in W, at most how many elements could be in G?

We've put this off to a later time so that we—ideally, at least—understand the game a bit better when we tackle it.

N is in W means that it's also in R. It has to be there with one of K or O. There are only 6 elements in the game, so we can eliminate (E) off the top. Similarly, we know from our deductions that there must be at least two elements in G, so we can eliminate (A).

The biggest number we could hope for after this is four: that would mean N is in R with one other element, and everybody else would be out. That would force N to be in A, which in turn would force P to be in R. Eliminate (D).

The next biggest number we can hope for is three. That means one of M or P, one of K or O, and one other element. Try M in G; that forces K into W, and therefore R; K in R forces O into G. P and H are the only elements left, and from what we've seen before, it's probably safest to put P in R and H in G. At this point, we can safely put N and P both in W with K, and then put N and P in A without violating a clue. We've found an example with three in G, so we pick (C) and run.

15. **D** What could be true?

Don't neglect your prior work on this one. As it turns out, we've just made an example of (D) in the previous question, and we should pick it without further ado.

Here are reasons for eliminating the others, for your reference:

In (A), H in W means that M must be in R; then P can't be in R, which is the contradiction.

In (B), M in G means that K is in W and H isn't. K in A means that either H or M must also be in A, but we've just deduced that H can't be in A, since it isn't in W, and M in G means it can't be in A, either. There's the contradiction.

In (C), N in A means P must be in R. Then M must not be in R, which means it can't be in W, either. There's the contradiction.

In (E), O in R means K must be in G; K in G means that K can't be in W, which means that M must be in R. Then P can't possibly be in W, since one or the other must be in G. There's the contradiction.

Game 4

b: c d
I: J K L

	1	2	3	4	5
first		I	d_b	I	
second					

switch:
I* → b*
b → I

L...K

[I I]   [I I I]   first
L...K   [b b]   second

19

	1	2	3	4	5
first	J_I	L_I ★	d_b ★	K_I	c_b
second	J_I	d_b	L_I	K_I	c_b

23

	1	2	3	4	5
first	c_b ★	L_I	d_b	K_I	J_I ★
second	J_I	L_I	d_b	K_I	c_b

21i

	1	2	3	4	5
first	c_b	L_I	d_b ★	J_I ★	K_I
second	c_b	L_I	J_I	d_b	K_I

21ii

	1	2	3	4	5
first	c_b	J_I	d_b ★	L_I ★	K_I
second	c_b	J_I	L_I	d_b	K_I

22i

	1	2	3	4	5
first	c_b	I	d_b ★	I ★	I
second	c_b	I	I	d_b	I

22ii

	1	2	3	4	5
first	J_I ★	L_I	d_b	K_I	c_b ★
second	c_b	L_I	d_b	K_I	J_I

Setting it up: We're ordering the figurines 1 through 5 twice—once for each week. A two-tier diagram with the two weeks' orders stacked on top of one another will work; we'll use upper- and lowercase letters to indicate the two types of figurines. The clues are fairly straightforward to symbolize for the most part, although you may need to improvise a bit on the switching clue. There are a number of deductions here. Since L can't be in 1 and also must be before K, K can't be in either 1 or 2; L can't be in 5. Since the b's can't be in adjacent spaces, both 2 and 4 must be I's during the first week.

This is somewhat complicated, although it certainly isn't as bad as the permissions game immediately before it. It's reasonable to estimate that this one is of comparable or slightly lower difficulty than the "Buzz the barrista" game, the second in the section.

19. **B** If d is in 2 during the second week, what must be true?

d in 2 during the second week means that the immediately adjacent spaces—1 and 3—must also be I's. That means the switch must have taken place between 2 and 3. Since everybody else has to stay put, that means 1 must have been an I in the first week, and 4 must be an I in the second week. 5 must be a b in both weeks. Now for who's who: The other b—in 5—has to be c in both weeks. In order to satisfy the L...K clue and also keep L out of 1, during week one L must be in 2, K must be in 4, leaving J for 1. Then the switch took place between d and L, and J, K, and c are all in the same positions for the second week. The only choice that's consistent with our deductions is (B), and that's the choice we want.

23. **C** If an I is in 5 during the first week but not during the second, then what doesn't have to be true?

An I in 5 during the first week means our other b—figurine c—must be in 1 during that week. It appears that there are several arrangements of I's that will work here. Since there has to be a b in 5 during the second week, we see that the only way we could do this is to switch 1 and 5. In the second week, then, we have an I in 1, c in 5, and everybody else stays put. Look at the second week: The only way to satisfy the L…K clue without putting L in 1 is to put L in 2, K in 4, and that forces J into 1. That means L and K must have been in the same locations during the first week, and J must have been in 5. The only choice that isn't consistent with our deductions here is (C), the choice we want.

18. **B** Which could be the labels on the figurines during the second week?

(A) has K with a lower-numbered label than L. (C) doesn't have two I's next to each other. (E) has the two b's next to each other. The problem with (D) is somewhat less obvious. In order to achieve this arrangement in the second week, we would have had to switch 1 and 3, and everybody else would remain in place. So, the first-week arrangement must have had d in 3 and c in 4, which would be a violation of other rules. (B) is the choice we want.

20. **E** Which could be true?

(A) would put two b's next to each other. (B) contradicts one of our deductions: Trying to do this would force us to put L in 1, a violation of the rules. (C) also violates a deduction: L in 5 leaves us no place to put K. (D) violates another deduction: Doing this would put two b's side-by-side. (E) could work: We'd have to switch 3 and 4 to do it, but there's no reason to think that can't be done.

21. **C** Where could J be during the second week?

We've already seen J in 1 and J in 5 during the second week. Unfortunately, these are both included in every answer choice. 3 is included in three of the choices, so this probably makes sense to try first. A quick check shows that it can be done: eliminate (A) and (B). It's best at this stage to try either 2 or 4: Let's say you try 2 first. That works, too, so we can eliminate (D). Sadly, we have to try 4 in order to be sure what the answer is here. In order for J to go in 4 during the second week, it has to have been there during the first week; there's no way it could switch to that space, since that would require two b's to have been side-by-side during the first week. Then the only way to make the example work, given J is

in 4 during the first week and doesn't switch, is to have c in 1, L in 2, and K in 5. The only switch here that keeps J in place would be a switch of 1 and 5, but that would force K into 1. It turns out that J can't be in 4 during the second week! Eliminate (E), and we'll pick (C), the only one that's left.

22. **C** If c is in 1 during the second week, then how many different arrangements could we have in the second week?

There are two ways c could wind up in 1 during the second week: It could either stay put, or it could switch into this spot. Consider the first possibility: If c is not involved in the switch, then during the first week 1 is a b and 5 is an I; there are three legal arrangements of the I's here, since no matter where we put J, we can still find locations for L and K. The only switch we could make would be between 3 and 4. That switch doesn't change the order of the I's or put any of them into 1, so any of the three arrangements of I's in the first week would also be legal in the second week. Our first possibility includes three different arrangements.

The other possibility is that c switched into 1. That means 1 must have been an I during the first week, which means that during the first week 5 must have been a b—namely, c. So the switch took place between 1 and 5. The only legal arrangement of I's in the first week would put J in 1, L in 2, and K in 3. The switch of 1 with 5 puts c in 1 and also results in a legal arrangement for the second week that hasn't been counted so far. This possibility includes one more possible arrangement.

The total of possible legal arrangements in this case is four, which is choice (C).

24. **D** What can't be true?

The best hope here is to try to find examples in our prior work. We've seen an instance of (A) in the first example we generated for question 21. We've seen an instance of (B) in our work for 23. We've seen an instance of (C) in the second example we generated for question 21. We've seen an instance of (E) in the second example we generated in 21. That leaves (D) as the only possibility, with no further work required.

As for why this can't be true, we have to realize that c must be in either 1 or 5 during week 1. There's no way c could be immediately before K if c stays put in either of these positions, since K has to be higher than L, so we'd have to move c in order to make this possible. But the only place we can move c into is 5—otherwise two b's would be side-by-side—so there's no way we could do this. (D) clearly isn't possible.

CHAPTER 15

PRACTICE SECTION 4: GAMES

Page 178

Note: All explanations in this section appear in the order in which you should have tackled the questions, based on difficulty level.

Game 1

HLMPT

	1	2	3	4	5
2B	H	P	T	L	M
3A	M/T	L	H	P	T/M
3B		H/P		L	M
3C	H	P	M	T	L
5*	T/M	L	P	H	M/T

HP

{ M...H(P) → H(P)...T
  T...H(P) → H(P)...M

{ L...T → L...(H)P

{ (H)P...L → T...L

Setting it up: This is a straightforward ordering task, with five elements, each used exactly once. The only thing that seems tricky here are those last two clues, both of which are conditional range clues. Note that both involve the block somehow. As for deductions, since the range clues are conditional, they can be difficult to make. If you happen to see it, there's one very helpful one that comes from the first conditional: Note that if M comes before the block, then at least one element has to come after it; similarly, if T comes before the block, then at least one element has to come after it; finally, if neither of these is true, then both M and T must come after the block, which means that two elements come after it. So there has to be, at a bare minimum, one element after the block, which means it can't go in 4 and 5. If you don't get this deduction at this stage, which is quite likely, chances are you'll find it in just a moment.

Certainly the familiarity of the task in this game gives the impression that it won't be too difficult; however, the difficulty of the last two clues should lead you to guess that this may not be the easiest game on the section.

1. **A** What can't be true?

Note that question 5, although it begins with the word "if," is actually a rule-changer, so we should work it last. We'll have to start from the top.

(A) is the deduction mentioned above: The block can't go in 4 and 5. If you have it already, pick this choice and move on; if not, if you simply start trying choices from the top, you'll come across it right away and should move on.

Although you shouldn't try the others under timed conditions, if you're curious at this point, here are quick sketches of examples that show how the other four could be true: H P M T L eliminates (B), (C), and (D); M L H P T eliminates (E).

Hopefully, you found that (A) was the answer without having to do this additional work.

2. **B** What could be true?

These choices are so specific that we'll just have to try them from the top. (A) can't work: L before T means that L also has to be before P, but this choice clearly violates that clue. (B), however, does work: Given the T L M-block in this choice, all we're left with is the H P-block; the only place it can possibly fit is in 1 through 2, but this doesn't violate any rules. Pick (B) and keep moving.

As for the others, if you're interested: (C) has L before T, which would mean that the H P-block would have to go after the block here, but that would put it in 4 through 5, which we know can't happen. (D) has T and M both before the H P-block, which contradicts our first conditional clue. (E) has the same problem that (C) does.

Hopefully you picked (B) as soon as you saw that it could be done.

3. **C** Which fact places all five of the elements?

Again, we have to try the choices from the top. (A) puts the H P-block in 3 through 4: The first conditional clue lets us know that either M or T has to go in 5, and that means L has to go in 2. Either M or T could still go in 1 without violating any of the rules, so (A) doesn't quite get the job done. (B) puts L in 4, which means the H P-block definitely goes before it, so T also has to go before it. That leaves M as the only element that can go in 5, but it seems that the H P-block and T can still go in 1 through 3 in either of two possible orders, so (B) doesn't do the job. (C) splits our diagram in half so that the H P-block has to go in either 1 through 2 or 4 through 5; since we know 4 through 5 isn't a possibility, the block has to go in 1 through 2. That makes it certain that the block will go before L, which means that T has to come before L; the only way we can do this is to have T in 4 and L in 5. (C) does the job, and you should pick it at this point.

For your reference, in (D) there are legal examples with L in 4 or in 5; in (E) there are legal examples with the H P-block in either 1 through 2 or 2 through 3. (C) is the one you hopefully picked as soon as you worked it out.

4. **B** Which doesn't have to be true?

Hopefully, prior work can help here. We're looking for counterexamples, and we find one for (B) right away in your work from question 3(A). None of the rest of these choices can be false.

5. **D** If we remove the H P-block and put as much space as we can between L and H, with L coming first, then what has to be true?

This is annoying, because we have to go back to our original symbols for the conditionals and modify them to take the removal of the H P-block into account. We know that L can't be in 1, so we'll want to try it in 2. We can make a similar deduction about H to the one we originally made about the H P-block, on the basis of the first conditional: At a bare minimum, either M or T has to come after H; let's try H in 4.

Now we have L in 2, H in 4, and either M or T in 5. Putting P before L would force us to put T before it as well, and there's no room for that, so let's put P in the only remaining space after L: 3. That puts the other of T or M in 1; either arrangement of these two elements in 1 and 5 will satisfy our new set of rules. The only choice that's consistent with our deductions is (D), the choice we want to pick.

Game 2

	V W X Y Z	A	M	J
	D	—		
	P	Y	V Z W/X	X/W
	S	—		

Block: [V Z] / [Y] [V Z] or Y_J

7

	A	M	J
D	V Z	X/W	Y W/X
P	Y	V Z W/X	X/W
S	W X	Y	V Z

9

	A	M	J
D	V Z X	W	Y
P	Y	V Z X	W
S	W	Y	V Z X

11i

	A	M	J
D	X/W	Y	V Z W/X
P	Y	V Z W/X	X/W
S	V Z W/X	X/W	Y

11ii

	A	M	J
D	W X	Y	V Z
P	Y	V Z X	W
S	V Z	W	Y X

Setting it up: This is a tough one to diagram. It seems clear that we need to put the months across the top, but the question is whether we should make the other axis of our chart the projects or the departments. It seems relatively clear that the clue relating V and Z is most easily represented if we put the departments down the side; then, the clue becomes a block. It also makes the clue relating Y with V (and therefore Z) a bit easier to symbolize. The game can likely be worked using the other diagramming possibility, but it doesn't seem nearly as straightforward. We'll put the departments down the side and organize our chart that way.

Once we've settled on a diagram and made our symbols, we have some deductions to make. The way we have it set up, we know we need each project to appear exactly once in each horizontal row (every department works on each project once), and also to appear exactly once in each vertical column (every project is worked on by one department each month). That being the case, the fact that three elements are in the P-row during May means there must be one element in the P-row during each of April and June. Similarly, there must be one element in each of the D- and S-rows during May. We know the VZ-block has to appear in the P-row; the only place with room for it is May. That means Y must be the element in the P-row during April. That leaves W and X for the two remaining spaces in the P-row; they could appear in either order. Finally, we see that we can't be sure what goes in the D- and S-row in May, except that Y goes in one of them and the other of X or W goes in the other. Still, we have a good starting point for this game.

As for difficulty, it seems fairly plain that this is going to be quite a difficult game. It's difficult to diagram, and even once you have, there's a lot of space to fill in and seemingly lots of possibilities. Even with all of our deductions, we still don't know about the distribution of elements in the D- and S-rows—it seems that it could either be 1, 2, 2, or 1, 1, 3. This would be a very good game to leave for last on the section.

7. **E** If Y and one other element are in the D-row during June, what must be true?

There are lots of deductions here. With two elements in the D-row during June, we know that there must be two elements in the S-row during the same month. Similar deductions let us know there must be two elements in each of the remaining spaces—D-row April and S-row April. So much for distribution. Now, since we know Y is in June in the D-row and April in the P-row, then it must be in May in the S-row; that puts the VZ-block in June in the S-row. That means W and X must go together in April in the S-row. The VZ-block goes in April in the D-row. The remaining spaces are occupied by either W or X; we don't know which goes where, although we know which spaces have to contain the same element. Fortunately, we've found the choice that we have to pick: it's (E).

9. **E** If the D-row has X before W and W before Y, then what doesn't have to be true?

The condition tells us exactly how the D-row has to look: W is alone in May, Y is in June, and X is in April. Since Y is in June in the D-row, this must be the row where the VZ-block goes in April. Y has to go in the S-row in May, which puts the VZ block in June in the S-row. Working down in April, we see that W has to go alone in the S-row in April, since it's the only element left and we have to fill that space. Working down in May, we see that X must be the third element in the P-row in May. That forces W into the P-row in June, and finally X has to go in the S-row in June. Our diagram is full! The only choice that isn't consistent with it is (E), the choice we want.

6. **B** Which could describe where Y and Z go?

At this point, it's a toss-up whether you want to go ahead with the specific count-the-ways question in number 11 or start on your general-question pass. The general questions may not be too tough at this point, and it's never bad to leave count-the-ways questions for near the end.

Check for outright violations of rules: Y has to be worked on immediately before Z in all cases. That gets rid of (A), (C), and (D). We know from our deductions that P has to be listed first for Y and second for Z; that gets rid of (E). Pick (B).

8. **D** What has to be true?

We have some work under our belt here that may help, but a first pass through the choices reveals that (D) was one of our initial deductions, and there's no need to go any further. It's a good thing, too, because we've only seen a counterexample for one of these choices—(C)—in our prior work. (D) is the one we want.

10. **B** What could be true?

From our deductions, we know that there has to be one element in the D-row in May; eliminate (A). We also know that there has to be one element in the P-row in April; eliminate (C). There has to be one element in the P-row in June; eliminate (D). There has to be one element in the S-row in May; eliminate (E). (B) is the only remaining possibility, and is the choice we want here.

11. **B** If neither W nor Z is in the S-row in June, then how many different orders can we get for X?

We can't put it off any longer. If neither W nor the VZ-block is in the S-row in June, then we have limited possibilities. We realize quickly that Y has to go here; otherwise, the only place it could go in the S-row would be May, which would force the VZ-block into this spot.

Once we know that Y goes in the S-row during June, the only remaining question is whether it's by itself, or whether X is here with it. Try each possible scenario.

Y alone here means there must be three elements in the D-row in June, three elements in the S-row in April, and one element in the D-row in April. We know, then, where Y and the VZ-block have to go in every row. The only elements left to play with are W and X, and it seems that either one could go in one of the open spots, but once we assign it, we can figure out who has to go in each of these spots. What that means is that there are two possible orders for X in this scenario.

It also appears to be possible that Y and X could go together in the S-row in June. In that case, there must be two elements each in the S-row in April, the D-row in April, and the D-row in June. We can easily locate the VZ-block and Y in the remaining rows, and since X is locked down in the S-row in June, that means we can tell that it also must go in the P-row in May and the D-row in April; W must go in the P-row in June, the S-row in May, and the D-row in April. That's one more possible order for X.

We've found a grand total of three possible orders for X: D, S, P; S, P, D; and D, P, S. Choose (B).

Game 3

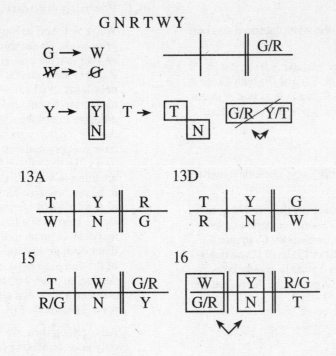

G N R T W Y

G → W
W̶ → G̶

Y → [Y/N]   T → [T]/[N]   [G/R̶ Y/T]

13A

T	Y ‖ R
W	N ‖ G

13D

T	Y ‖ G
R	N ‖ W

15

T	W ‖ G/R
R/G	N ‖ Y

16

W	Y ‖ R/G
G/R	N ‖ T

Setting it up: This is a spatial arrangement game—four slots in two rows—with two "out" slots for the two elements that aren't included in the banner. Most of the clues are conditional, although they're all fairly easy to symbolize. The only real deduction here involves N: Since putting either Y or T in requires us to have N in as well, there's absolutely no way we could have N out. Even if R/G weren't occupying one of the "out" slots, we still wouldn't have room for Y, T, and N. So N must always be in.

As for difficulty, this one seems a bit odd but not outrageously difficult. It looks to be a good deal easier than the previous game, and is likely more or less equivalent to the first game in difficulty. Given the rest of the games on this section, this seems like a reasonable one to work early on.

12. **B** Grab-a-rule

(A) puts T beside R, which violates rule 6. (C) puts T in but N in the lower-left, which violates rule 4. (D) puts G in without W, which violates rule 2. (E) puts Y in but N not below it, which violates rule 3. (B) is the choice we want here.

13. **E** If W isn't in either of the top slots, what must be true?

Tough to make deductions off the top on this one, and although the answer choices are also a bit difficult to work with, you have to start somewhere. Try (A): To work on this one, we'll want to make it false. A good place to start is to try Y in the upper-right. That puts N in the lower-right, and tells us that neither R nor G can go in the upper-left. We can do several things from here: Try W in the lower-left and T in the upper-left. That example lets us eliminate (A), (B), and (C). We can adapt this example slightly to eliminate (D): If we put Y in, then there's still room to put W out, which forces us to put G out. We can still make a legal example by putting R in the lower-left and T in the upper-left. That eliminates (D), leaving us with (E), the choice we should pick.

15. **E** If Y is out, what has to be true?

If Y is out, then the "out" column is full. That forces T, N, W, and the other of R or G in. The arrangement of T and N is set by the T-conditional, and whichever of R or G is in, it can't go next to T, so W has to go there. (E) is the only choice that's consistent with our deductions, and is the choice we should pick.

14. C What could be true?

We're leaving the count-the-ways question, number 16, for later.

(A) can't work, we know, because N has to be in. (B) has the same problem. (D) and (E) both fail to list R and G, and we know that at least one of them has to be out. (C) is the only possible choice here.

17. A What must be true?

We're leaving the count-the-ways question, number 16, for last.

This is a deduction we made off the top: N has to be in, which is (A). We've seen counterexamples for three of these in our prior work: (C) in question 13 (D); (D) in 13 (A); (E) in 15. Even if you don't have the deduction in hand already, it only takes one example to see that (A) has to be the choice we want.

16. C How many different banners can be made?

We've put it off as long as we can. Reviewing our prior work, we see the following. In number 13 (A) we saw the one and only possibility in which R and G are both out. In 13 (D), we saw the only possibility in which W is out (W out means G also has to be out, and this is the only possible arrangement of the remaining "in" elements). In 15, we saw the two possibilities in which Y is out. We have four possibilities so far. Since N can't be out, it looks like the only examples we have left to generate are those in which T is out. Since either R or G has to be out, we must have Y, N, W, and the other of G or R in. Y has to go above N; since neither R nor G can go next to Y, it has to go on the bottom, which leaves W to go on top. It looks like our two vertical blocks can go in either position, so for each location of the vertical YN-block, we have two arrangements depending upon whether R or G is the "out" element. That's two sets of two arrangements each, for a grand total of four more arrangements.

All together, then, we have eight arrangements. The only issue remaining to consider is whether there are any possibilities we've missed in which R is out. We've already seen it with G, Y, and T out, and since N can't ever be out, and W out means G has to be out, we can see that we haven't missed any possibilities in which R is out. So eight is the grand total, making (C) the choice we want.

Game 4

rtvwyz

		M	P	Q
$v_P \rightarrow w_M$	D	r/v/y _	r/v/y _ _	r/v/y _ _
w̶$_M$ → v̶$_P$	18	v/y z	r t z	y/v w z
	19	v/y z	r/y t w	r/v/y t w
r → $\boxed{r\ t}$	20	r t	y w z/t	v w t/z
#t = #w	21	v/y w	r t w/z	y/v t z/w
	22	y w	v t w/z	r t z/w
	23	v/y z	r/y _ z	_ _ z

Setting it up: This is a three-group game where the elements can be used more than once. Since we have three elements, no two of which can be in the same group—r, v, and y—and since all of the elements have to be used, we know that one of the three elements goes in each of the three groups, and none of them can be used more than once. That leaves t, w, and z to fill out the remaining five spots. Take a look at the clue that requires t and w to be used the same number of times: In order to fill five spots, we have to use each of them once or each of them twice. In the first case, z will have to be used three times, which means z will be in every group; in the second, z will be used exactly once. We'll want to keep track of these two possibilities as we work the questions.

Difficulty on this one is a little difficult to judge. It's not exceptionally difficult, but the distribution factor here means that it certainly isn't easy. It looks as though the second game is definitely the most difficult on the section, and the others are of approximately similar difficulty, with this game a shade more difficult than the first and third games.

18. E If t is only in P, then what has to be true?

t only in P means t is only used once; this means that w is only used once, and that r must be in P. With each of w and t used once, we know that z has to be in all three groups. So the only space remaining is in Q, and it must be occupied by w. We don't know where v and y have to go, but we've deduced plenty to get to the answer: (E) is the choice we want here.

19. D If z is not with either t or w, what could be true?

z with neither t nor w means that t is used twice, w is used twice, and z is used once. In order to avoid both t and w, z would have to go in M; since that means w can't be in M, we know that v can't be in P. Since there's no space for t, r must not go in M. Finally, although we can't tie the r/v/y triplet down any further, we do know that t and w have to go in both P and Q. (D) is the only choice that's still possible here.

20. C If r is in M, then what has to be true?

r in M means that t must also be in M. Since w can't be in M, v can't be in P, which means that y must be there. That leaves v to be in Q. Look at what's left: We have to place z and w, and that'll leave two spaces left. There's no way z can occupy both of them, since it can't occupy two spaces in any group, so that means the two remaining slots must be occupied by second copies of w and t. So w goes in each of P and Q, and t or z go in P and Q, but we don't know which goes where. The only choice that's consistent with our deductions is (C), the choice we want.

21. **E** If w is in M, which can't be a listing of the elements in Q?

w in M means that r can't be the member of the triplet there, although it could be either v or y. rt goes in one of the remaining groups, and the other of y or v in the other. Since z can't be in all three groups at this point, we know there must be another use each of w and t and only one use of z. Since t is already in one of the other groups and we have to use it twice, it must be in both P and Q. There's the key: Choice (E) doesn't have t listed, which makes it the choice we want.

22. **A** If v is in P, then what has to be true?

v in P means that w has to be in M. That leaves Q as the only group that can accommodate the rt-block. So y has to go in M. Since z can't be in all three groups, that means we have one more occurrence each of w and t, and the single occurrence of z left to place. Since t is already in Q, the second t must go in P. That leaves w and z to flip back and forth in P and Q. The only choice that's consistent with our deductions is (A), the choice we want.

23. **A** If z is used as many times as possible, what can't be true?

To use z as many times as possible, it'll have to be in all three groups. M is full now, so in particular w can't be in M. Since w can't be in M, v must not be in P. We still have to place the rt-block, and it can go in either P or Q; the other group contains the single occurrence of w. Right off the bat, we can see that (A) can't work: The single occurrence of w has to be in either P or Q, and the single occurrence of t has to be in the other one.

24. **D** What can't be true?

This comes straight from our distribution deductions. The only choice here that isn't a possibility is (D), the choice we want.

CHAPTER 19

PRACTICE SECTION 5: READING COMPREHENSION

Page 216

Passage 1

The disaster of land reform in Zimbabwe illustrates the poisonous legacy of colonialism in that country in at least two ways. The first paragraph describes the historical origins of land ownership problems in Zimbabwe from the founding of the colony of Rhodesia and the eventual establishment of majority rule in independent Zimbabwe. The second paragraph describes the land reform approach adopted in the postcolonial period and indicates why it was not successful. The third paragraph describes the failure of new efforts at land reform, assigning blame for the failure to President Robert Mugabe's adoption of a colonial style of rule.

1. **D** General: What is the main point of the passage?

   (A) is too specific; although this fact is mentioned, it doesn't cover the subject of the whole passage. (B) is off the mark; among other things, it doesn't even mention Zimbabwe specifically. (C) isn't terrible, but like (B) it seems to generalize in a way the passage doesn't; its primary focus isn't the overall difficulty of postcolonial government in Africa. (E) tries to blame everything on the postcolonial rulers of Zimbabwe, which is not in line with the passage. (D) is the closest to the main point we've identified, and is the one we should pick.

2. **C** Specific: What does the passage say about the Lancaster House agreement?

   This is mentioned briefly in the first paragraph in connection with Zimbabwe achieving independence, and in more detail in the second paragraph in terms of the "willing buyer, willing seller" principle that ultimately failed to achieve land reform. (A) isn't in line with the passage; although the author does say that the scheme sounded reasonable, the author indicates that it was unlikely to work. (B) seems decent, although it seems a little more partisan than the passage itself does; the passage doesn't include a judgment that the agreement didn't go far enough. (D) says more than the passage does; the author doesn't lay the blame for the forced land seizures on just the Lancaster House agreement. (E) also seems decent, but it isn't strictly supported by the passage. (C), however, is: It's clear that the agreement included protections for white landowners, and the description of how the land was initially claimed seems to support the statement that their claims were of questionable legitimacy. (C) is the best choice here.

3. **B** Specific: Which of the choices is included in the passage?

   Although the passage asserts that the Rhodesian government was racist, it doesn't include a specific example of a racist policy; eliminate (A). We can eliminate (C) for similar reasons; the structural reforms are mentioned but are not further explained. We don't have any specific statistics about land reform; eliminate (D) and (E). (B), however, is included in the passage: In the final paragraph, the author indicates that land reform had become a means by which Mugabe maintained his power in government. Choose (B).

4. **A** Specific: What does the passage say about the proposed constitution of 2000?

This is mentioned at the end of the second paragraph and extensively in the third. (B) is a little too strong; the passage doesn't indicate approval for the constitution. (C) is pretty much the opposite of the passage's description. (D) is also too strong; the passage doesn't indicate disapproval of the constitution either. "Outrage," in (E), is far too strong. (A) seems the best choice here: The passage does say that an alternative to the Lancaster House principles was "inevitably" sought, indicating that its approach to land reform was in some sense necessary.

5. **B** General: What is the author's purpose in the passage?

(A) is pretty good, but it seems focused a little too much on the land reform issue, at the expense of discussions of colonialism. (B) is similar to (A) but has the emphasis on colonialism that we're looking for. (C) talks about the international community, which isn't really part of the passage's main point. (D) mentions a comparison of several problems, which isn't really the point here. (E)'s use of the word "interference" isn't like anything else in the passage. (B) is the best of the answers here.

6. **C** Specific: What is the purpose of the referenced text?

The text in question describes the reasons why the "willing buyer, willing seller" principle established in the Lancaster House agreement wasn't effective at instituting land reform. (A) seems more or less in line with this. (B) is tough, but it doesn't seem as good as (A); the author isn't really interested in claiming that "willing buyer, willing seller" is unreasonable. (C) also seems like it has a chance. (D)'s mention of the 2000 constitution makes it worth eliminating, since that isn't mentioned until later. (E) should go for similar reasons.

The choice between (A) and (C) is tough. The author doesn't make as strong a value judgment about the principle as (A) does in its use of the term "inadequate." The purpose here isn't to criticize "willing buyer, willing seller" so much as to explain why it didn't work and therefore had to be replaced. It's close, but (C) is a hair better.

7. **A** Complex: Weaken the assertion in the last sentence of the passage.

The assertion in question is that Zimbabwe's current problems can ultimately be laid at the feet of the land reform effort. We're looking for some other possible explanation of the problems. (B) doesn't seem to explain what might be responsible for the problems, aside from land reform. (C)'s impact on the situation isn't particularly clear. (E) doesn't really do the job we need, since the IMF reforms are identified as being associated with land reform.

We're left with (A), which identifies a similarity between the current conflict and past precolonial conflicts, and (D), which indicates that drought has had an effect on the region. (A) is probably stronger, since although (D) might help to explain the famine, it only says that crop yields have "decreased," and the scale of the problem it describes is in some doubt. (A), on the other hand, might indicate some source completely unrelated to land reform that might have contributed to the country's problems. It's close, but (A) is the best choice here.

Passage 2

The Fourth Amendment protection against unreasonable search and seizure has been enforced using the exclusionary rule, but the weakness of the rule itself, its further weakening through court action, and the court's increasing willingness to consider warrantless searches not "unreasonable" all show that Fourth Amendment protections have never been very strong. The first paragraph presents the Fourth Amendment and introduces the exclusionary rule. The second paragraph describes the exclusionary rule and its limited application. The final paragraph describes further weakening of the rule through the "good faith" exception and the likely future of the exclusionary rule.

8. **E** General: What is the main point of the passage?

(A) puts it a bit strongly, and the passage never really talks about anything like "egregious abuses," but instead focuses on the exclusionary rule itself. (B) focuses solely on the future, which is not the main concern of the passage. (C) is too specific, and also takes the wrong side in the discussion about the protection of Fourth Amendment rights. (D) is close, but it's a little too neutral; the author's opinion isn't really in this choice. (E) is the one we want.

9. **E** Specific: What is the purpose of the cited text?

The text describes instances in which evidence obtained in an illegal search is not subject to exclusion. (A) pertains to the "good faith" exception, which isn't mentioned until the following paragraph. (B) seems decent, although the statement on which it is based is some distance from the cited text, and isn't really directly related to these exceptions. (C) is a bit too strong; the whole point is that the exclusionary rule doesn't prevent all evidence that might be considered the fruit of an illegal search from being introduced. (D) is also a bit off the mark; the author certainly believes that the exclusionary rule isn't strong enough, but the passage never actively advocates an expansion of the rule's application. In fact, the author never suggests a solution to the problem being identified. (E) is the safest choice here.

10. **C** Specific: What does the passage say about "popular sentiment?"

The referenced statement is at the beginning of the last paragraph, and indicates that popular sentiment is against the acquittal of offenders on perceived technicalities. (A) is rather strong; it recommends the use of tainted evidence in every case. (B) doesn't suggest a particularly specific course of action; it seems too weak to be in line with the statement from the passage. (D) talks about excluding exculpatory evidence, which isn't really something the passage registers an opinion on. (E) is more or less the exclusionary rule, but the passage indicates that popular sentiment is in favor of something that permits the inclusion of evidence that could be said to be tainted. (C) is something that the point of view would almost certainly agree with: A defendant who is guilty should not be allowed to go free simply because important evidence must be excluded for legal reasons. (C) is the choice we want.

11. **A** Specific: Which statement about the exclusionary rule is consistent with the passage?

(B) starts off sounding good, but its application to criminal defendants only is not a problem identified in the passage. (C) is not the author's opinion. (D) sounds similar to some of the things said in the passage, but there's no indication that the type of case that's being tried changes the way the rule is applied. (E) is way outside the passage. (A) comes from the passage statement, in the first paragraph, which says that courts have settled on the exclusionary rule "not without vacillation."

12. **C** Complex: Which situation is most similar to that of an investigator conducting a search on the basis of a flawed warrant?

This comes from the area of the passage that discusses the "good faith" exception. (A) talks about something that's done on the basis of an error, but the passage discussion involves cases where, even though a mistake is involved, the result of that mistake is found to be in some way acceptable or useful. (A) doesn't include this idea. (B) is very similar. (D) talks about an error but, once again, doesn't talk about the result of the error being acceptable or useful. (E) has the same problem. The only choice that talks about an error having an acceptable or useful effect is (C), and that's the choice we should pick.

13. **D** Complex: What principle would support the courts' decisions as they are described in the last sentence?

This is the statement that talks about the courts' increasing willingness to find that searches conducted without a warrant are not "unreasonable." We want a choice that supports this decision. (A) couldn't do the job; this is a means for deciding that a search is unreasonable in certain cases, not that it isn't unreasonable. (B) has the same problem, as do (C) and (E). The only principle that could support the statement in question is (D), and that's the choice we want.

Passage 3

Simple readings of Franz Kafka's work as allegory of whatever type miss the true depth of his work, which speaks most broadly of the futility of any search for ultimate meanings. The first paragraph introduces Kafka's work as it is commonly read and understood and uses his novel *The Castle* to indicate that these readings constitute a misunderstanding of the novel. The second paragraph provides a second example—"In the Penal Colony"—in which Kafka's work itself indicates the folly of trying to impose a single interpretation on it.

14. **B** General: What is the main point of the passage?

(A) isn't exactly right; the passage's point isn't that Kafka's work has no meaning, but that ascribing a single meaning to it constitutes a misunderstanding of the text. (C) is a bit too general; the passage is only about readings of Kafka's work, not about readings in general. (D) gets the emphasis of the passage a bit wrong; it isn't primarily concerned with talking about how wonderful Kafka is, but instead how those who read him in particular ways are mistaken. (E) is along the right lines, but it isn't as specific as (B), which is the best choice here.

15. **D** Specific: What is true of the two types of interpretations cited?

This pertains to the discussion in the second paragraph. Simply put, the passage believes that both make the mistake of seeking a single meaning in the story. (A) is backwards; it's the fact that they try to read the text as allegory that is the problem. (B) is associated with psychological interpretations, but not sociological ones, and isn't even a complete description of what the passage says about psychological interpretations. Mainly, though, we want to remember that the question asks about what all these interpretations have in common. The thing they share is the shortcoming of ascribing a single meaning to the image, not the meaning they ascribe to it. (C) is trying to go the correct direction, but the emphasis here is a bit off: The passage's complaint isn't that these interpretations don't correctly understand the "mechanism," but that they don't fully understand the consequences of their act as trying to interpret it as meaning the same single thing. (E) has to do with the previous paragraph. (D) is the best summary of the meaning of the second paragraph, and correctly describes the passage's opinion about these types of readings. Let's pick that one.

16. **D** Specific: What does the passage tell us about treating *The Castle* as an allegory of an individual's search for social acceptance?

Basically, the passage's opinion is that reading the text only in this way represents a misunderstanding of it. (A) is too strong, as is (B). (E) is in the wrong direction. It's a bit much to say that the passage dismisses this idea, and there's no evident amusement in the discussion. (D) is the safest statement of the passage's treatment of this reading.

17. **E** General: What is the primary purpose of the passage?

The passage talks about why a particular way of reading Kafka isn't right. (A) doesn't talk about readings of the author's work, which is the passage's main focus. (B) talks about defending the assertions of other critics, which isn't something the passage does. (C) mentions chronology, which isn't really present anywhere in the passage. (D) refers to interpretations of a person, rather than the person's work. (E) is a good summary of what we were hoping for; let's pick it.

18. **C** Specific: What does the word "Kafkaesque" mean in connection with *The Castle*?

(A) and (E) are both out of the question. The passage describes the adjective as pertaining to an individual's feeling of helplessness when acted on by "institutional power." Although (D) might work, and (B) might work better, the best choice of all is (C), since the passage describes *The Castle* as a story about seeking permission to stay in the village.

19. **B** General: What is the organization of the passage?

(A) seems decent, although it doesn't match the organization as closely as we might hope; the passage doesn't really talk about all of the positions before it criticizes them. (B) has a similar problem, but it's better than (A) because it includes mention of the work to which these interpretations are applied, which is definitely something the passage does. (C) isn't right; we don't get several different evaluations of the readings described in the passage. (D) is pretty bad; the passage isn't really concerned with questions of "accuracy" here. (E) is also off the mark; the passage doesn't mention two theories specifically. (B) is the closest fit to the passage, and is the choice we should pick.

Passage 4

Although the genetic modification of organisms represents use of a powerful technology that must be pursued carefully, we have an obligation to develop this technology because of its potential to solve long-standing human problems. The first paragraph describes GMOs, especially commercially important food crops, and provides the example of *Bt* corn. The second paragraph describes the benefits of GMOs cited by those who support the development and implementation of the technology. The third paragraph describes past instances of the careless use of new technology; this is the portion of the passage where the author advocates the technology's cautious use.

20. **C** General: What is the passage's main point?

(A) is too one-sided; the author does agree that opponents of the technology have valid fears. (B) is also too one-sided, but in the other direction. (D) emphasizes the role of scientists in deciding how to use the technology, which is not something that's recommended in the passage. (E) is far too neutral. (C) gets both sides of the author's point, and is the choice we want.

21. **E** Complex: Which situation would be an illustration of the danger mentioned in the cited text?

The danger in question is that allowing genes to become more mobile may cause "drastic" changes that aren't anticipated. (A) talks about the use of antibiotics having unanticipated effects, not genetic modification technology. (B) does talk about the movement of introduced genes, but these changes cannot really be said to be drastic. (C) doesn't talk about the movement of introduced genes in unanticipated ways; neither does (D). (E) sounds pretty serious, and it talks about unanticipated effects of the movement of an introduced gene; this is the choice we want.

22. **B** Specific: Which isn't described as a benefit of GMOs?

(A) is mentioned in the second paragraph as the potential to "increase a food's nutritional value." (C) is mentioned as the potential to engineer plants "better suited to [their] growing environment." (D) is mentioned as the potential to reduce the use of "possibly dangerous insecticides." (E) is mentioned in connection with the potential to engineer crops that require less fertilizer, "a major source of environmental pollution." (B) is the odd choice out here.

23. **A** Specific: What does the passage say about *Bt* corn?

The passage states that the protein in *Bt* corn has never been shown to harm any organism other than the corn borer. On this basis, we can clearly eliminate (B), and (A) is looking good as a choice, since the protein must not have been shown to harm people. (C) is incorrect: The protein occurs naturally in the bacteria from which the gene is taken, not in the corn. Although the passage does mention that the protein is used as an insecticide in organic corn farming, we can't conclude from that that *Bt* corn can itself be considered organic: eliminate (D). We know that it is a successful and widespread GMO, but we don't know how the number of farmers growing it compare to the number who aren't growing it: eliminate (E). (A) is clearly the best choice here.

24. **A** Specific: What is the purpose of the mention of zebra mussels?

It is presented as an example of a case in which placing a naturally occurring organism in a new environment caused environmental disaster. (A) is along the right general lines, although it isn't particularly appealing because of its wording. (B) definitely isn't right; nothing in the passage tells us that zebra mussels are GMOs. (C) has a similar problem; we don't know any way in which a global technology is related to the zebra mussel problem. We can eliminate (D) because we don't know that the introduction of the mussels was intentional, but we also don't know that the introduction was part of a natural process, so we can eliminate (E). (A) is the best choice we have.

25. **C** Complex: What would opponents of GMOs say about a proposal to prevent scurvy in an area by growing a crop modified to produce vitamin C?

Basically, they'd be opposed to it. Unfortunately, the only choice that isn't in line with this idea is (E), which we can easily eliminate. The passage characterizes these opponents as not trusting science and industry, so (D) is a good one to eliminate. Both (A) and (C) seem to propose natural solutions, whereas (B) doesn't, so we can eliminate (B). Between (A) and (C), (C) is the better choice because it includes the stipulation that the plants must occur naturally in the area, a piece that (A) is missing. It's tough, but (C) is the smartest choice on this one.

26. **D** General: What is the organization of the passage?

(A) doesn't include any mention of the opponents of GMOs, which are a main topic of the third paragraph. (B) focuses too specifically on a single GMO, which is not what the passage does. (C) seems to be saying that the author advocates the wide adoption of the technology, which is not consistent with the passage. (E) includes the idea of "limited usefulness," which isn't really anywhere in the passage. Also, genetic technology is not presented as a single "controversial problem." (D) is a very nice play-by-play of the passage, and is the choice we should pick.

Need More?

If you're looking to learn more about how to raise your LSAT score, you're in the right place.

As you know, the LSAT is weighted heavily in your law school application and since most top law schools average multiple LSAT scores, you should take the test only once. So if you're experiencing some trepidation, consider all your options.

We consistently improve prospective law school students' scores through our books, classroom courses, private tutoring, and online courses. Call **800-2Review** or visit *PrincetonReview.com* for details.

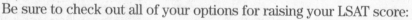

Be sure to check out all of your options for raising your LSAT score:
- *Hyperlearning* LSAT Classroom Courses
- Online Courses
- Private Tutoring
- *Cracking the LSAT*